For Geets
From Ban
Christmas 2005

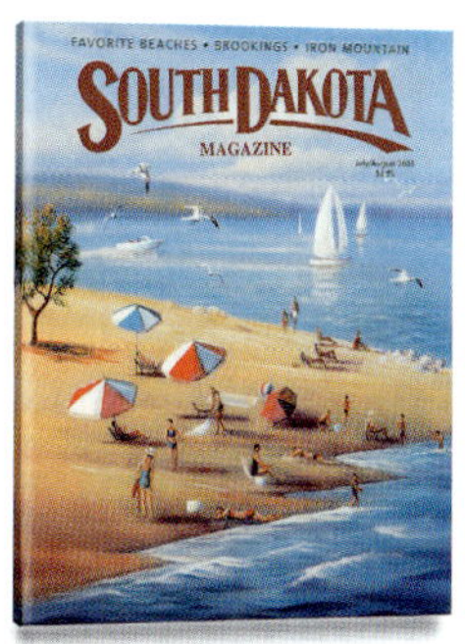

Founded in 1985
with the express purpose
of exploring South Dakota
in words and pictures
on the printed page.

Written by
Bernie Hunhoff and Roger Holtzmann

Creative Director
Ben Hanten

Production design by
Donna Bollich and Mary Johnson

Also produced and presented by
Katie Hunhoff, Jerry Wilson, Barb Hanson, Alma Korslund,
Ruth Steil, Jana Jonas, Courtney Freng and Andrea Clark.

With special thanks to our freelance photography friends.

Library of Congress Catalogue Number
2004110434
Printed in Korea

ISBN 0-9744044-1-1

Published by
Middle Border Books
P.O. Box 175, Yankton, S.D. 57078
Phone (605) 665-6655

We dedicate this collection
of photographs
to all the people pictured within these pages
and to all the talented photographers
who have helped to make South Dakota Magazine
possible since 1985.

— From all of us at *South Dakota Magazine*

CONTENTS

We devoted a special chapter in this book to the Missouri River in recognition of the bi-centennial of the 1804-1806 Corps of Discovery led by William Clark and Meriwether Lewis.

JOEL STRASSER

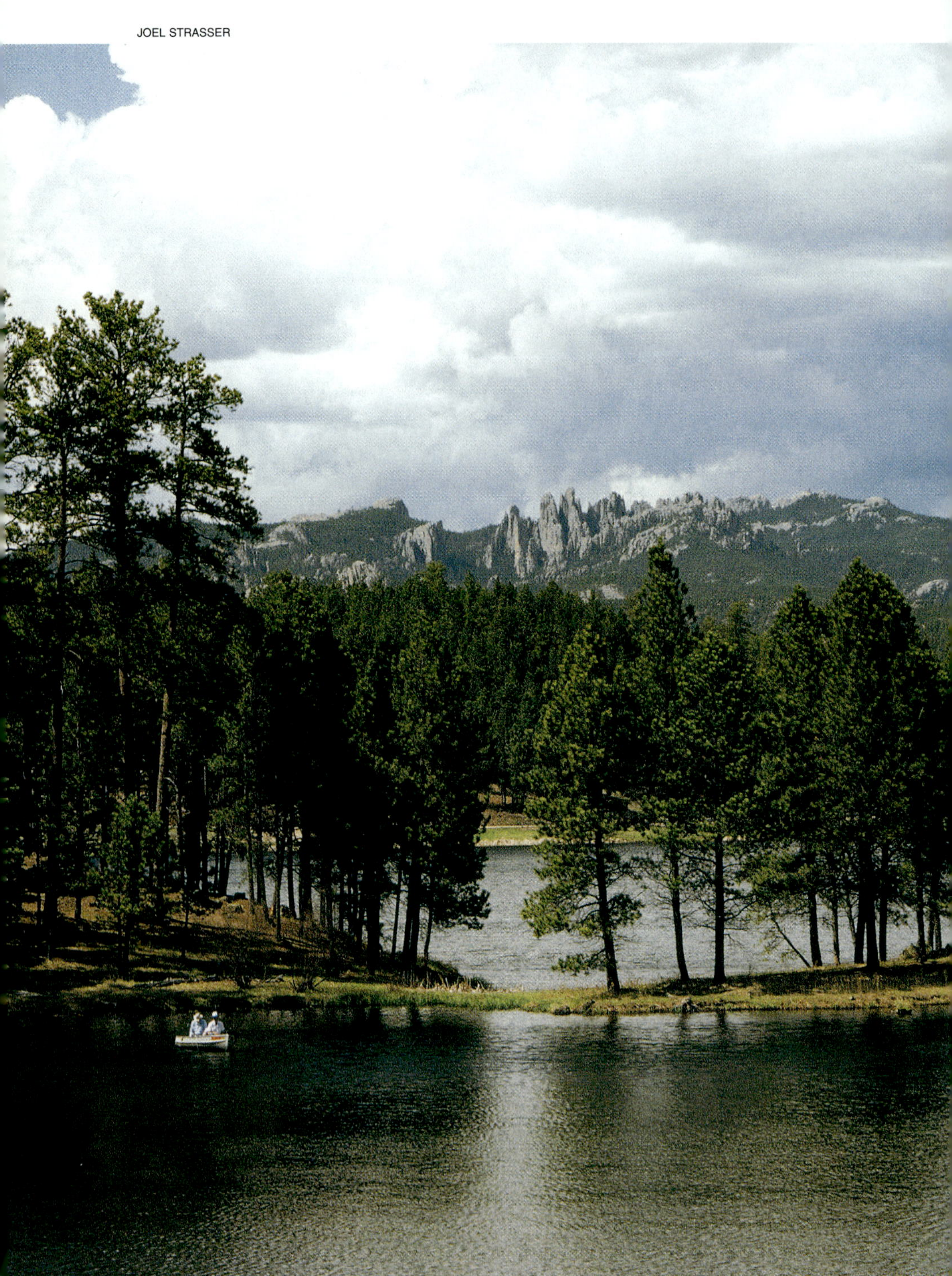

A boat ride on Stockade Lake.

Introduction

A ONE-OF-A-KIND

By Bernie Hunhoff

Did you ever watch a red-tailed hawk surveying the landscape for prey? That's our magazine staff the past 20 years, no feathers or fangs, but with cameras in hand, looking for photographs rather than mice — photographs that show the spirit of South Dakota.

My editorial crew and I shot many of the pictures in this book. But we've also constantly encouraged our state's best photographers to contribute their work, and many of their pictures are also within these covers.

Joel Strasser of Sioux Falls was one of the very first to be featured in *South Dakota Magazine* when we started publication. He has a huge collection of wonderful photos. Whenever we stopped at his studio, which in the 1980s was near Newton Hills south of Canton, we also got the added benefit of his wife Lavonne's homemade cookies and — if we'd listen carefully — common sense from Joel.

On a particularly nice summer morning I was in a hurry to get to Sioux Falls to call on advertisers. When I arrived at the Strassers I told Joel that I'd seen several beautiful scenes along the way — including a perfect sunrise over the Volin Lutheran Church steeple — but I didn't have time to stop to take the picture.

"What's your hurry?" he asked. "That church will never

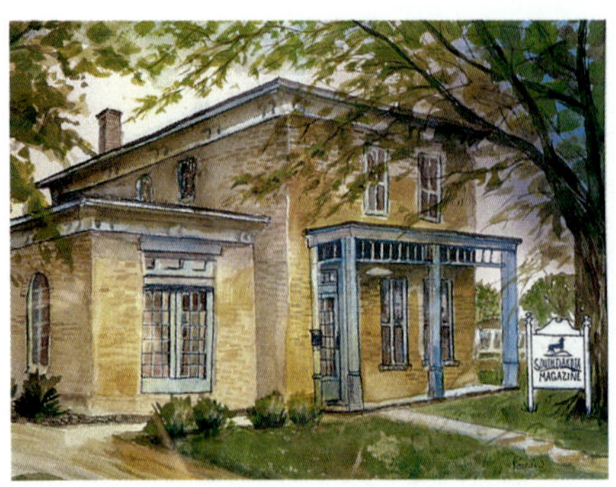

The Pennington House, home to South Dakota Magazine since 1987.

look the same again." That was about all he said but it was enough. It was his version of "stop and smell the roses," blended with some publishing advice that I never forgot.

He was right. Volin Lutheran Church never looked as pretty. So I learned to stop for kids and old men and mule deer and rainbows and anything and anybody that I thought our readers might like to see. And I encouraged all of our traveling staff members to leave time for surprises when on the road.

Many excellent photographers followed Joel Strasser in helping us to capture South Dakota on the printed page — people like Greg Latza, Paul Horsted, Johnny Sundby, Chad Coppess, Mark Kayser, Phil Henry and countless others.

I've noticed that good photographers view their subject matter like a young man might eye his beloved — let nothing come between them and the picture in their minds. Latza once worked for the Sioux Falls *Argus Leader*. He was traveling on the Cheyenne Indian Reservation with Terry Woster, the paper's veteran writer, when he grabbed Woster's arm and said, "Stop the car."

Woster was puzzled because the street seemed empty. Latza got out of the car and crawled half-a-block on his belly through icy mud to get a picture of a shaggy dog gnawing on the bone of a deer. He walked back with mud, weeds and ice hanging from his clothing and with a big smile on his face. "I got it," he said.

That's why he's a professional photographer. He just had to take that picture — like a writer has to write and a good mother has to feed her family and a farmer has to plant in the spring.

Thanks to our own staff and people like Latza and Strasser and so many others, we've captured moments in South Dakota history — landscapes, lakescapes, townscapes, people at work and play, flora and fauna and just about everything else that makes up South Dakota. Most of the pictures in this book were lifted from the pages of *South Dakota Magazine.* A few never made the magazine, but not because we didn't like them. We're pleased to have this second opportunity to show them.

A lot of the photos are mine because I've been here longer than anybody else. (Also, as editor, I got the final say.) I photographed a charming recluse in his shanty by the Bad River, Hutterite girls who delighted at instantly seeing their image on the digital camera, the moon rising over Sheep Mountain in the Badlands, heirs to the sacred pipe playing with their dog on the Cheyenne Reservation, mysterious stone effigies of snakes on Hughes County hilltops, lutefisk lovers at Nordic Hall in Sioux Falls and Deadwood dancehall girls.

In 2003 I photographed George Voigt, a blind farmer who lives by Avon. On my way back to Yankton I was pondering the unhappy fact that he would never see his picture. I remembered, however, that he grew a garden, built several sheds, repaired tractor motors, cut wood with a chain saw and cared for a herd of cattle. Obviously, he had developed skills and senses I don't have.

Pictures can do the same. They expand our senses. Most of us will never get to live like Beryle Seaman, the recluse on the Bad River, but seeing him in photographs gives us a sense of what it might be like to be Beryle. The same is true of boiling lutefisk or exploring the mystery stones or watching the moonrise at Sheep Mountain.

Others have published photography books on South Dakota; few if any, however, featured so many of our state's top photographers. No other book took 20 years to accumulate. And no other book emphasizes our people the way we do. We've always found people to be the most interesting species in South Dakota.

If you love South Dakota, then you want to experience all of her vagaries and beauties. We hope our 20th anniversary book of photographs brings you enjoyment. You won't see the same people and places in any other book or in person because, as Joel Strasser said long ago, "the church will never look the same."

This book, like South Dakota, is one-of-a-kind.

Bernie Hunhoff and his wife, Myrna, started South Dakota Magazine in 1985. He has been the editor and publisher ever since.

BERNIE HUNHOFF

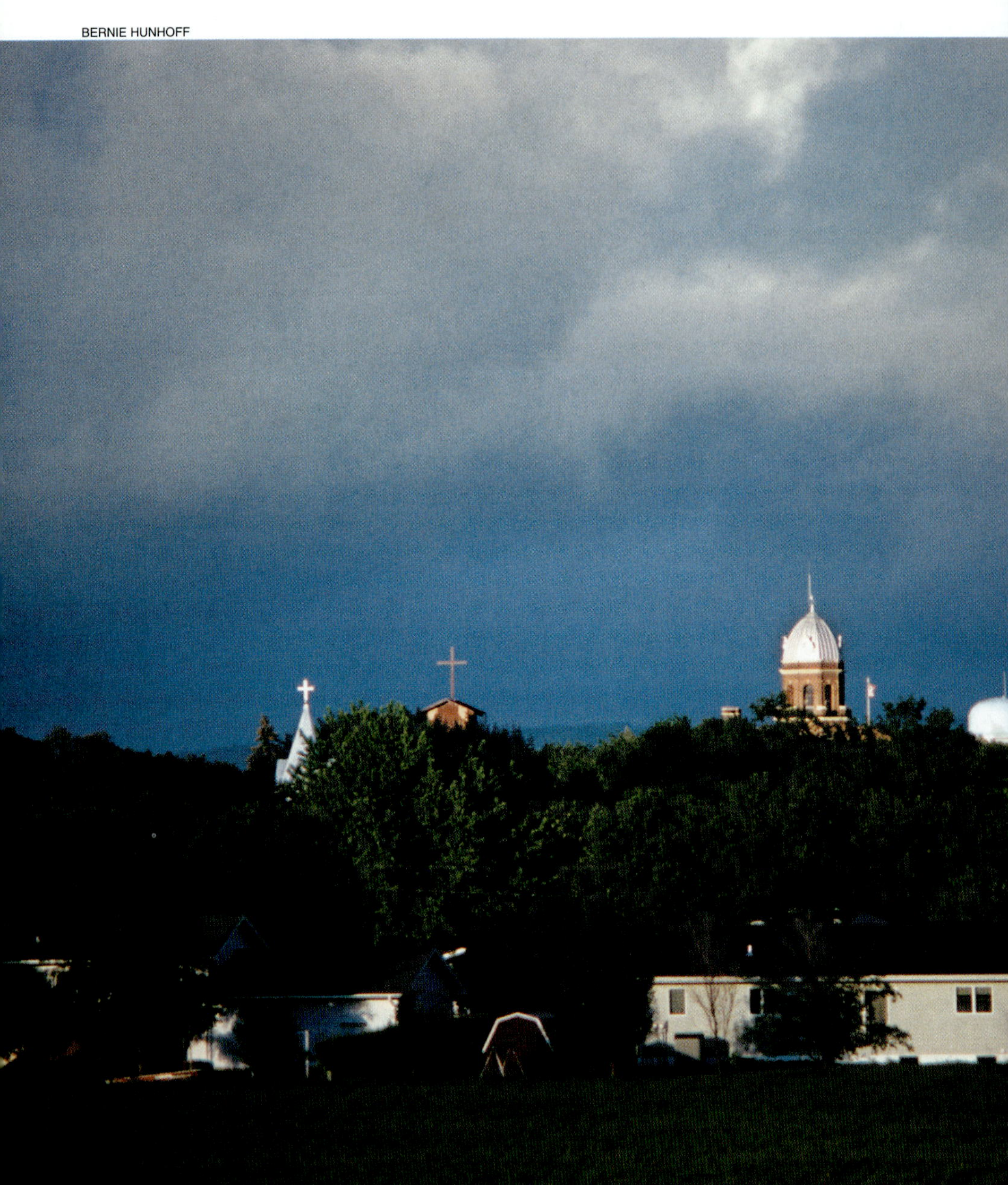

The Roberts County Courthouse steeple has towered above treetops in ***Sisseton*** *since 1902.*

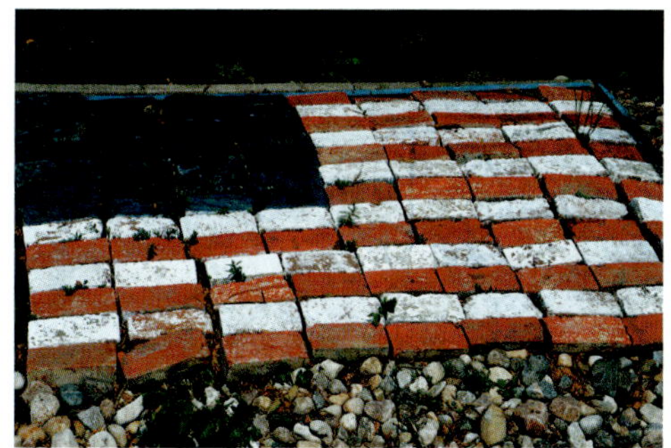

Towns We Like

We humans are herd animals, and that accounts for our love of towns and cities. We are attracted to places where the basic necessities of life are provided, as well as a few niceties like a good steakhouse or movie theater or fishing pond or bookstore.

South Dakotans seem especially protective of their hometowns. That's because we're only a few generations removed from the people who founded them. We can still point to historic buildings constructed by our grandparents. In worldly terms, it takes centuries for a town to mature. Ours are all just fragile fledglings. We haven't lost any to old age. Those that died were in their infancy.

South Dakota Magazine explores a community in every issue. We send a writer and a photographer there for a day or two. They try to find its personality — what makes it interesting and different. The "town stories" have become one of the most popular features in the magazine.

Gathered here are some of our favorite photographs from those stories, dating back to 1985. They are a collage of urban living, South Dakota style.

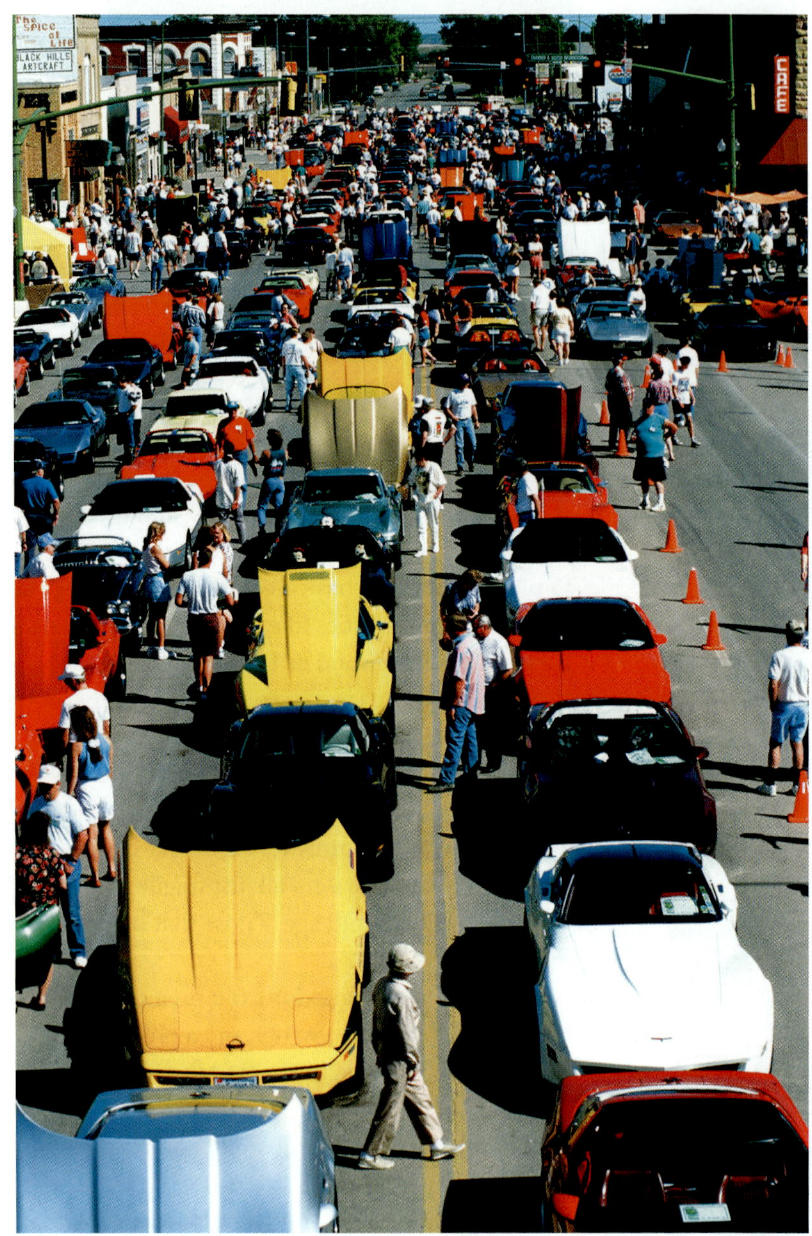

SD TOURISM

***Spearfish's** main drag is dubbed Vette Street every July for the Black Hills Corvette Classic. Over 700 of the popular Chevys, old and new, line the street as their owners share food, fellowship and story-telling.*

BERNIE HUNHOFF

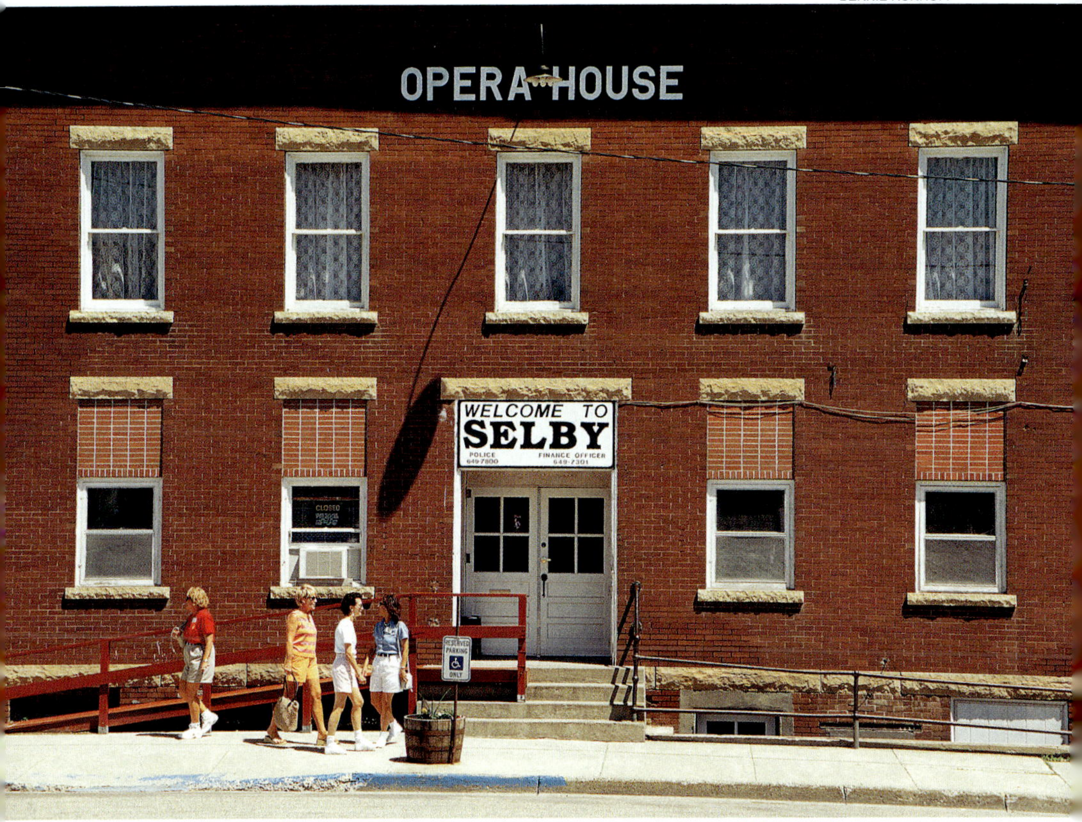

Century-old cedar trees surround the Walworth County Courthouse square in ***Selby****. They were planted in 1908, three years before the courthouse was finished. Above, the community's old Opera House is now city hall.*

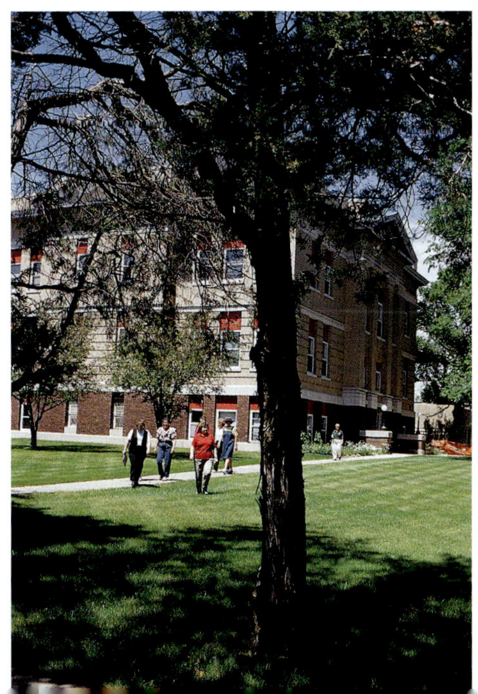

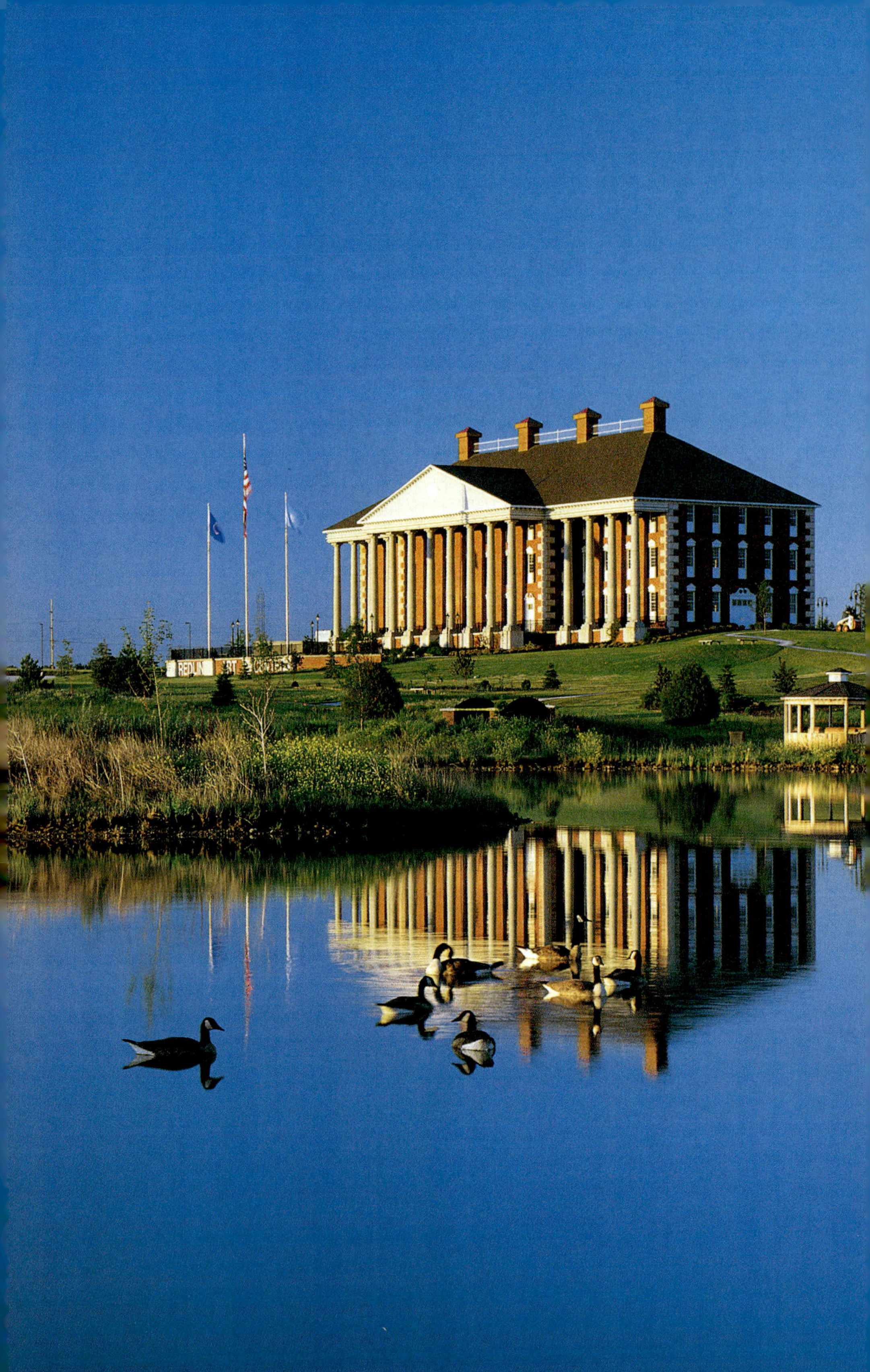
REDLIN

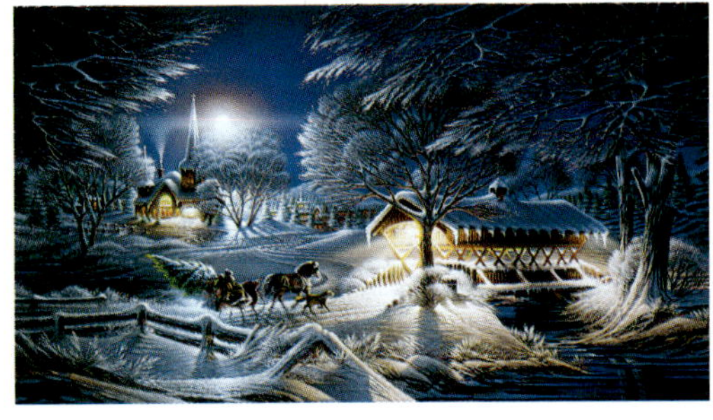

Terry Redlin, one of America's favorite artists, returned to ***Watertown*** *in the 1990s with 100 of his original oils, including "Evening Frost" (left) and built a $10 million art center (opposite page) as a gift to the community that gave him a start.*

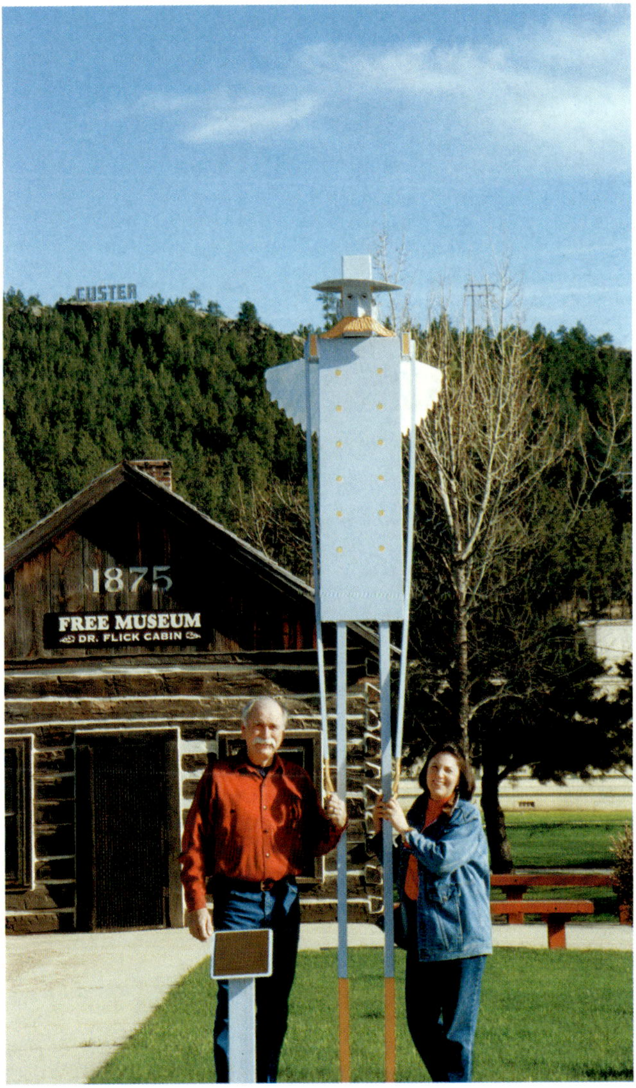

In the Black Hills city of ***Custer****, a main street statue of the town's controversial namesake shows the general with wings — leaving townspeople to argue whether he was an angel or a devil.*

BEN HANTEN

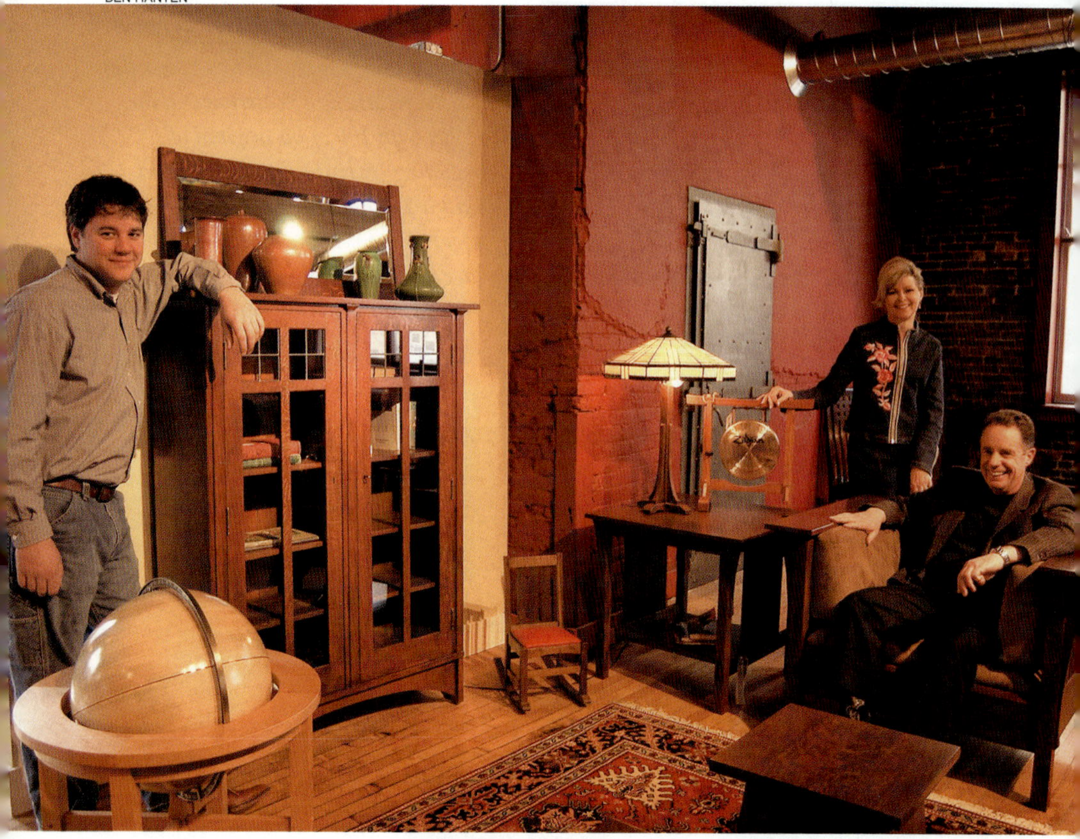

A trend toward living and working downtown has emerged in South Dakota's larger cities. Above, the old Harvester Building in downtown ***Sioux Falls*** *hosts a design business on the main floor and lofts above.*

KATIE HUNHOFF

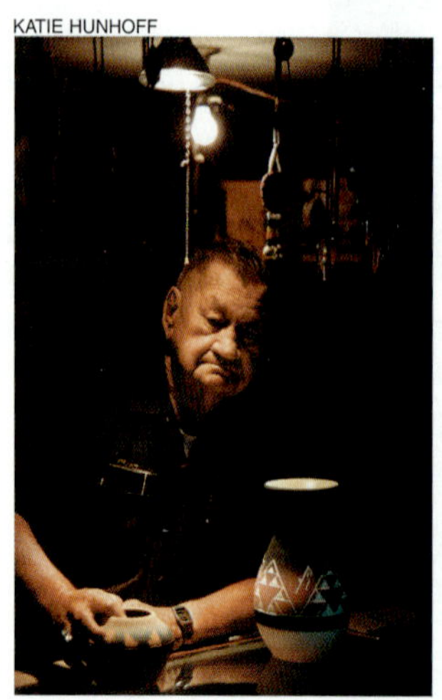

Business owners are colorful characters. Glenn Jesperson of ***Wagner*** *retired from the oil business and then sold art and crafts. Prior to that, he fought in WWII. He lay in a 3x8 foxhole for nine days without water or food during the Battle of the Bulge. He was the sole survivor in his unit. On a happier note, he once gave a box of cigars to Winston Churchill.*

BERNIE HUNHOFF

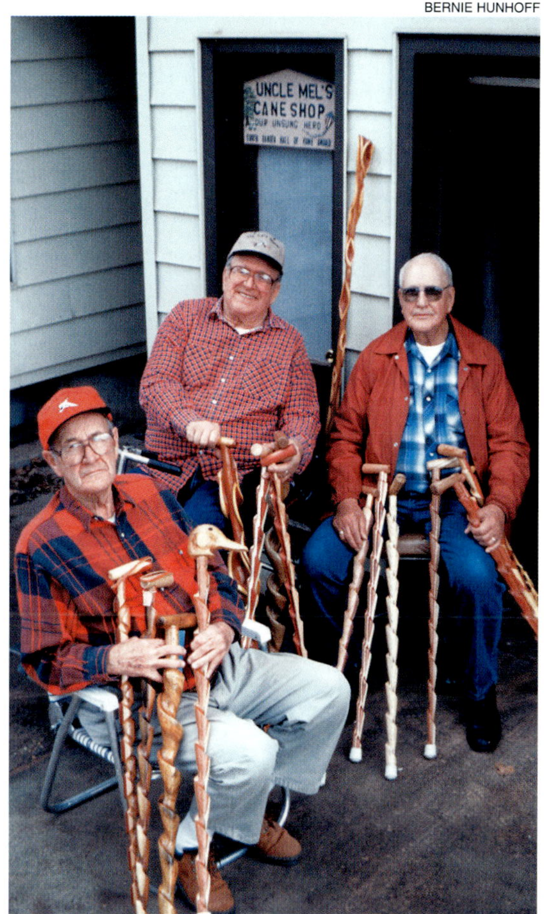

South Dakota's only cane factory was located in Mel Hanthorn's garage in ***Watertown****. He and his buddies used jackknives and wood lathes to produce over 3,000 canes. They gave them all away to people who needed them.*

The arts flourish on the Augustana College campus in ***Sioux Falls****. Pictured below are potters Julie and Gerry Punt.*

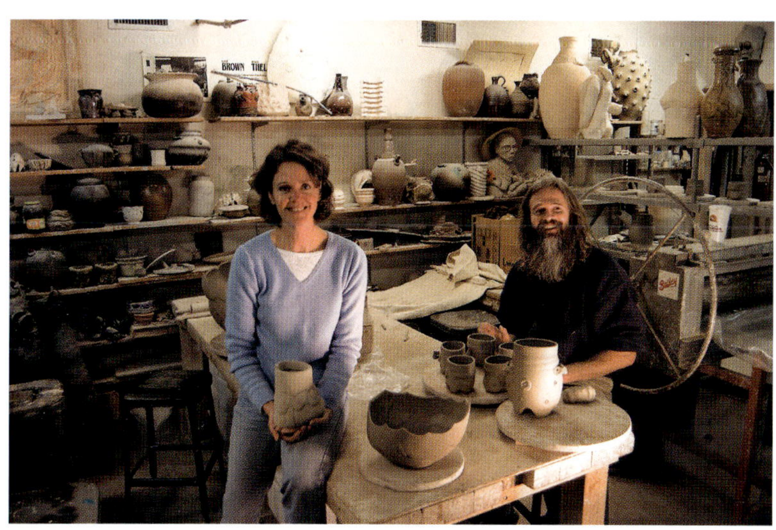

JOHNNY SUNDBY

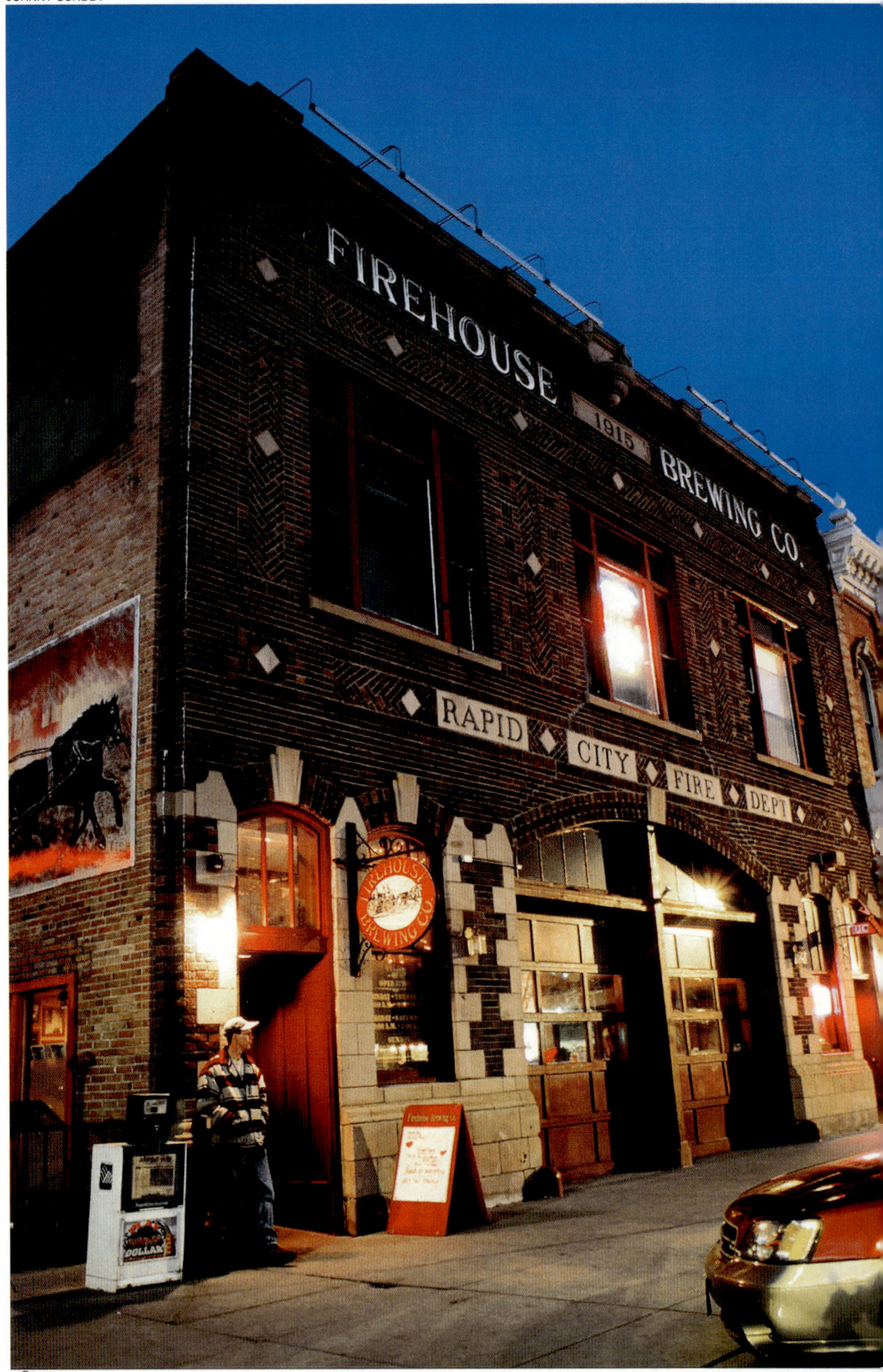

BERNIE HUNHOFF

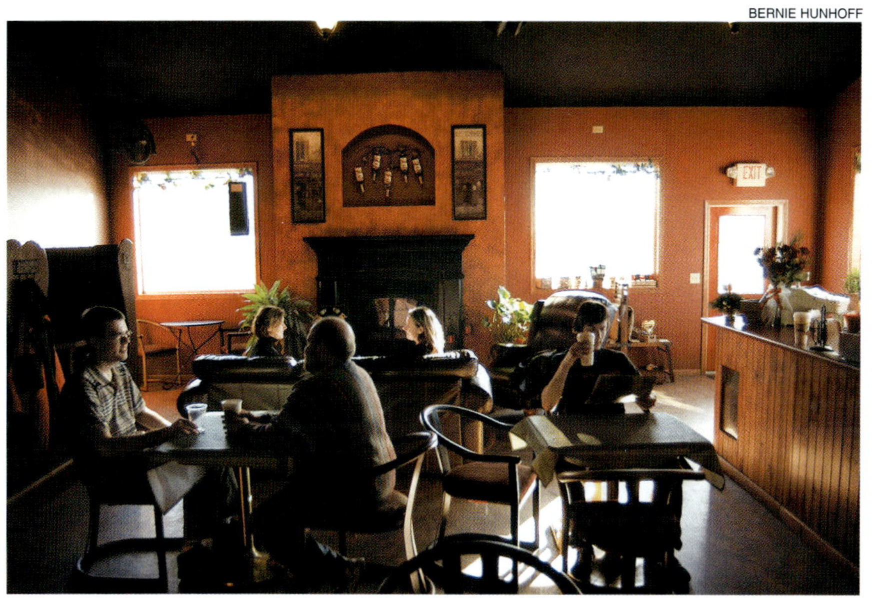

*Interesting eateries give a town panache. The Firehouse Brewing Co. in downtown **Rapid City** (opposite page) hasn't dampened that city's reputation. Other such spots include The Neighbors Coffee House in **Brandon** (above) and the Old Bowdle Hospital and Inn in **Bowdle**. Yes, the latter was a real hospital before it became a restaurant.*

STAFF PHOTO

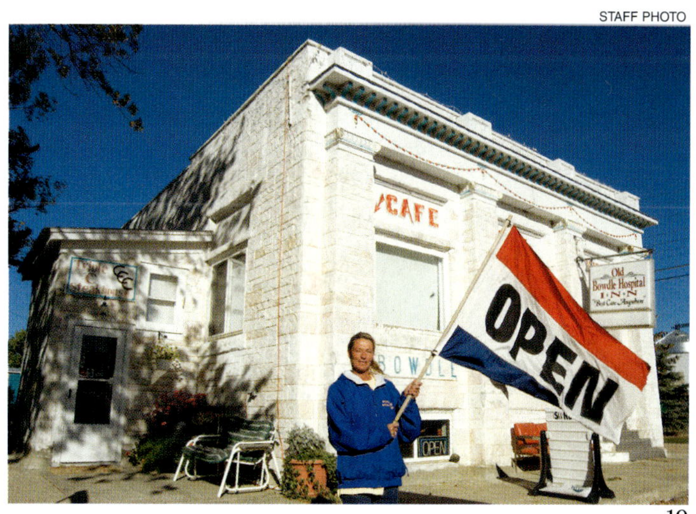

KATIE HUNHOFF

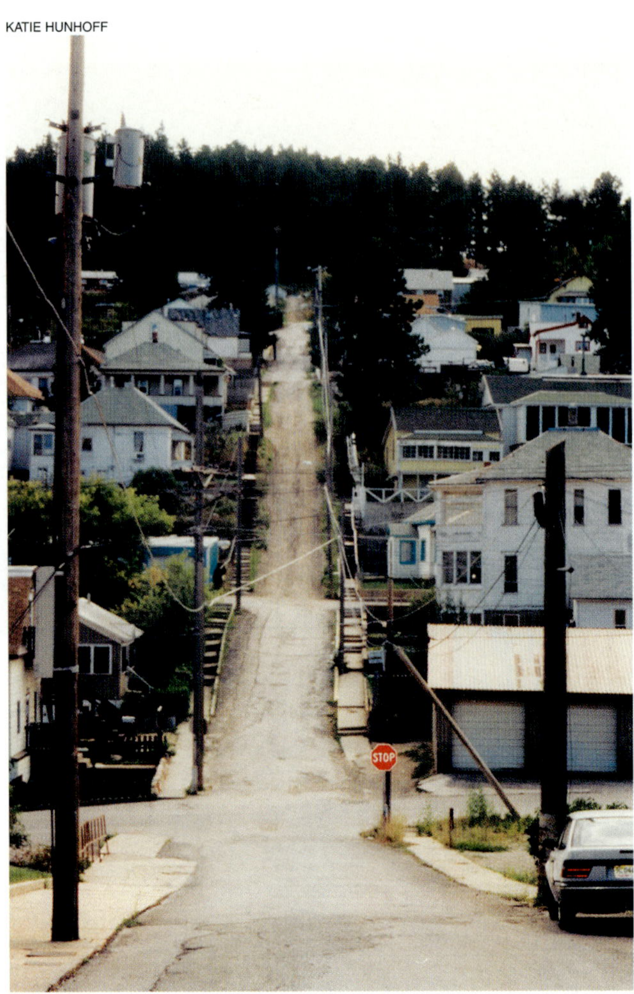

Forest towns are different from their prairie cousins, in ways good and bad. Not so good on icy days are the steep streets to be found in ***Lead*** *(above) and most other Black Hills communities. Growth and mountainous terrain have caused some communities like* ***Black Hawk*** *(opposite) to sprawl in the valleys.*

JERRY WILSON

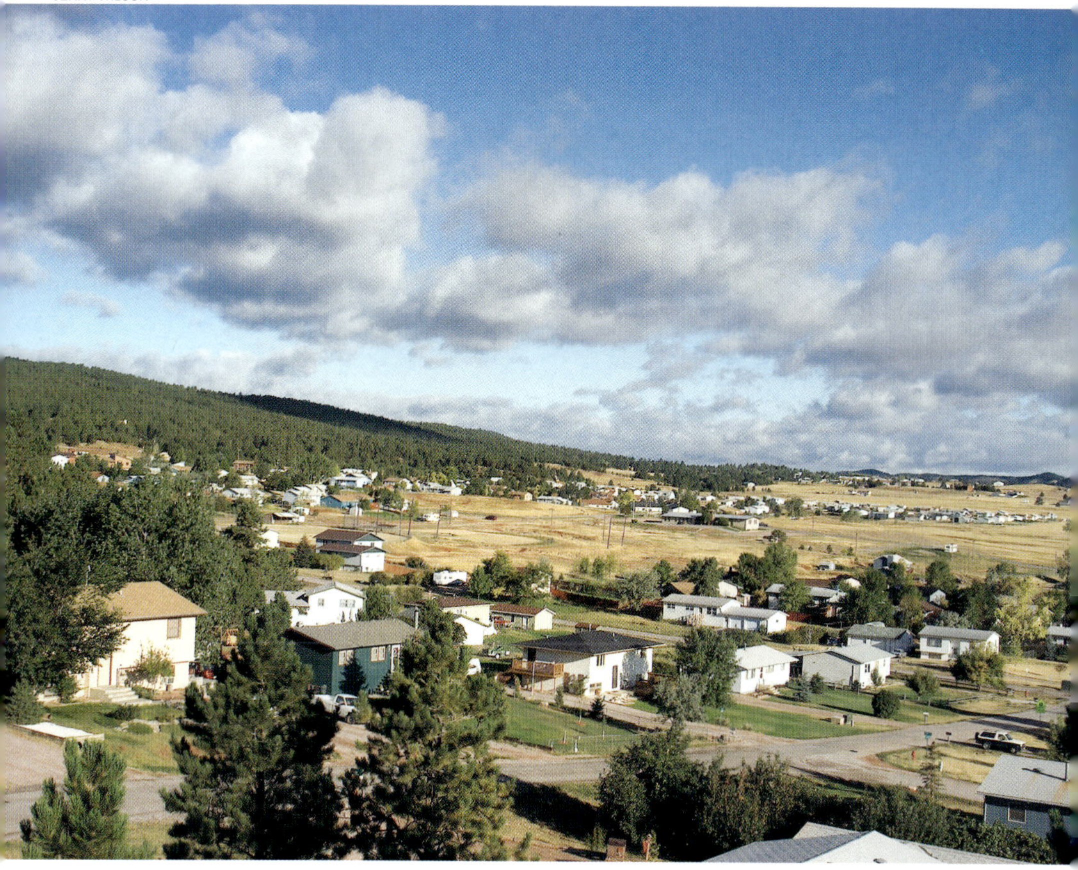

PAUL HIGBEE

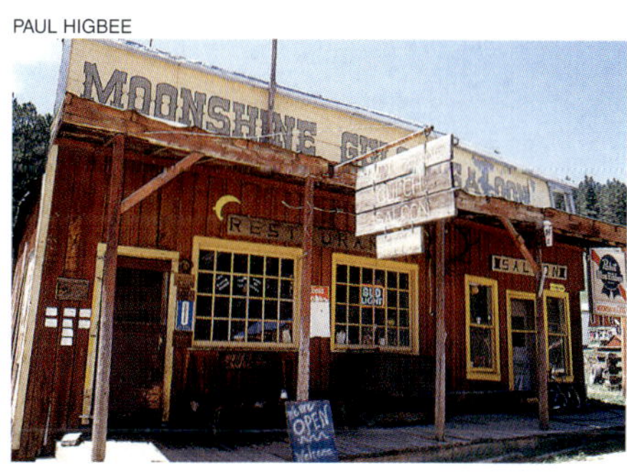

PAUL HIGBEE

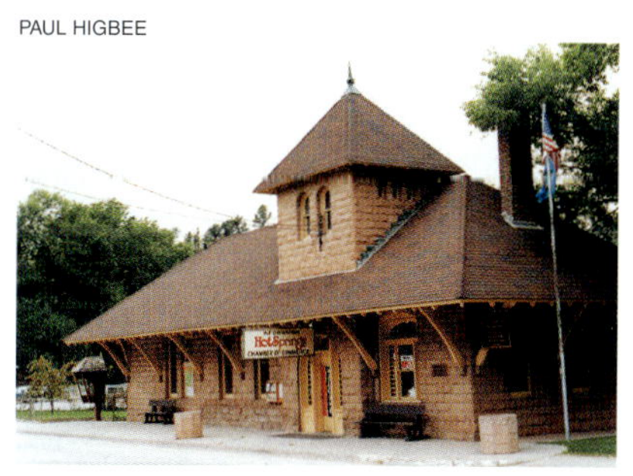

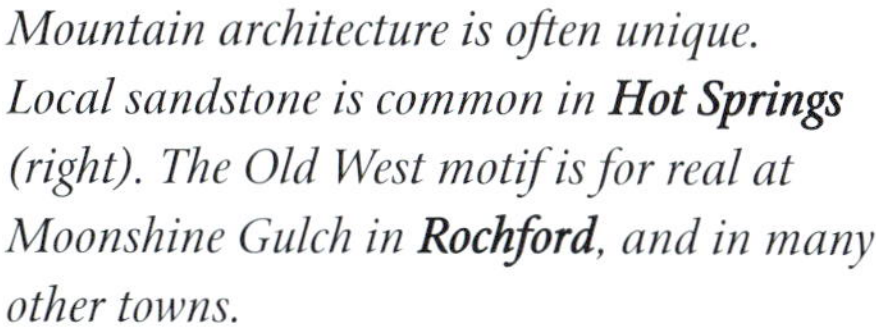

Mountain architecture is often unique. Local sandstone is common in ***Hot Springs*** *(right). The Old West motif is for real at Moonshine Gulch in* ***Rochford****, and in many other towns.*

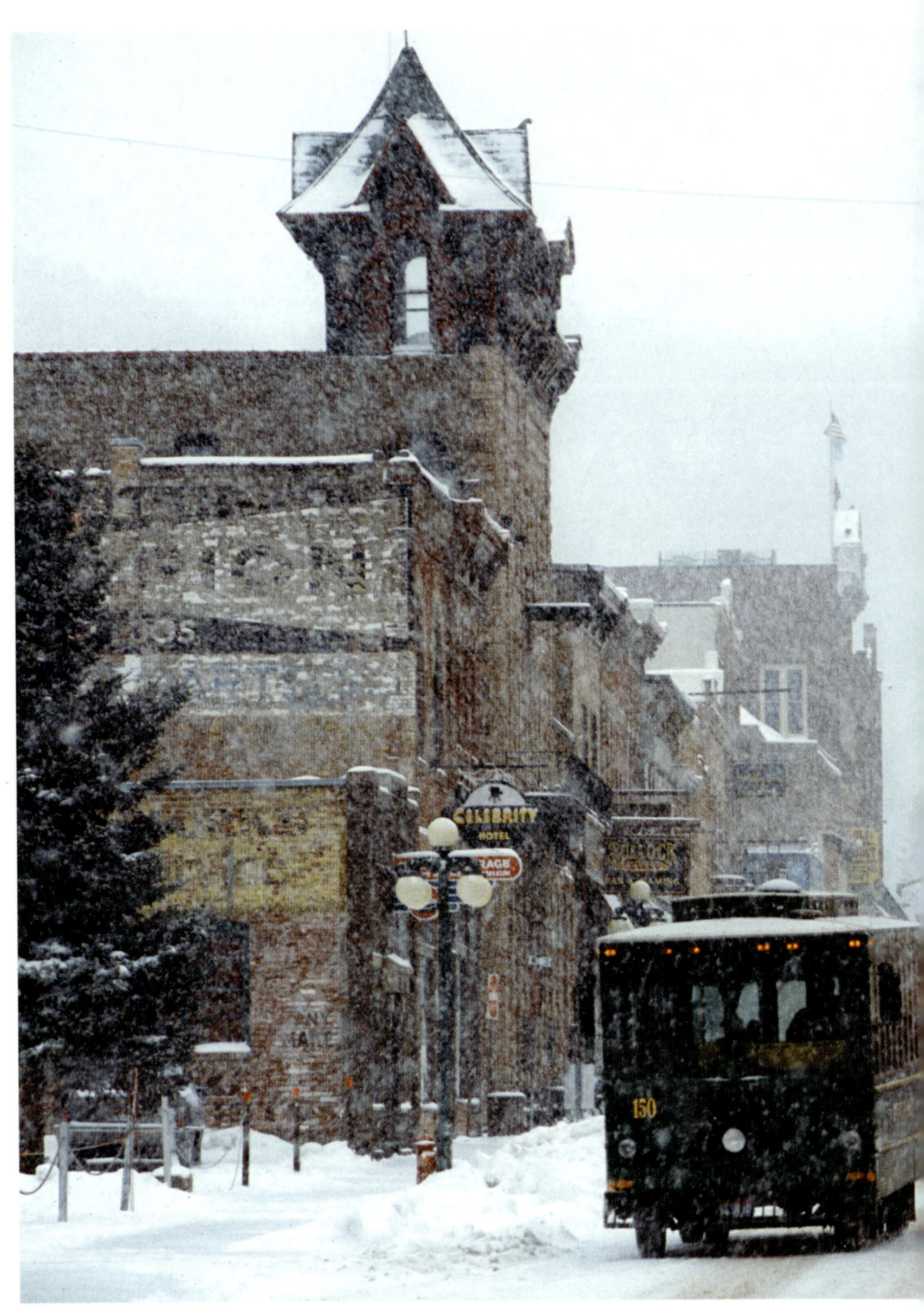

When voters legalized gambling in 1988, ***Deadwood's*** *luck changed. Tens of millions of winnings have been invested in historic restoration and preservation. Some now consider it South Dakota's "little Las Vegas," but with less glitz and more class.*

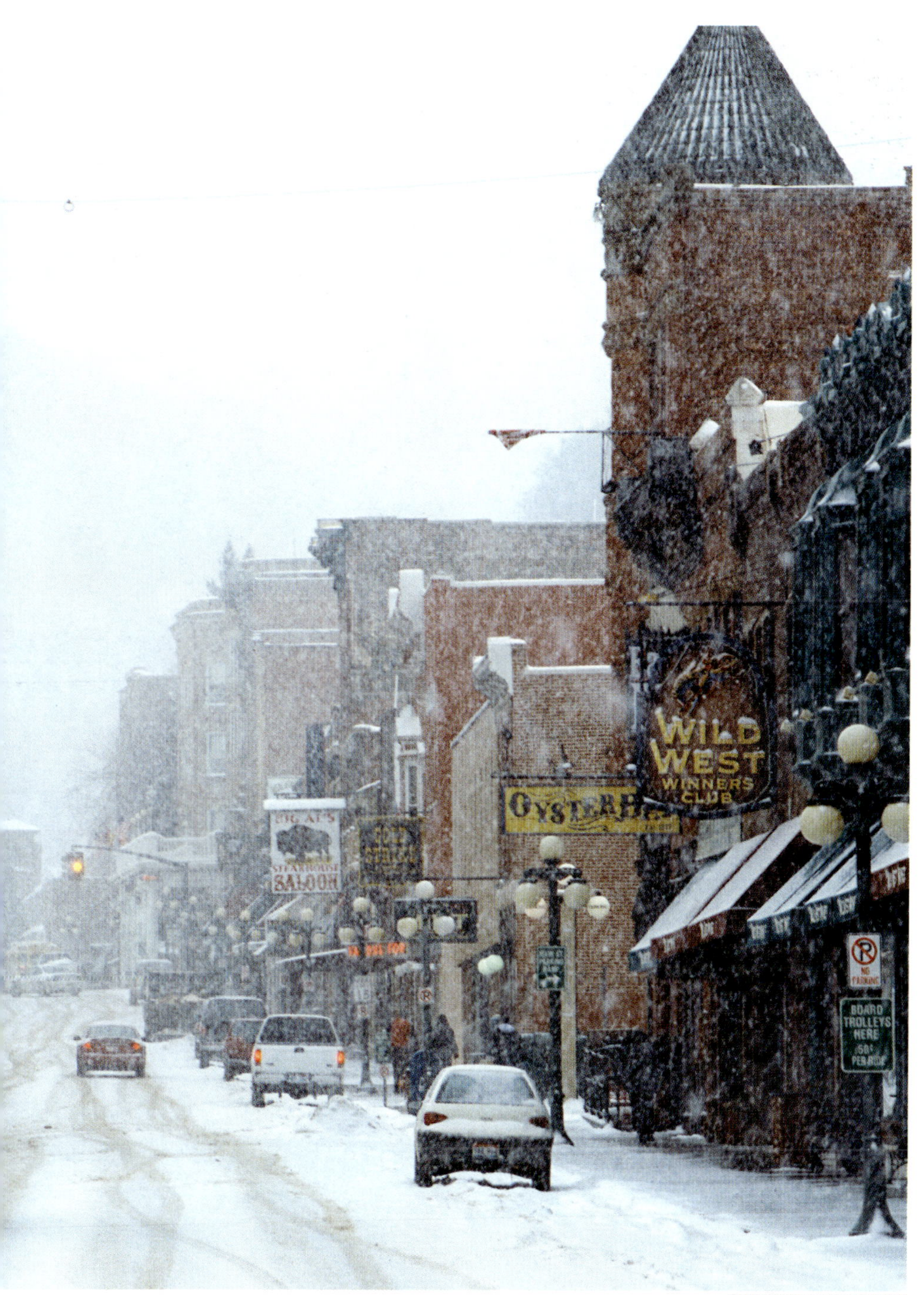

CHAD COPPESS / SD TOURISM

BEN HANTEN

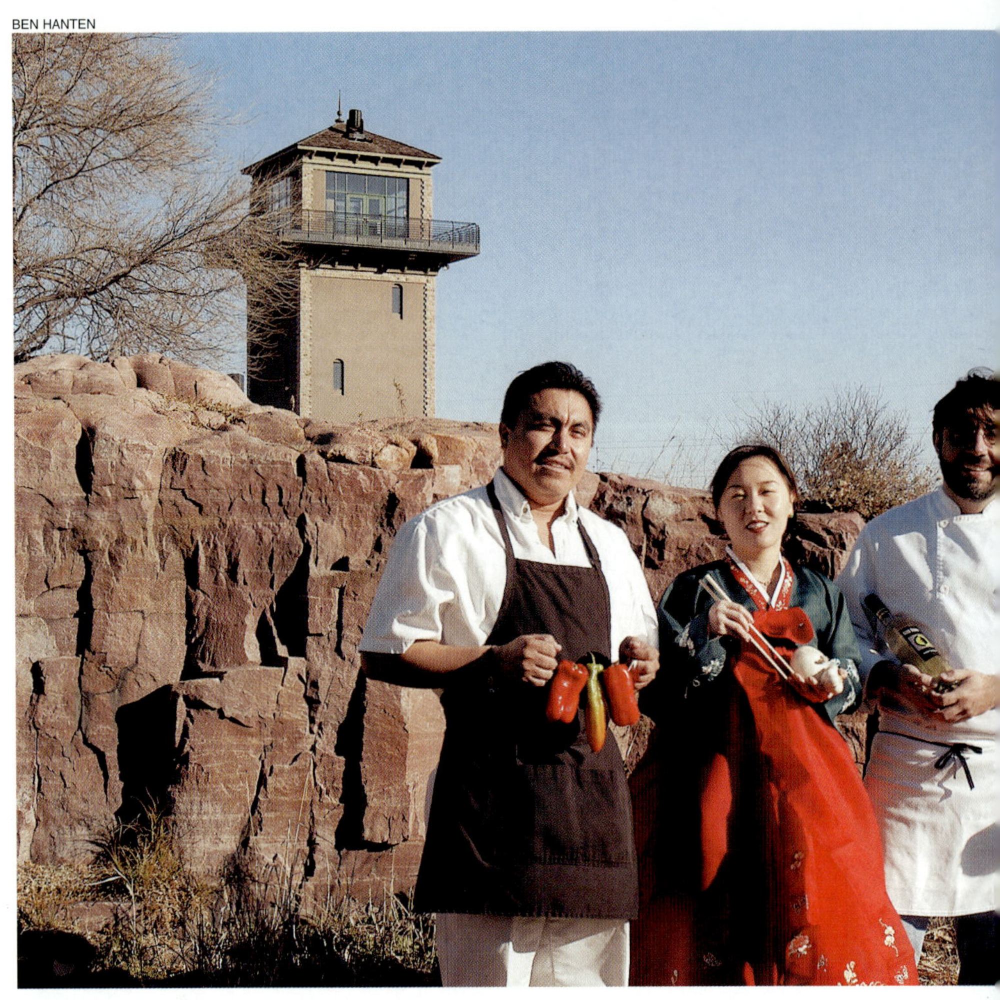

South Dakota was built by immigrants, so it's no surprise that the citizenry enjoys ethnic foods. ***Sioux Falls*** *leads the parade — its chefs (from left) range from Gustavo Vasquez (Salvadoran) to Anna Sim (Korean), Dominique Fontenille (French), and Rosie Warner (down-home American). Other interesting places include (right, top to bottom) an English pub in* ***Spearfish****, Highland Laddie's brewery in* ***Watertown*** *and a kuchen bakery in* ***Eureka****.*

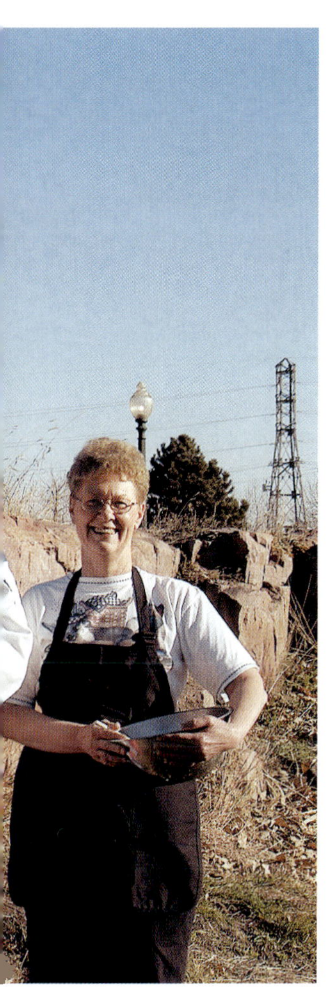

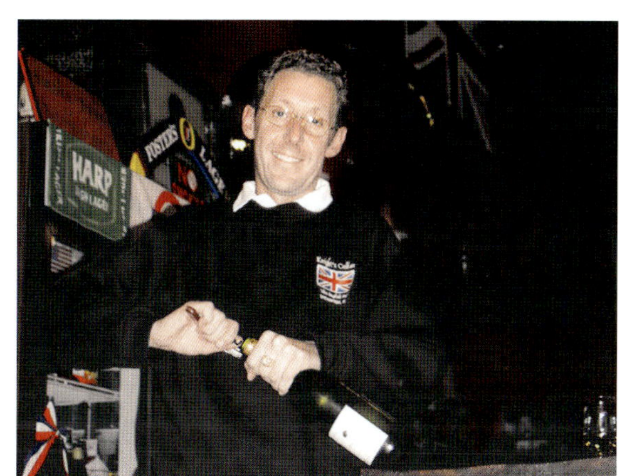

STAFF PHOTO

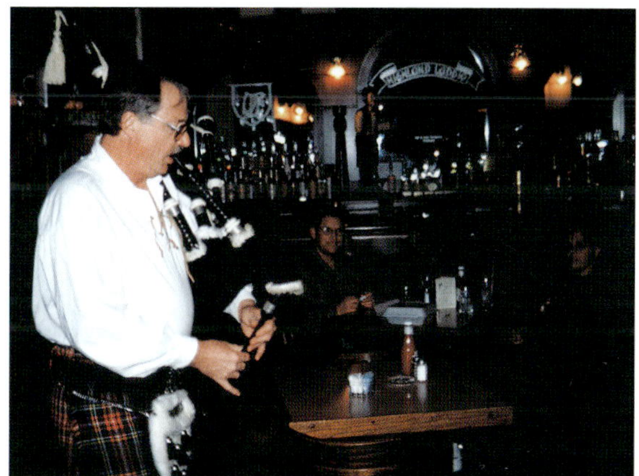

STAFF PHOTO

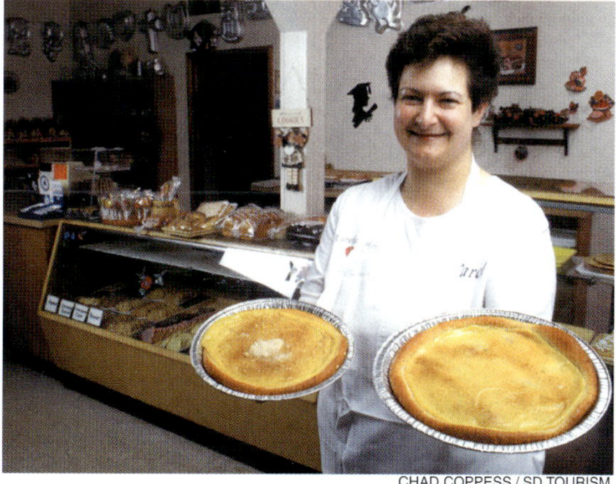

CHAD COPPESS / SD TOURISM

STEPHEN GASSMAN

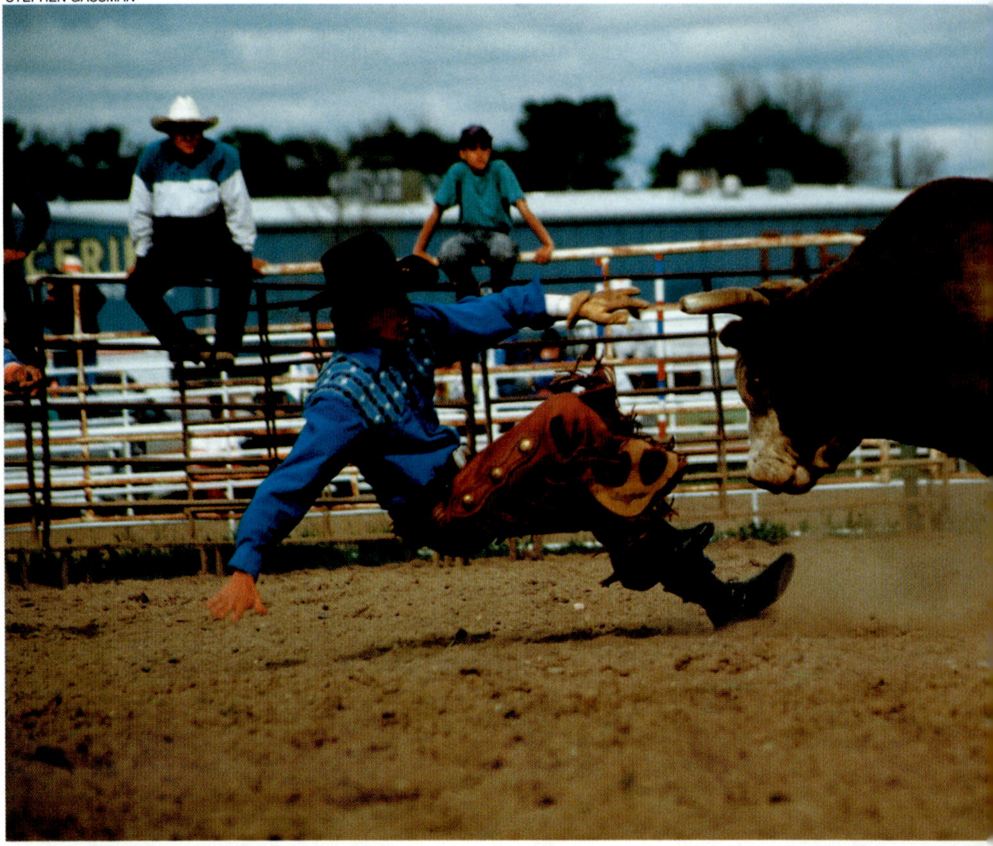

STAFF PHOTO

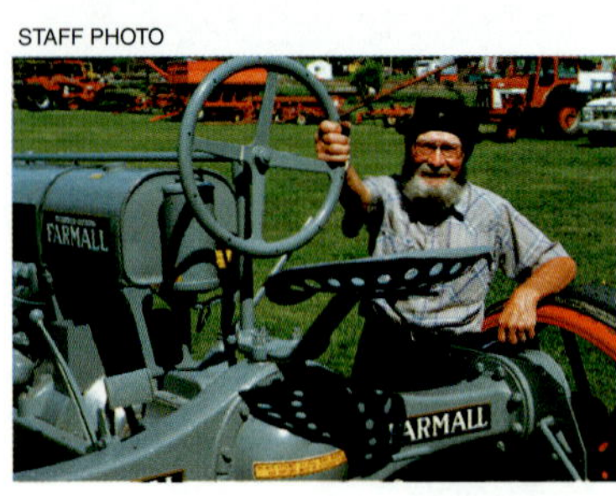

How a town celebrates says much about its people. For starters, wild creatures are often part of our partying; bucking horses and bulls, for example, or racing turtles, walleye and pheasants. Bull-riding may be the oddest example. The rider pictured above was competing at a high school rodeo in ***Wall****.*

We surely lead the nation in the number of parades and parties that feature old farm equipment, like Walt Zabel's popular tractor collection in ***Selby*** *(left) or the venerable Prairie Village near* ***Madison***

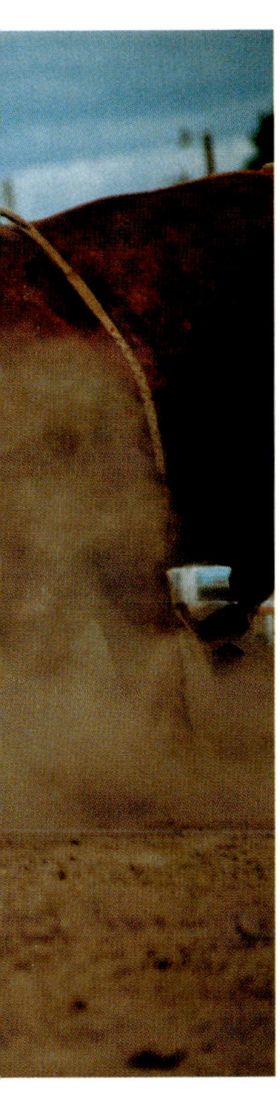

BERNIE HUNHOFF

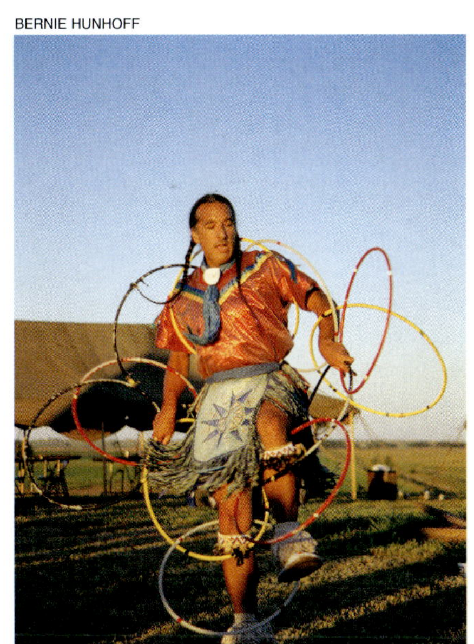

SD TOURISM

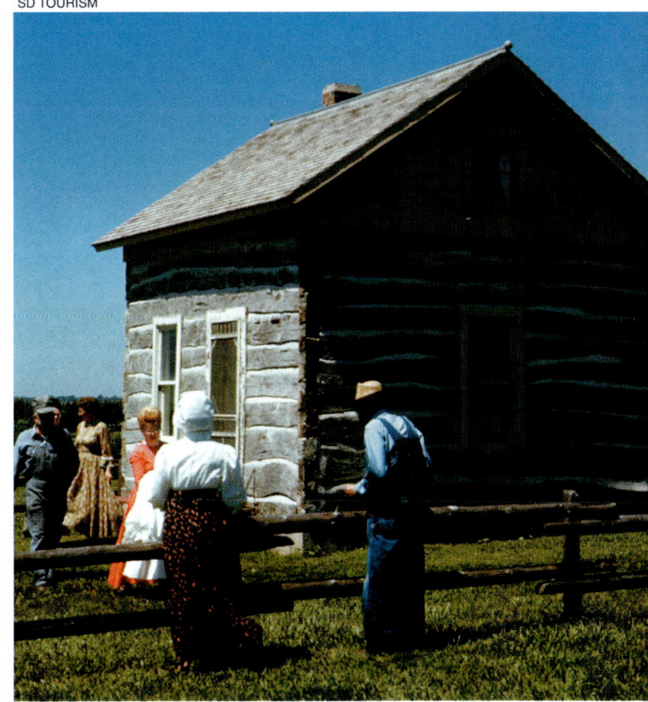

(right) where a steel-wheeled tractor once rolled over a small sedan parked too close to the parade route. The tractor driver shrugged and proceeded. Old tractors have the right of way at the village.

*Towns and cities both on and off our reservations like to display the Native American culture by including music, pow wows and other Indian arts in their celebrations. Kevin Locke of **Wakpala** (above) has educated thousands of non-Indians to Lakota spirituality and his vision of global unity through elaborate hoop dances.*

ROBERT WONG

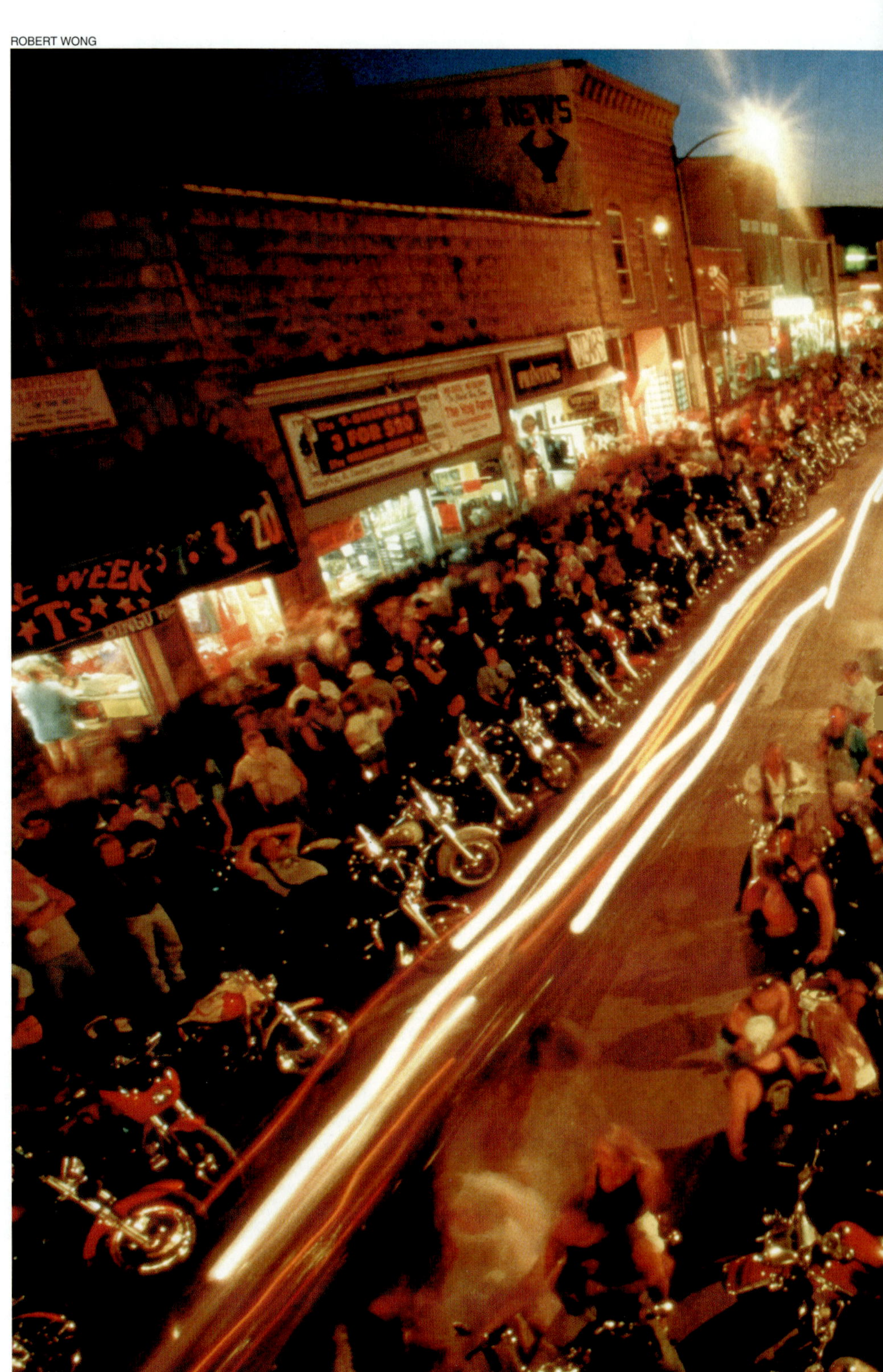

The Sturgis Motorcycle Rally is one of South Dakota's oldest and most successful celebrations. It dates to 1937, and now attracts more than 500,000 bikers and sight-seers every August.

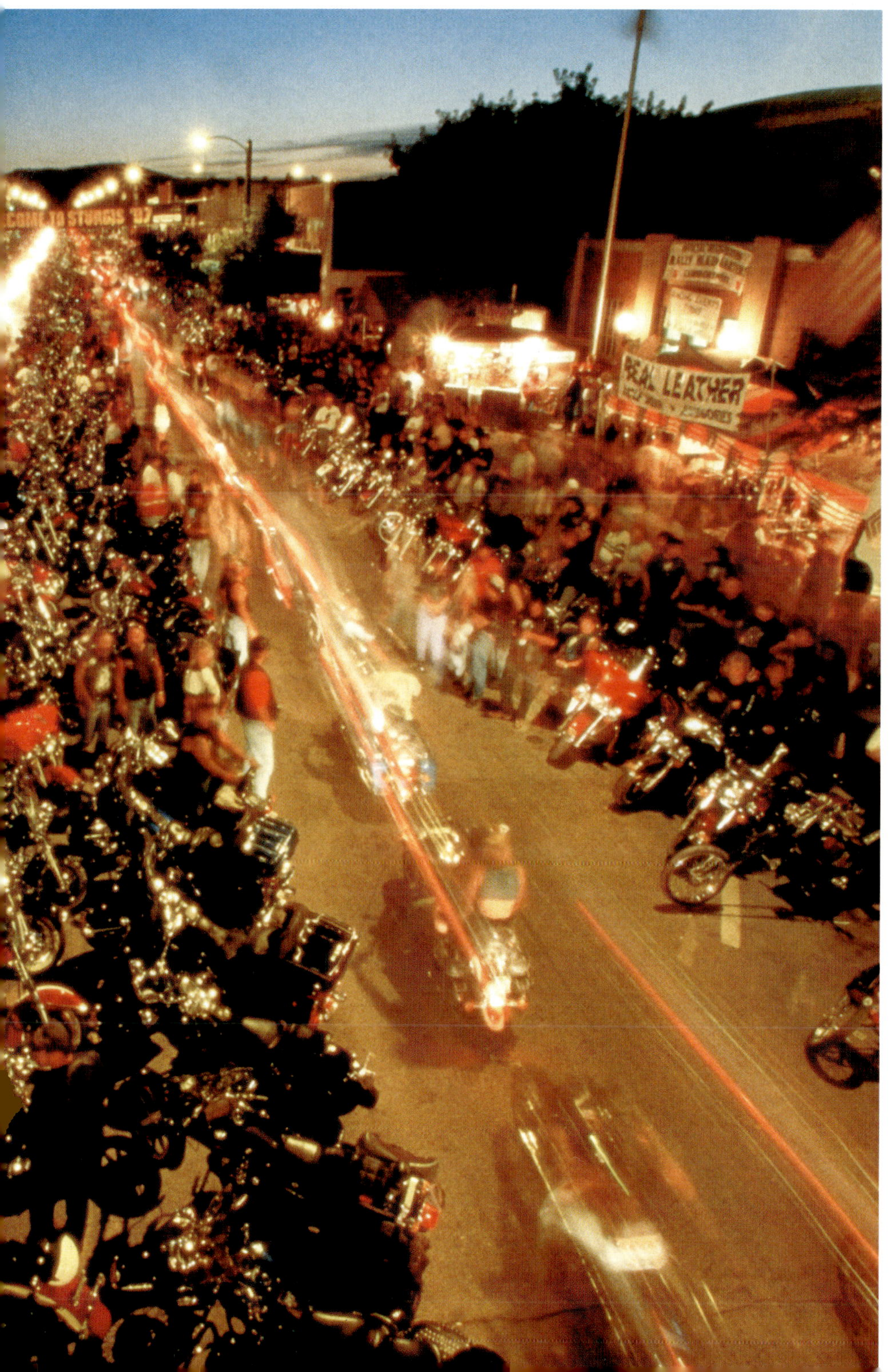

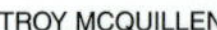

TROY MCQUILLEN

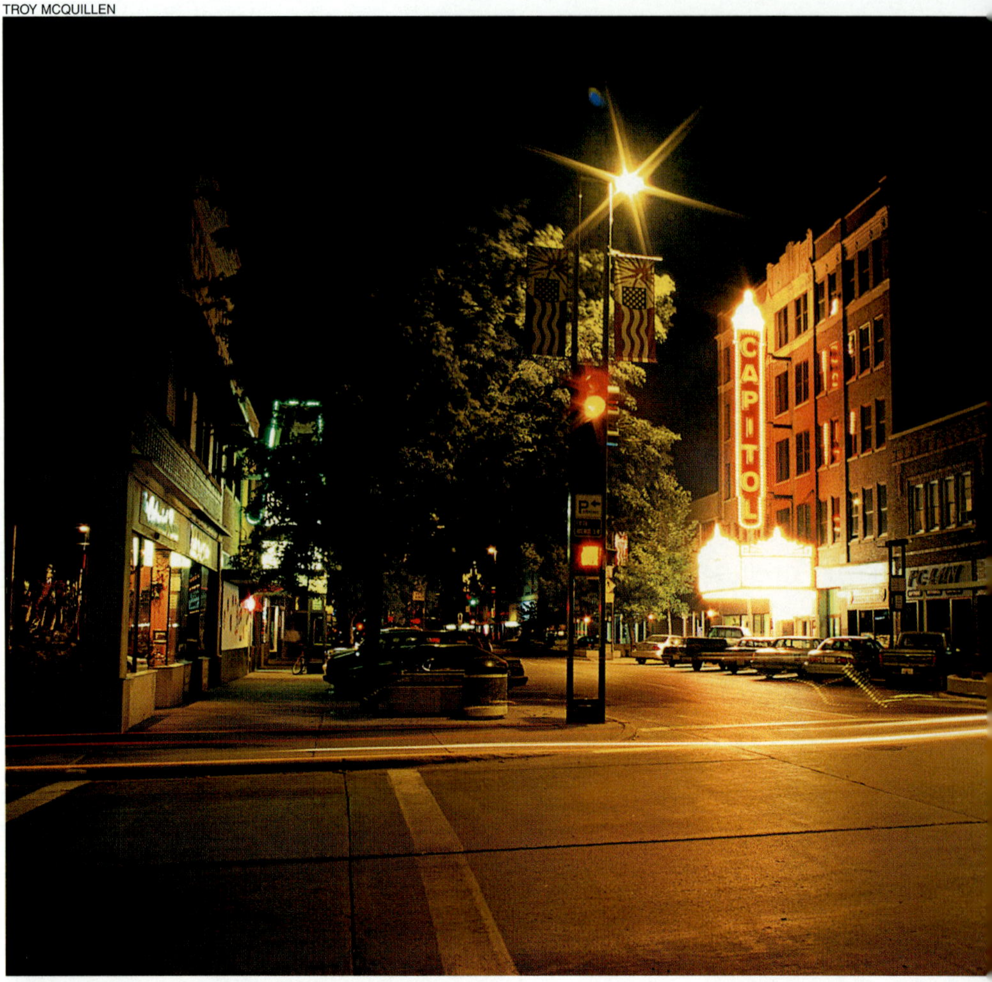

STAFF PHOTO

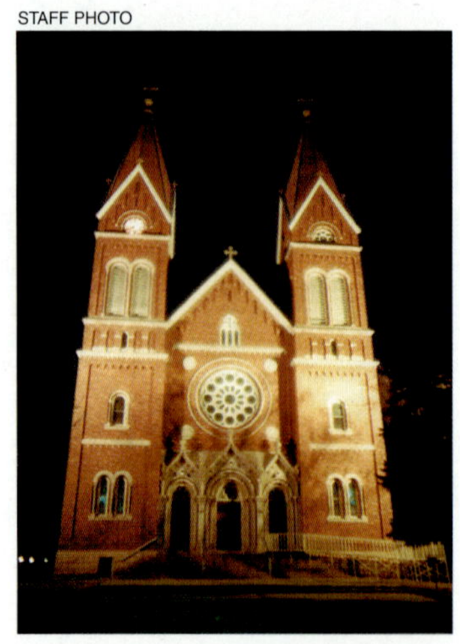

A town's appearance changes at night because you see only what people choose to illuminate. At ***Hoven*** *in northern South Dakota, they light the Cathedral of the Prairie (left), a Catholic church that opened in 1921 after nearly a decade of fundraising and work.*

The Capitol Theater (above) stands

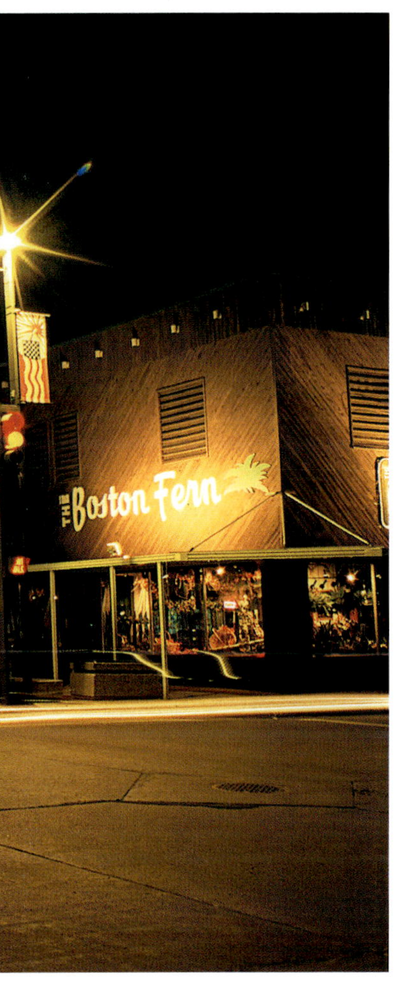

STAFF PHOTO

STAFF PHOTO

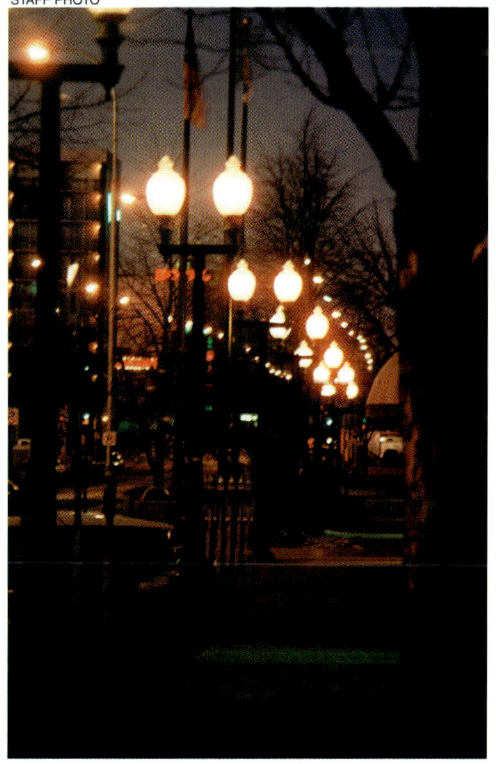

*out on **Aberdeen's** main street when the marquee is lighted. It is now a community theater.*

***Sioux Falls'** famous 41st Street (above) surely burns more electricity than any other road in the state, but no matter the wattage, it's hard to compete with the same city's downtown district (right) for evening charm.*

KATIE HUNHOFF

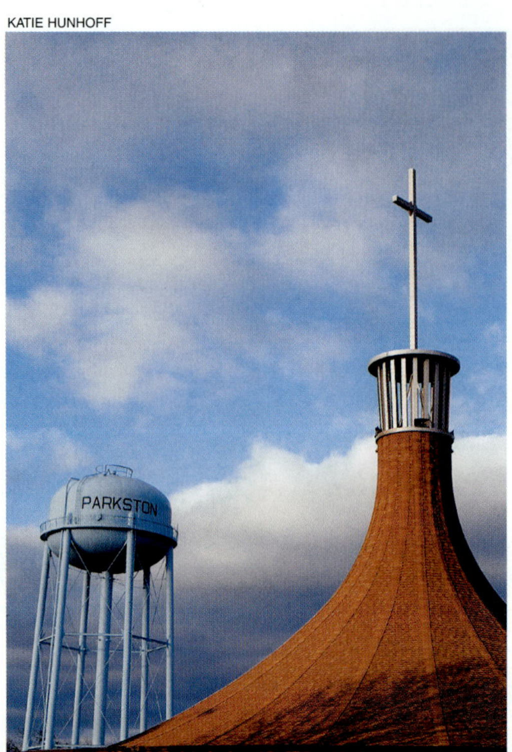

*Architecture is a town's most visible art. South Dakota has appealing modern examples – the Catholic church at **Parkston** (above) and a mini skyscraper in downtown **Rapid City** (below). However, many travelers prefer the classical prairie pioneer styles like the Carnegie Library on the University of South Dakota campus in **Vermillion** that has housed the world-class National Music Museum (opposite) since 1973.*

SD TOURISM

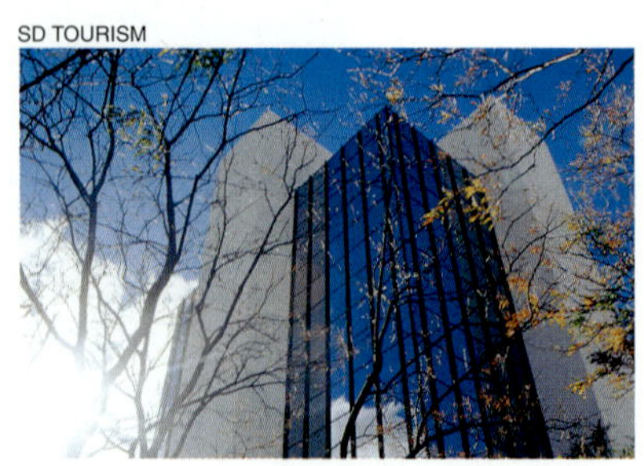

SIMON SPICER

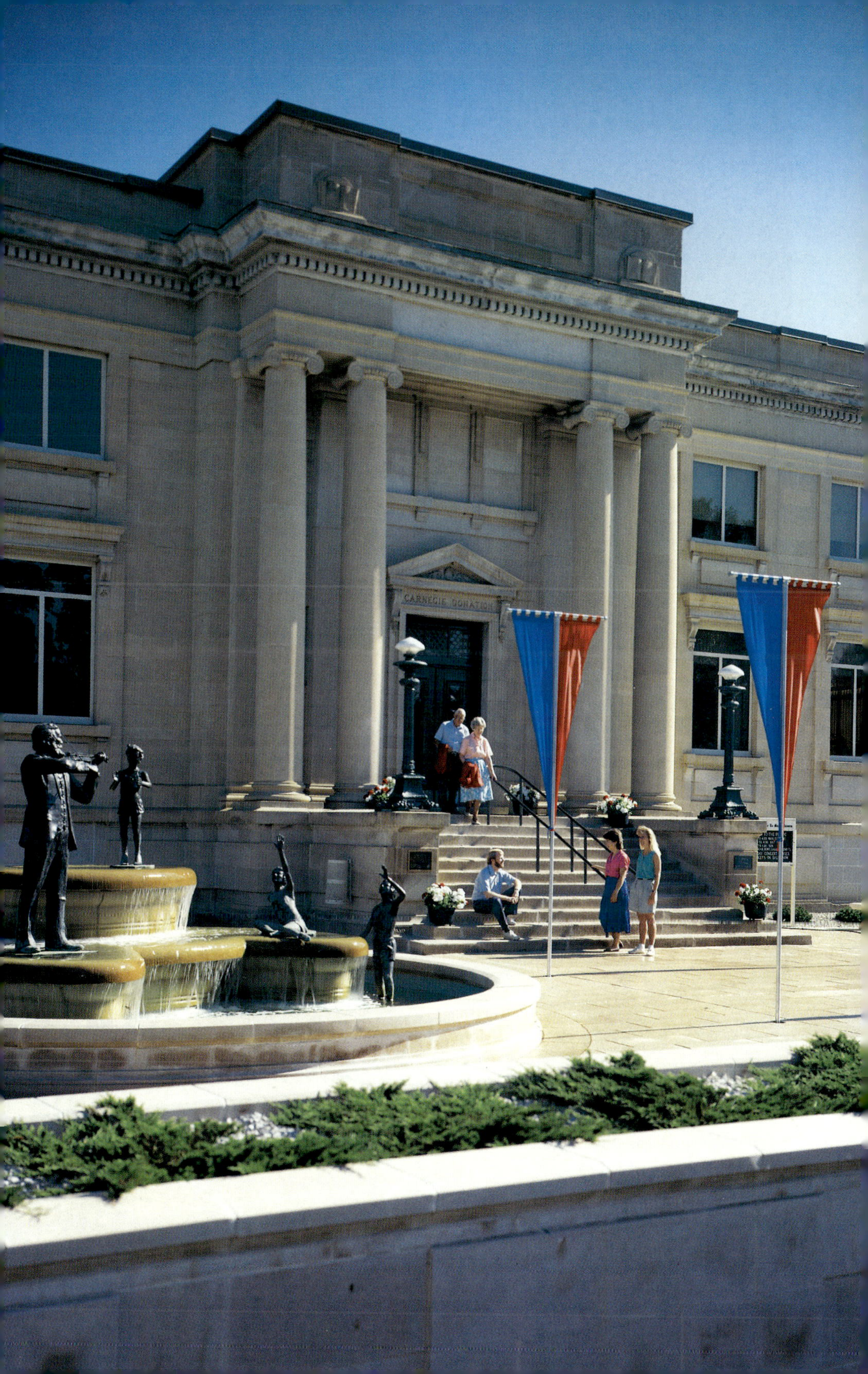
CARNEGIE DONATION

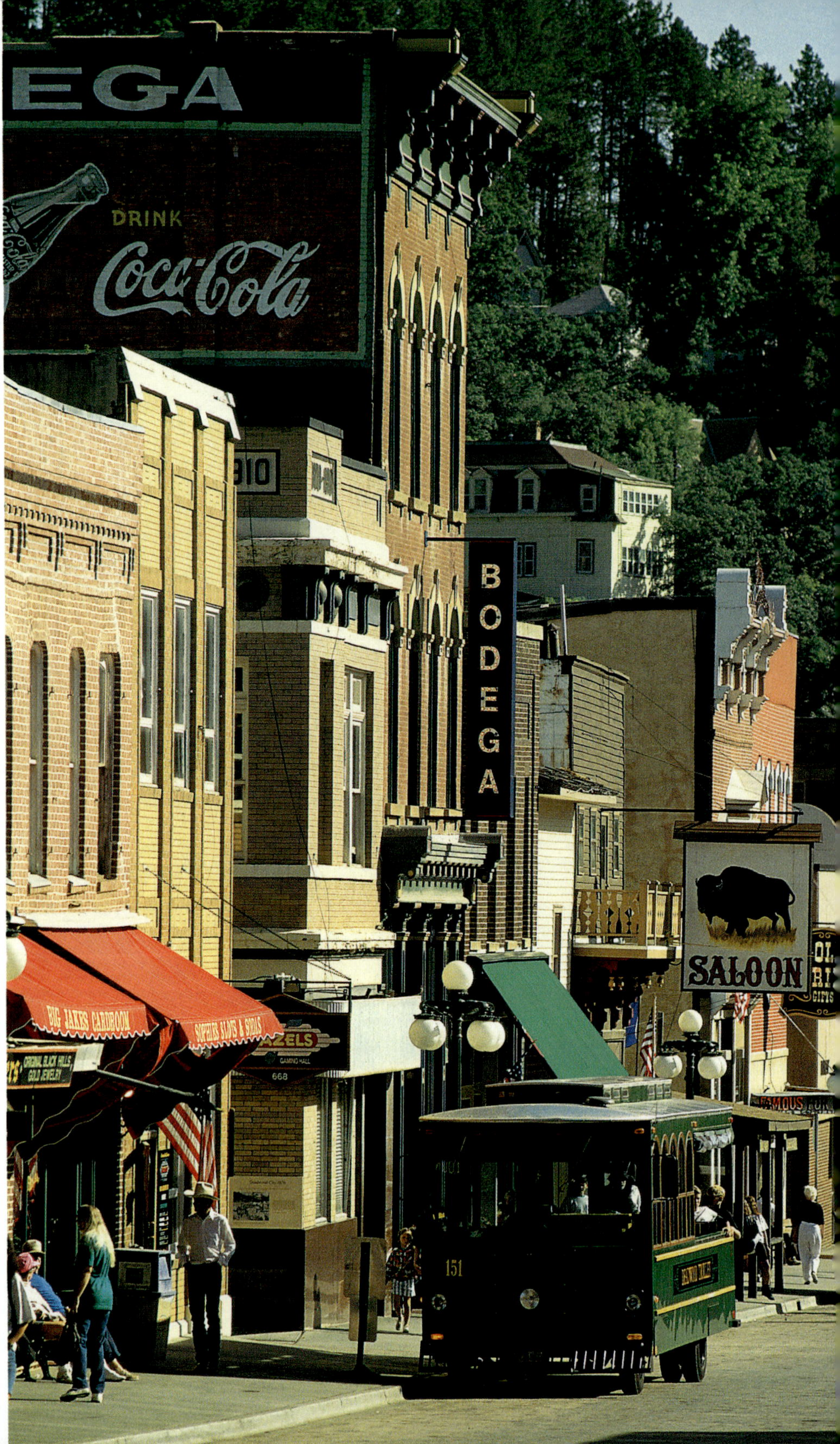
EGA
DRINK
Coca-Cola
BODEGA
SALOON
BIG JAKES CARDROOM

BEN HANTEN

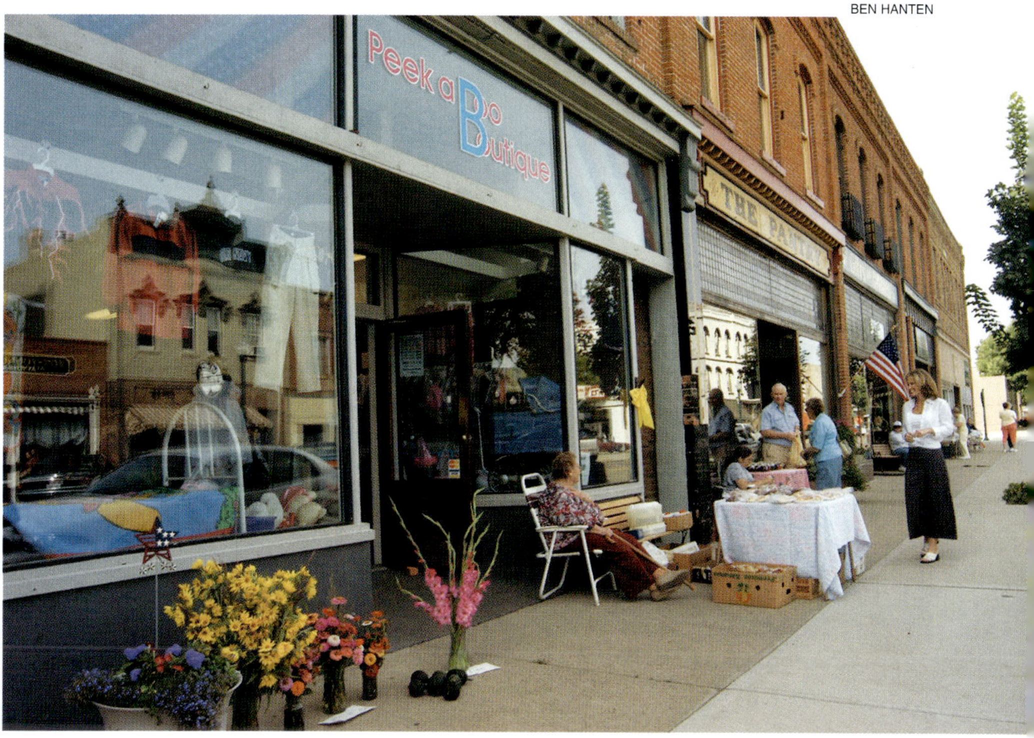

STAFF PHOTO

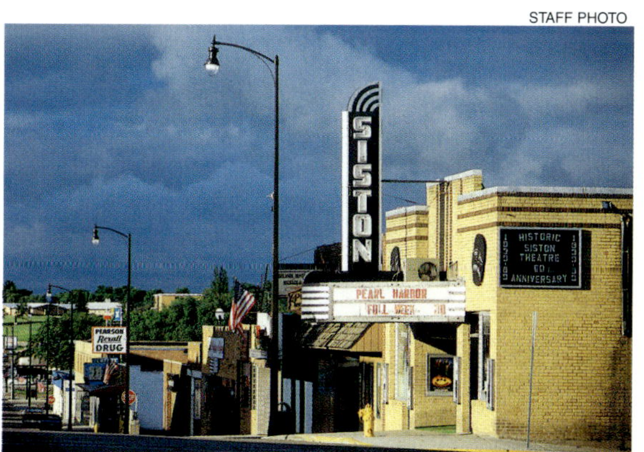

*Old West towns like **Deadwood** (opposite page) and **Yankton** (above) originally had wood structures on main street, but fires usually convinced merchants to try brick around the end of 19th century, and we still enjoy that "new" look today. **Sisseton** (right) has worked to preserve its main street's original appearance.*

KATIE HUNHOFF

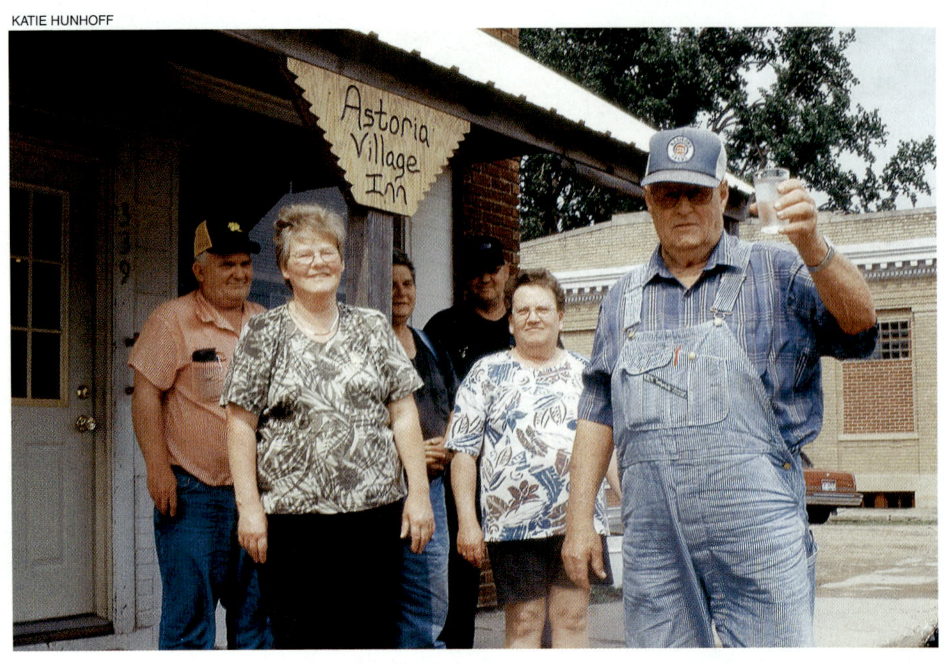

STAFF PHOTO

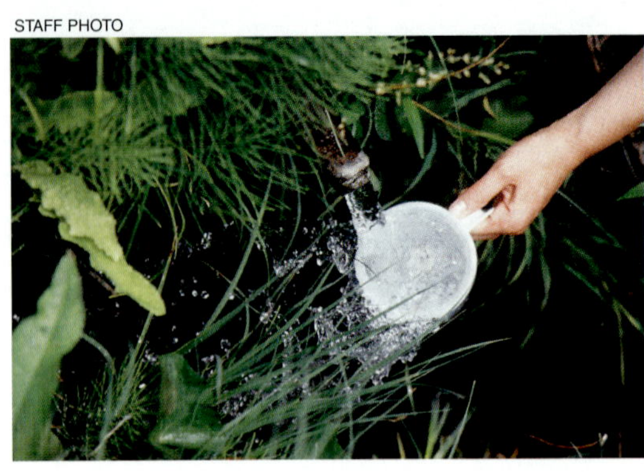

Some South Dakota towns are blessed with being close to water. River towns are common, and some communities have lakes near the city limits. ***Astoria*** *has Lake Astoria, but it also has an unusual resource known as Jorstad Spring, a sand point well two miles northwest of town that has been bubbling clean, tasty water 75 years or more. Out-of-towners often pull off Highway 28 to fill jugs with the water. At the Village Inn, Astoria's lone restaurant, the regulars tell stories about the spring and its surrounding bog that can "swallow a big cow."*

STAFF PHOTOS

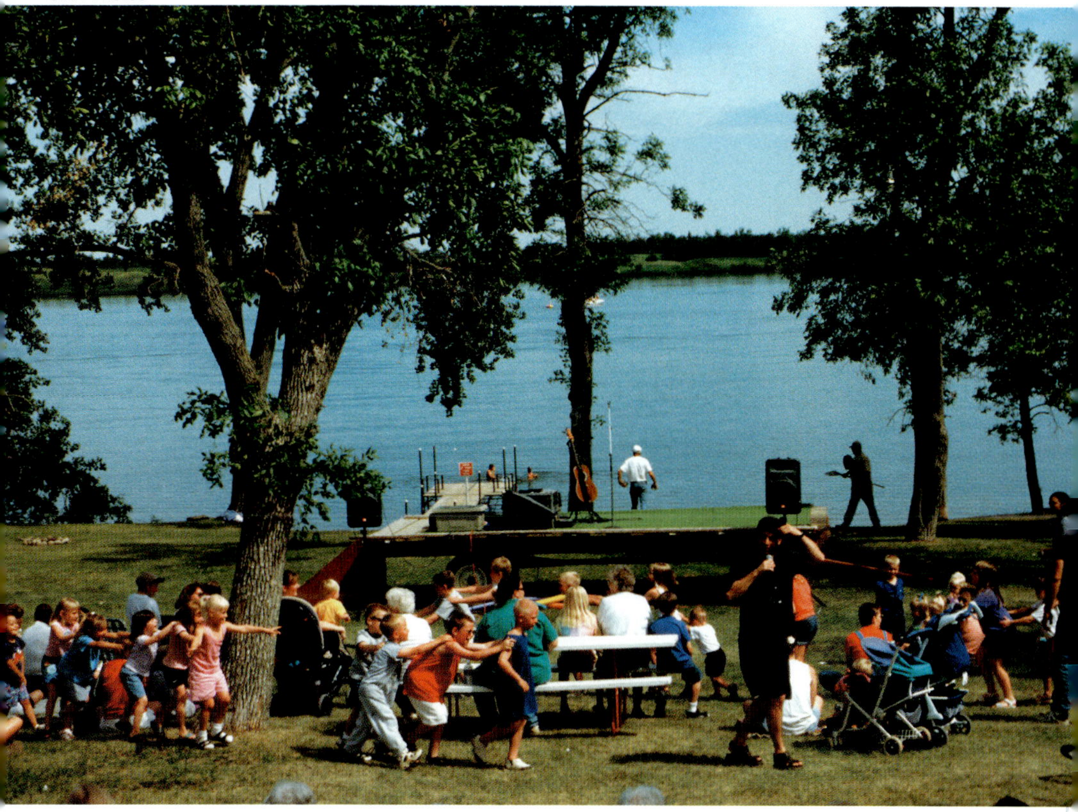

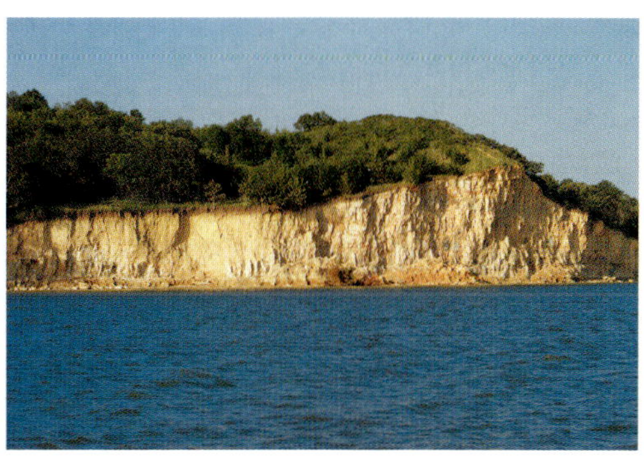

***South Shore** citizens cleaned Punished Woman's Lake (above) on the town's north side as a centennial project in 2001. Named from an Indian legend about a warrior and his lover who were killed by a jealous chief, it is now a popular gathering place. Phil Baker entertained kids for the centennial. **Yankton** has Lewis and Clark Lake, framed by yellow bluffs (left).*

STAFF PHOTO

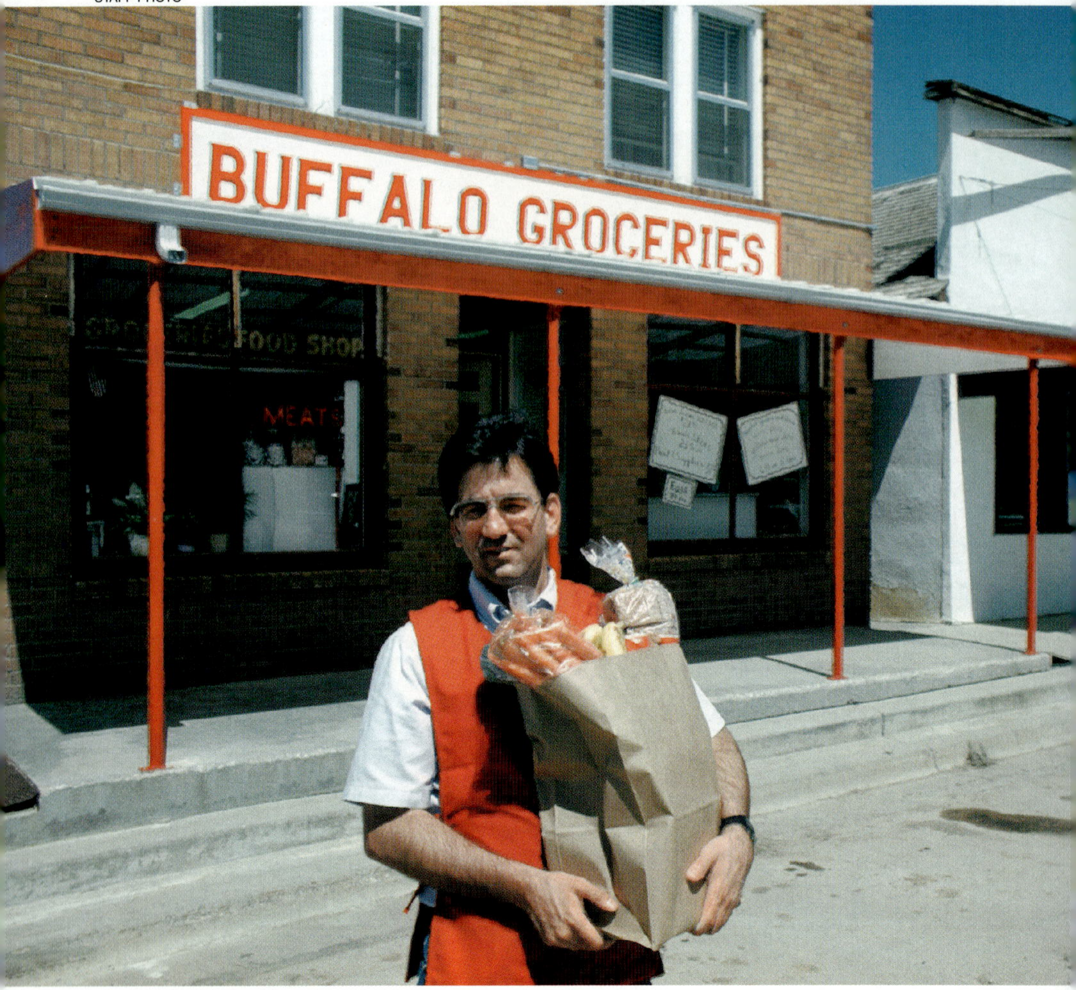

*Colorful characters and tireless leaders are always easy to find in a good business district. We photographed **Buffalo** grocer Terry Medley carrying sacks for a customer. When he bought the store in 1992 he received 17 bouquets of flowers, including one from his competitor. "You could have knocked me over with a flower!" he said.*

*We shot a picture of **Wall Drug Store** founder Ted Hustead at his desk in the state's most famous pharmacy. His bulletin board was thick with positive messages and quotes.*

BERNIE HUNHOFF

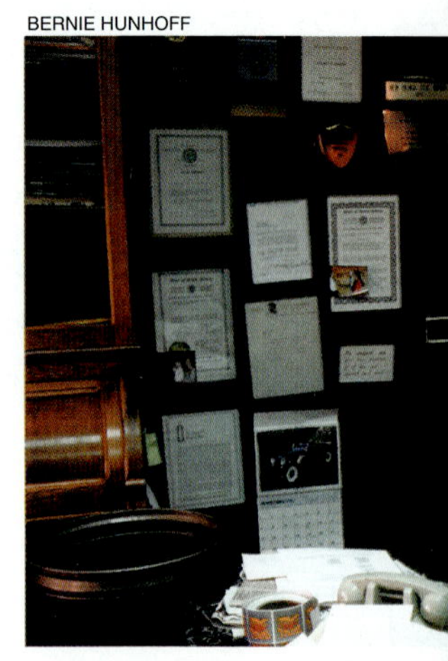

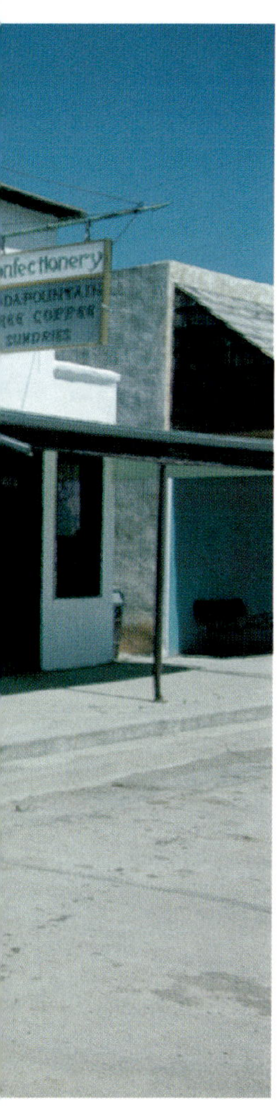

STAFF PHOTO

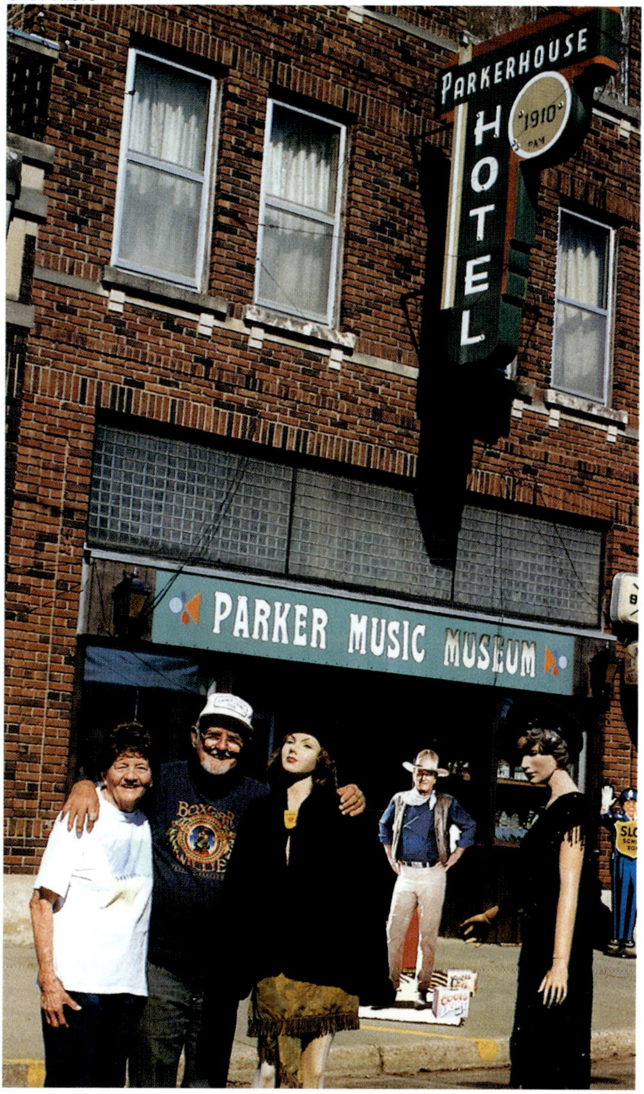

Milo and Dorothy Preheim turned a lifelong collection of memorabilia into a music museum in ***Parker****. Milo said he bought the second television set sold in South Dakota. He put an antenna on his 60-foot windmill tower to catch a signal.*

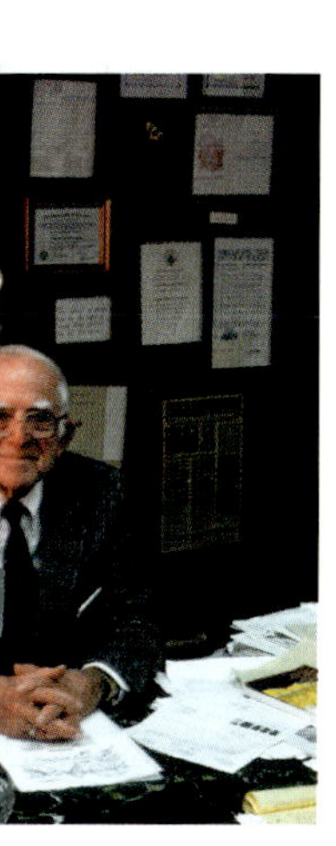

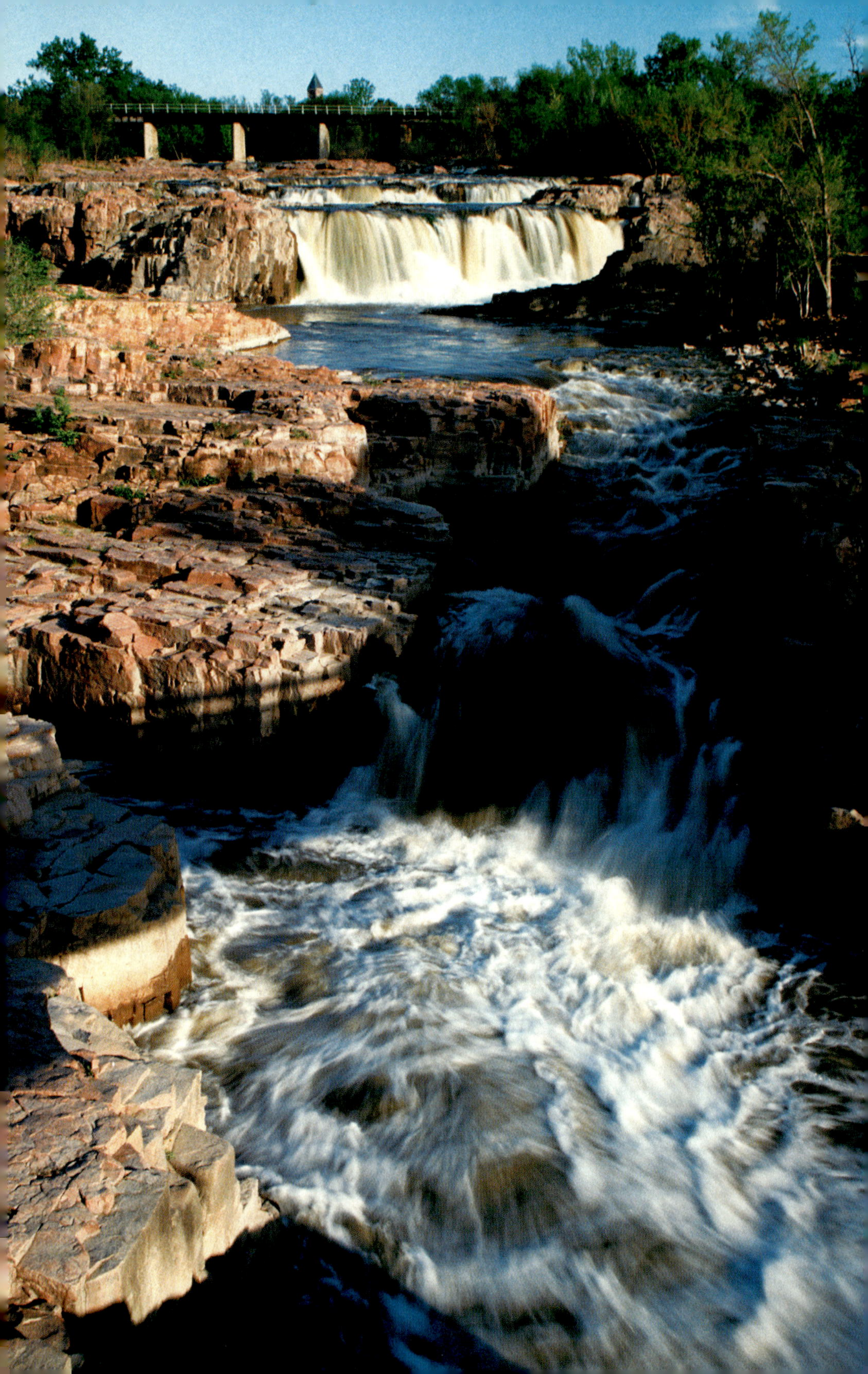

SD TOURISM PHOTOS

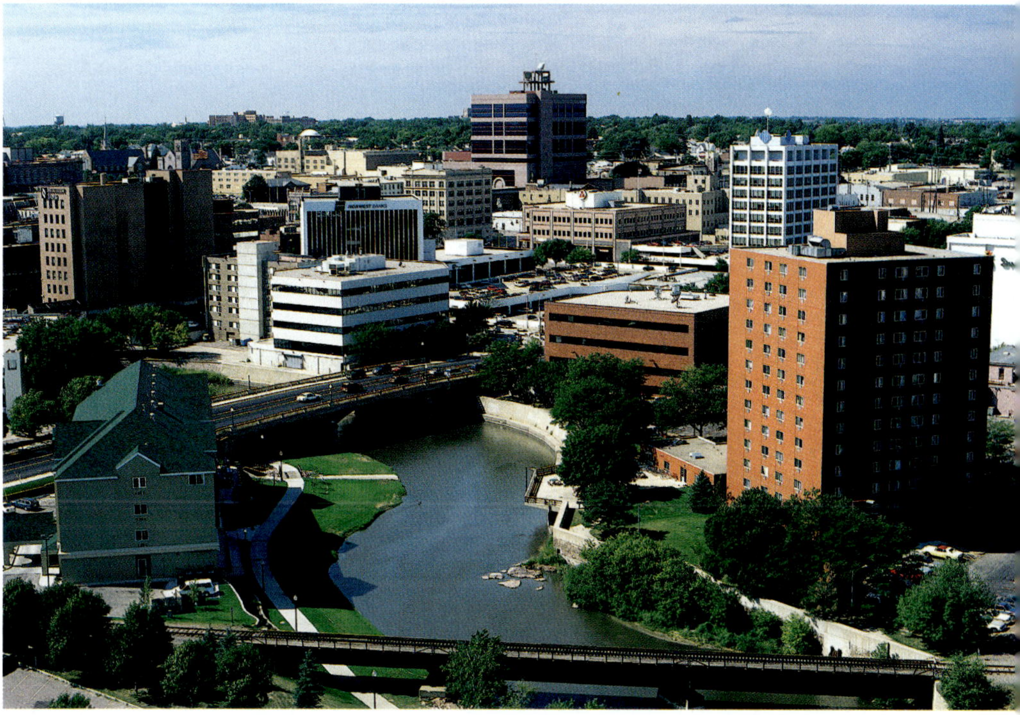

Sioux Falls, *the state's largest city by several miles, gives the state an economic engine, culture, a unique park along the Big Sioux's granite falls (opposite page), beautiful architecture like St. Joseph's Cathedral (right) and even a metro skyline (above).*

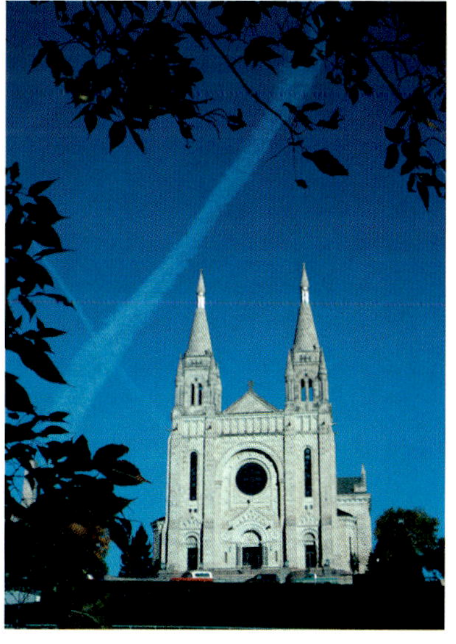

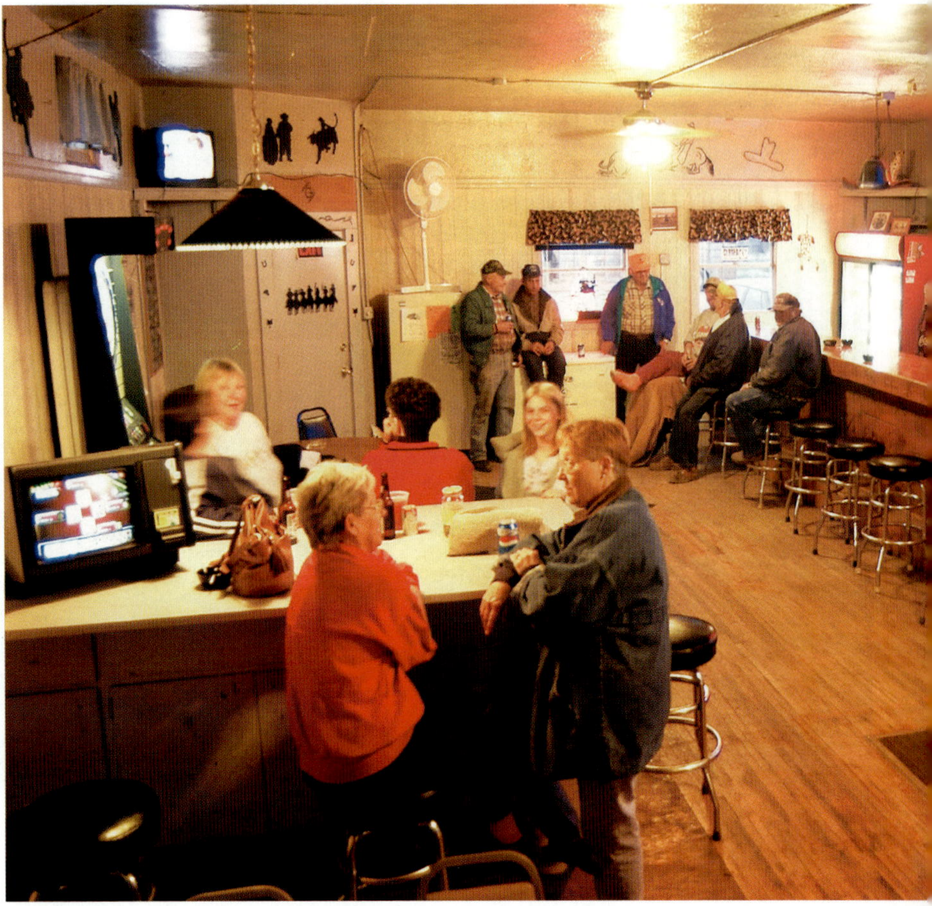

Public institutions and residential neighborhoods are important, but most of a town's personality — at least from a traveler's perspective — shows up in the business district. At the Roundup Bar (above) in ***Ree Heights****, ranchers burned their brands in the pine bar. At right, a warehouse roof in* ***Wagner*** *shows some age.*

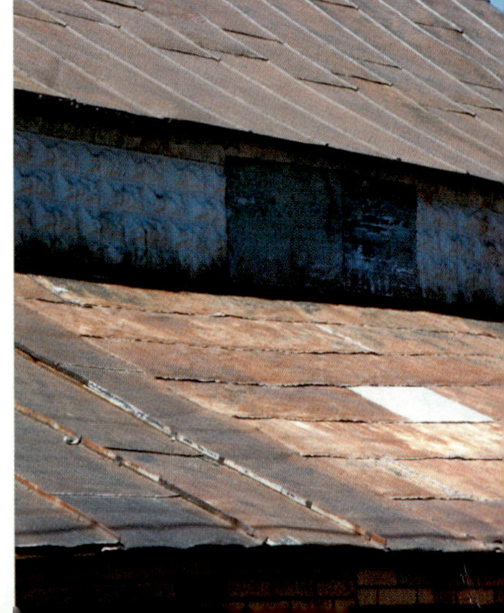

KATIE HUNHOFF

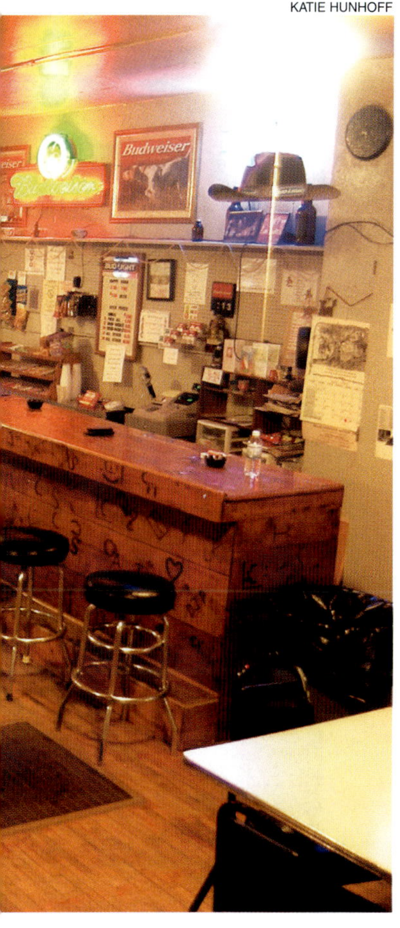

KATIE HUNHOFF

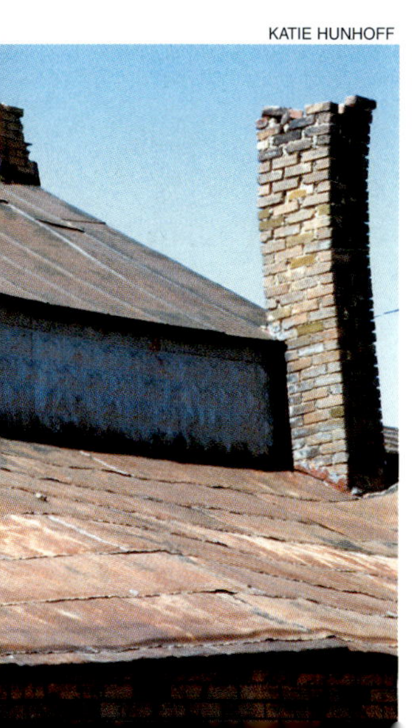

CONTRIBUTED PHOTO

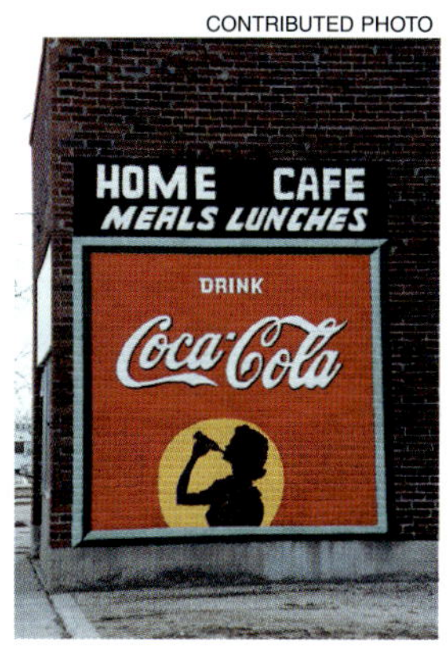

A soda pop mural in downtown ***Willow Lake*** *harkens to an earlier day. Citizens in that small Clark County town have worked to build up a local library. Flowers and a customer's bike create a still-life by the Roberts County National Bank in* ***Sisseton****.*

STAFF PHOTO

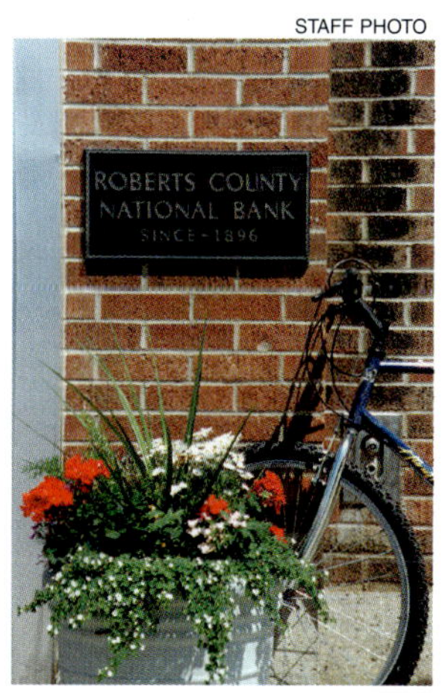

STAFF PHOTO

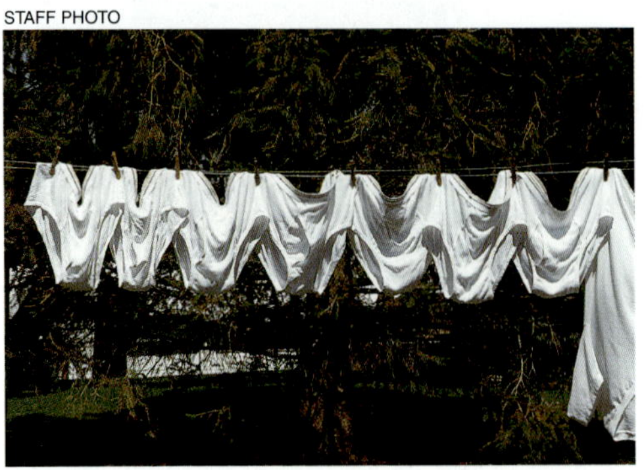

Sometimes its funny what catches the eyes of our photographers as they explore South Dakota's cities — like (clockwise from above) a man's underwear hanging out to dry in ***Parker****, a park made of petrified wood in* ***Lemmon****, a sculpted flying pheasant that welcomes visitors to the Cabela's store in* ***Mitchell****, and Ken Bell's auto-sculpture of Ford LTDs along Highway 212 west of* ***Clark*** *that he titled "The Parade."*

STAFF PHOTO

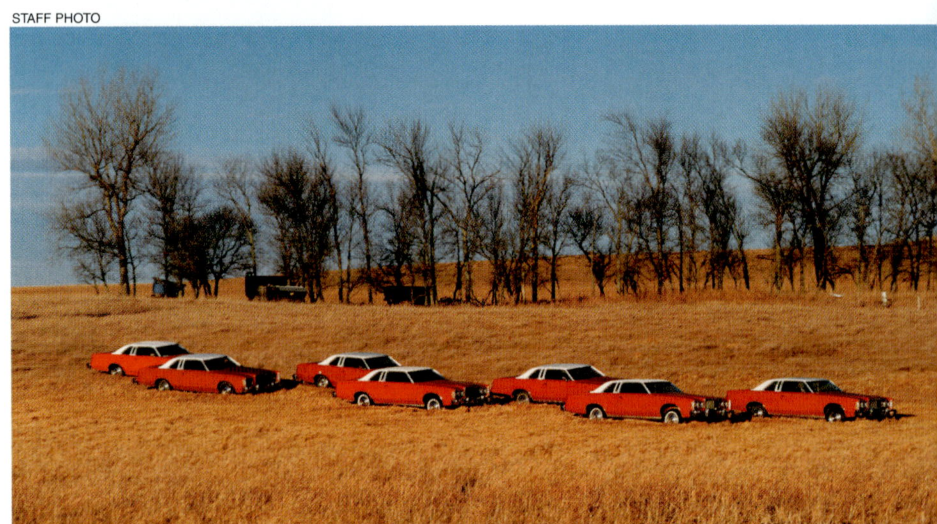

BERNIE HUNHOFF

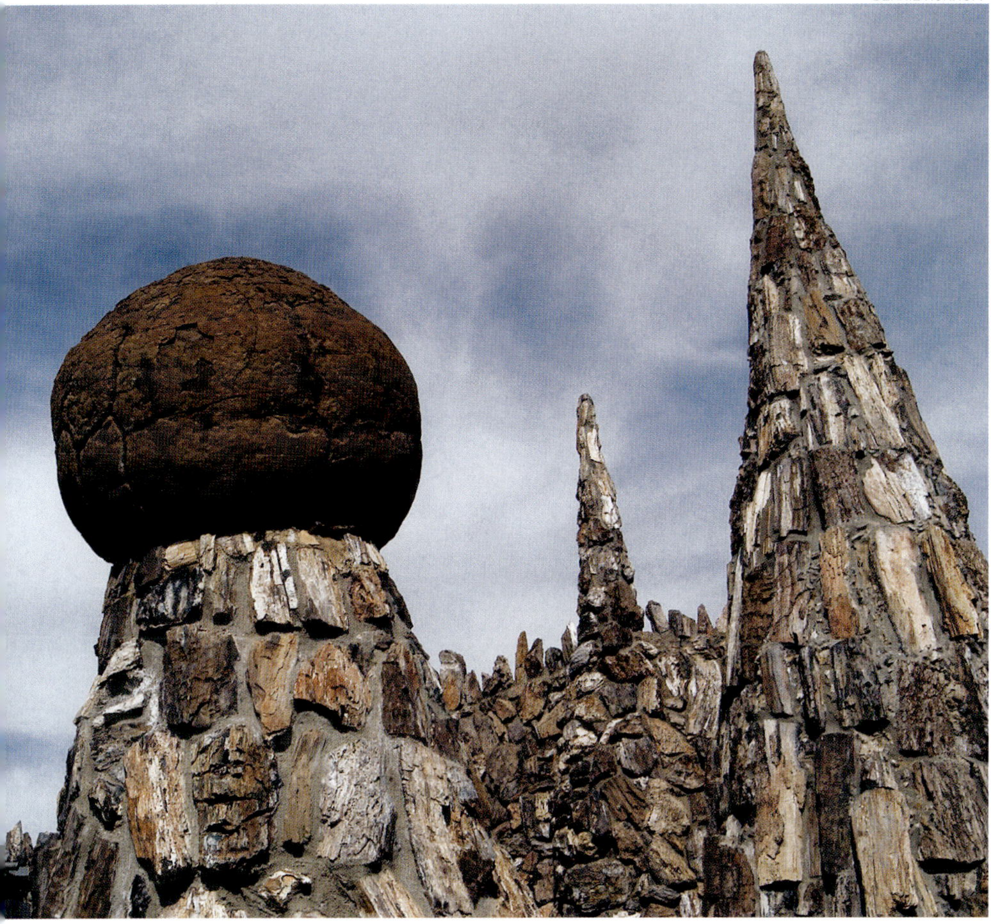

STAFF PHOTO

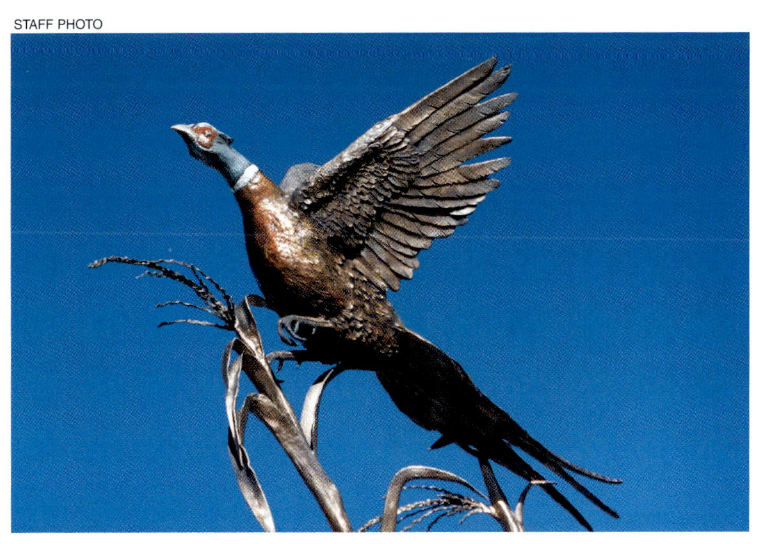

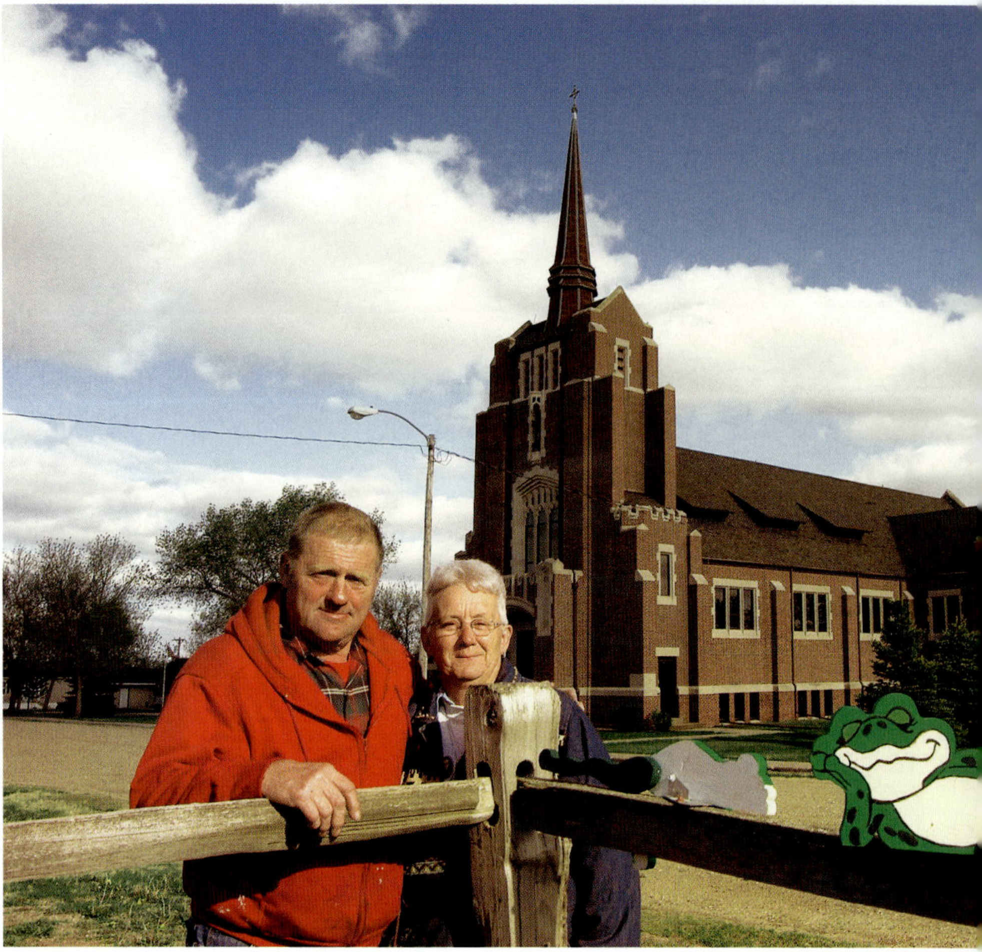

STAFF PHOTO

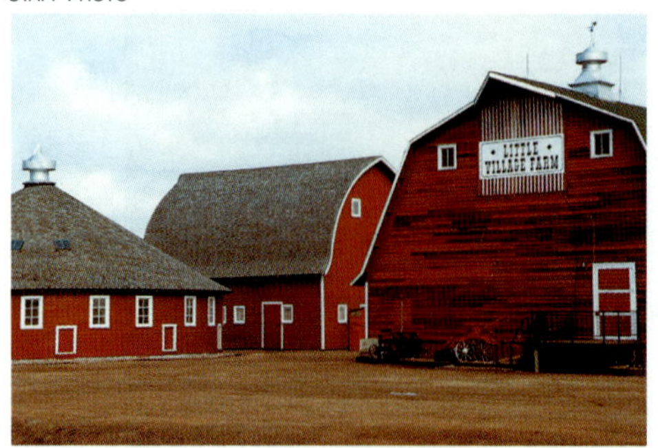

Everybody loves to be surprised when they visit a town. In South Dakota, the biggest surprises often come in the smallest of towns. ***Turton,*** *with just 61 people, has several historic churches and an annual Frogtown Festival. Joe and Betty Barrie used the frog theme to decorate their home. Near* ***Trent,*** *north of Sioux Falls, is Little Village Farm, a nostalgic collection of buildings, equipment and oddities.*

KATIE HUNHOFF

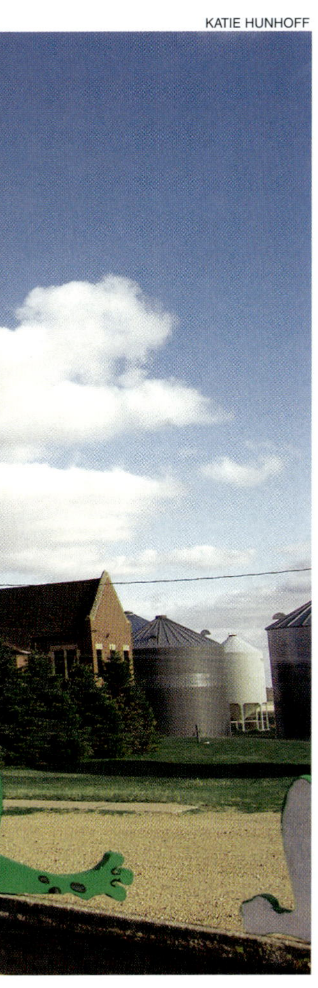

KATIE HUNHOFF

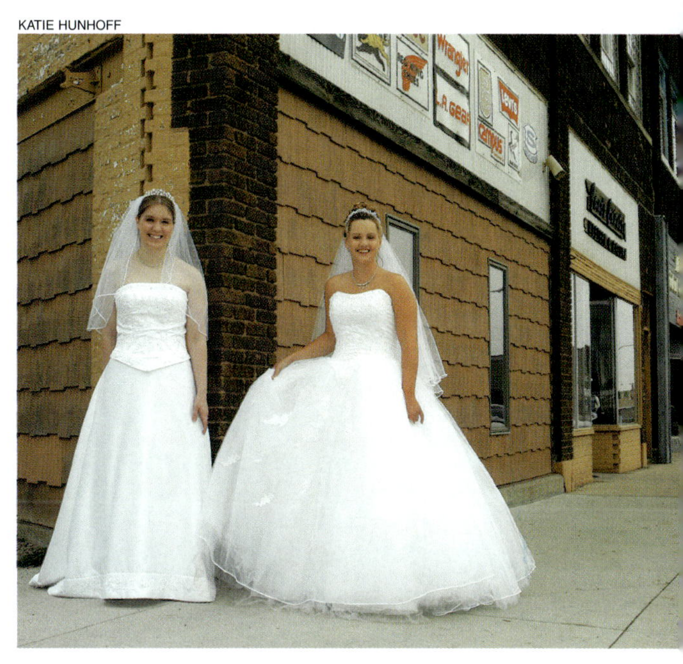

Small towns have lost much of their retail trade, but many still have specialty shops that cater to people from miles around. For decades, brides-to-be have journeyed to ***Wagner*** *for wedding apparel. Travelers can also be surprised in the bigger cities: a concrete section of the Berlin Wall (below) is displayed in a park near downtown* ***Rapid City****.*

CONTRIBUTED PHOTO

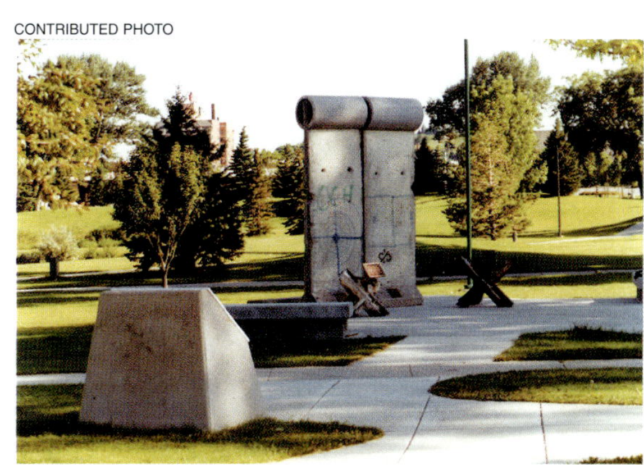

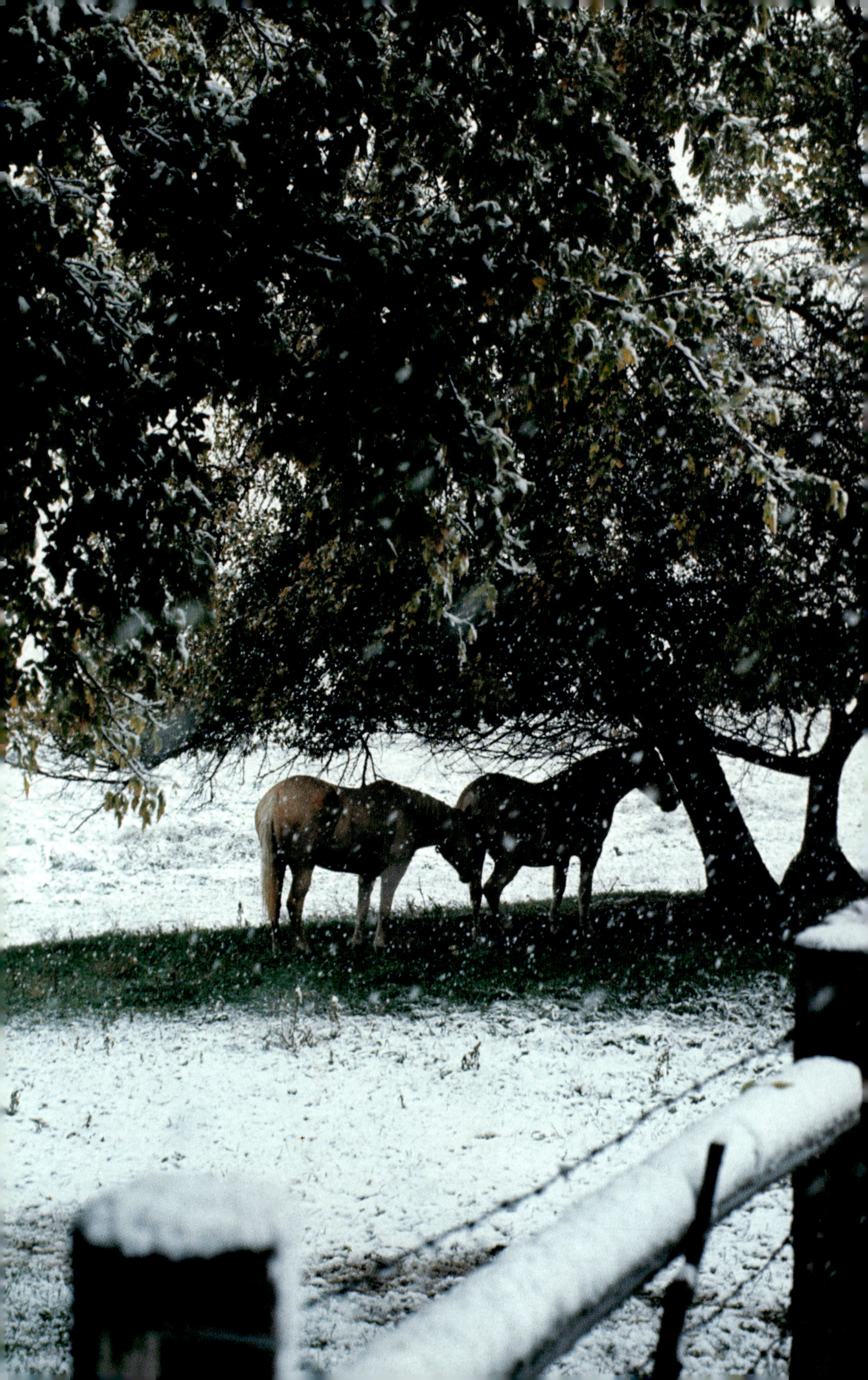

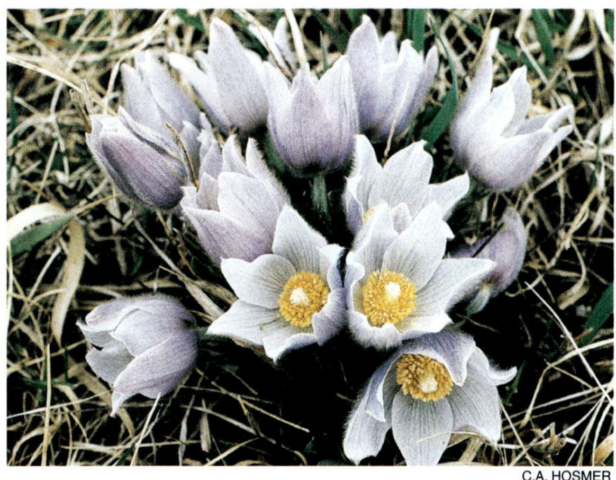

C.A. HOSMER

Spring

Long winter nights retreat at last, and noonday shadows recede with the snow. Tomorrow the sun will warm us a few minutes longer than today, its rays softening the frosted Earth. And below the crust the roots of spring awake. Any day now the quickening will come.

The pasqueflower is the first to arrive. Like the joyous occasion for which it is named, the pasque signals the resurrection of life. The Hebrew word *pesah,* meaning Passover, entered English as *pasche,* or Easter. The transparent-purple symbol of rebirth has been the official flower of South Dakota since 1903.

But it is only one harbinger of spring. Meadowlark music, willow buds, thawing streams and rivers, children on bikes — all are signs and sounds of hope for new beginnings.

SD TOURISM

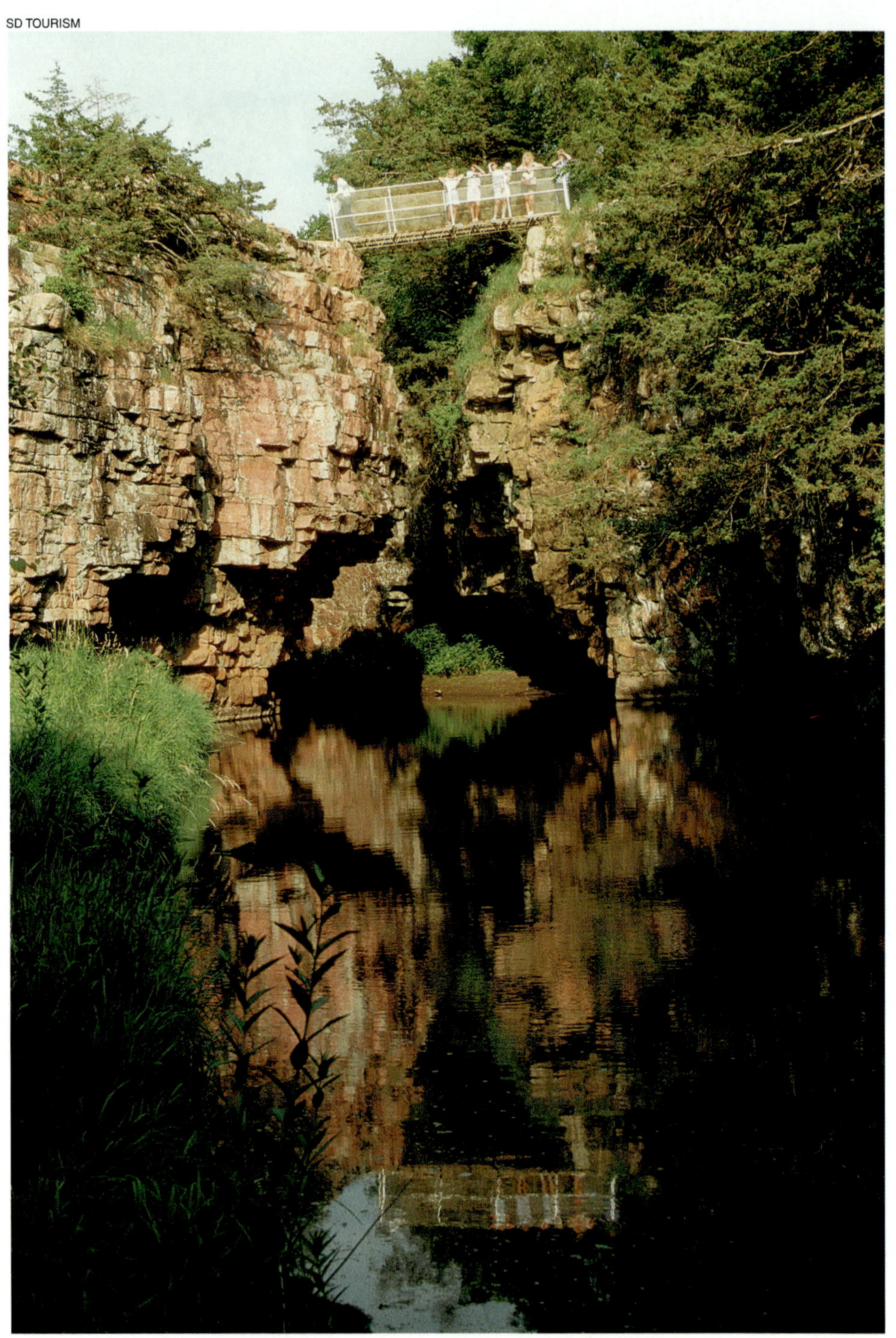

Spring comes to Devil's Gulch in Garretson, where legend has it that Jesse James leaped the 30-foot gorge on horseback to escape a posse.

BERNIE HUNHOFF

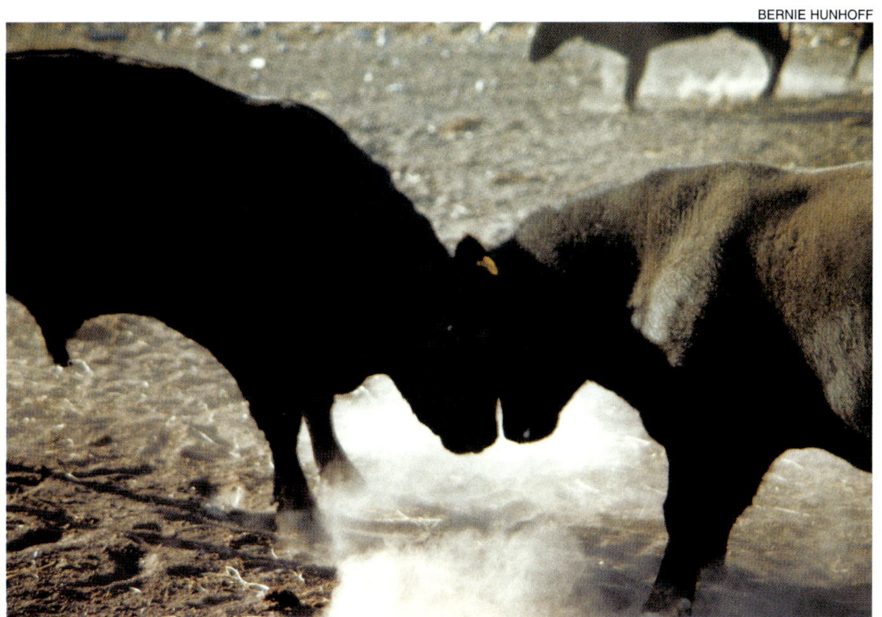

Bull fights are a spring ritual in cattle country, as one-ton beasts establish their pecking order. Below, a more tranquil critter relaxes on a log at Bear Country near Rapid City.

BEN HANTEN

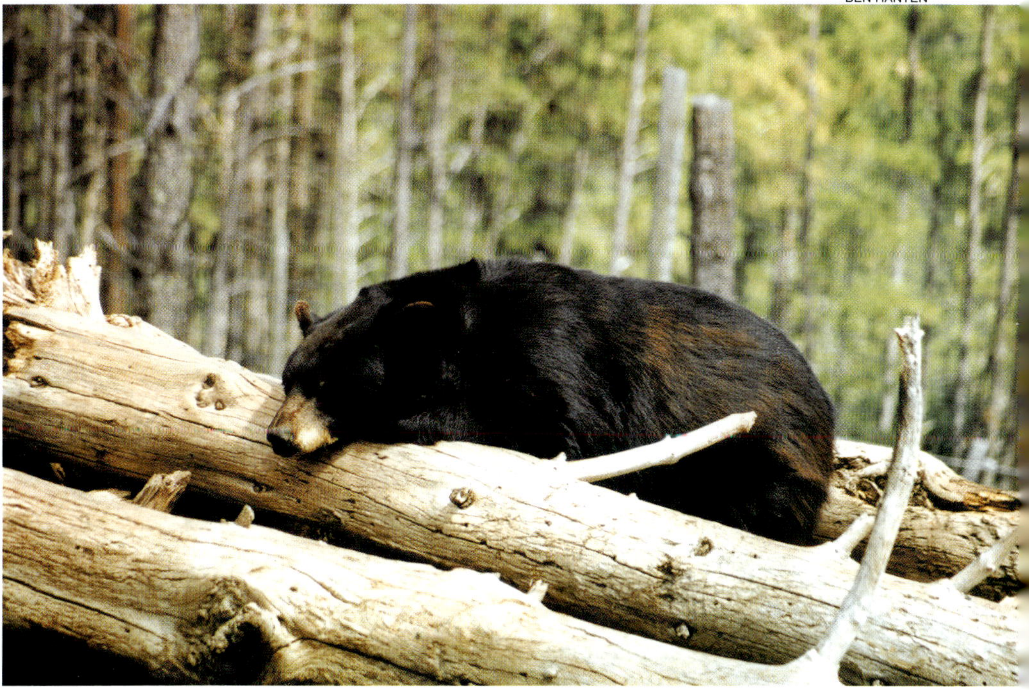

ROY DAVID FARRIS

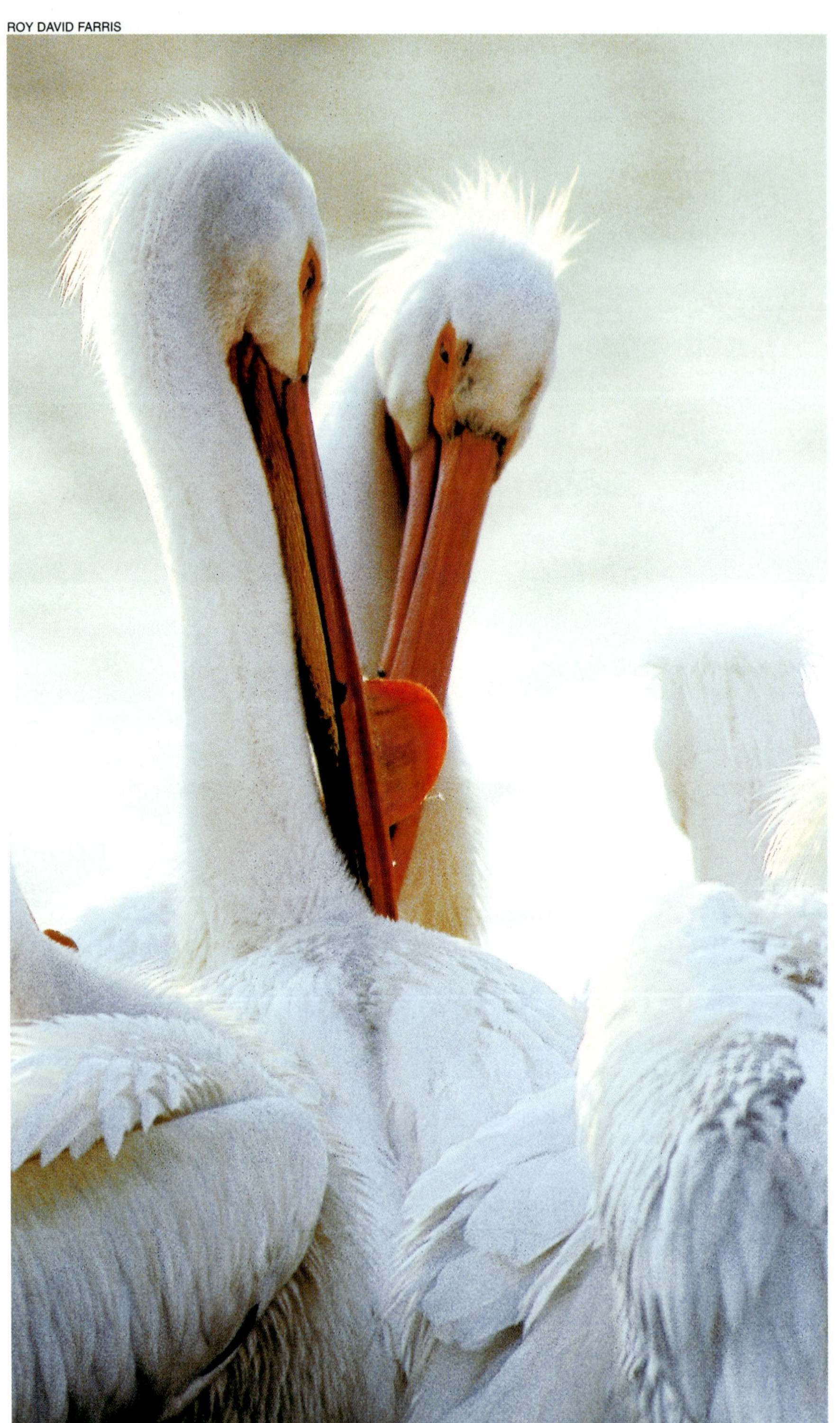

Chuck Post

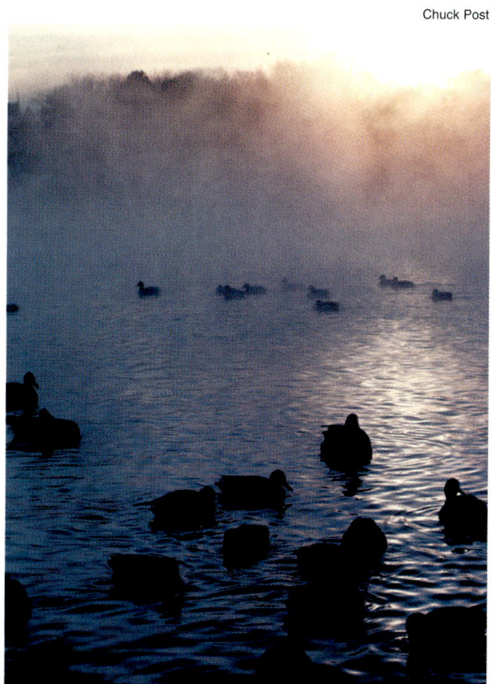

Warm weather brings back the birds. At left, pelicans mate at LaCreek Wildlife Refuge near Martin. Ducks (above) relax on Pierre's Capitol Lake, and (below) a lone mourning dove rests on barbed wire.

MARK KAYSER / SD TOURISM

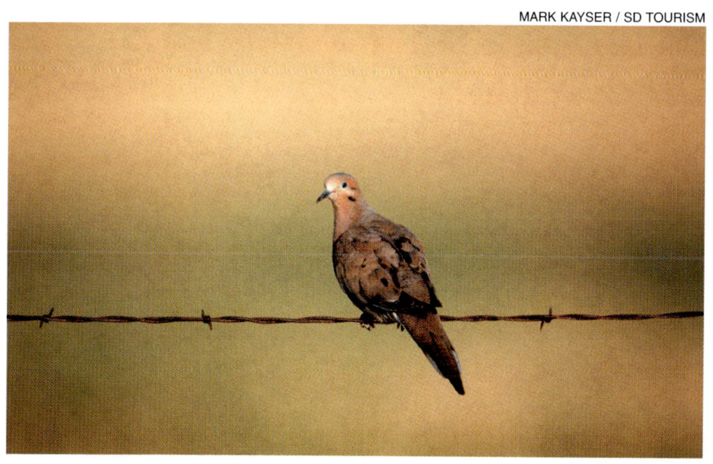

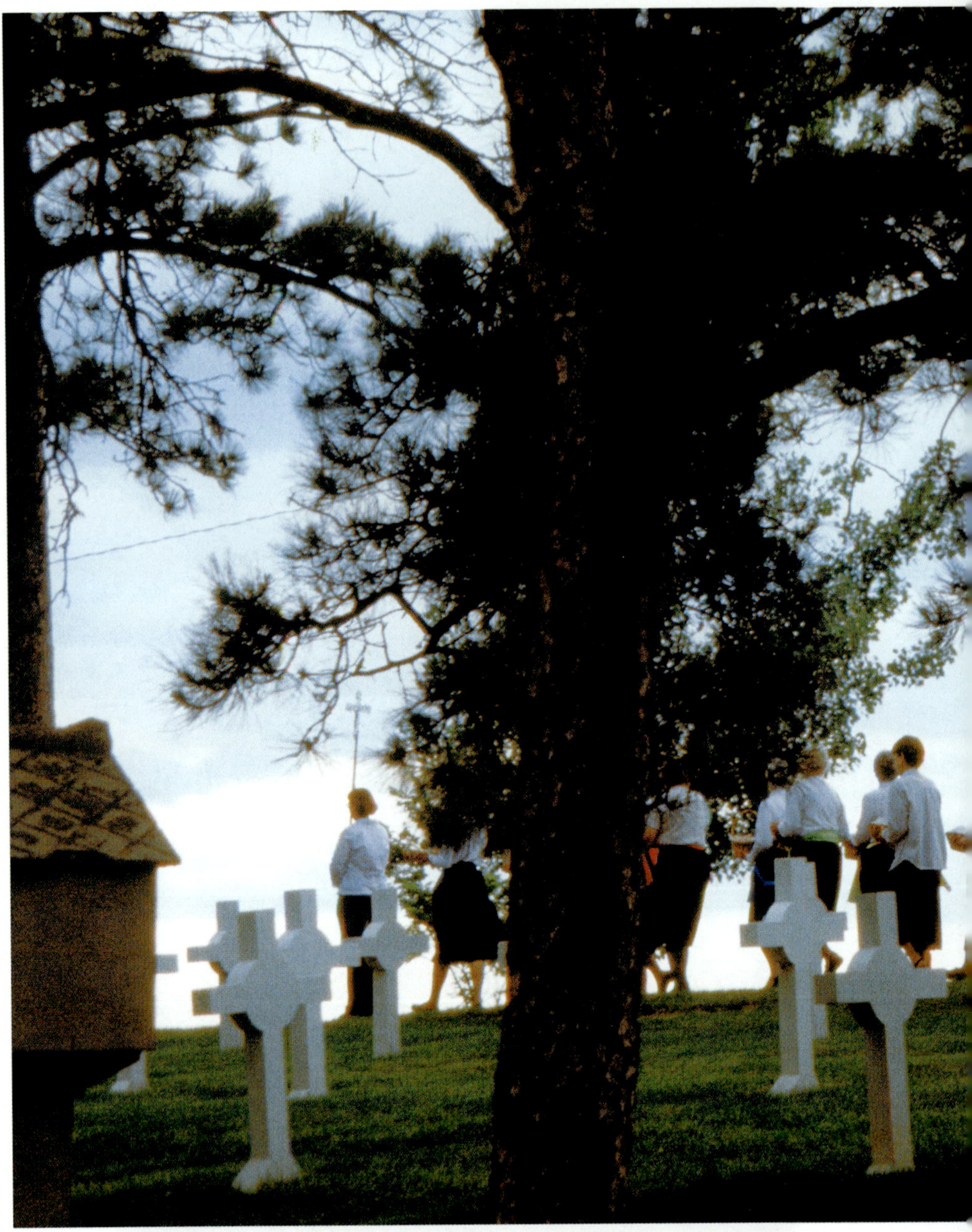

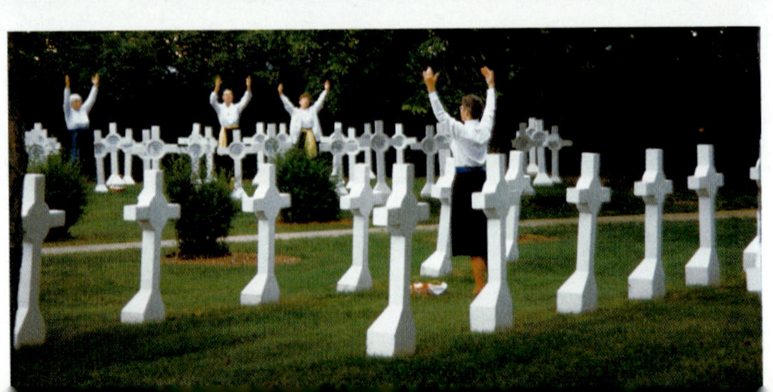

BERNIE HUNHOFF

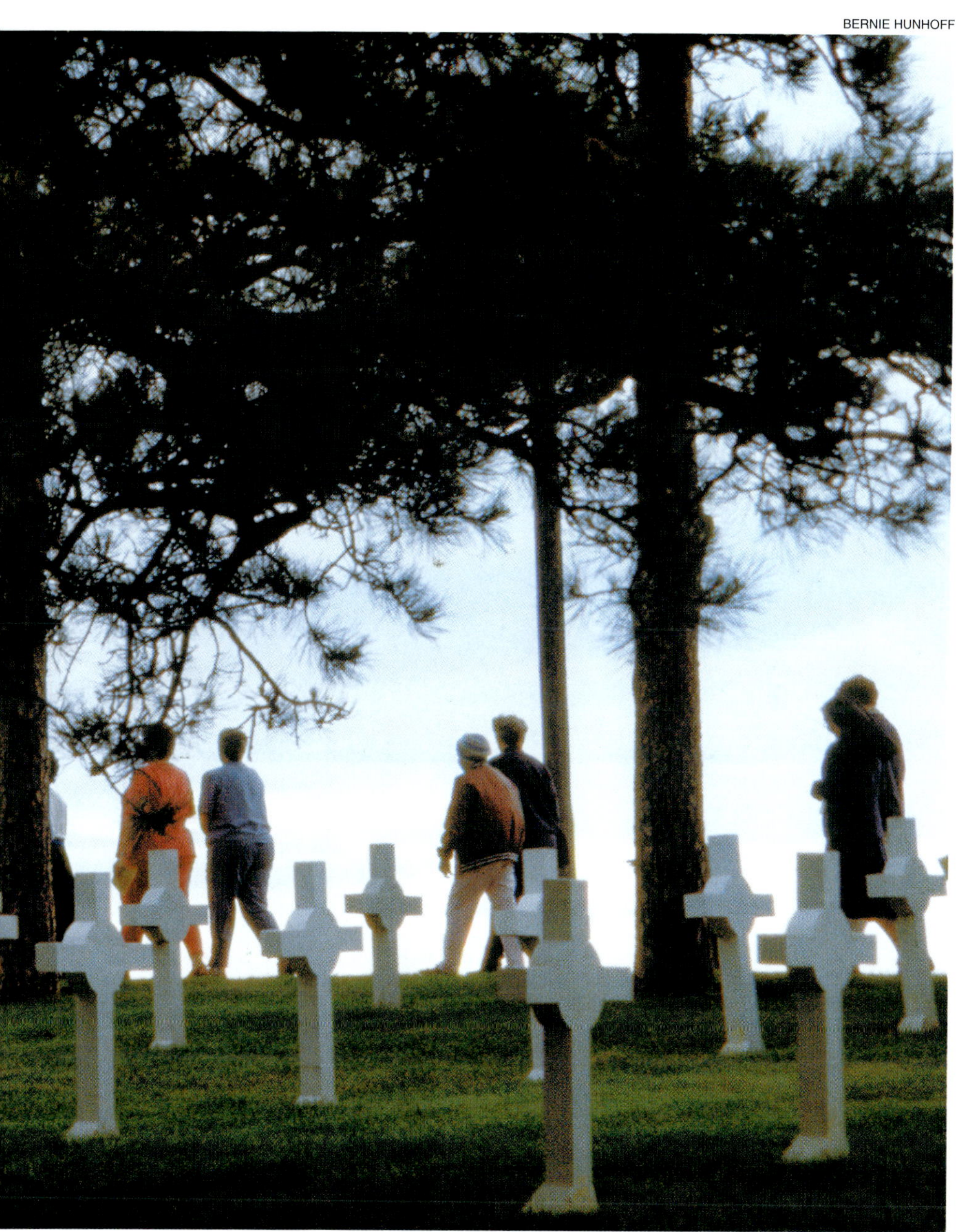

The women of Sacred Heart Monastery work in far-flung places, but they all meet in June at their monastery above the Missouri River in Yankton for Community Days. One of the annual traditions is a procession to the cemetery to remember their deceased sisters with songs and prayer.

JAY DAVIS

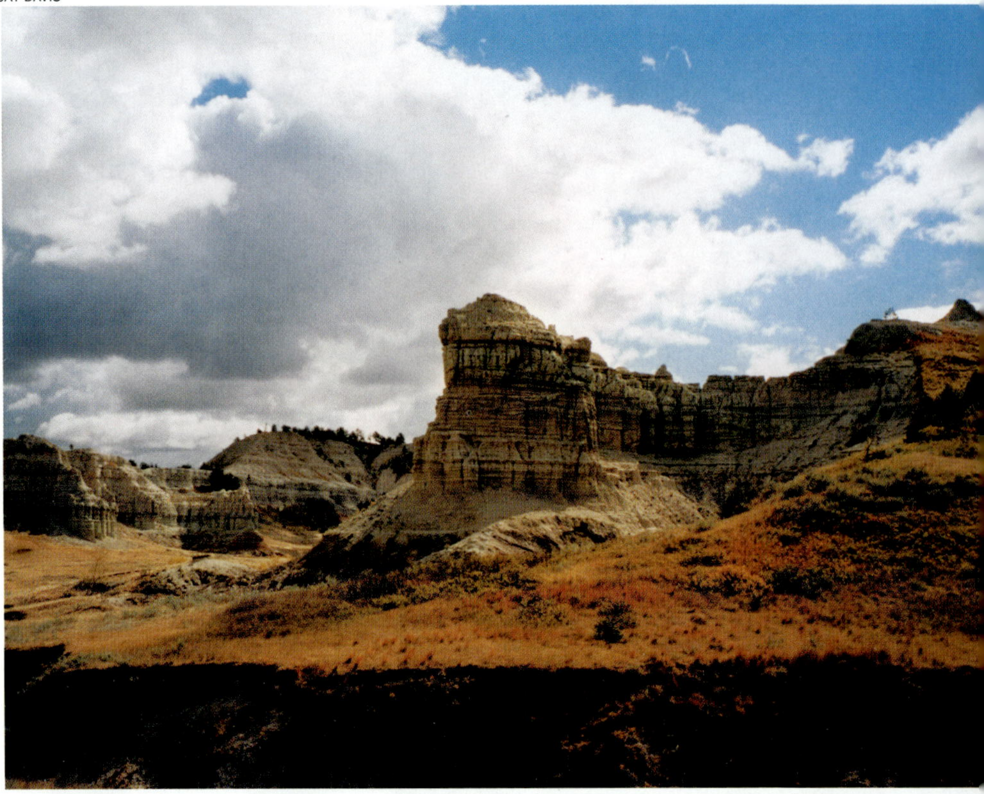

Slim Buttes, the scene of a battle between Crazy Horse and the U.S. military in the bloody year of 1876, is now a quiet spot in Harding County. At right, brightly-clad cowgirls await their turn to ride at a West River horse show.

STEPHEN GASSMAN

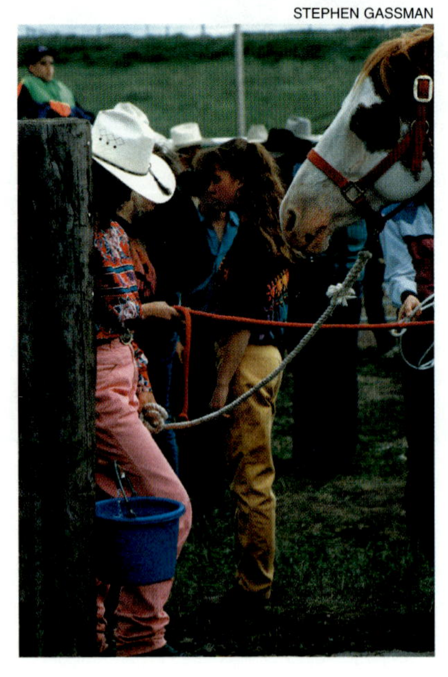

BERNIE HUNHOFF

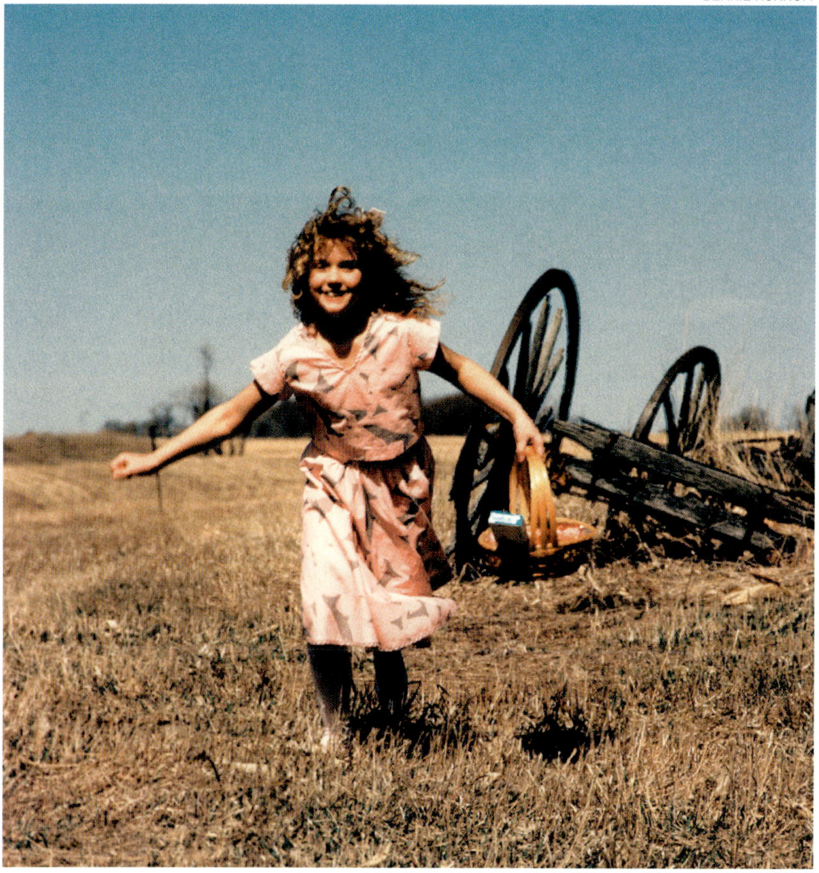

An early Easter in South Dakota can mean candy eggs hidden in brown grass. Right, a female badger prepares her underground home for the spring litter, which generally arrives in April. You can usually count a badger's babies on one hand.

DAVE COFFIN

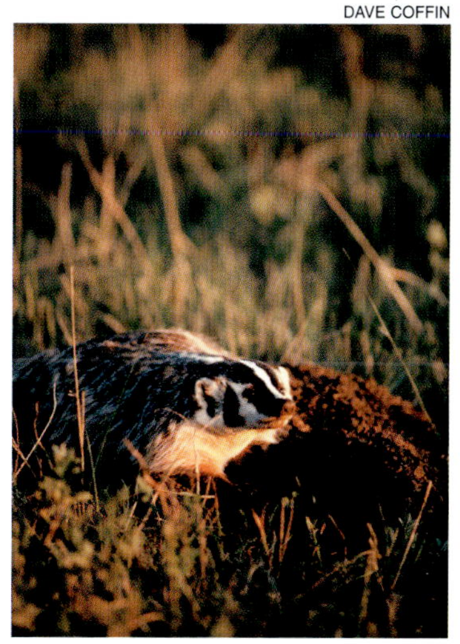

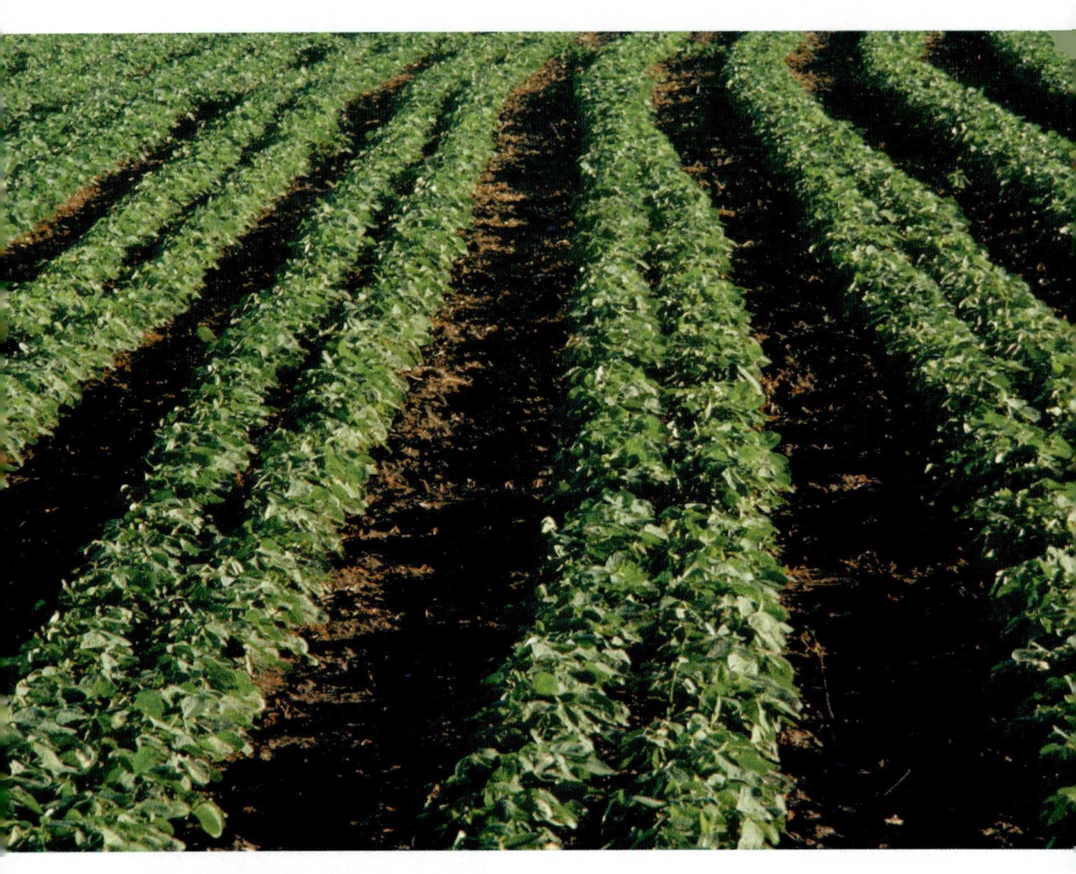

Soybeans have emerged as one of South Dakota's biggest cash crops. Four million acres are planted every spring. The beans are used for foods, fuel and fabric.

BERNIE HUNHOFF

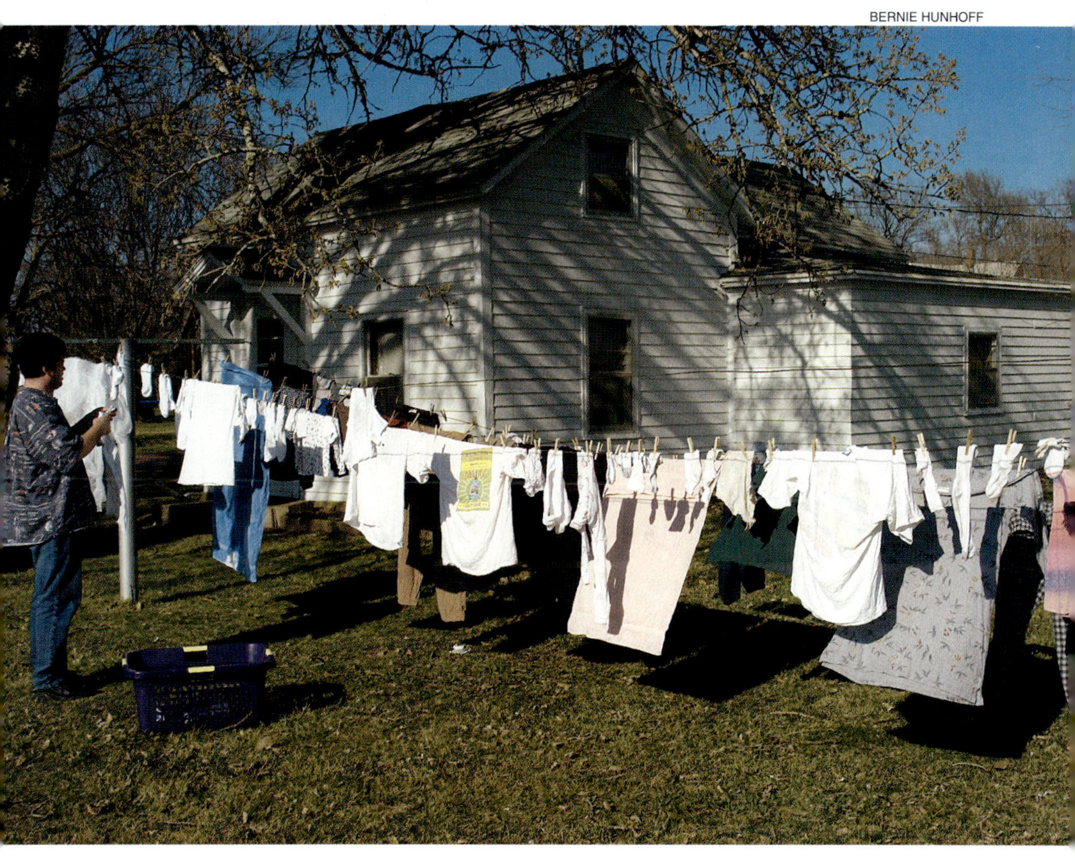

Spring breezes save electricity, but spare privacy, for a young man in the small town of Bridgewater. A clothes line is wind energy at its simplest.

STEPHEN GASSMAN

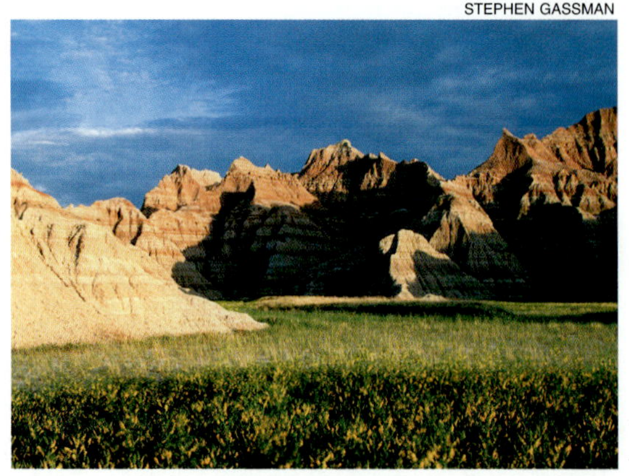

The valley east of Sheep Mountain Table in Pennington County greens with spring rains (above), and that is when the male sage grouse (below) spikes his tail feathers and coos to the females in one of nature's most interesting courtships.

SD TOURISM

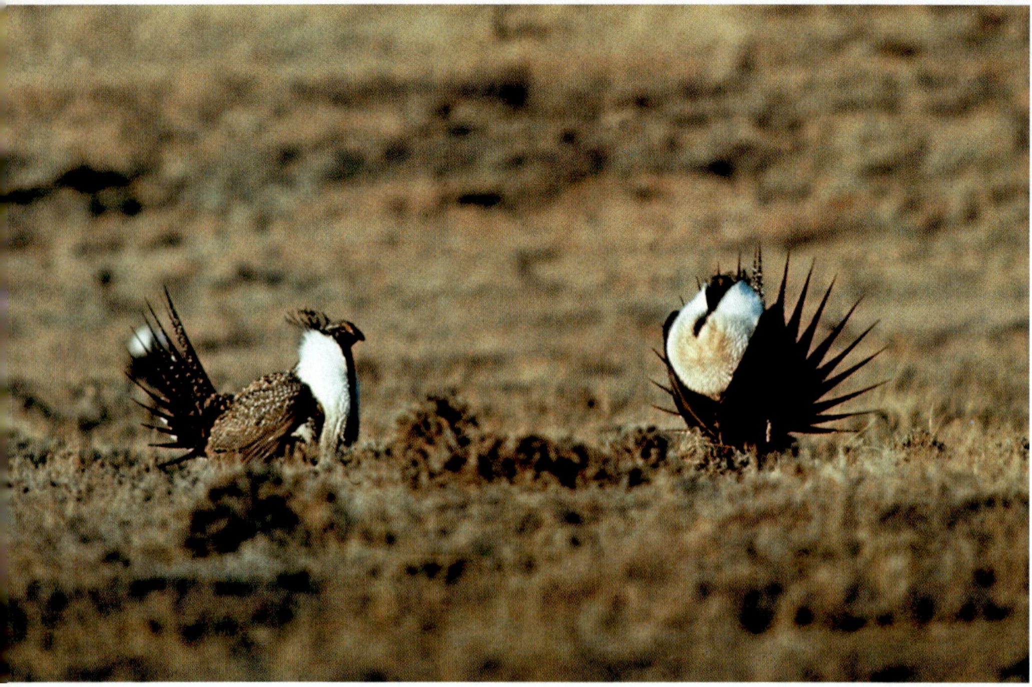

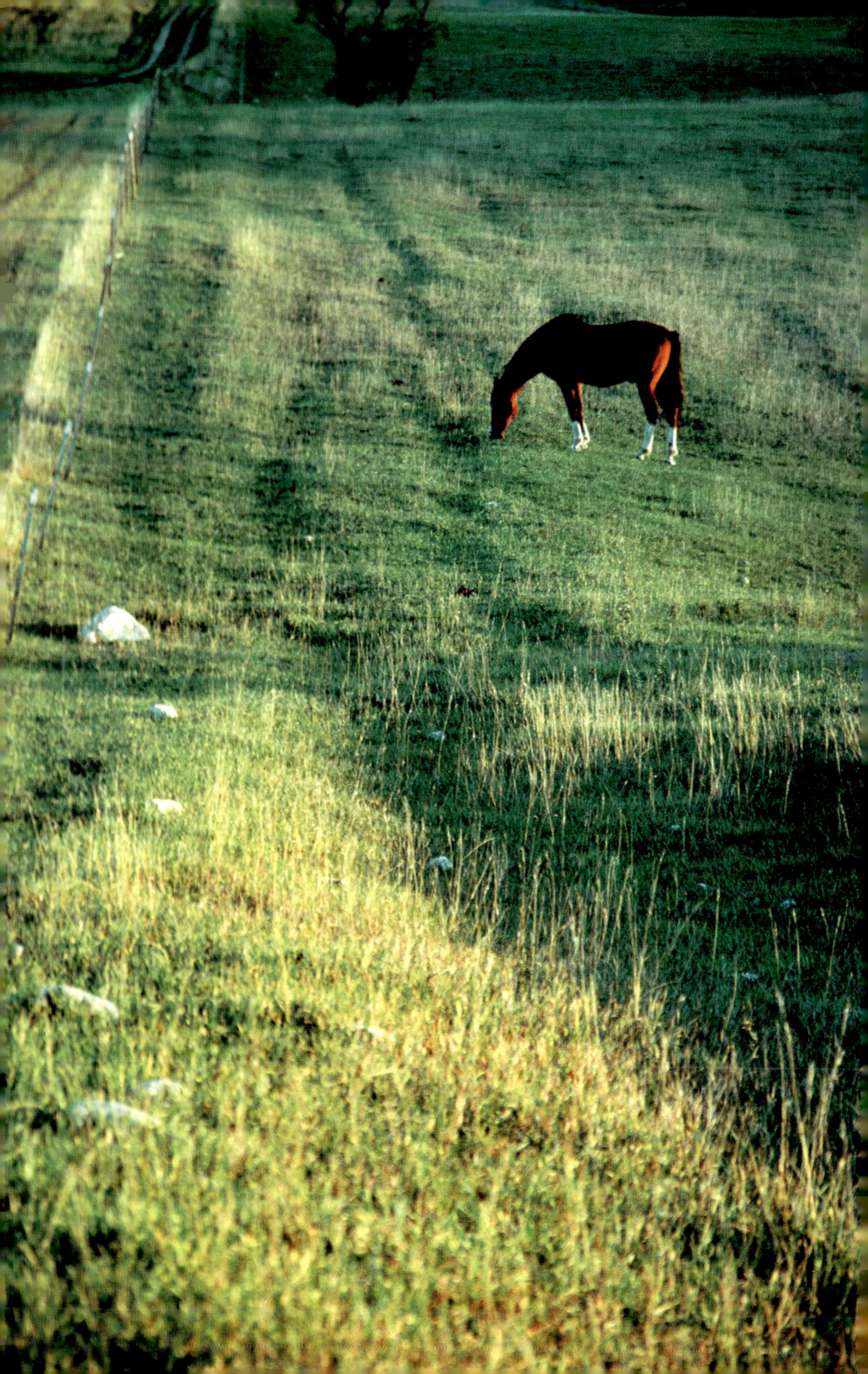

BERNIE HUNHOFF

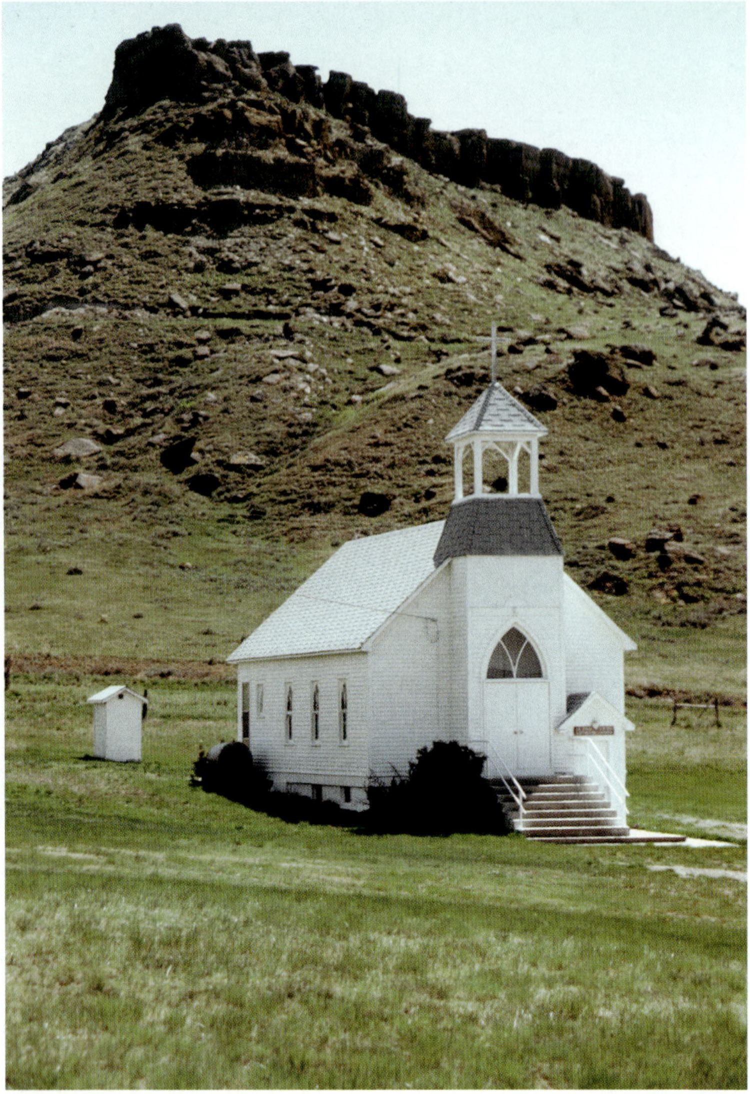

Finnish immigrants founded the Cave Hills Church north of Buffalo in northwest South Dakota. The settler who gave land for the church died soon after it was built. He was the first man buried in the cemetery.

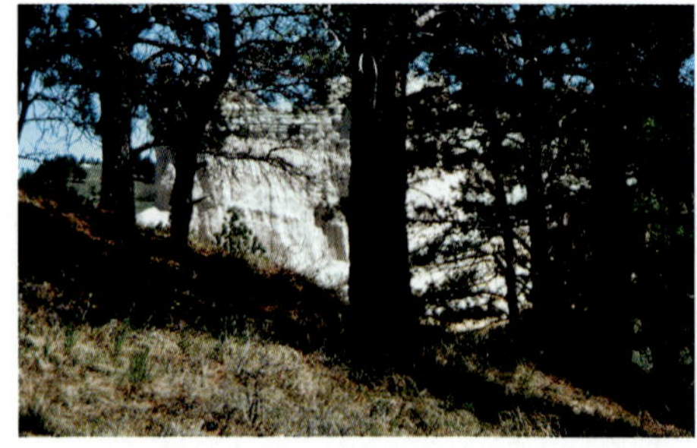

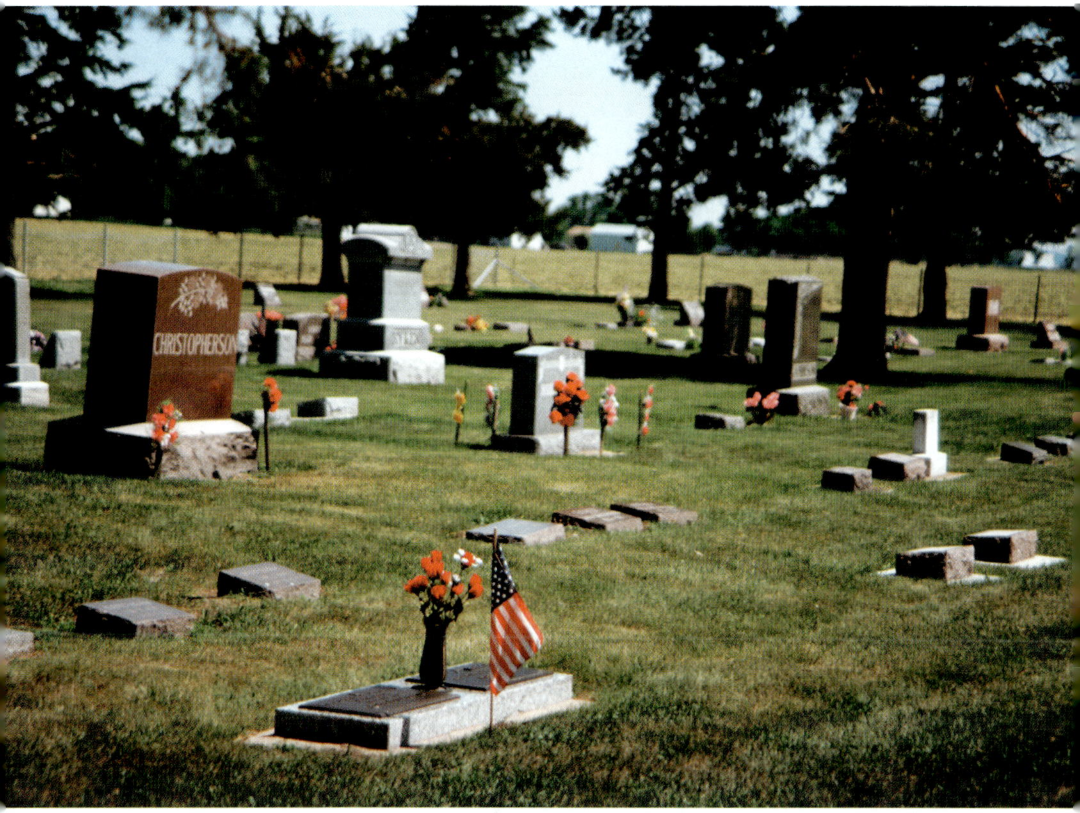

Graves of veterans are flagged in springtime at the Gayville Cemetery in Yankton County. Buffalo Lake Lutheran Church (right) stands on a hill west of Sisseton.

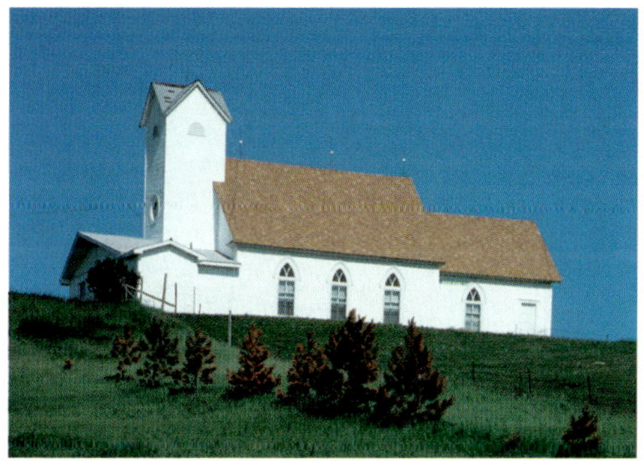

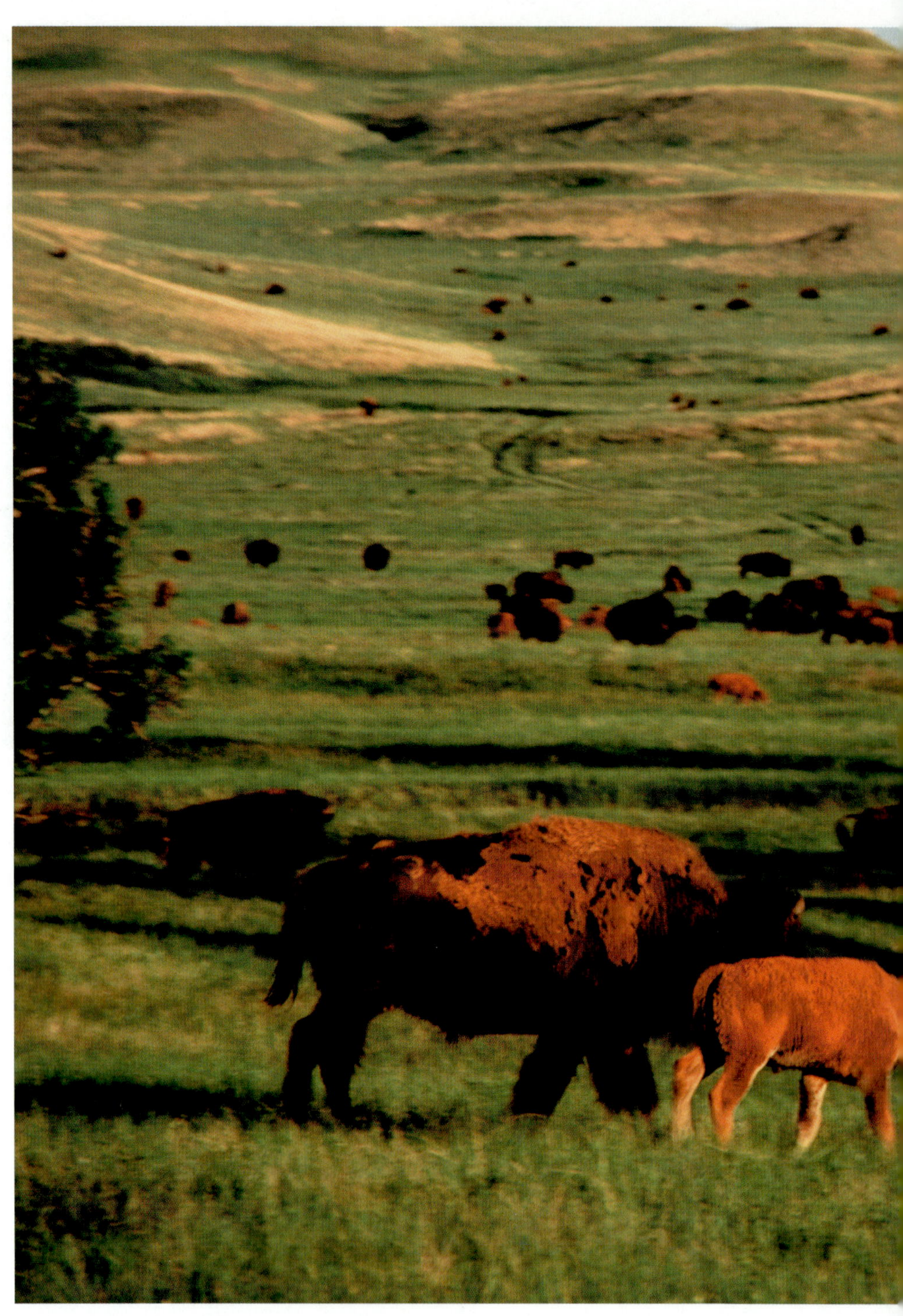

Calves follow the buffalo cows in Custer State Park.

STEPHEN GASSMAN

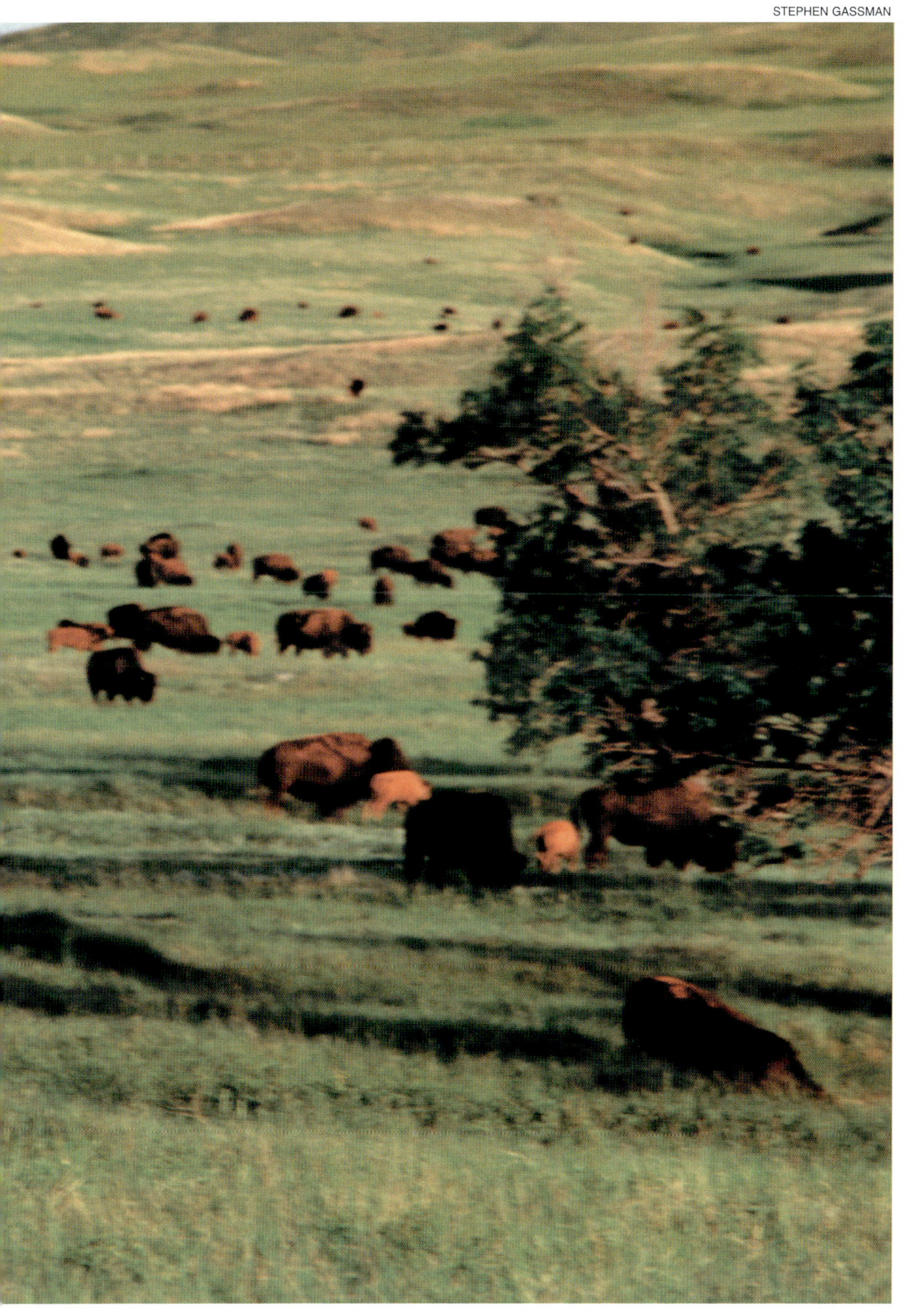

GREG LATZA

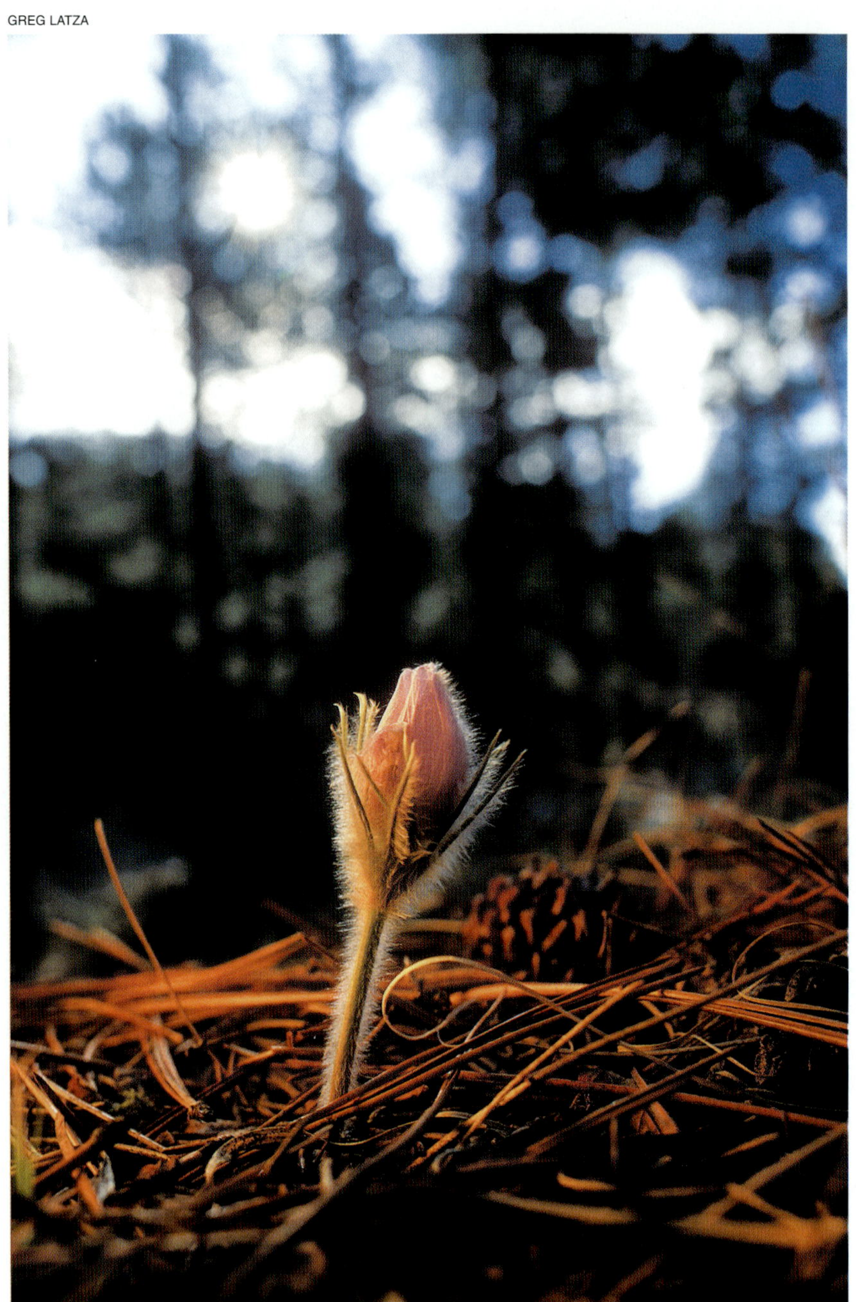

Even before grass turns green, the delicate pasque blooms. A harbinger of spring's hope, it is our official state flower.

BERNIE HUNHOFF

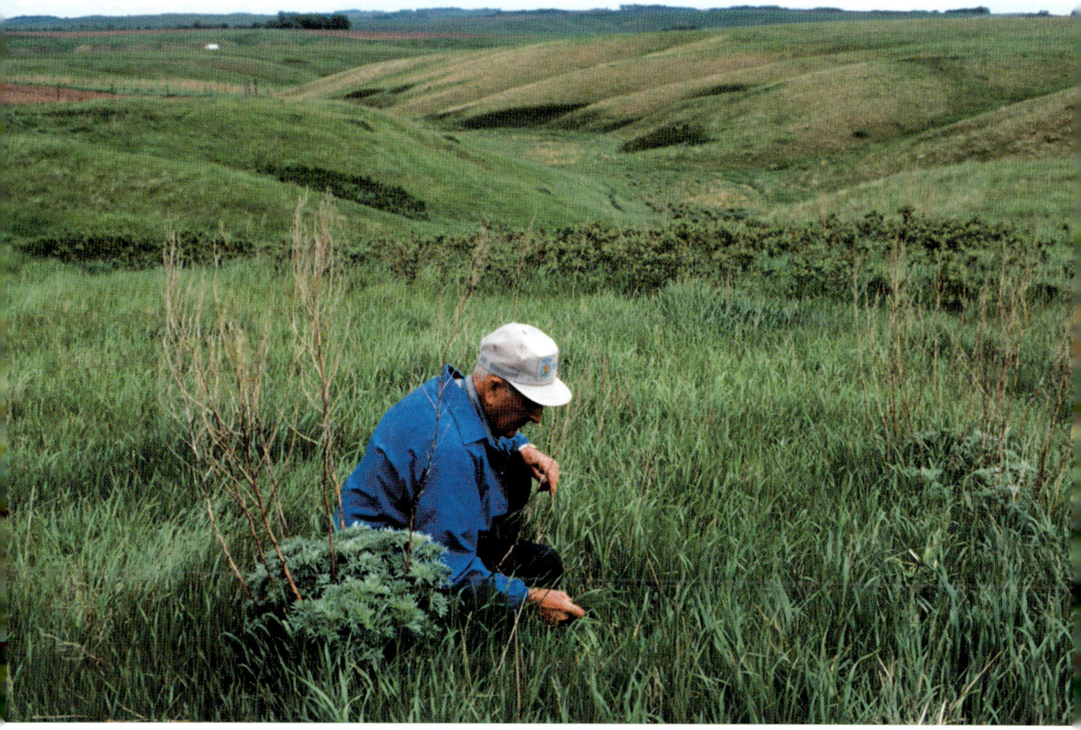

Graves of a homesteader's wife and daughter lie nearly forgotten in the Hidewood Hills near Castlewood. The widower planted blue flag flowers on the graves and left the area All would be forgotten today, except for the flowers which bloom every year in early May — century-old reminders of a man's grief. Floyd Haug (above) farmed near the graves for years and kept watch over the flowers.

A whitetail fawn (right), wary but resting in spring grass.

CHUCK POST

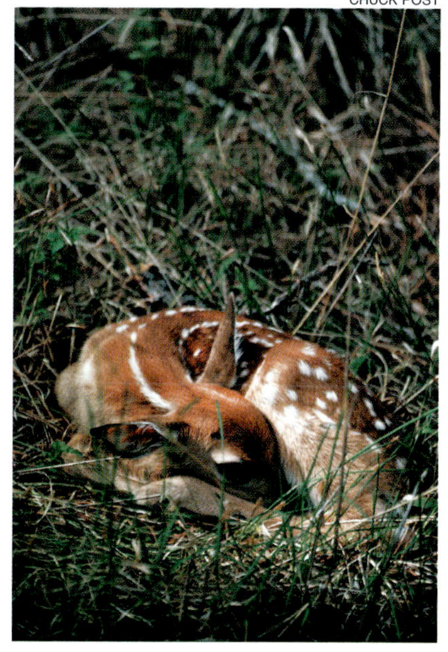

JERRY WILSON

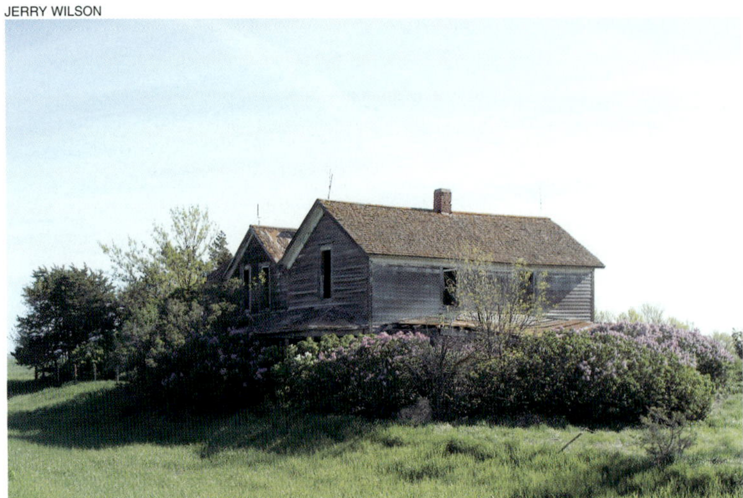

Lilacs grow near an empty house north of Artichoke Creek in Potter County (above), and adorn the altar of Holy Spirit Chapel on the Standing Rock Reservation (opposite page).

Spring is an opportunity for main street "stool time" for some small town merchants.

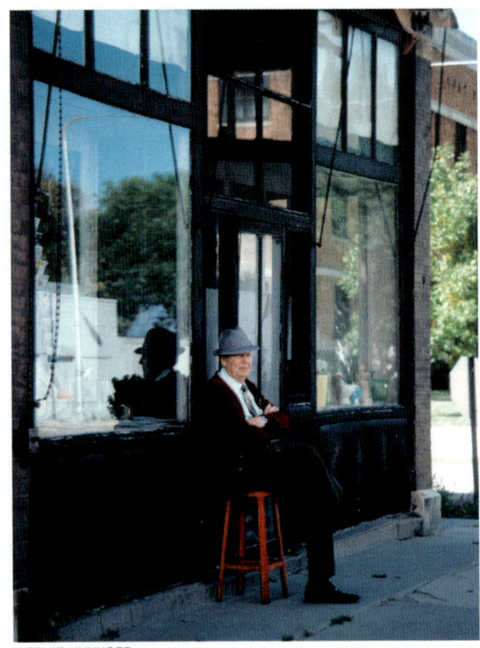

BERNIE HUNHOFF

JERRY WILSON

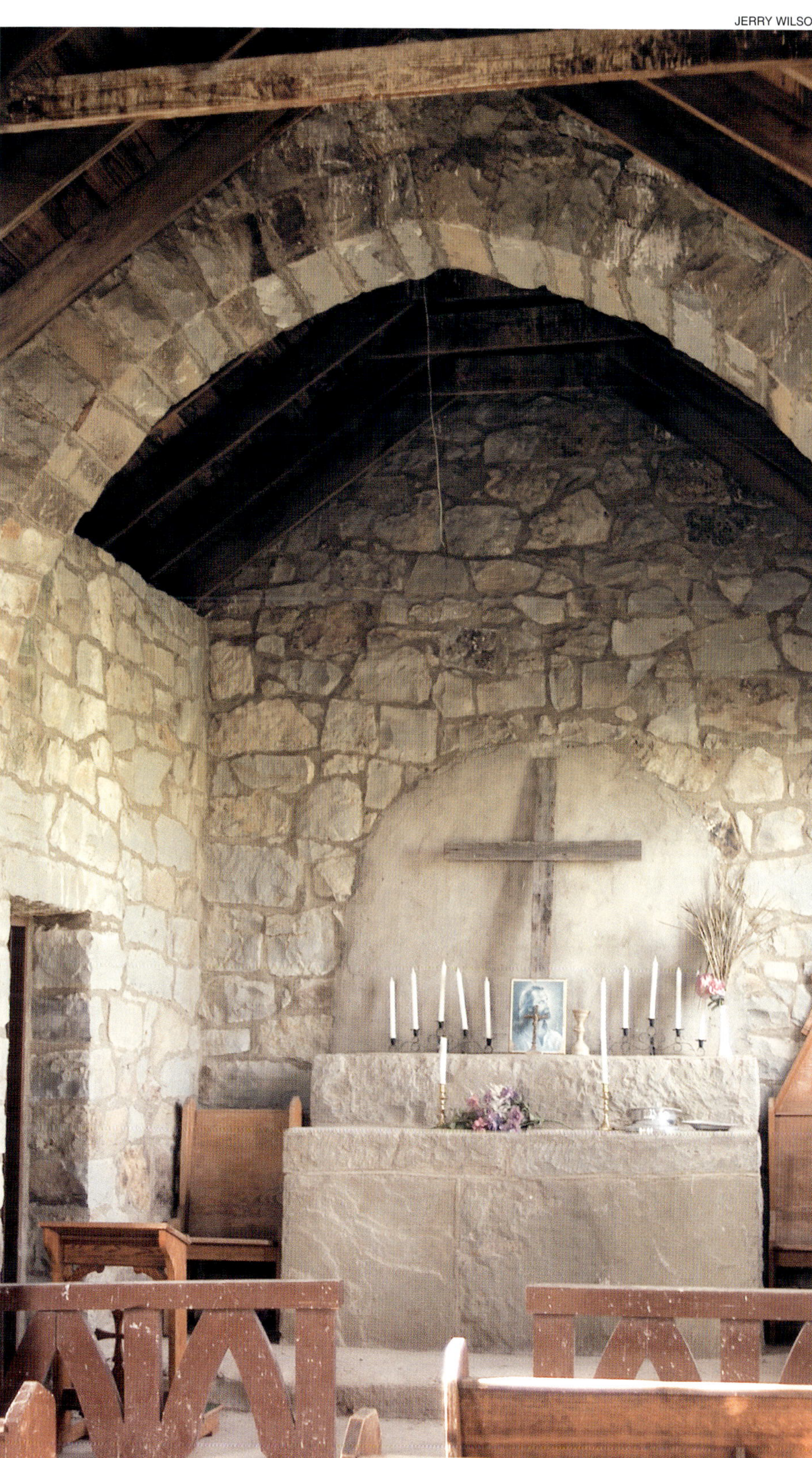

BERNIE HUNHOFF

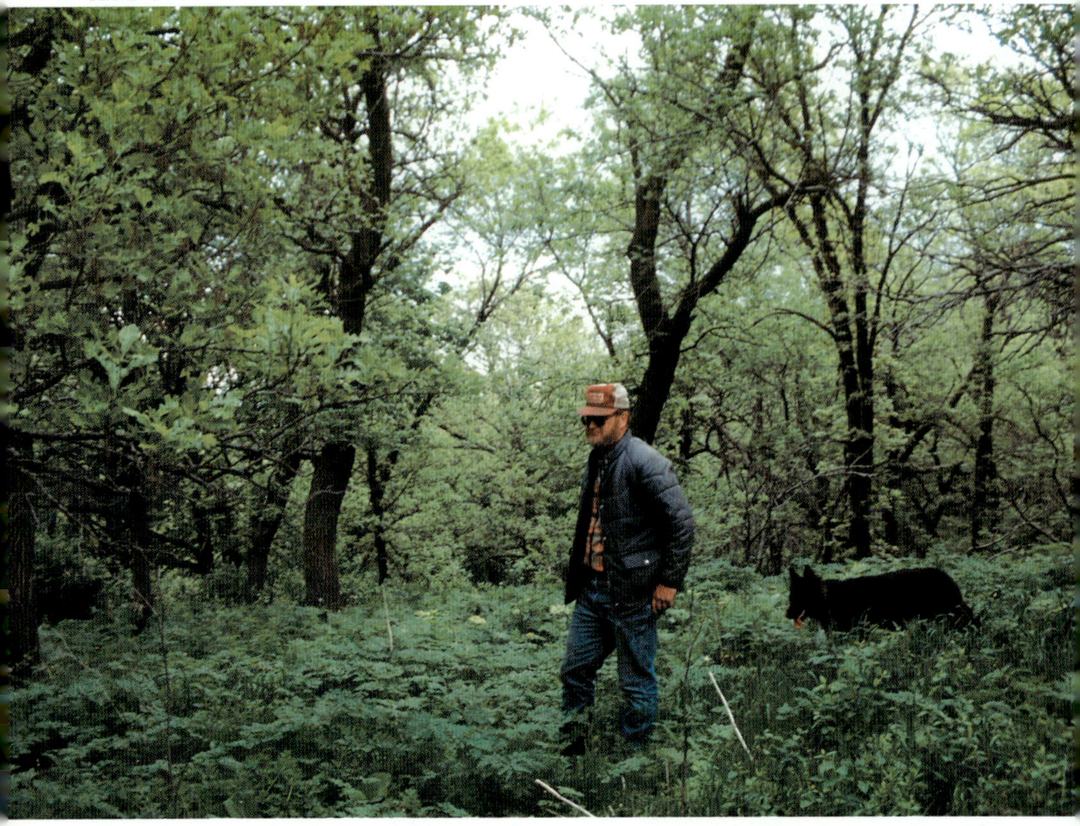

The Hidewood Hills of Deuel County were named by the Dakota Indians, who called it the Hidden Woods. In the summer of 1862, Indians involved in bloody conflicts with white settlers in Minnesota fled across the border and hid in the valley. Many of the same slow-growing oaks still shade the 30-mile stretch of hills between Clear Lake and Estelline.

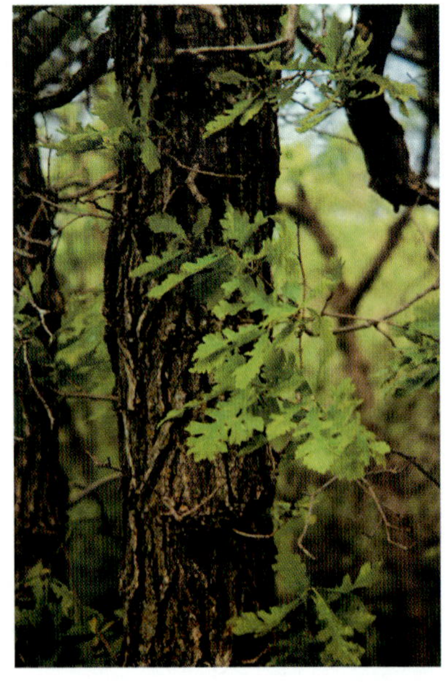

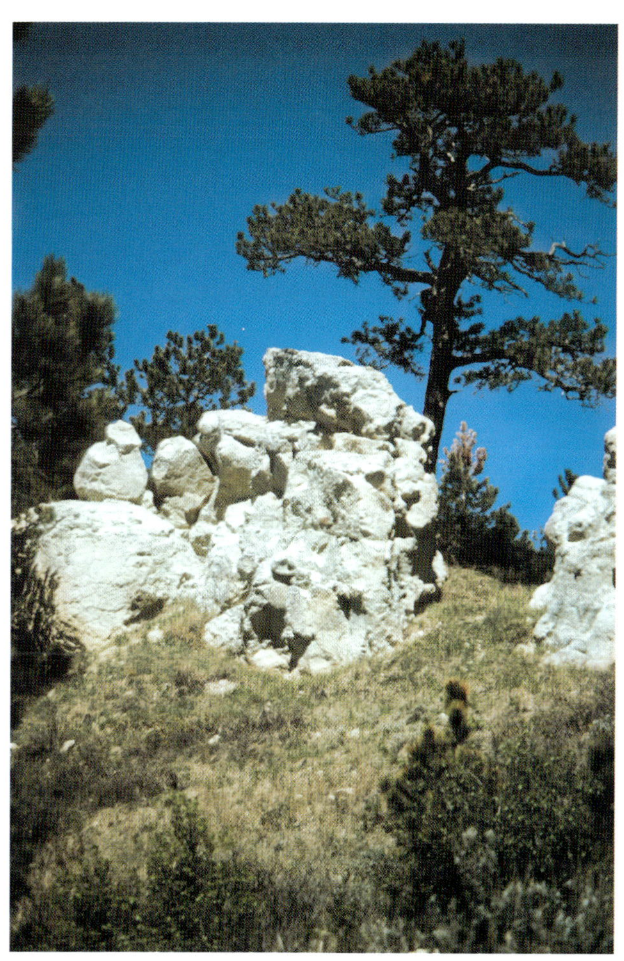

Harding County, in South Dakota's northwest corner, ironically has a very sparse population and some of the Great Plains' best scenery. The terrain includes the Slim Buttes, Ludlow Cave, the Short Pine Hills, the Jumpoff Country, Sheep Butte and the Moreau River valley.

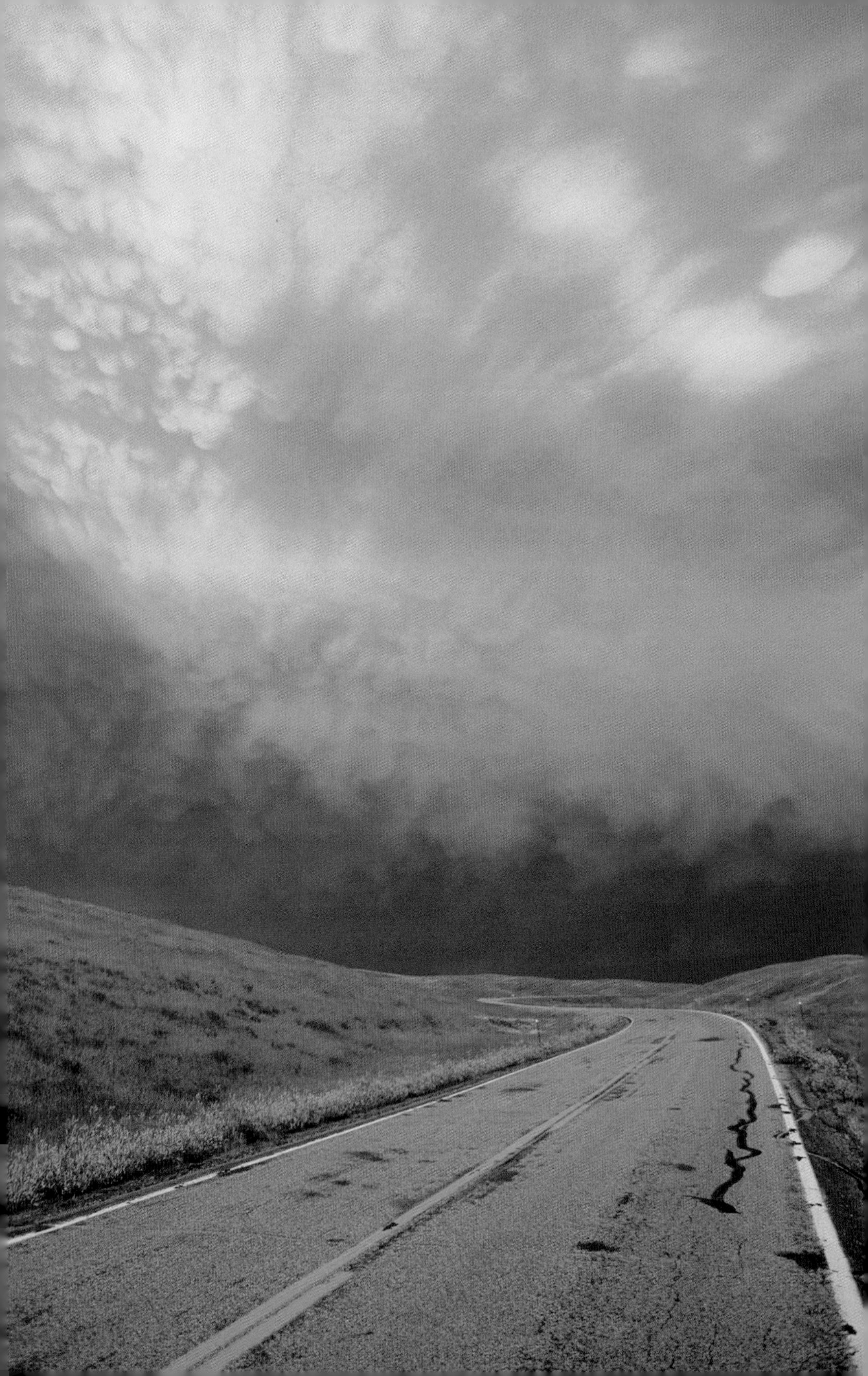

SD TOURISM

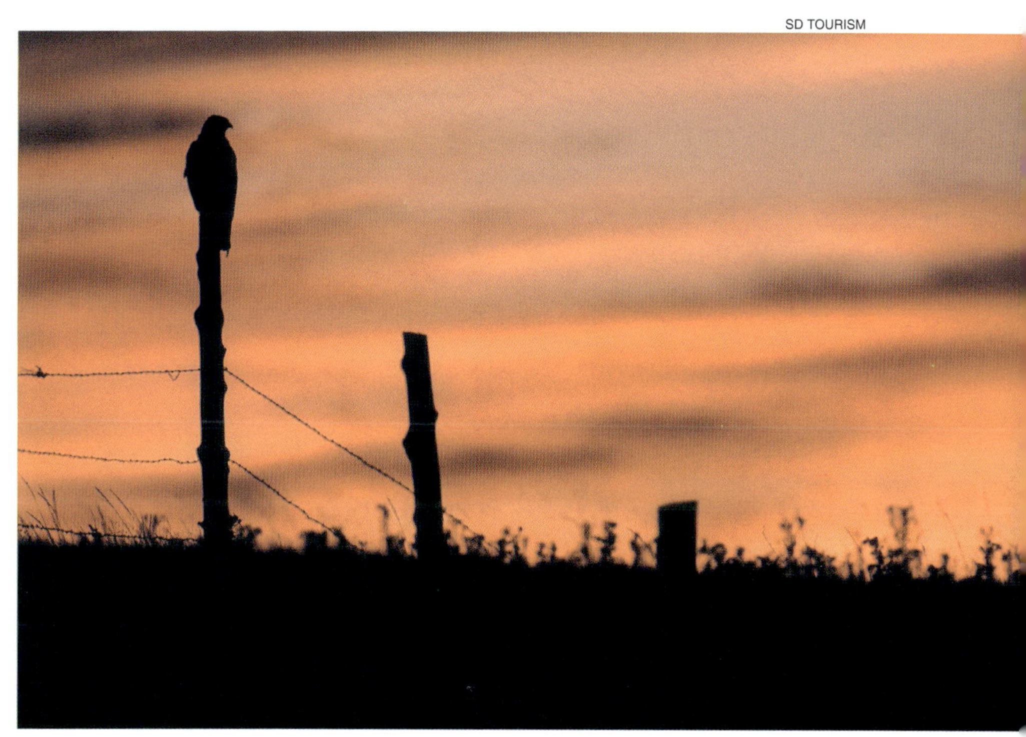

South Dakota's skyscapes are awesome, and never the same. Storm clouds loom ominously over Highway 1806, southeast of Fort Pierre (left); above, a red-tailed hawk watches the day end.

GREG LATZA

CHAD COPPESS / SD TOURISM

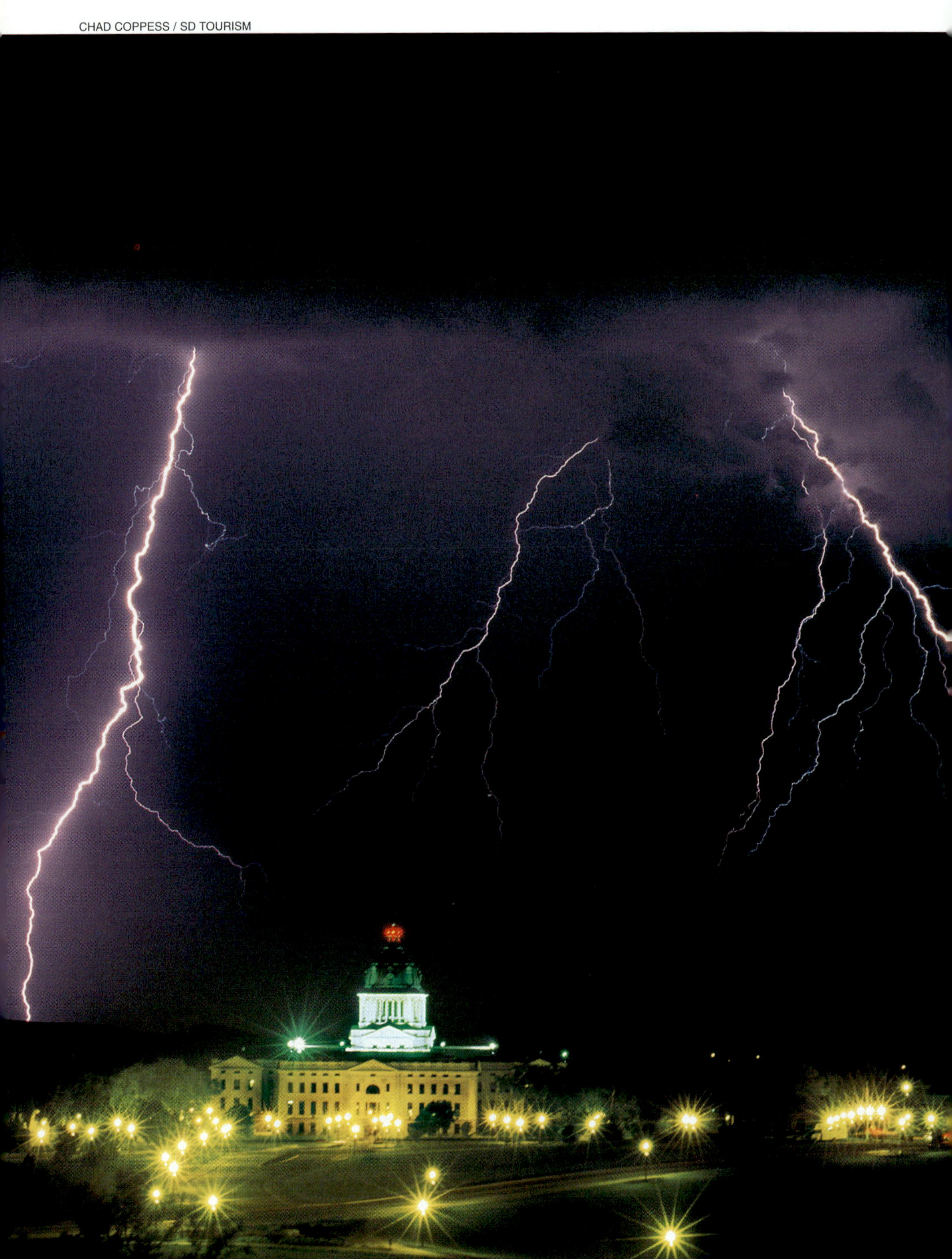

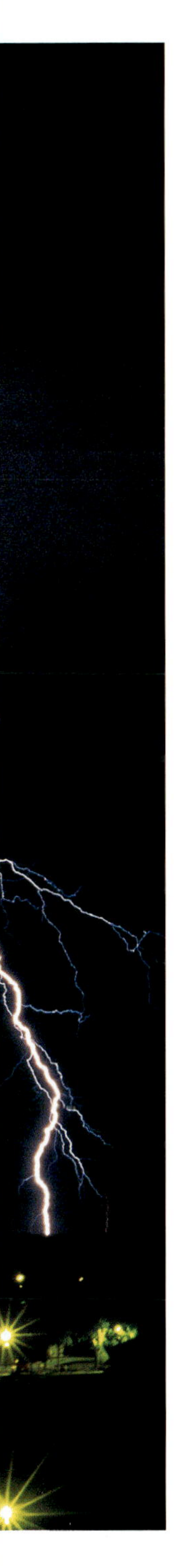

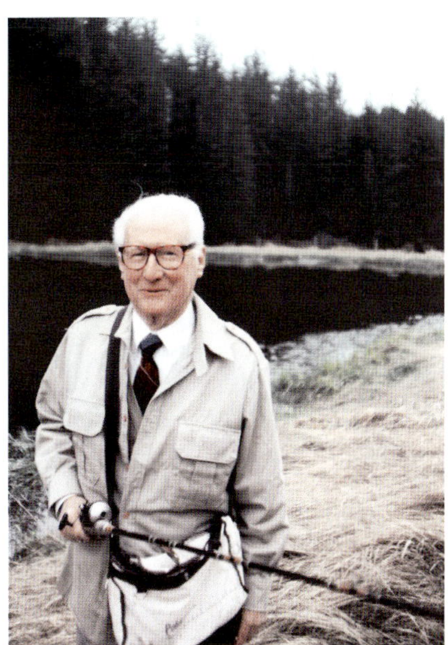

Summer

Summer is surely the most photographed season in South Dakota. Green landscapes (brown in dry years), blended with big blue skies and cumulus clouds, make everyone a photographer. We also cram most of our community celebrations — at least the outdoor events — into the dozen or so weeks that summer lasts.

In summer, you can almost see the corn grow. It is probably inches high in early June, but taller than an NBA center by Labor Day. The same is true of pasture calves and hollyhocks and sunflowers. You can also see the children grow as they test themselves with farm work, fishing, ball games and bike rides.

Summers are generally too hot, too dry, too busy and too long. But as soon as one summer ends we begin to yearn for another. We must like the season more than we want to admit. Perhaps that's part of South Dakota's collectively cautious psyche — if we say we like it a lot we might get even less than the 12 (or so) weeks.

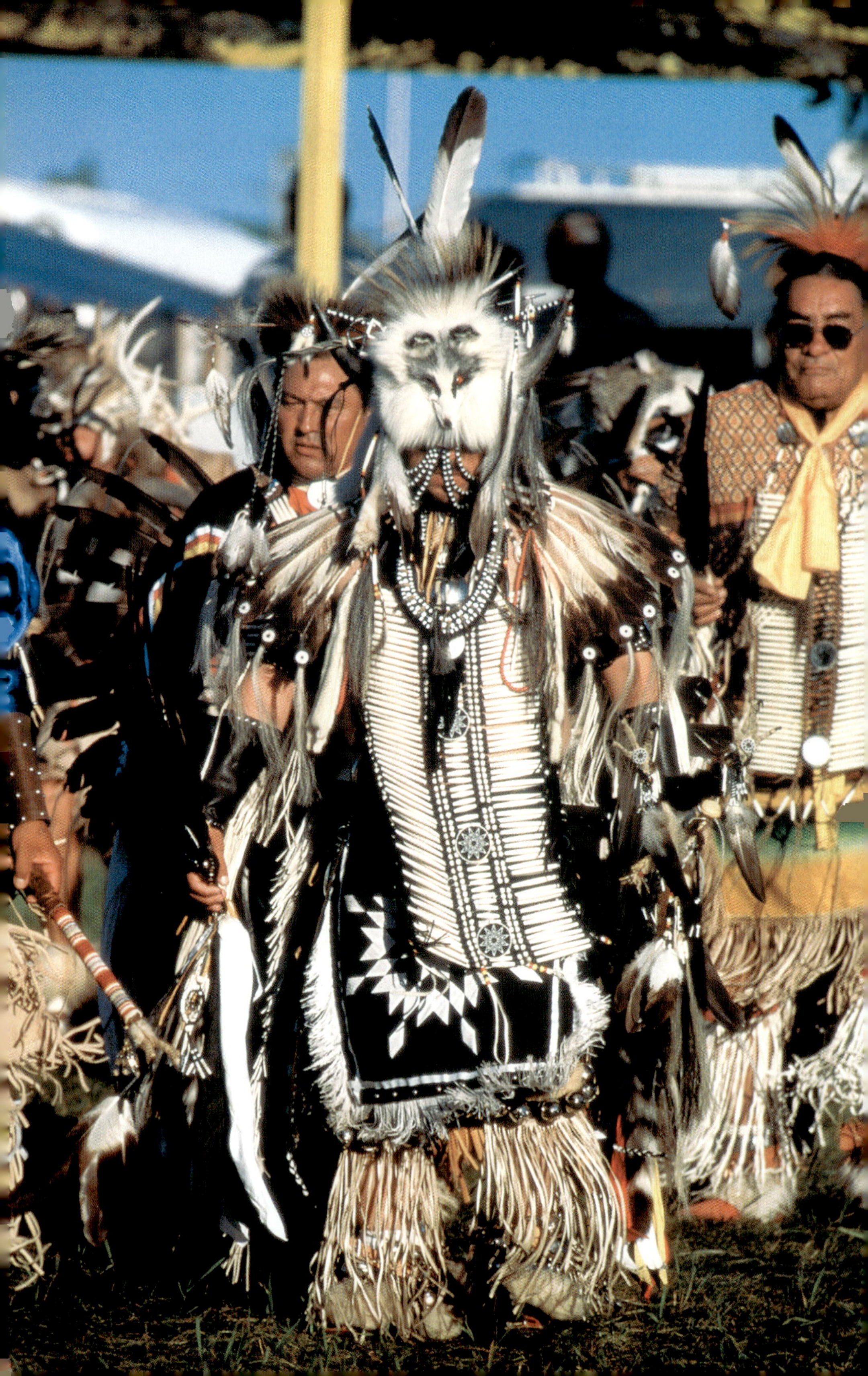

STEPHEN GASSMAN

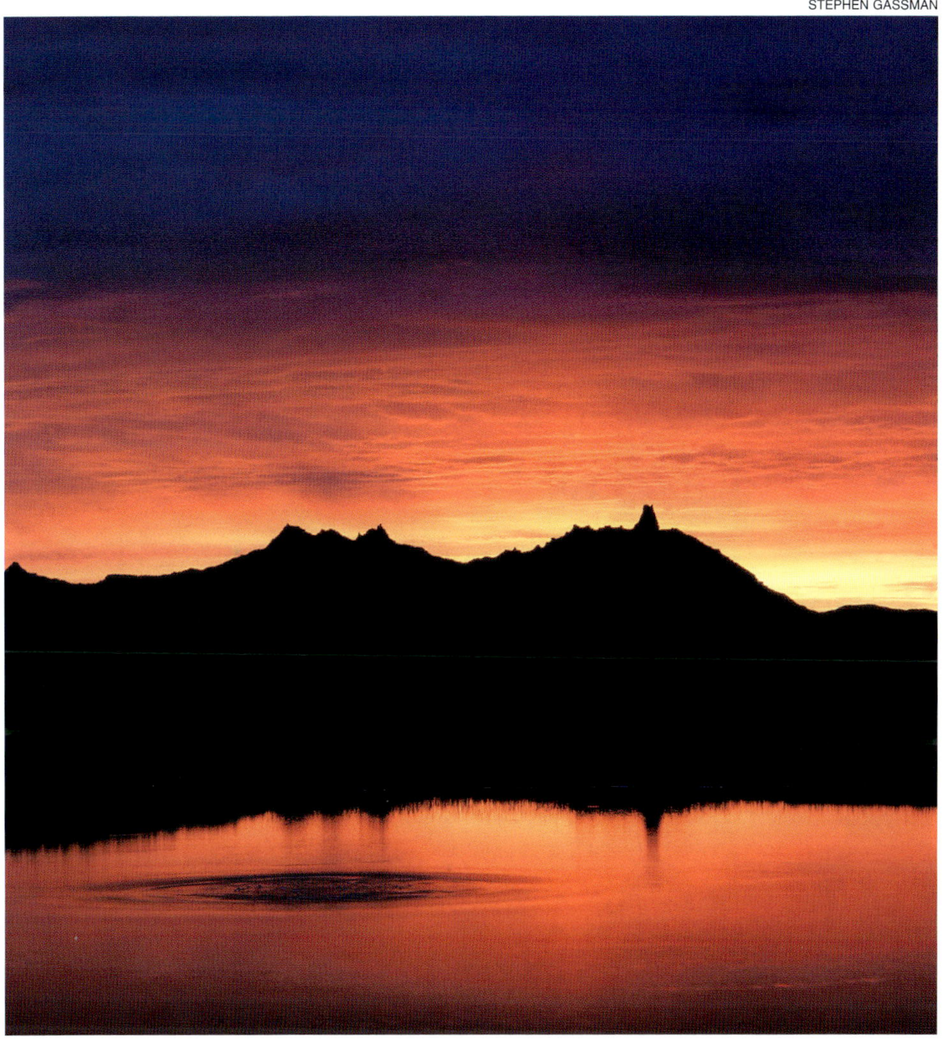

Summer is a season of celebrations, and none are more colorful than those involving South Dakota's Native American dancers. Some dancers (opposite page) relate to winged and four-legged relatives through bones, quills and feathers that adorn their regalia. Badlands buttes (above) near Interior — on the northern edge of the Pine Ridge Indian Reservation — are shadowed between a sunrise and its reflection.

GREG LATZA

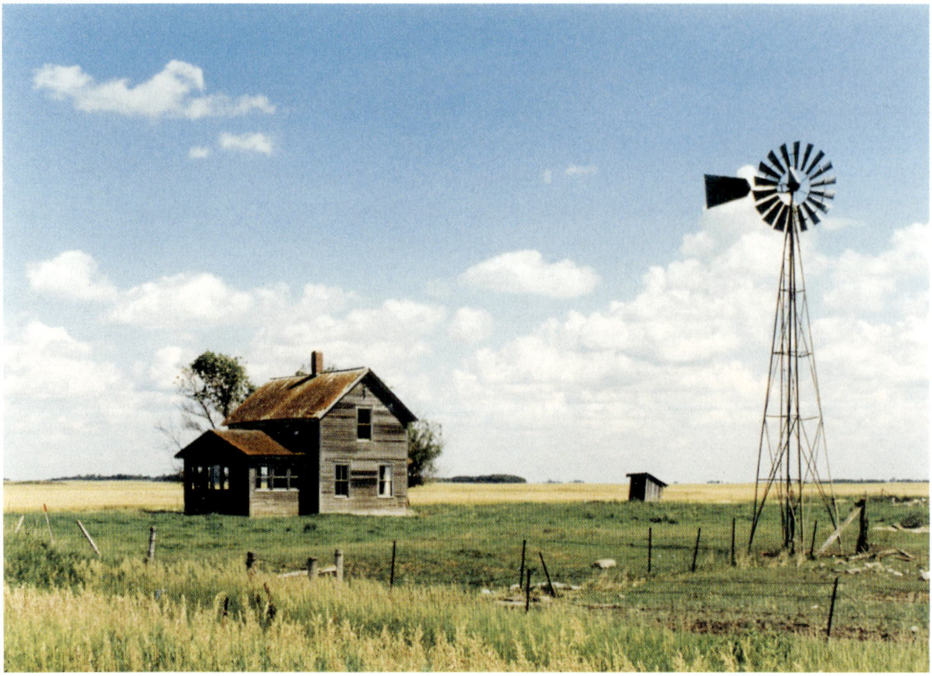

MARIANNE LARSEN

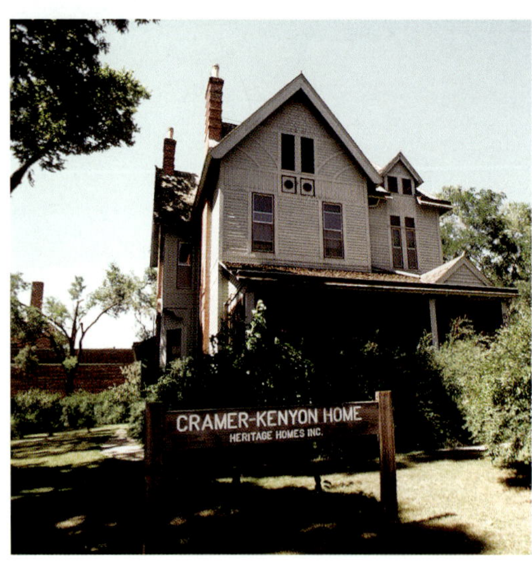

The two-story wood frame house, a South Dakota staple, seems suited to summertime. The Kingsbury County farm house (above) is long abandoned, but the Victorian style Cramer-Kenyon home (left) on Pine Street in Yankton is well-preserved and open to the public.

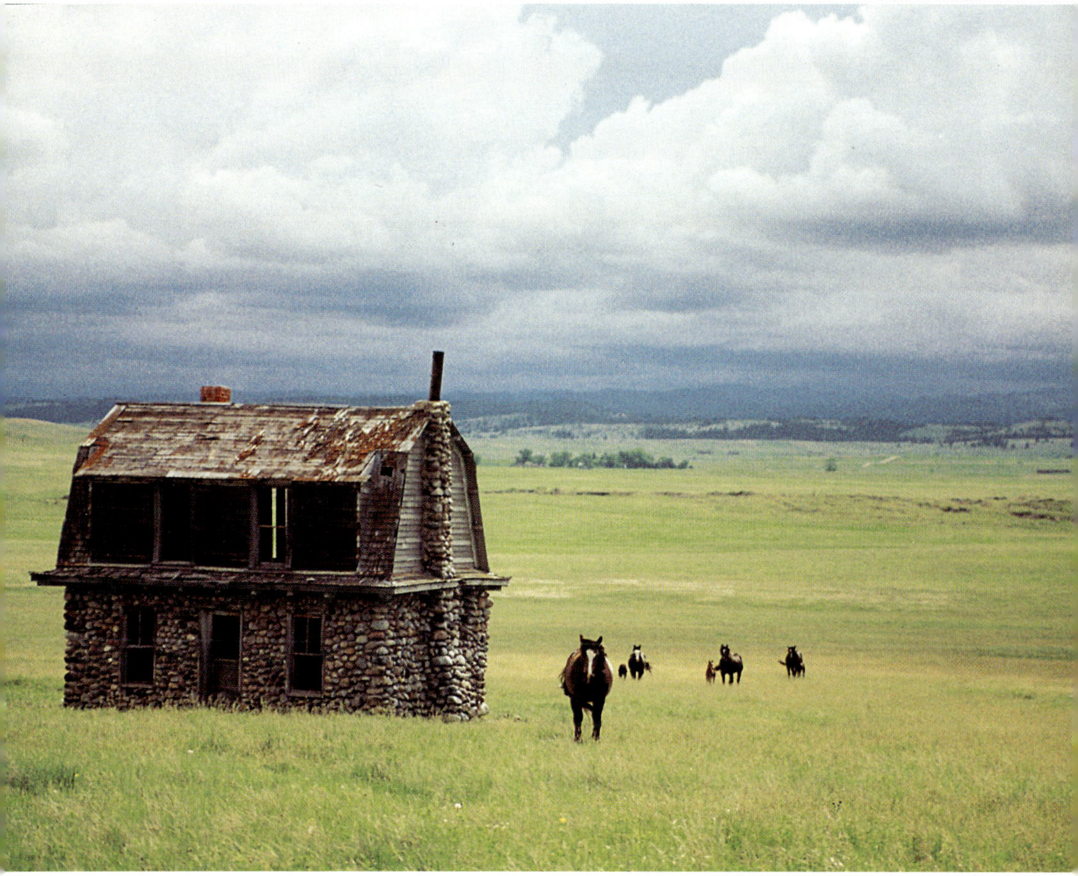

RUBY R. WILSON

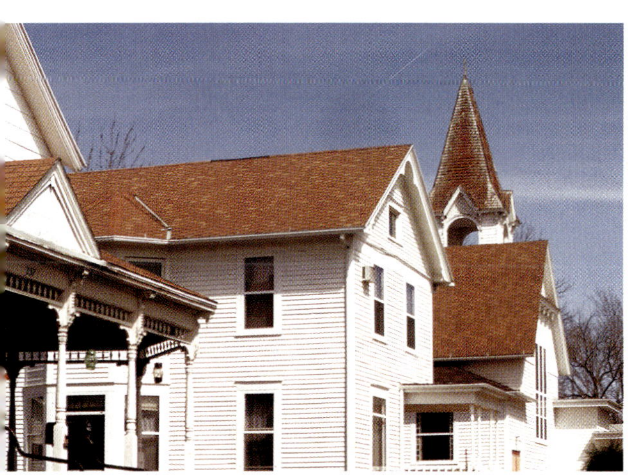

Horses graze near a stone house in the foothills of the southern Black Hills (above). White is still a favorite color for old houses in Parker (left) and elsewhere, because it's easy to mix and match for touch-ups and it reflects the summer heat.

JOHN FRONT

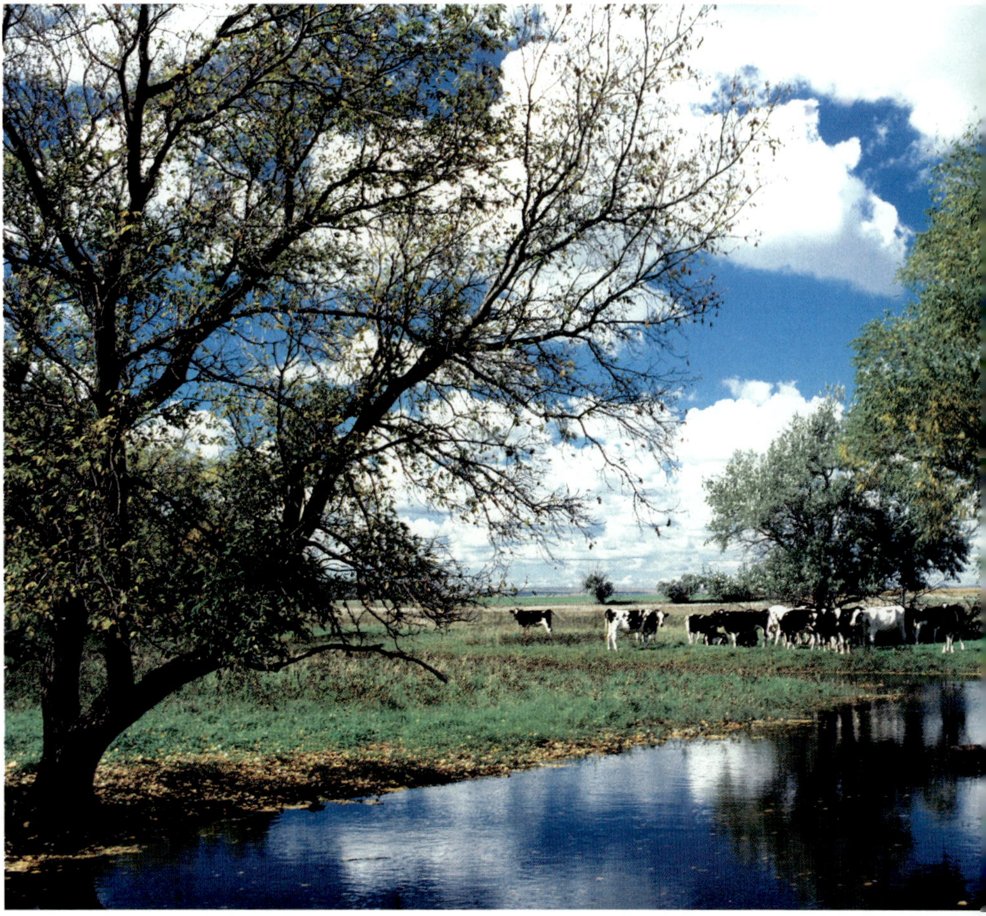

MARK KAYSER / SD TOURISM

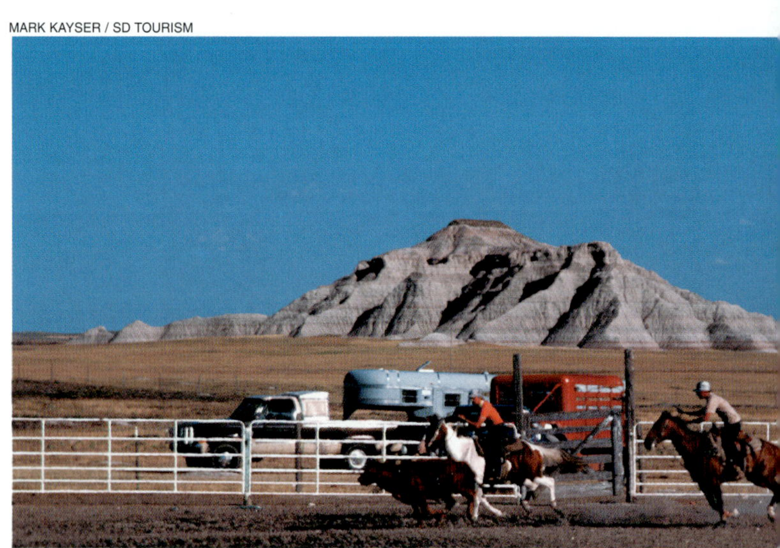

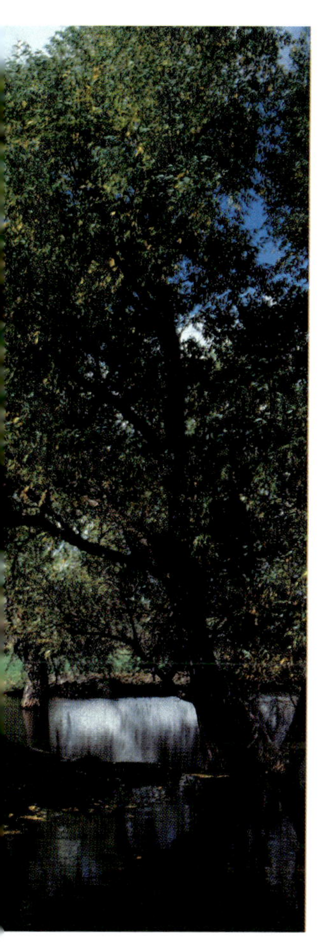

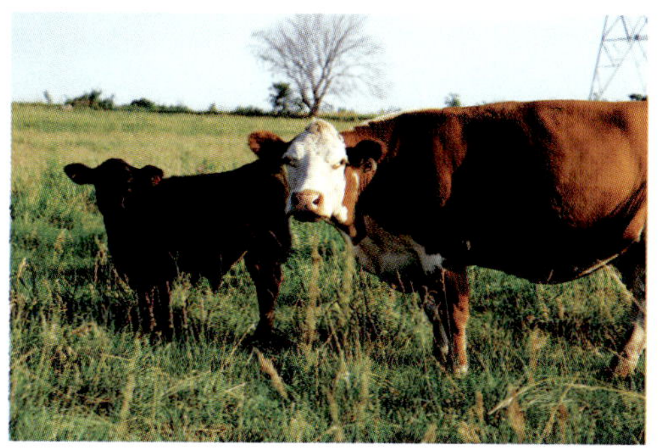

South Dakota is cattle country. About 1.6 million beef cows and a few dairy cows roam our pastures and grasslands. Most have a calf every spring. There are at least 100,000 breeding bulls. Beyond dollars and cents, cattle also provide much of agriculture's romanticism. Cowboys always get the girl. Rodeos glorify the ranchers' skills. And many of our best restaurants are called the Cattleman's Club, the Black Steer and other variations. Have you ever eaten at a Joe's Soyhouse or The Sheepman's Club?

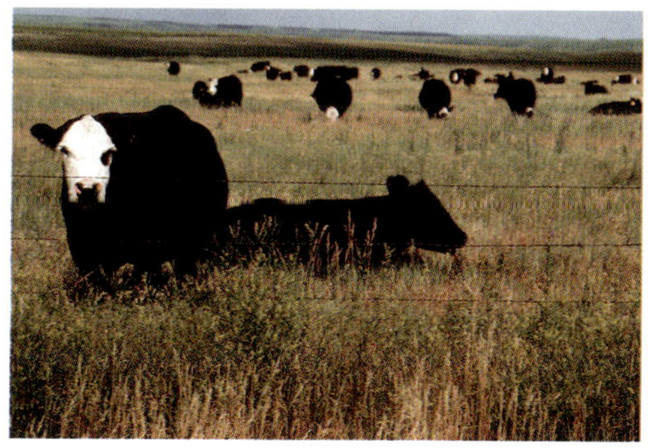

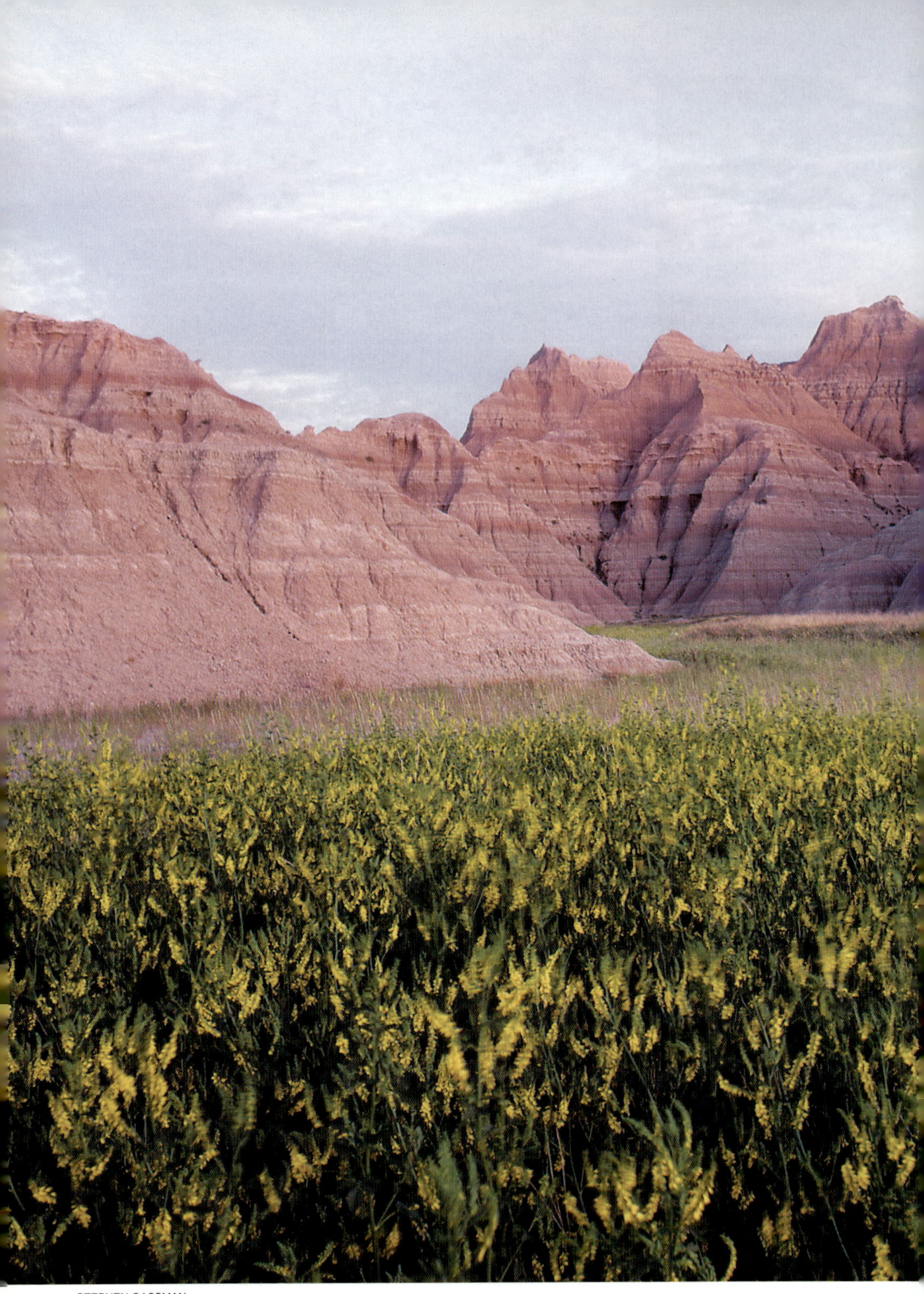
STEPHEN GASSMAN

Sweet clover blooms in the Badlands (above) and throughout most of South Dakota. It tolerates dry weather and thrives with rain. Honey bees

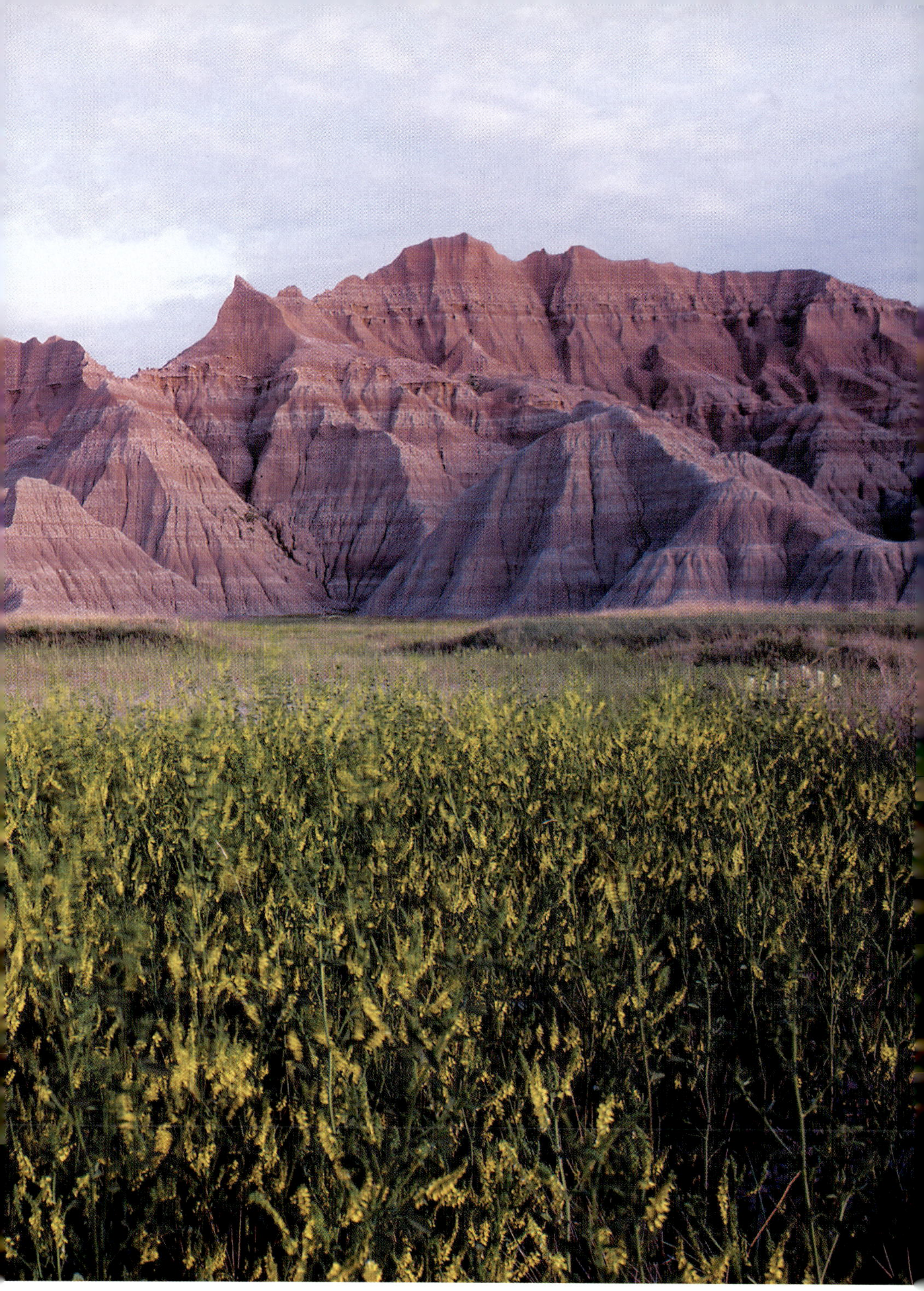

and cattle both enjoy its yellow flowers, but only the bees are allowed to dine among the buttes and valleys of Badlands National Park.

STEPHEN GASSMAN

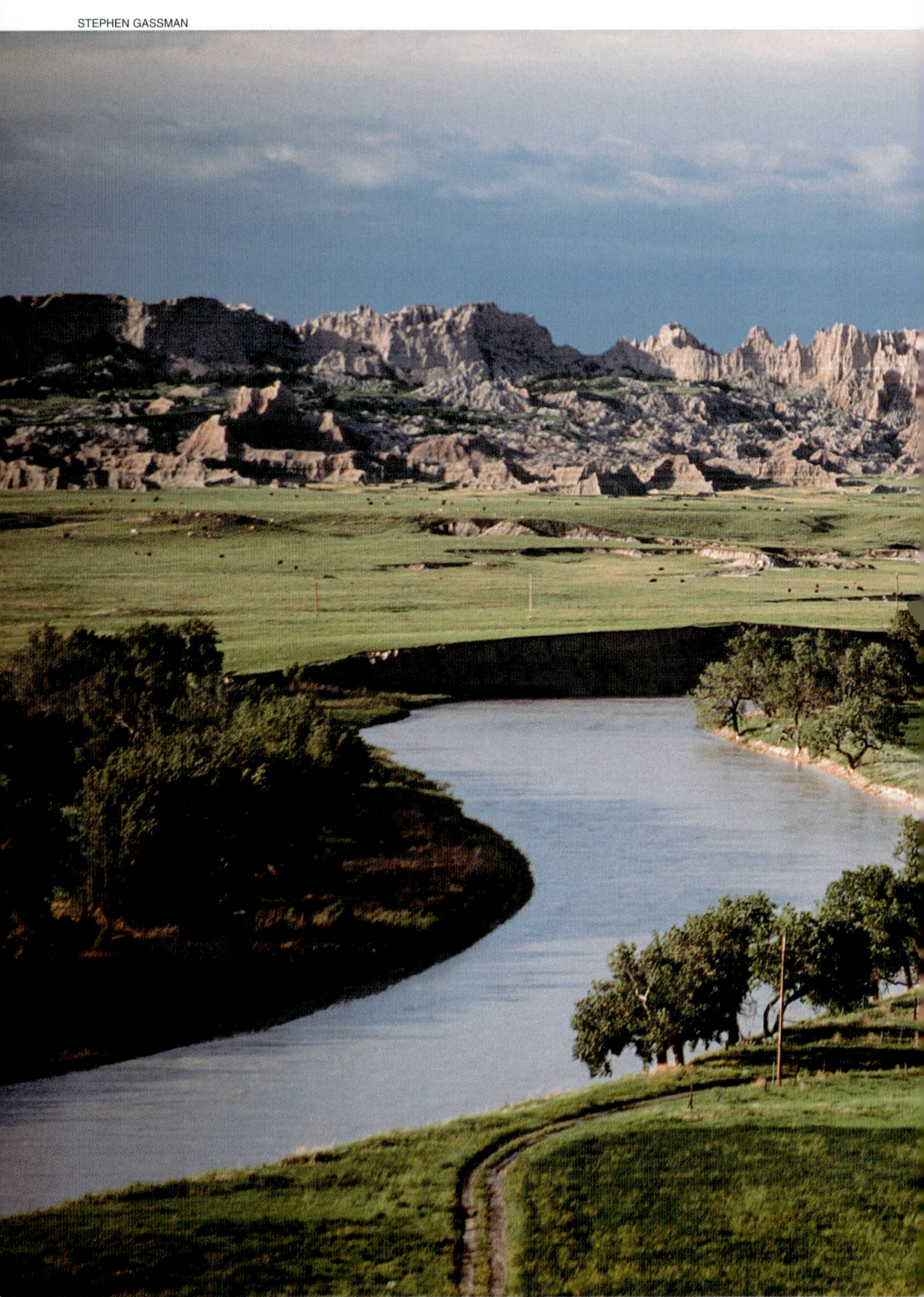

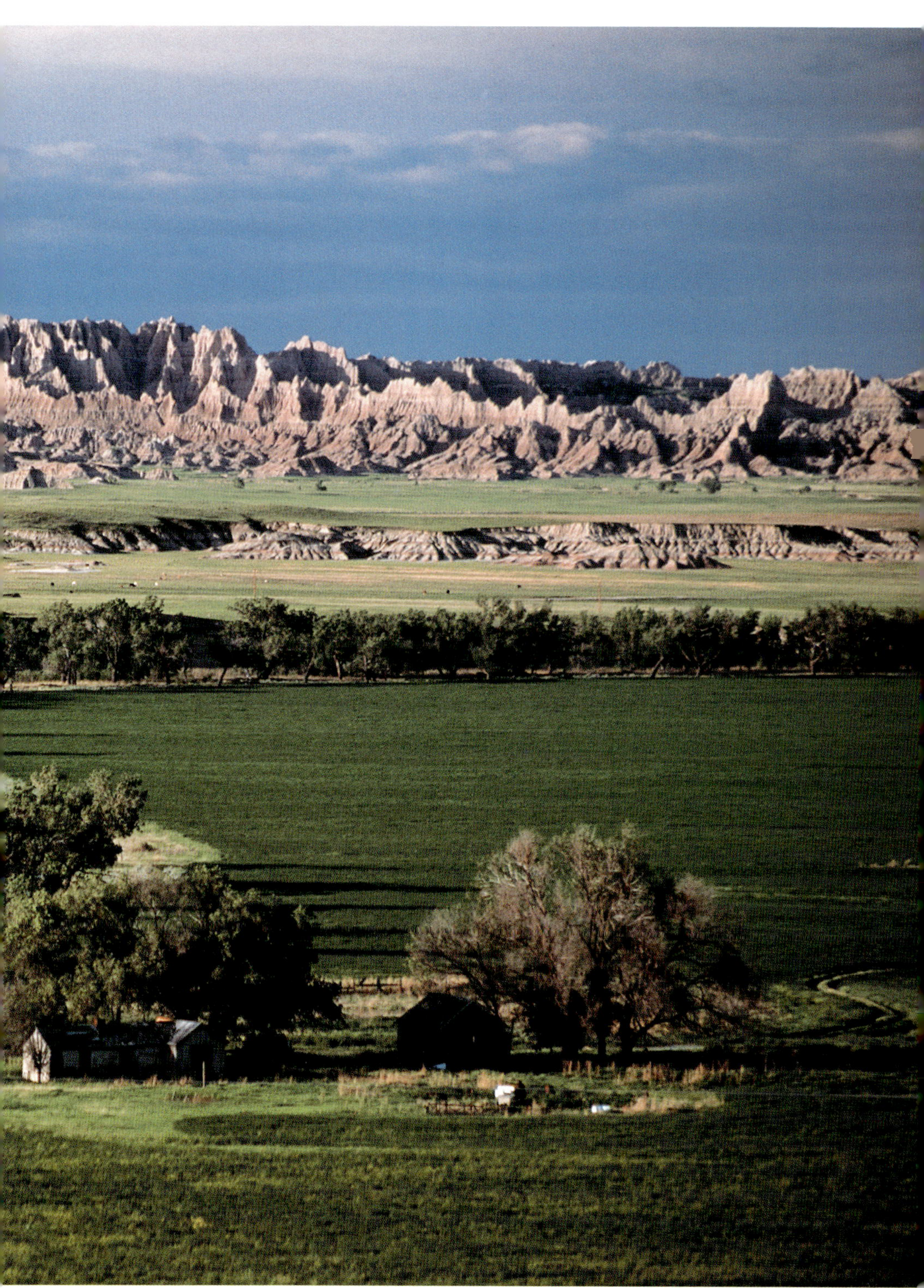

White River cuts through scenic valleys in the Pine Ridge country on its way east to the Missouri River. This scene is near Interior.

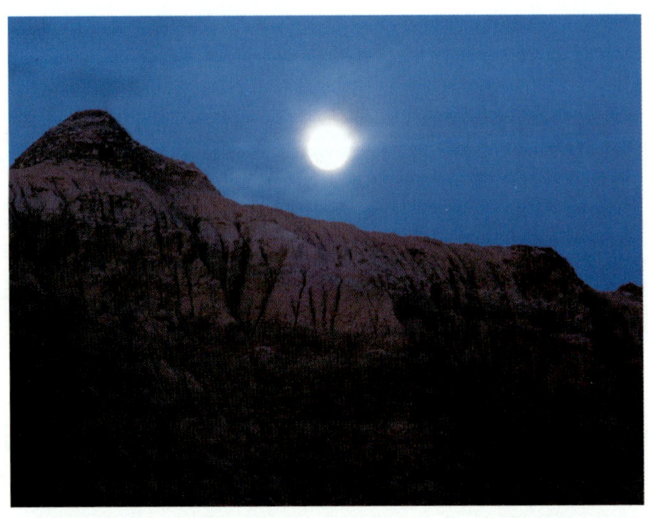

Few people see the moon rise over Sheep Mountain, a tabletop in the Badlands south of Scenic. Mary Hynes and her 11 children homesteaded on the mountain because all of the more accessible land was claimed when they arrived. They clawed and carved a road to the top. Once there, however, Mary and her kids were delighted with the view and the rich soil. How they must have loved summer's moonlit nights.

KATIE HUNHOFF

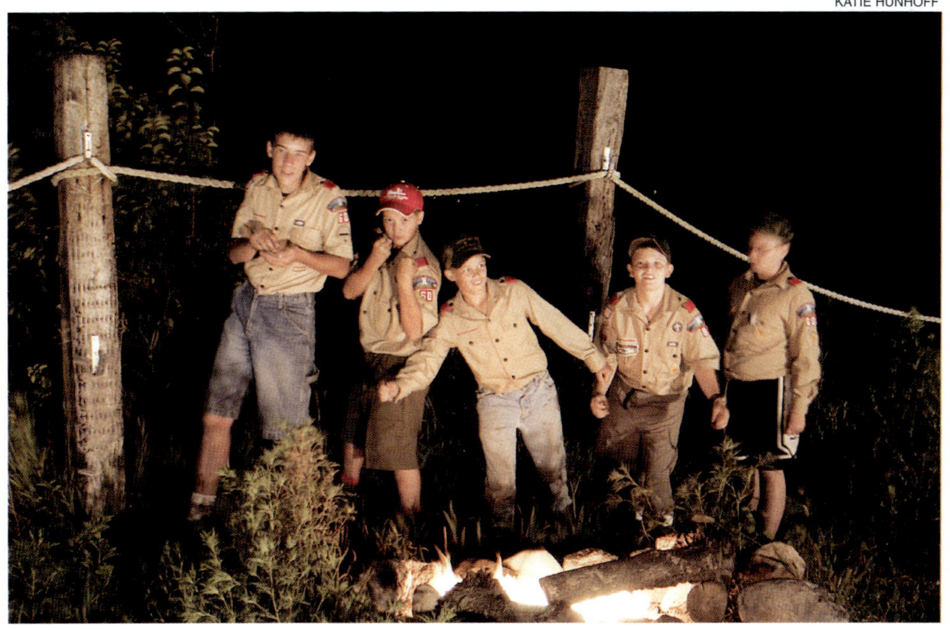

Darkness doesn't come until nearly 10 p.m. in the thick of summer, but South Dakotans wait up. Above, scouts at the Lewis and Clark Boy Scout Camp near Tabor hold a campfire talent program. Below, bikers and others party at the legendary Ice House, an outdoor establishment near downtown Yankton.

BEN HANTEN

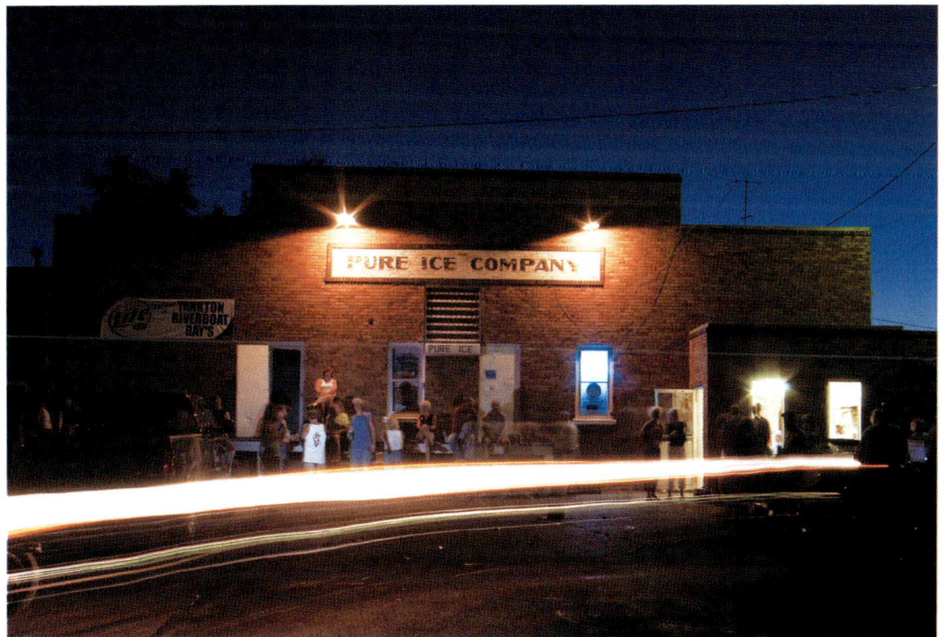

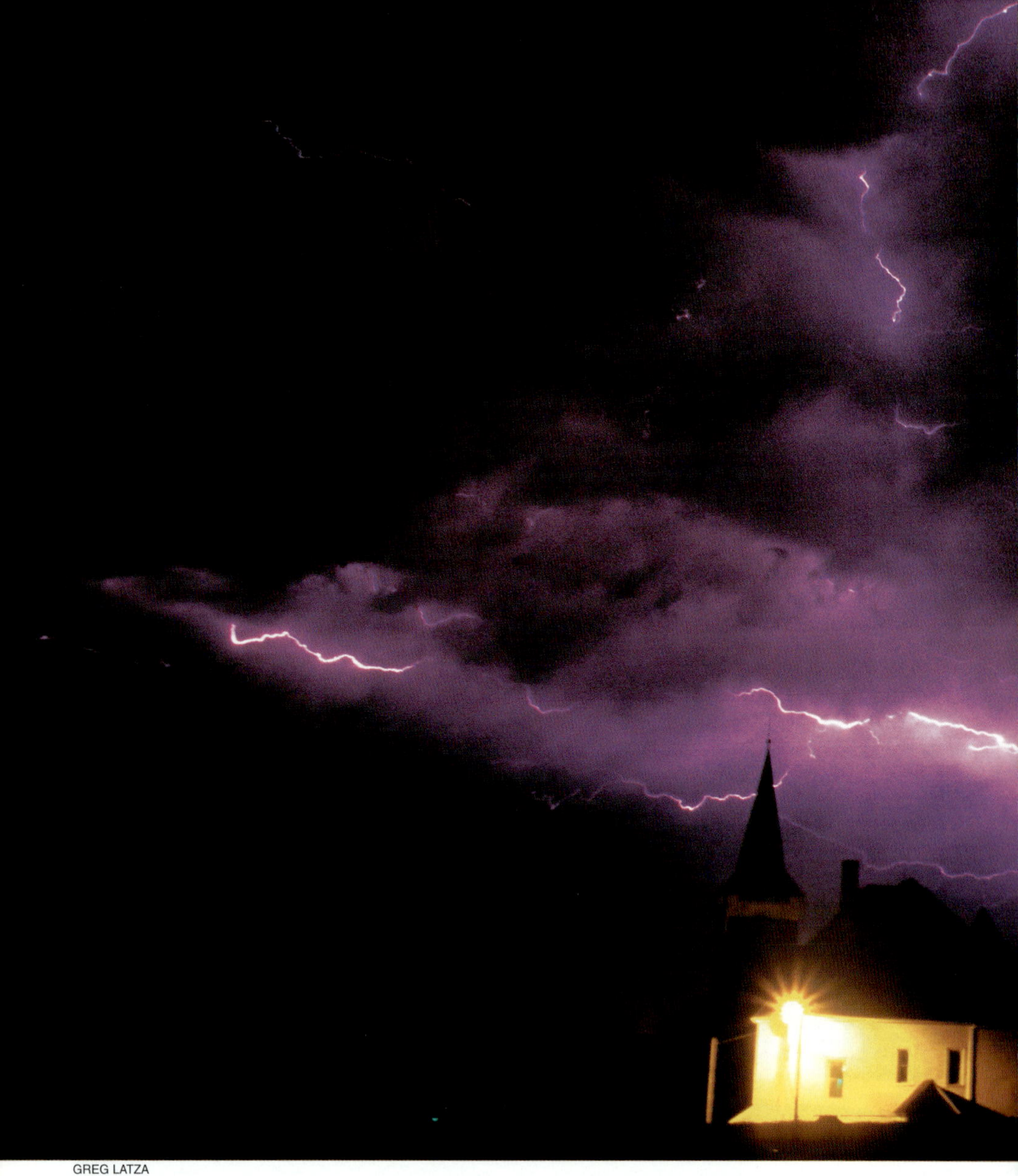

GREG LATZA

West Nidaros Lutheran Church, in the country near Baltic, is illuminated by a summer lightning storm.

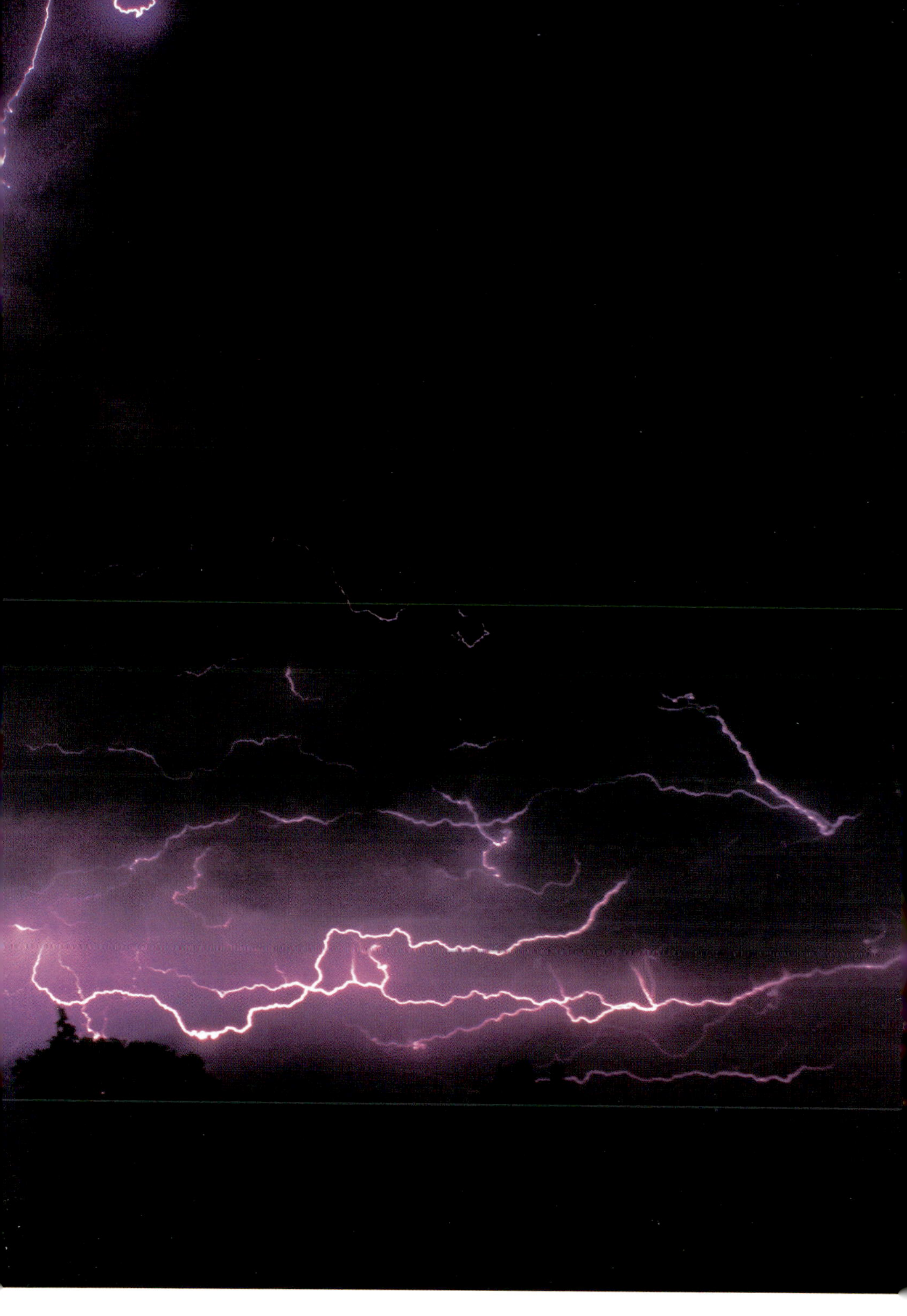

South Dakota's second largest industry is tourism, thanks primarily to millions of summer visitors who ride, hike, row and steer their ways around the state's roads, paths and waterways.

MARK KAYSER / SD TOURISM

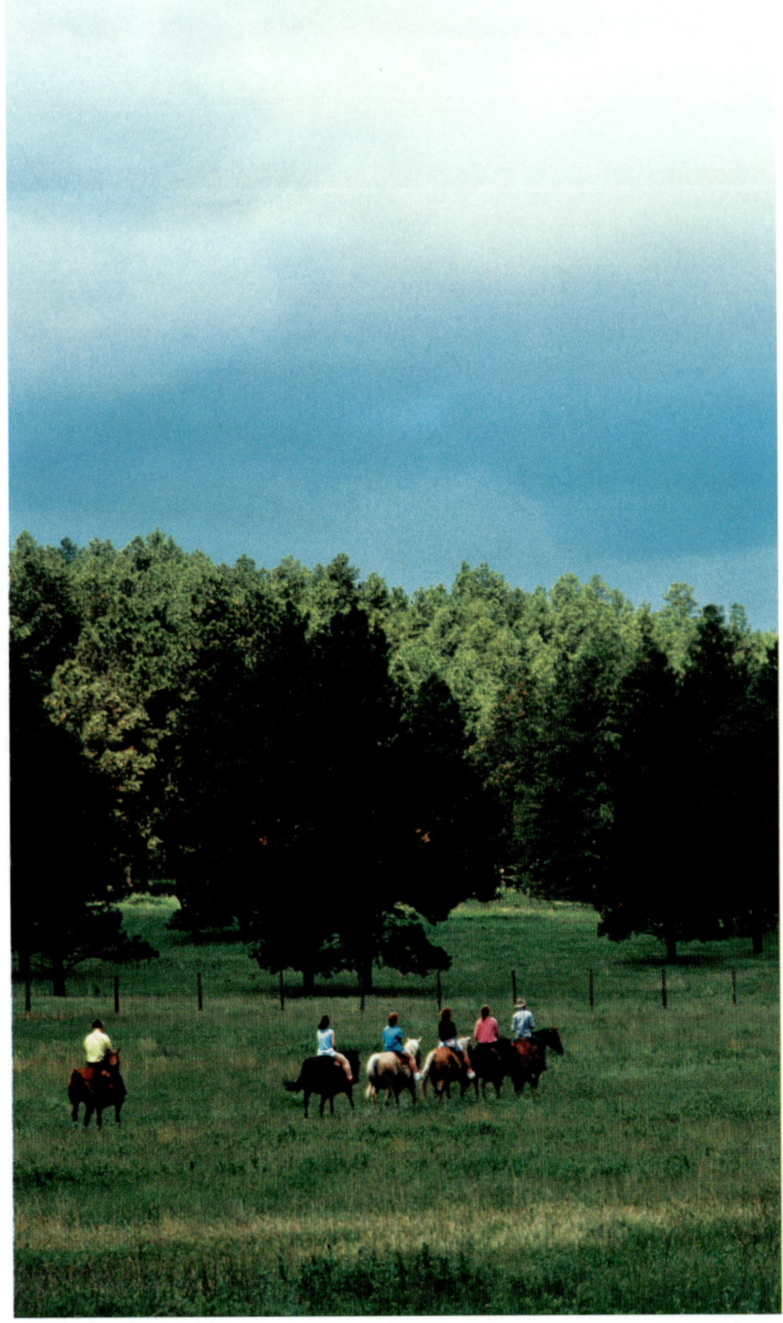

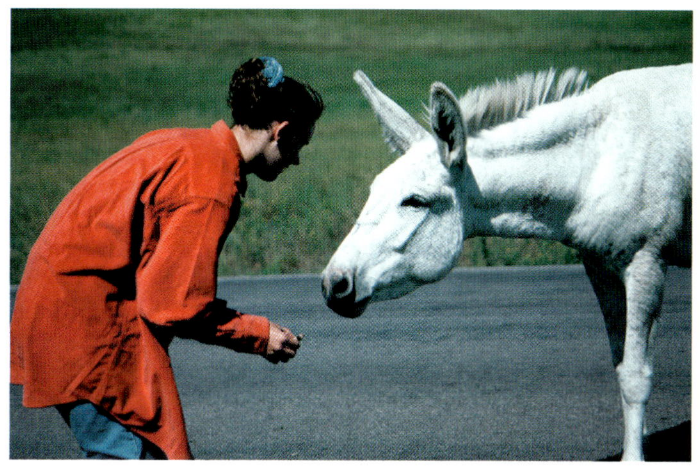

Panhandling donkeys, a favorite of visitors on the Custer State Park wildlife loop, may be descendants of early settlers' work teams.

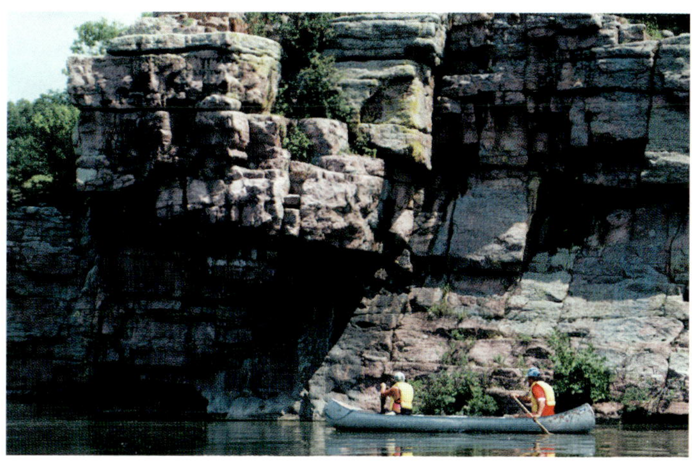

Split Rock Creek's granite walls are a favorite of canoeists in the Sioux Falls area. Below, the Mickelson Trail attracts bicyclists and hikers.

GREG LATZA

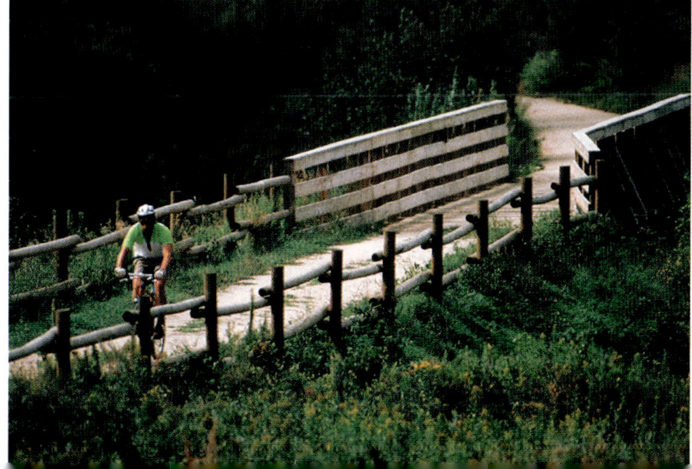

MARK KAYSER / SD TOURISM

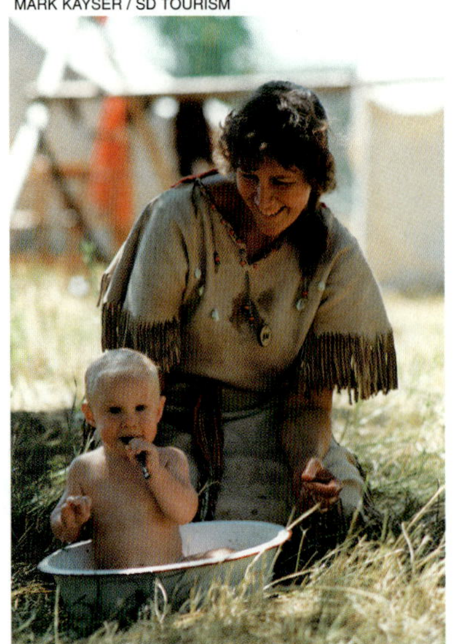

STAFF PHOTO

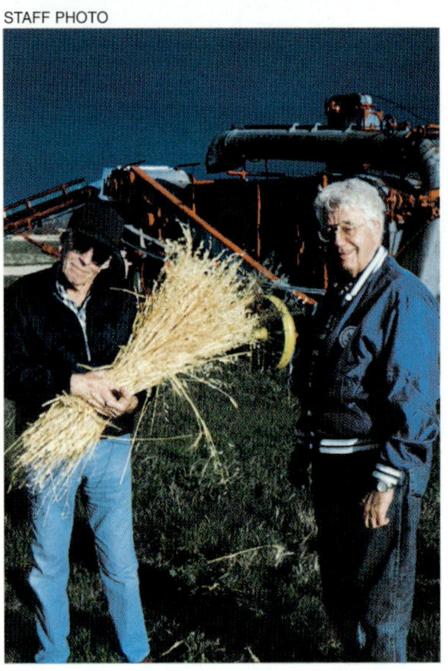

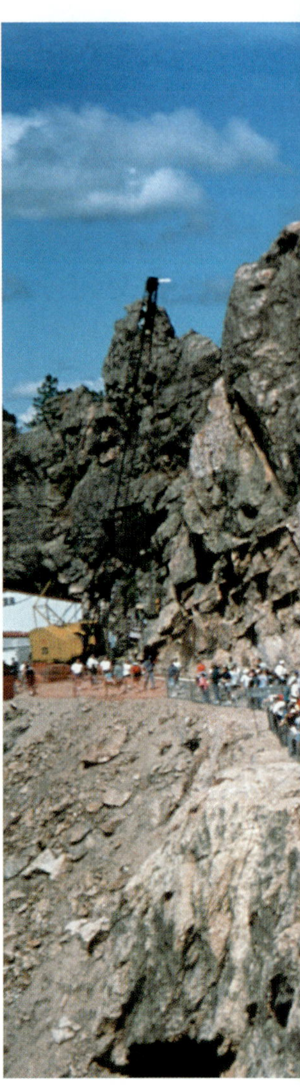

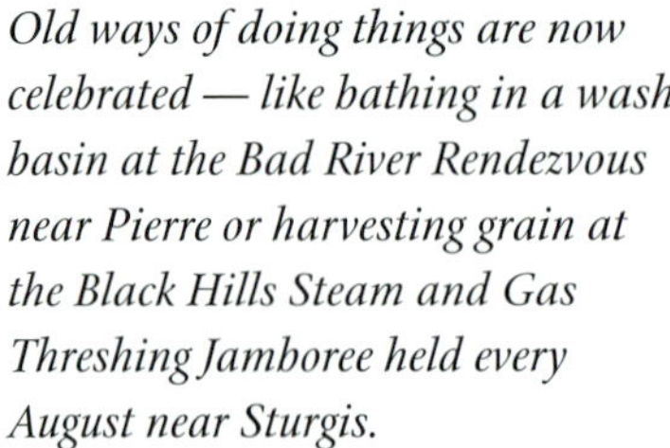

Old ways of doing things are now celebrated — like bathing in a wash basin at the Bad River Rendezvous near Pierre or harvesting grain at the Black Hills Steam and Gas Threshing Jamboree held every August near Sturgis.

SD TOURISM

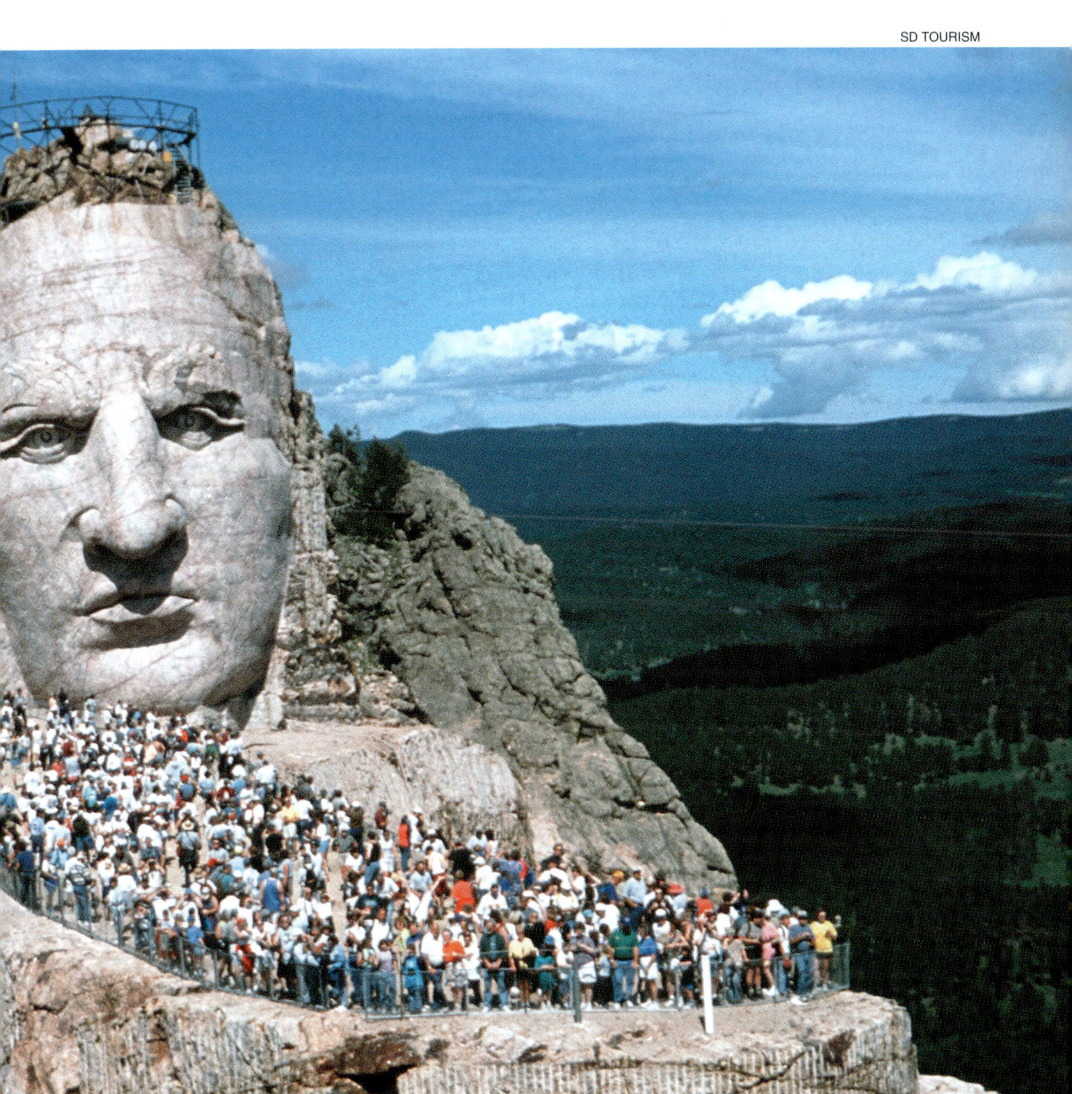

South Dakota's biggest community walk is the Crazy Horse Volksmarch, held the first weekend in June. In some years, as many as 15,000 people have hiked the six mile roundtrip to the face of the mountain carving near Custer.

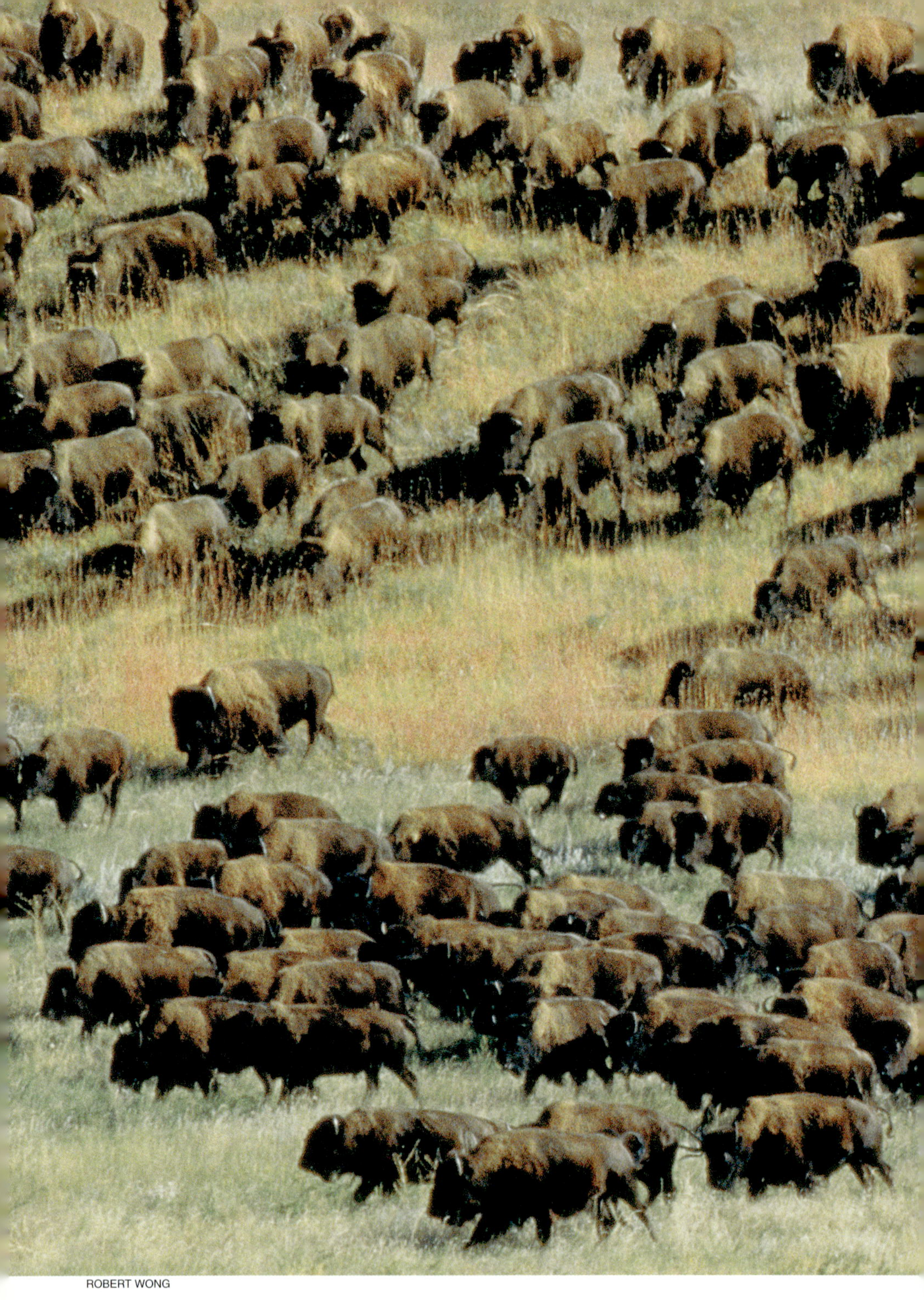

ROBERT WONG

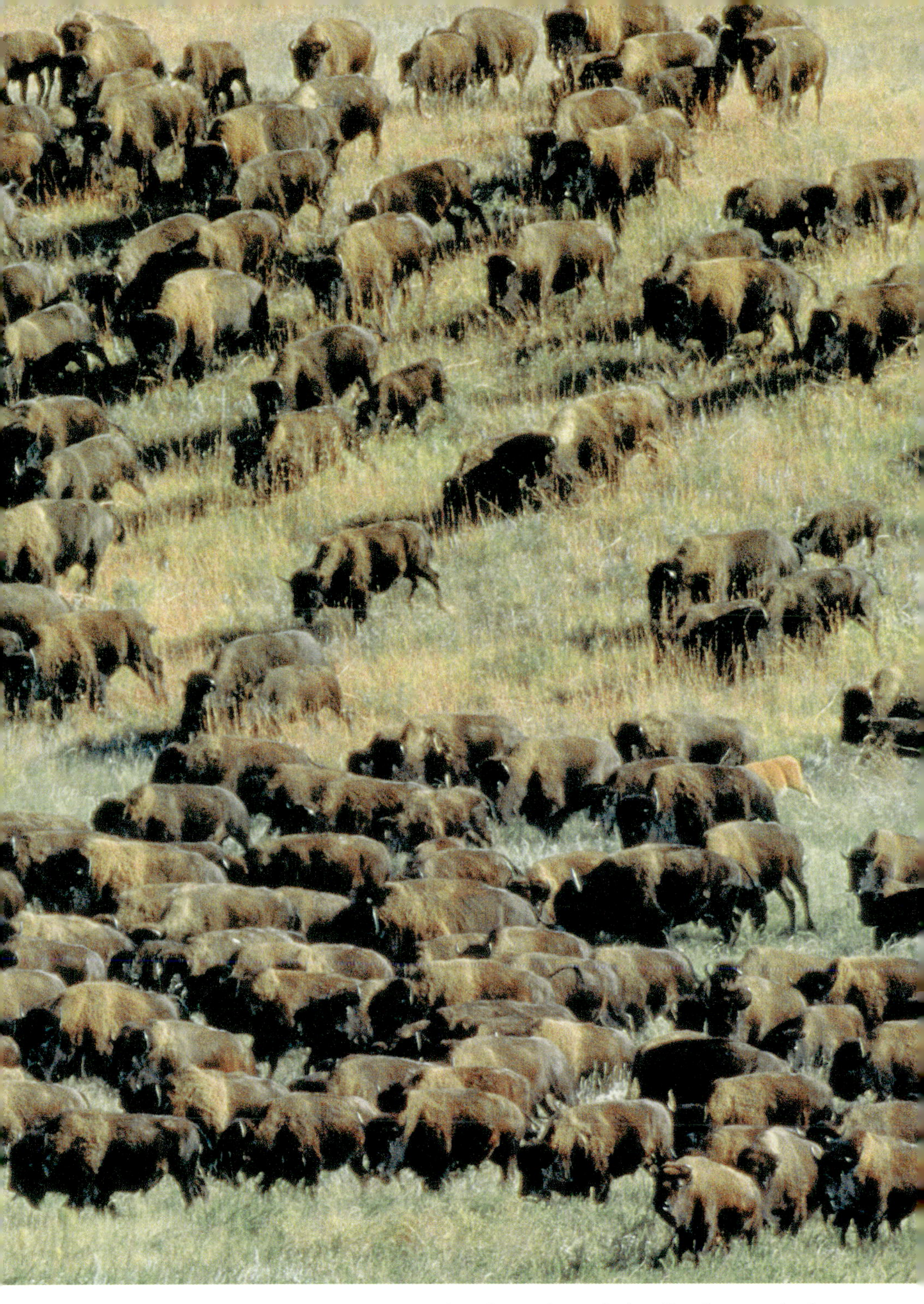

Bison are the star attraction in Custer State Park in the southern Black Hills. They can also be seen on farms, ranches, reservations and other parks throughout the state. The bison, or buffalo, has gained a prominent place in the state's culture.

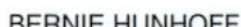
BERNIE HUNHOFF

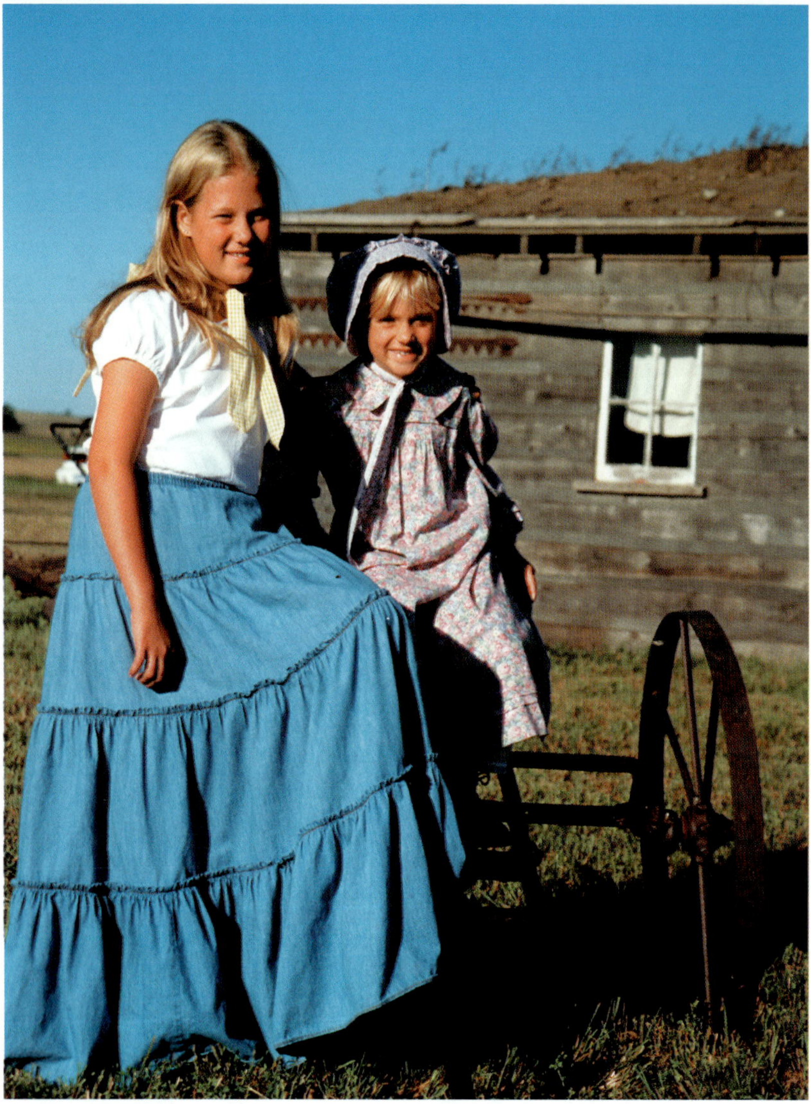

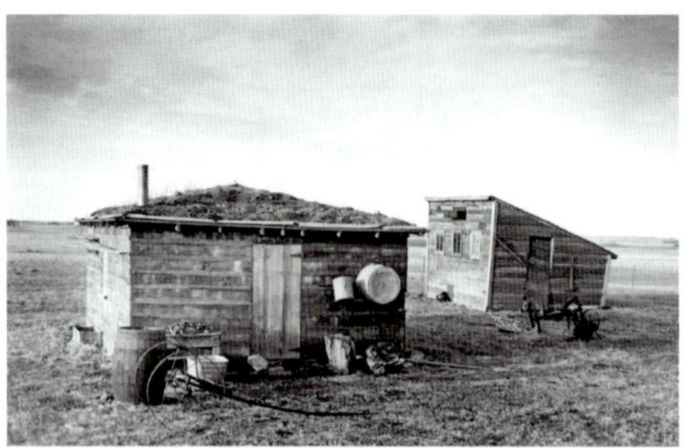

Children and adults alike enjoy the Oscar Micheaux Film Festival held every August in Gregory. Some attendees wear period costumes to the event. At left, local promoters erected a replica of the black film-maker's shanty. Micheaux loved South Dakota, and couldn't understand why all young black men didn't want to homestead here.

SD TOURISM

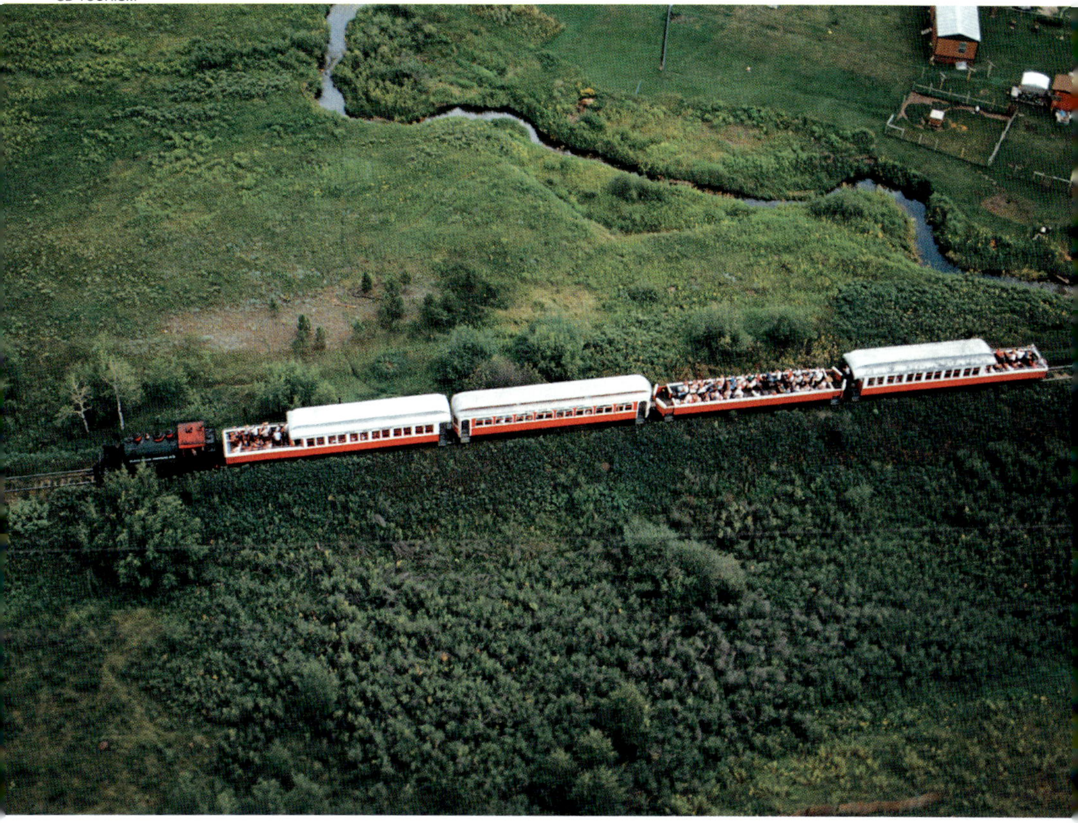

MILBANK CHAMBER OF COMMERCE

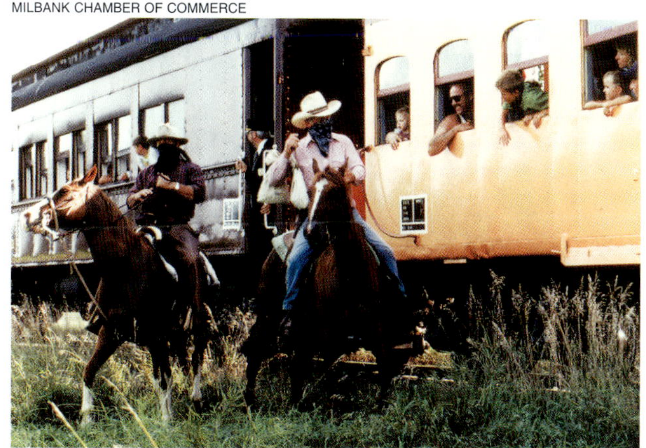

Railroads were important to the development of the Black Hills, even though it was difficult to build tracks around the mountains. That heritage remains alive, thanks to the 1880 Train that carries passengers from Hill City to Keystone in the summer months. Across the state, a Train Festival at Milbank features a robbery on every trip to nearby Corona.

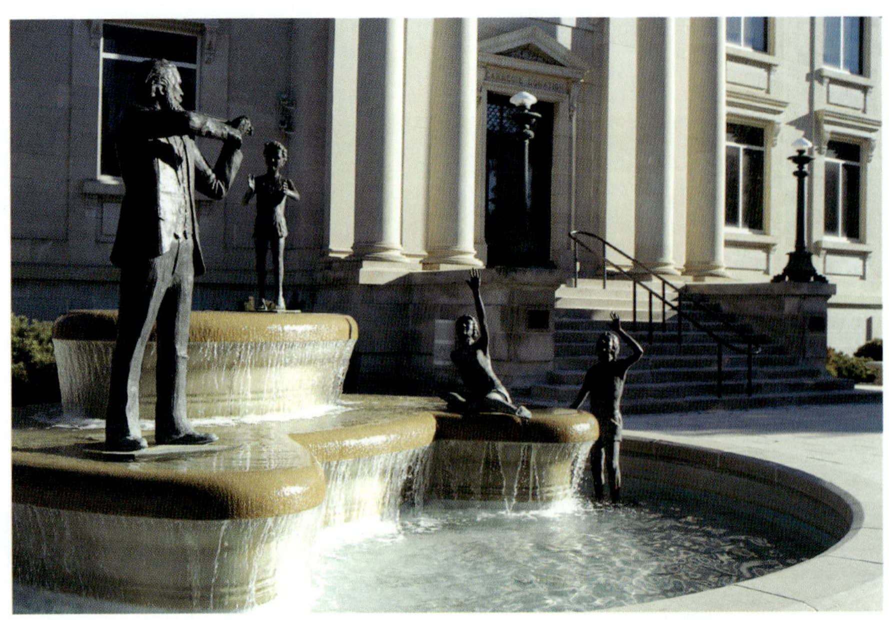

SD TOURISM

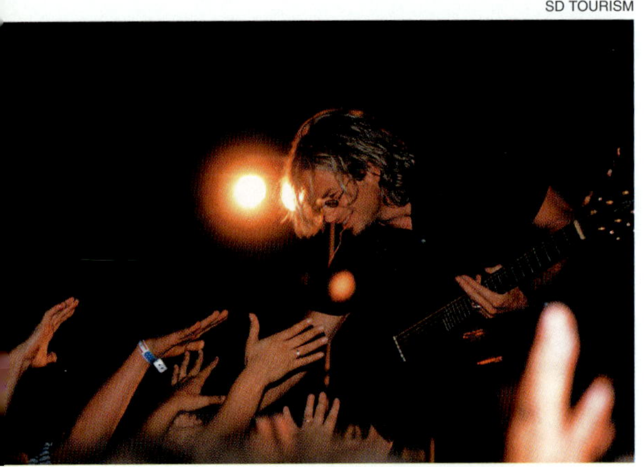

Music of all types adds to summer's aura. At the National Music Museum in Vermillion, "brown bag lunches" are as likely to feature folk music as Bach and Beethoven. The museum, a world-class display of musical instruments, grew from the private collection of Brookings teacher Arne Larson.

On the other end of South Dakota's music spectrum, a Sioux Falls band known as Kory and the Fireflies entertains enthusiastic fans.

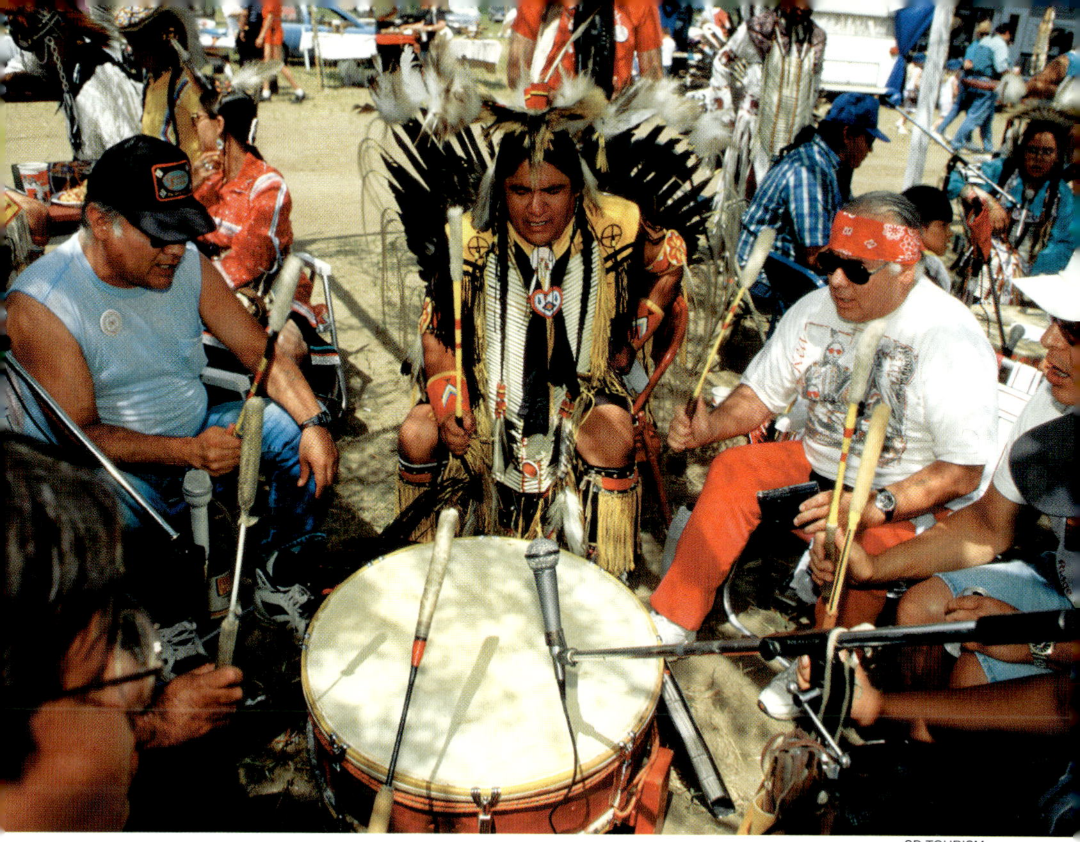

SD TOURISM

Native American music doesn't make America's pop charts, but it has many fans. Drummers (above) perform at pow wows. The band Brule gained fame for soulful instrumental recordings and personal performances. The leader, Paul LaRoche was adopted at an early age and discovered his Lakota heritage as a young adult. Brule's guitarist (below) and other band members also have Indian ancestry.

SD TOURISM

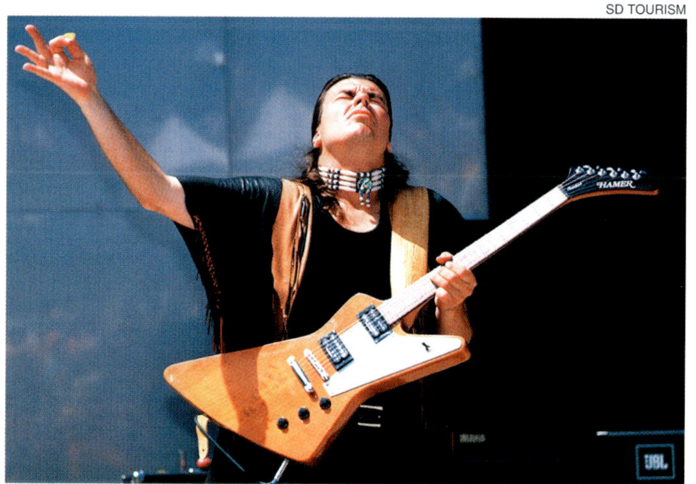

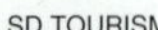
SD TOURISM

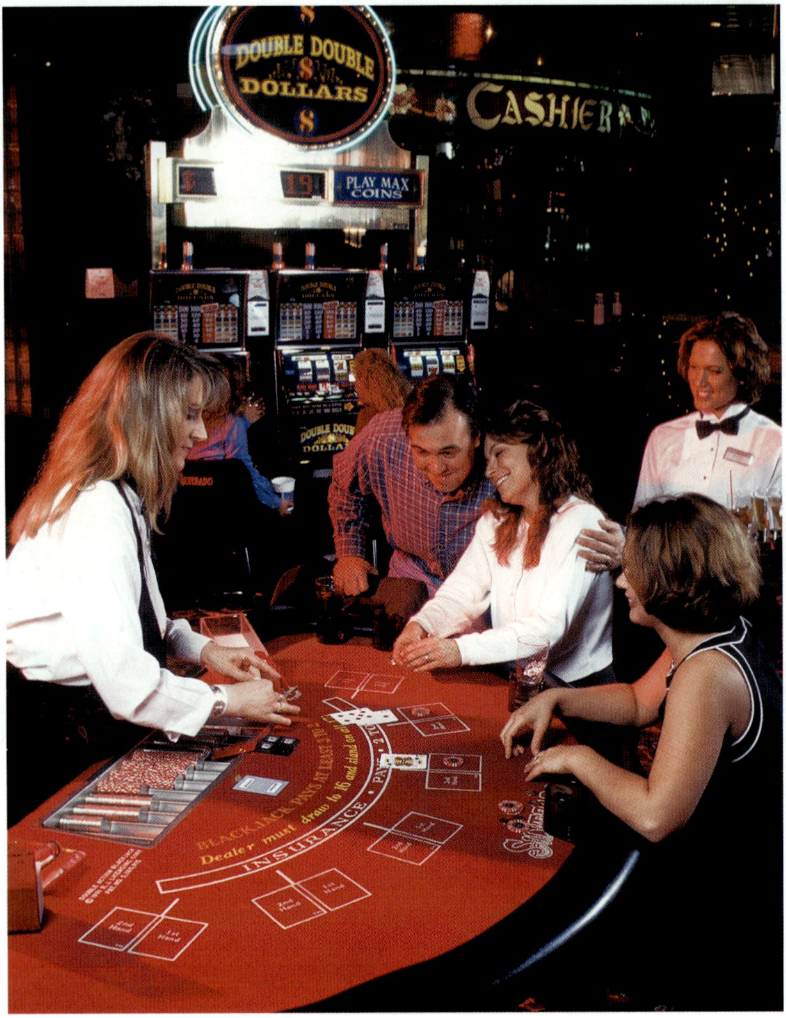

Entertainment venues vary wildly from town to town, especially in West River. Tens of thousands of people journey to Deadwood (above) for casino gambling. For even wilder action, some like Wall's annual high school rodeo (right). Local spectators chat between calf ropings at an arena near Swett in Bennett County (top right).

STEPHEN GASSMAN

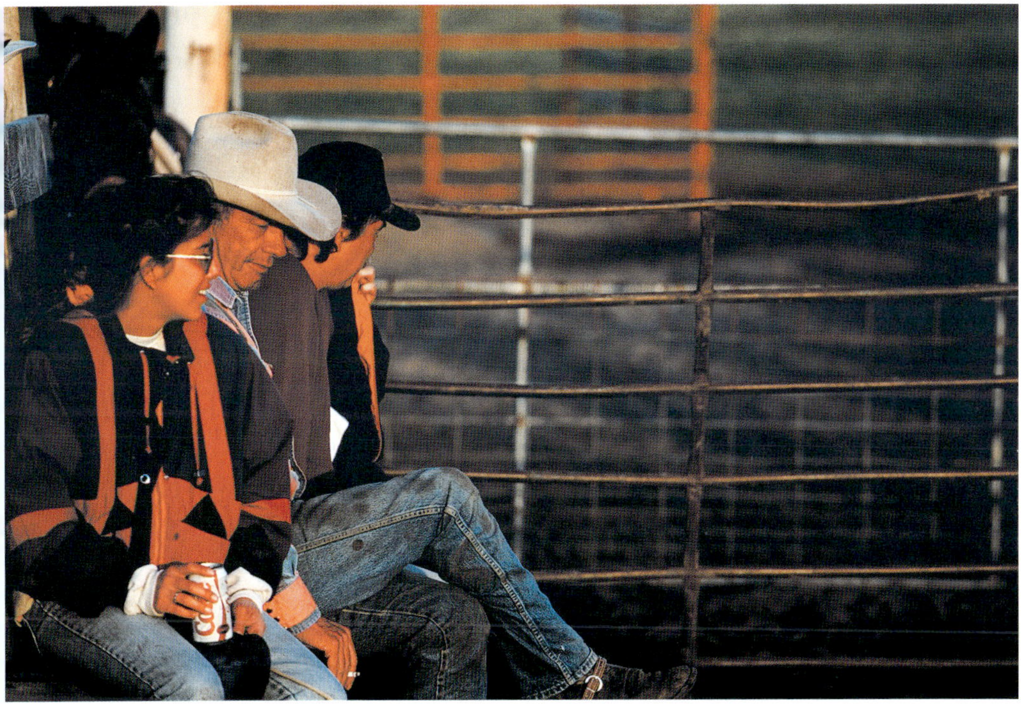

STEPHEN GASSMAN

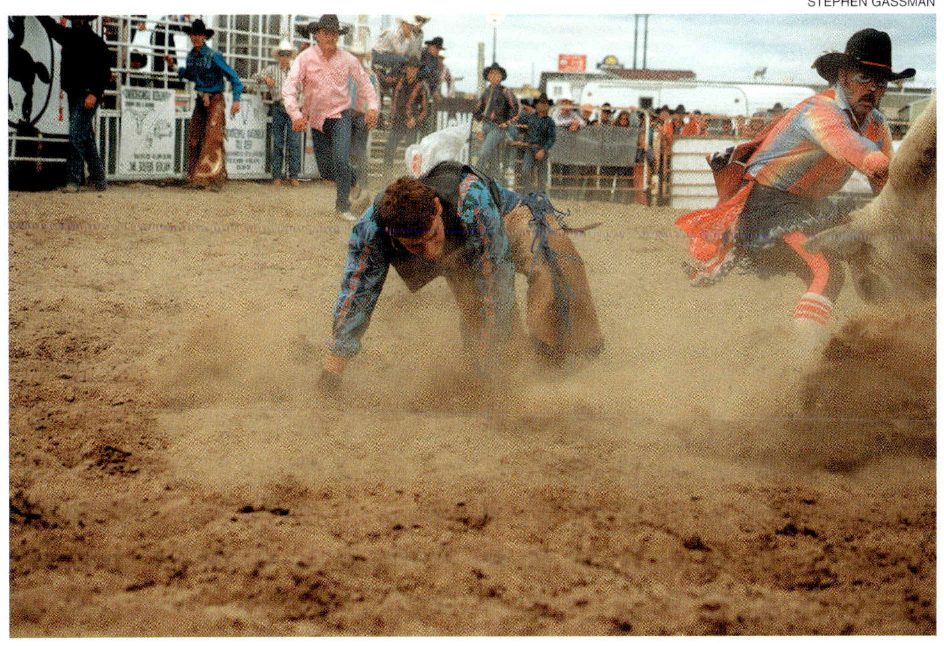

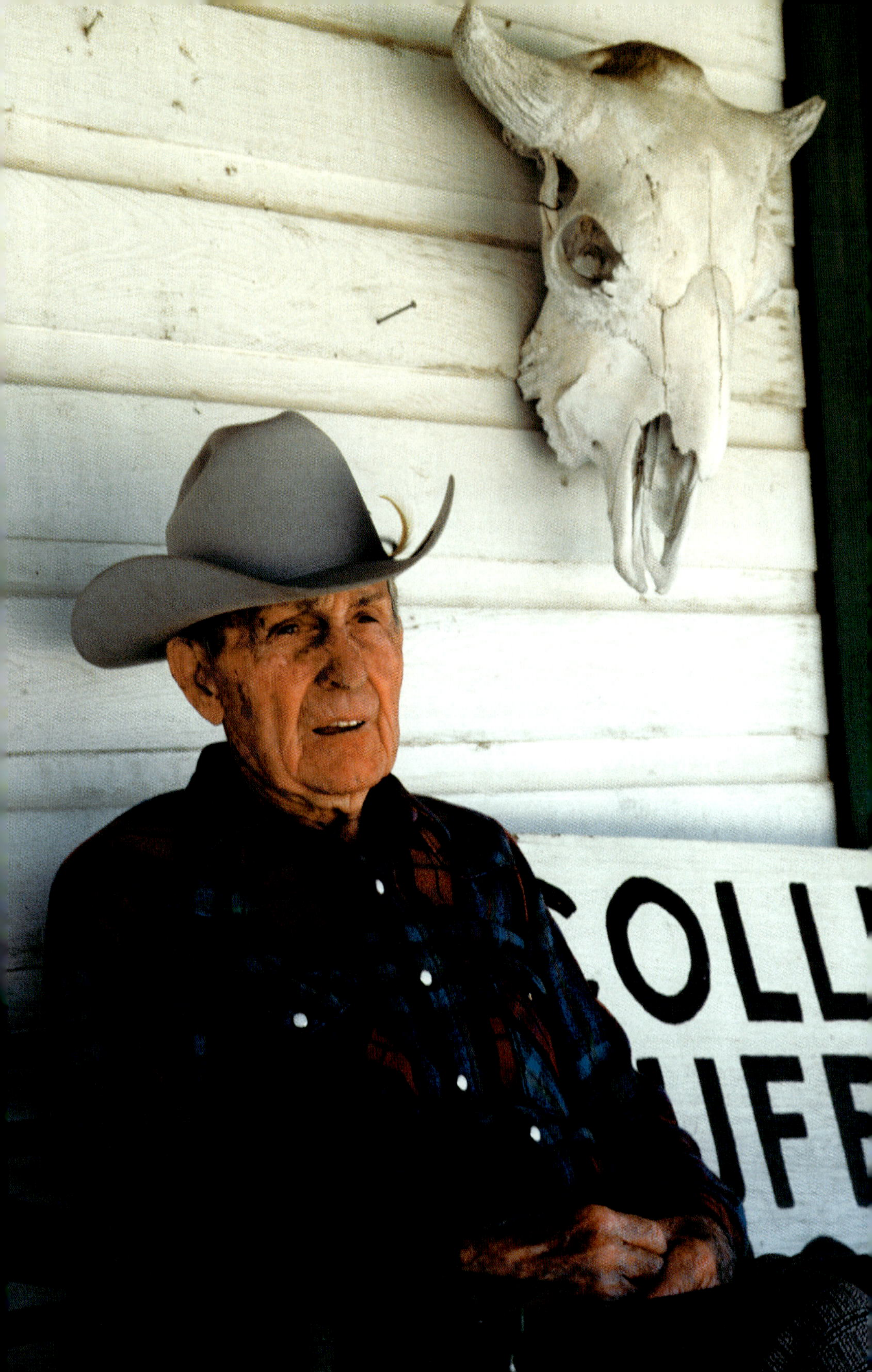

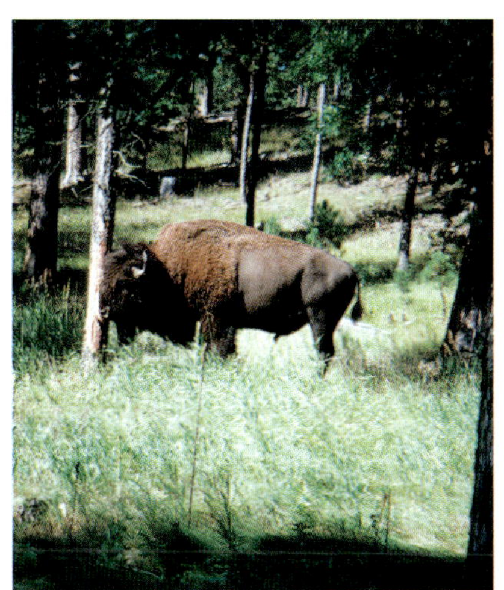

Martin Collins and his wife raised seven children on a small ranch along Highway 385 near Hill City by corralling a few buffalo. Tourists stopped to take pictures and most dropped coins in a donation box. Collins never charged admission. By the 1990s buffalo had become too common, so he added other animals, including a bear that bit off part of the old man's finger. He came to South Dakota by covered wagon in 1902.

BERNIE HUNHOFF

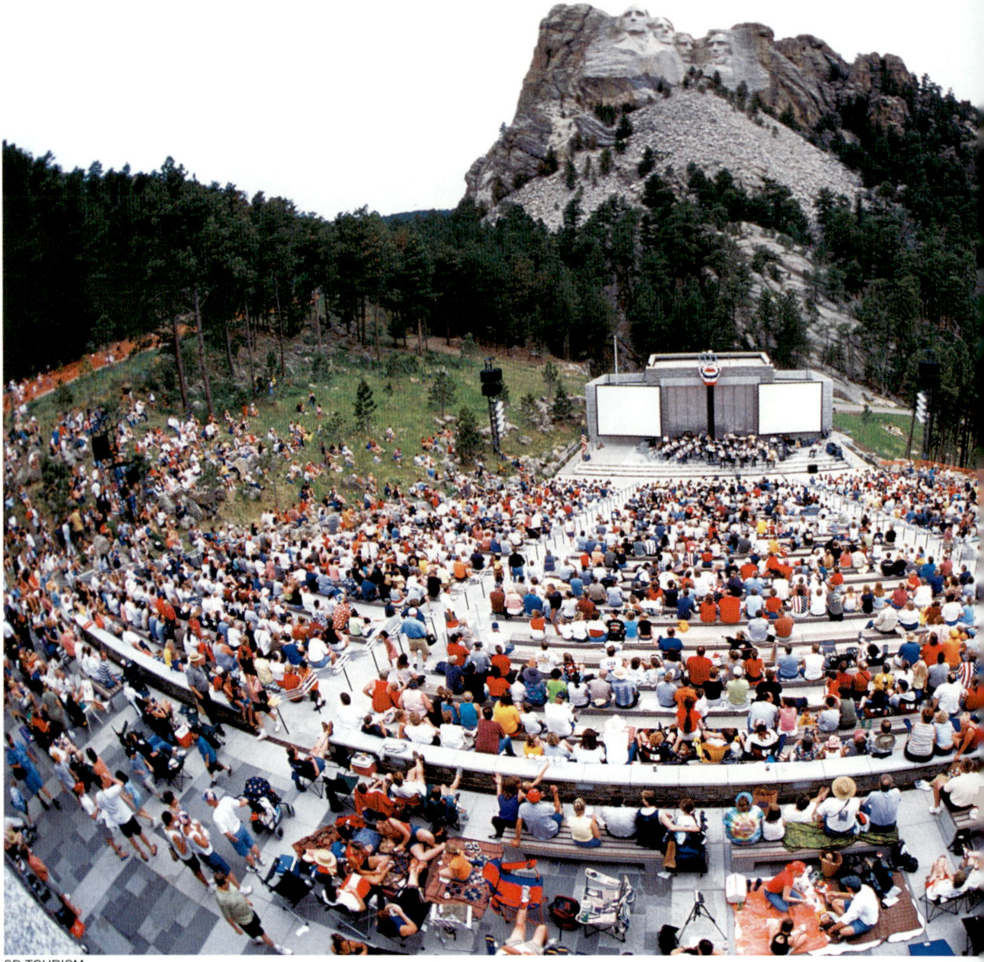

SD TOURISM

Mount Rushmore is among the world's best-known landmarks. The 60-foot-high faces carved by sculptor Gutzon Borglum and his crew were completed in 1941. Only $1 million was spent on the project. It became the Midwest's leading tourist attraction and, more importantly, a symbol of American democracy. Fourth of July celebrations on the mountain are memorable.

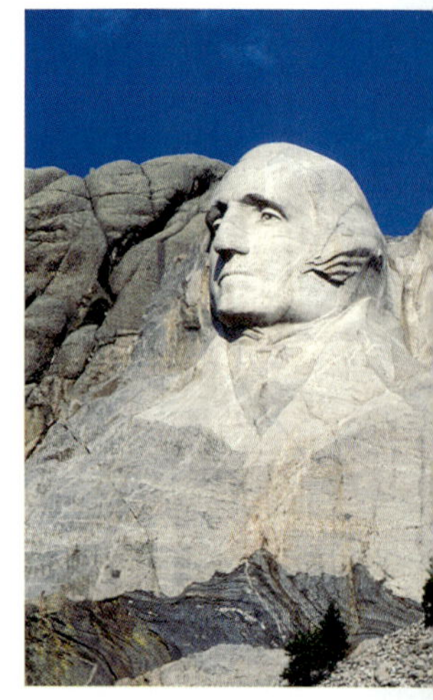

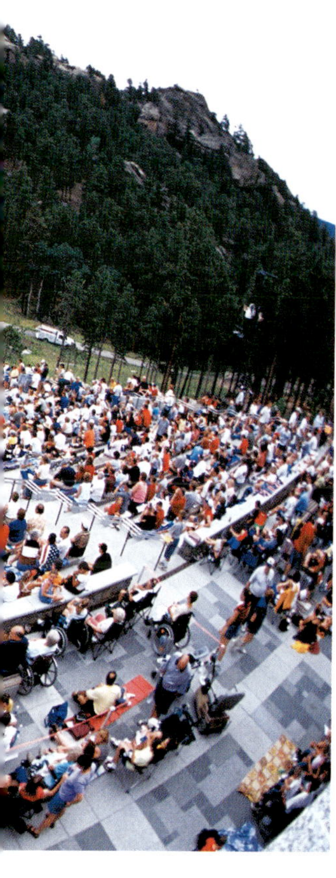

SD TOURISM

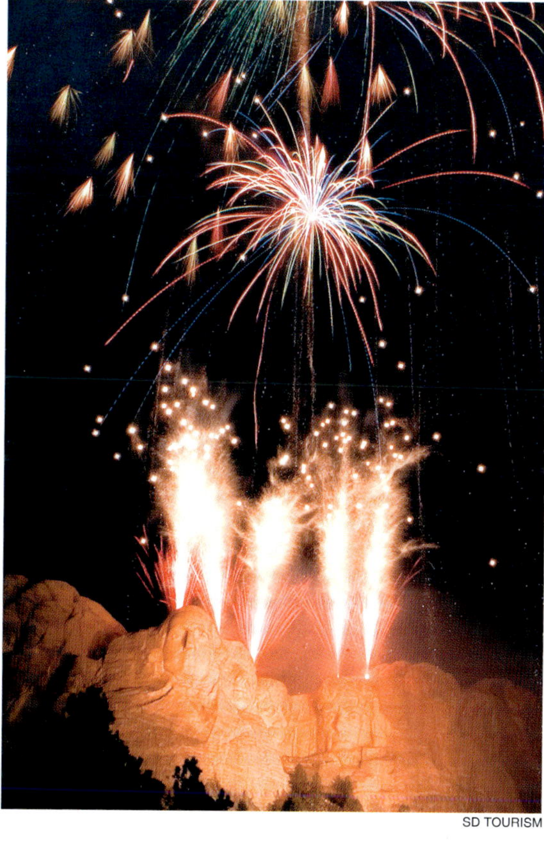

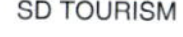

SD TOURISM

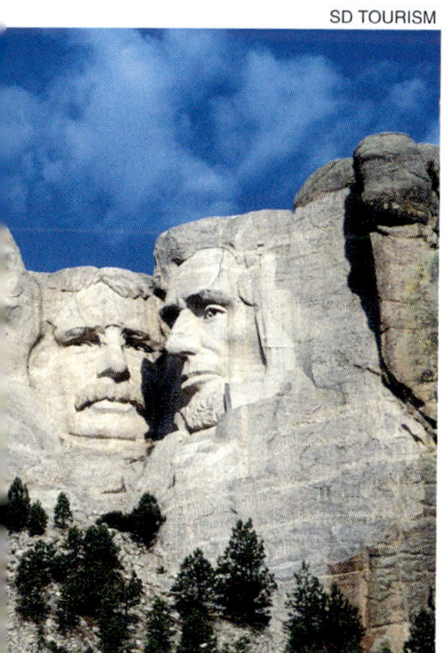

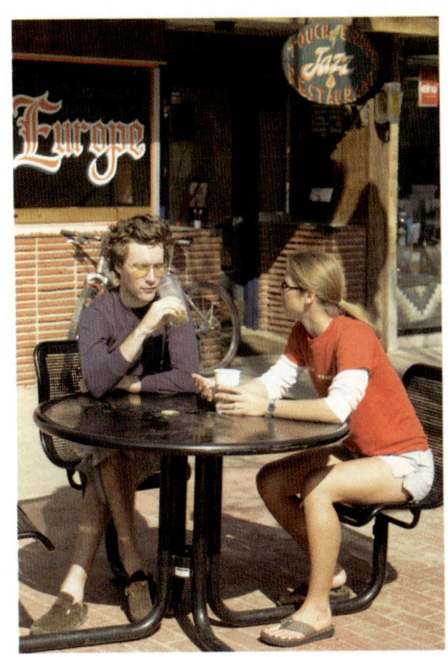

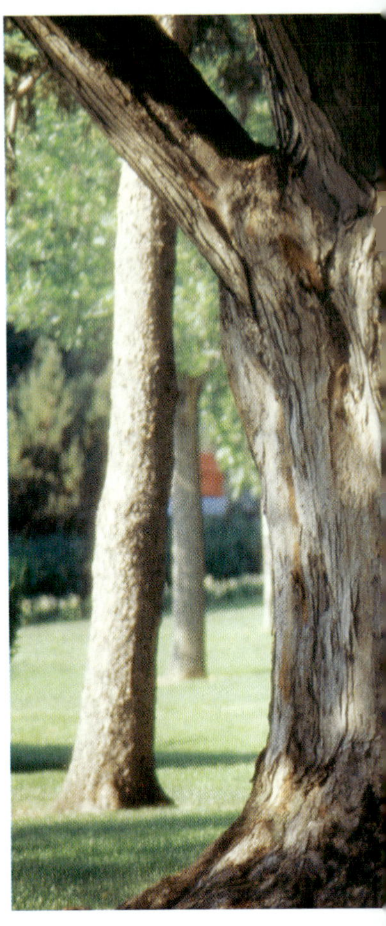

As much as people love nature and South Dakota's rural regions, they eventually converge on our cities in their summer travels. In Sioux Falls, couples enjoy downtown cafes (above) and the historic McKennan Park (right). Hill City, near Mount Rushmore, has become known for regional art. In the southeast, an Elk Point drug store draws motorists from Interstate 29 to a quaint soda fountain called Edgar's.

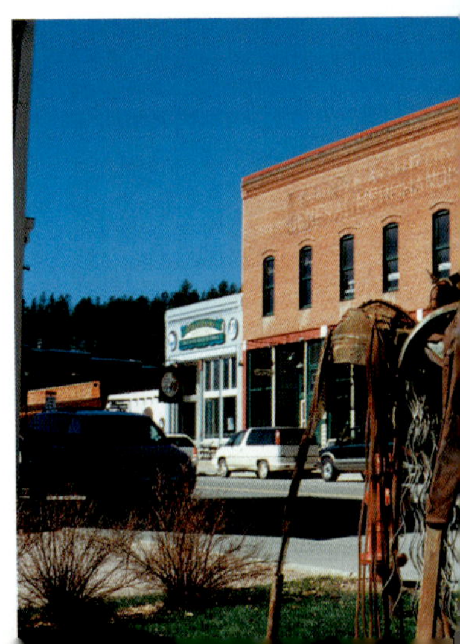

BERNIE HUNHOFF PHOTOS

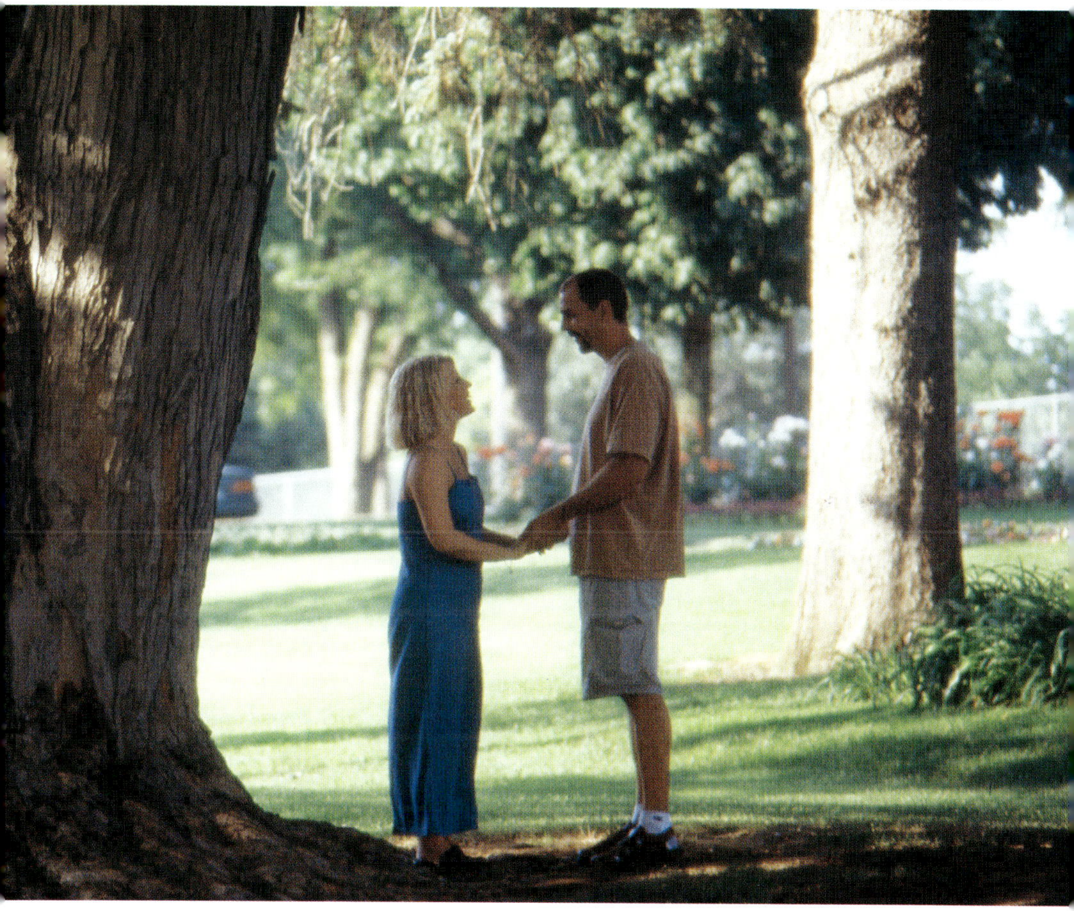

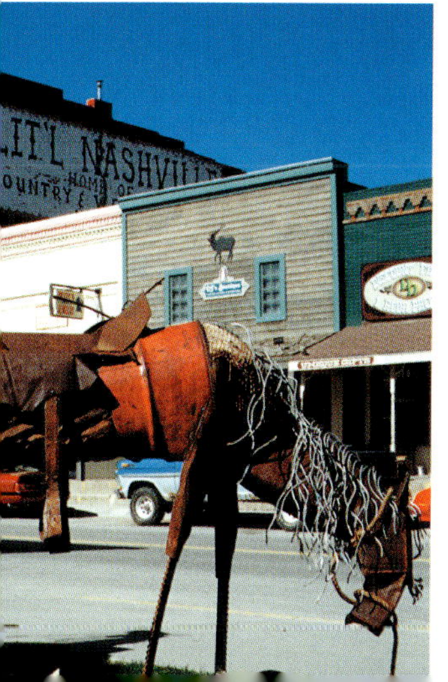

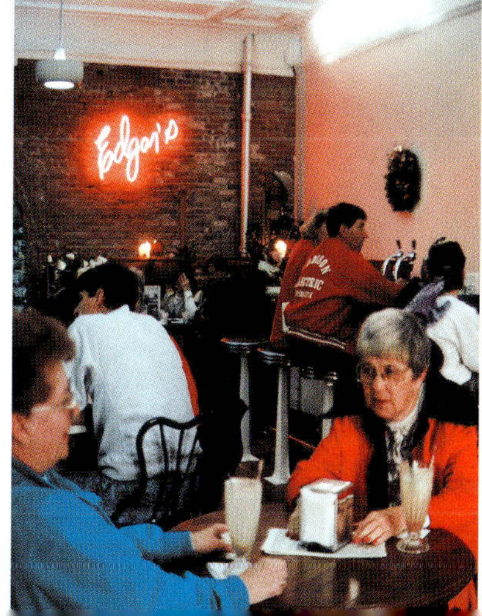

STAFF PHOTOS

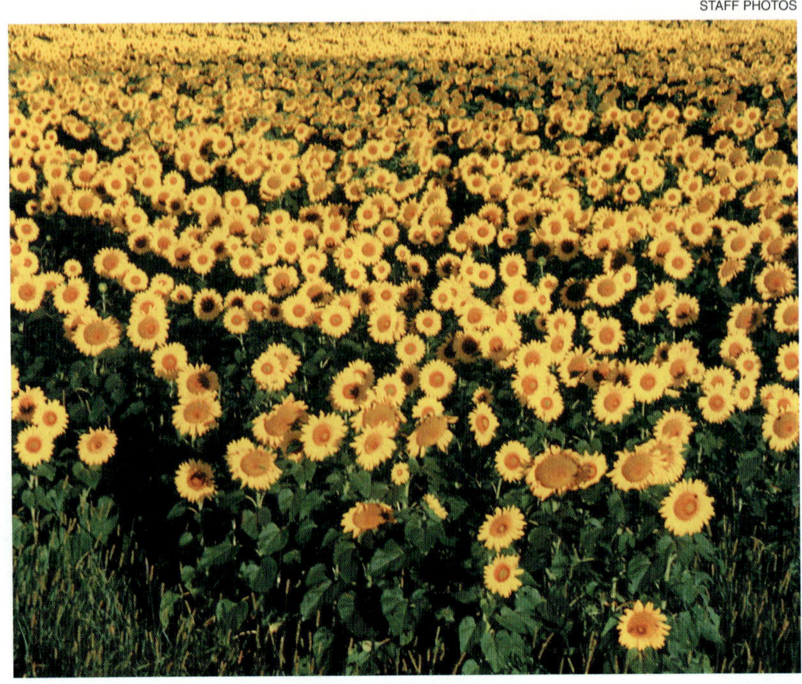

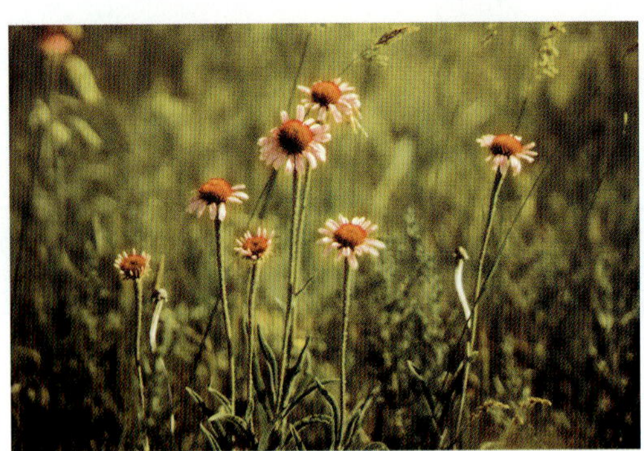

Farm country scenery changes as summer progresses. Sunflowers begin as row crops and eventually look like a giant bouquet. The Echinacea flower (left), sought for medicinal purposes, grows wild in grasslands. Below, a butterfly rests on a common weed called stick-tight.

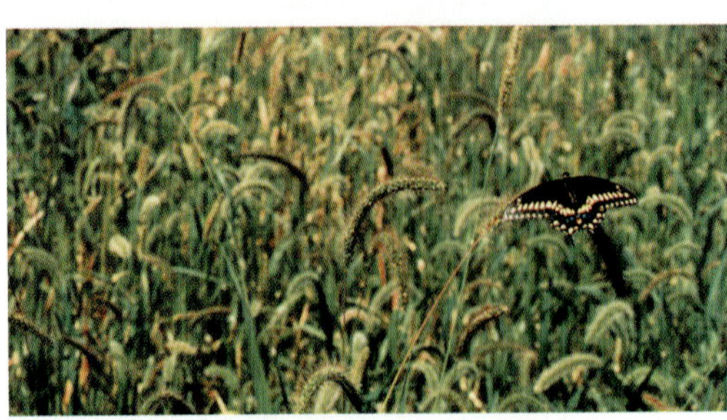

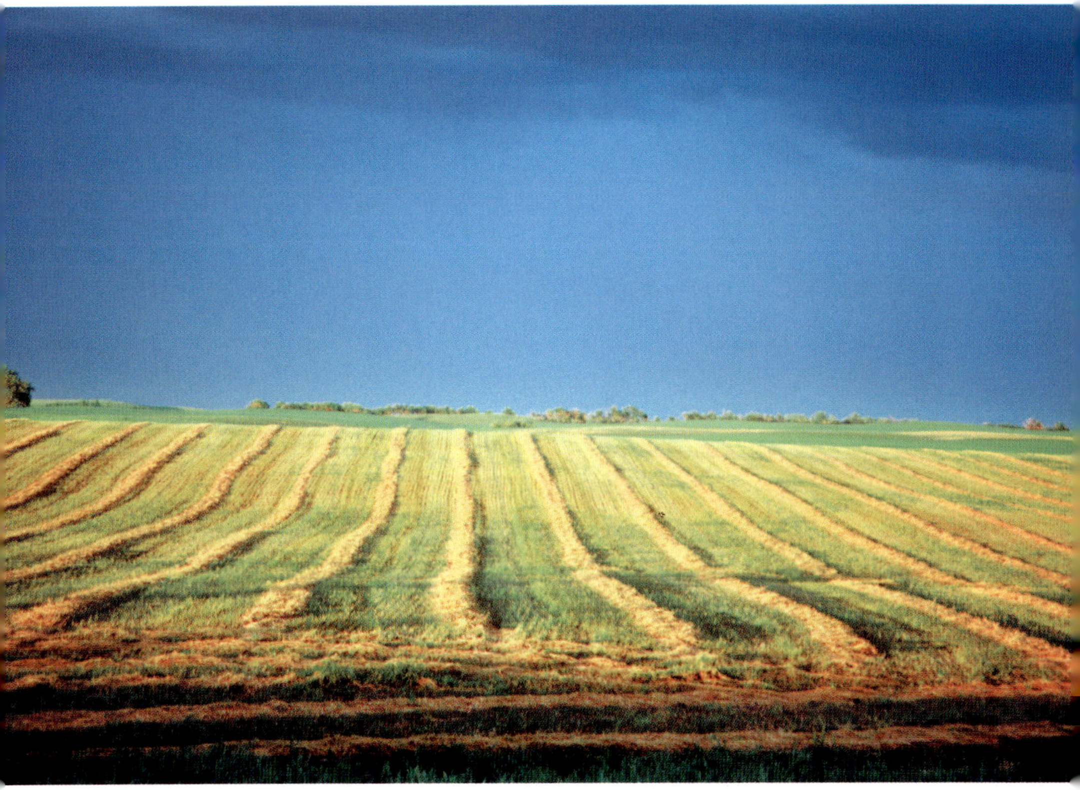

Windrows of fresh-cut hay dry in the golden sun of late afternoon near Watertown. Hives of honey bees stand in a hayfield near Winner (right). South Dakota beekeepers usually spread 230,000 colonies in white wooden boxes across the state.

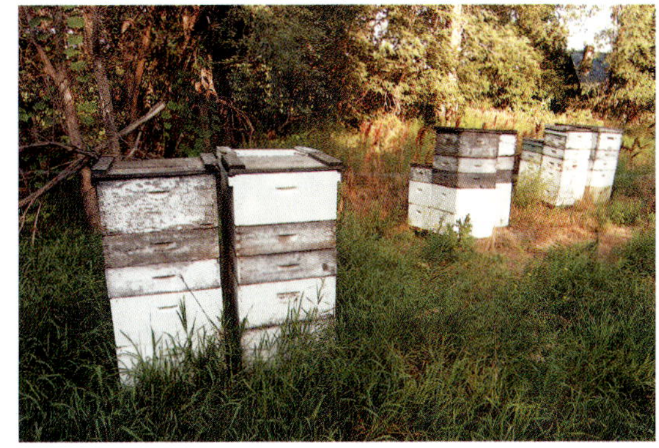

BERNIE HUNHOFF

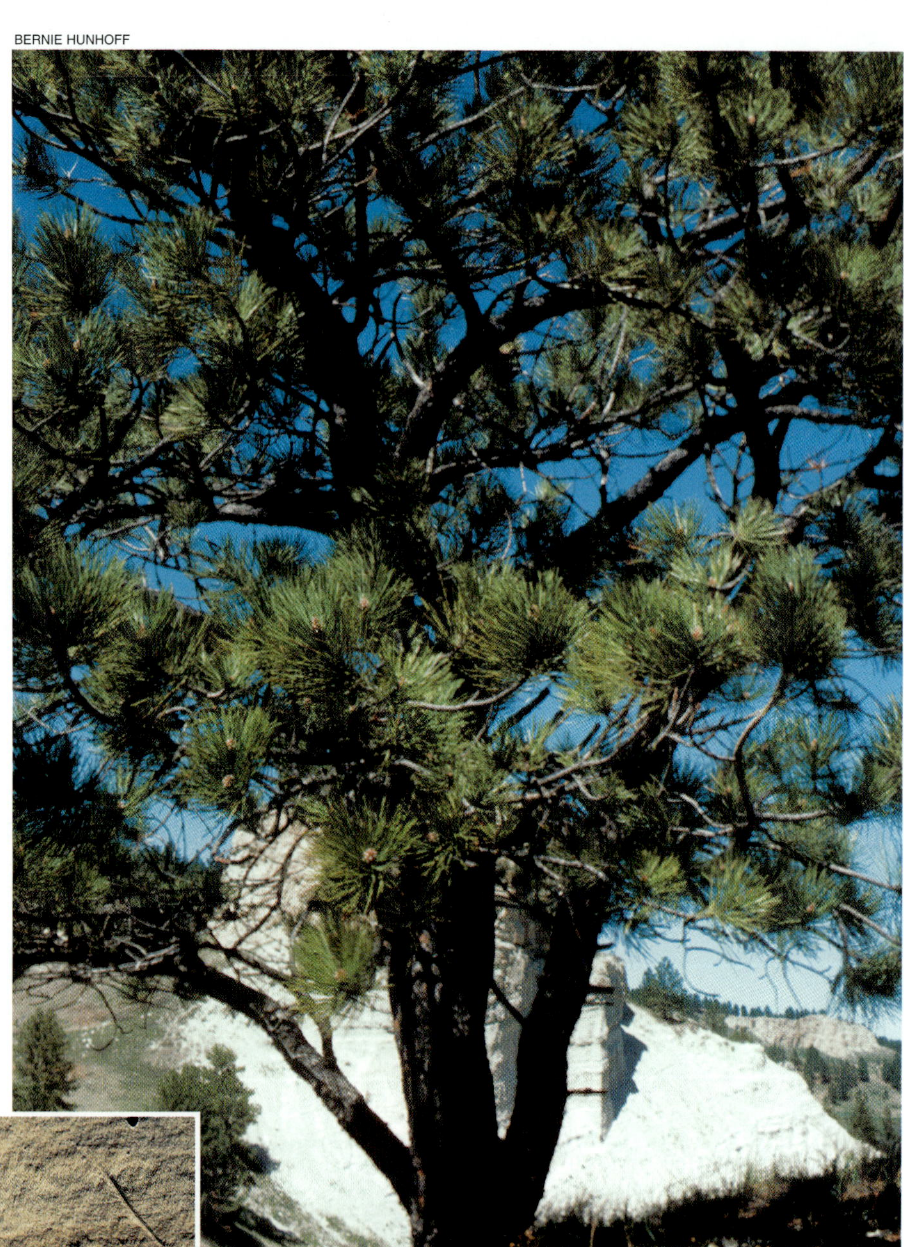

Harding County's Cave Hills may be South Dakota's best-kept historical and geological secret. Native American petroglyphs survive in the soft sandstone of caves and cliffs. Custer's cavalry carved their initials in 1874. Theodore Roosevelt proclaimed the area a National Forest Reserve when he became president.

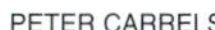

PETER CARRELS

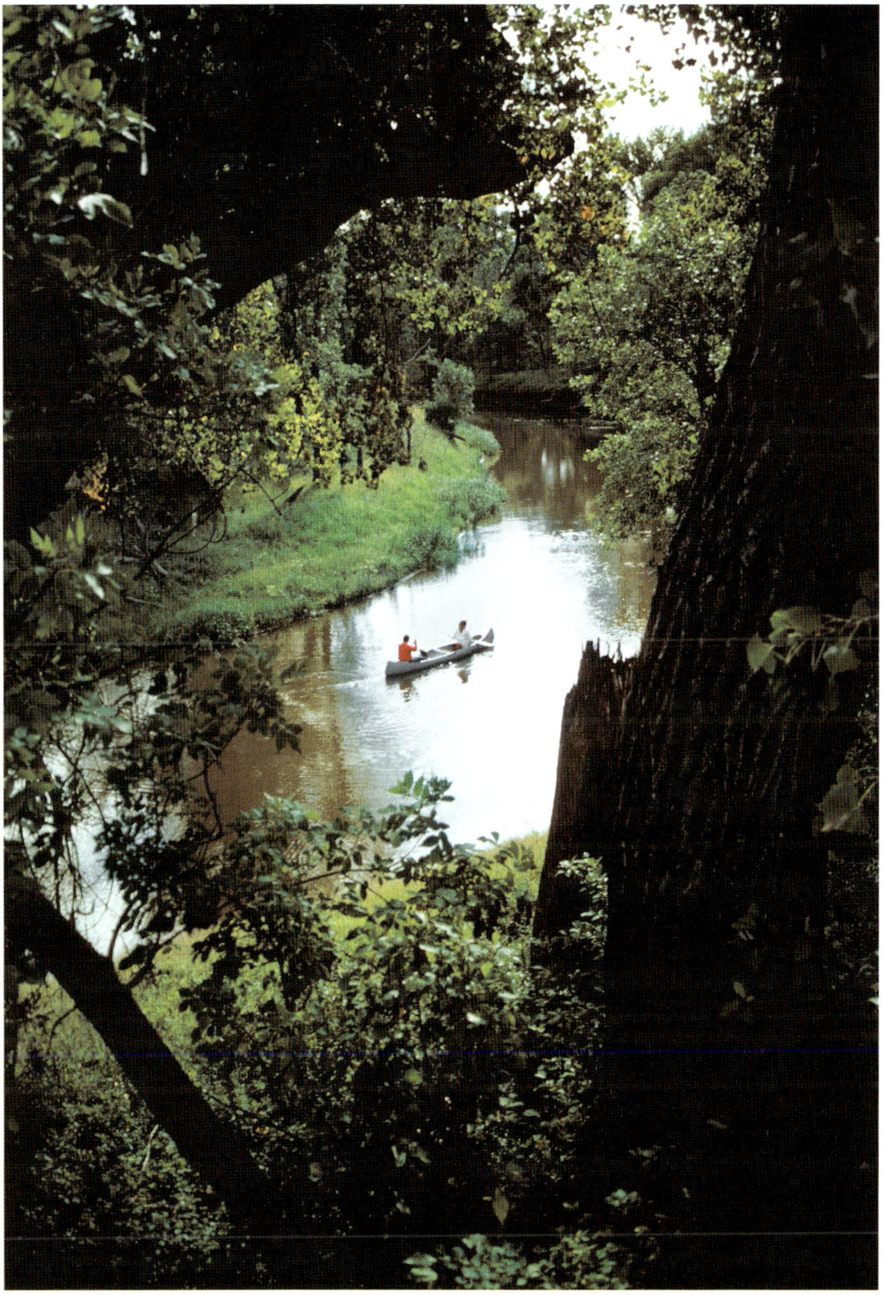

Canoeists paddle near the border of Brown and Spink counties on the James River, which nearly parallels the Missouri River's north-south trip across South Dakota. The meandering James is one of the flattest rivers in the world, dropping an average of a few inches to the mile.

BERNIE HUNHOFF

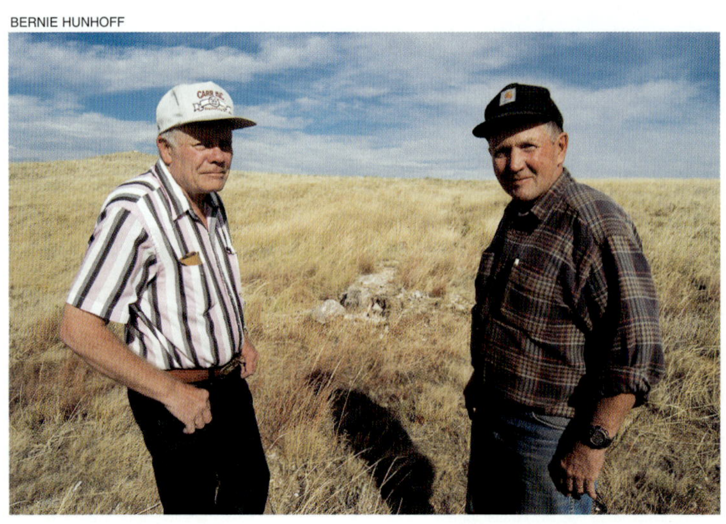

The northwest corner of South Dakota has the state's market on oil and petrified wood. Both come from fossilized plants. Two Perkins County ranchers, Keith Carr and Clyde Jesfjeld (above), showed a photographer the stump of a 100-foot petrified redwood buried in a hill near Bison. Below, oil wells pump money into the pockets of Harding County families.

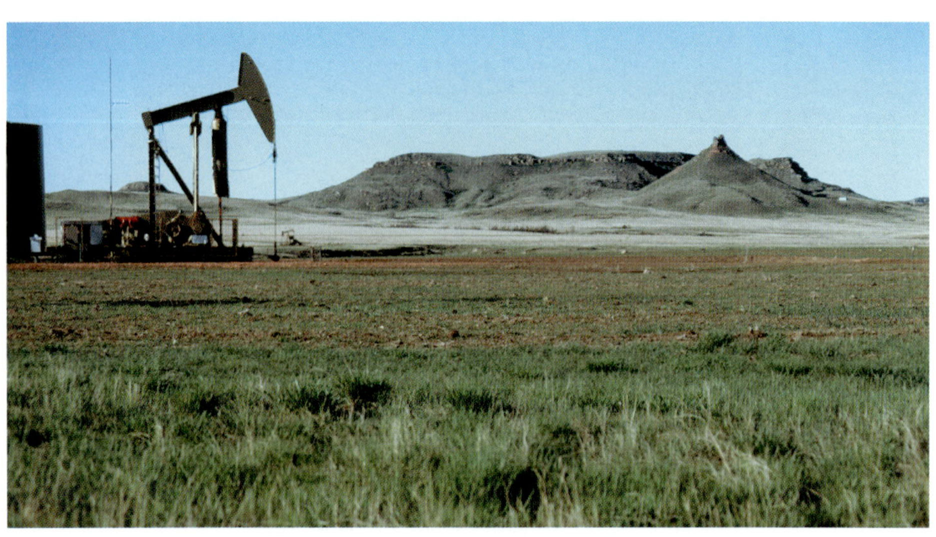

ROB POWELL

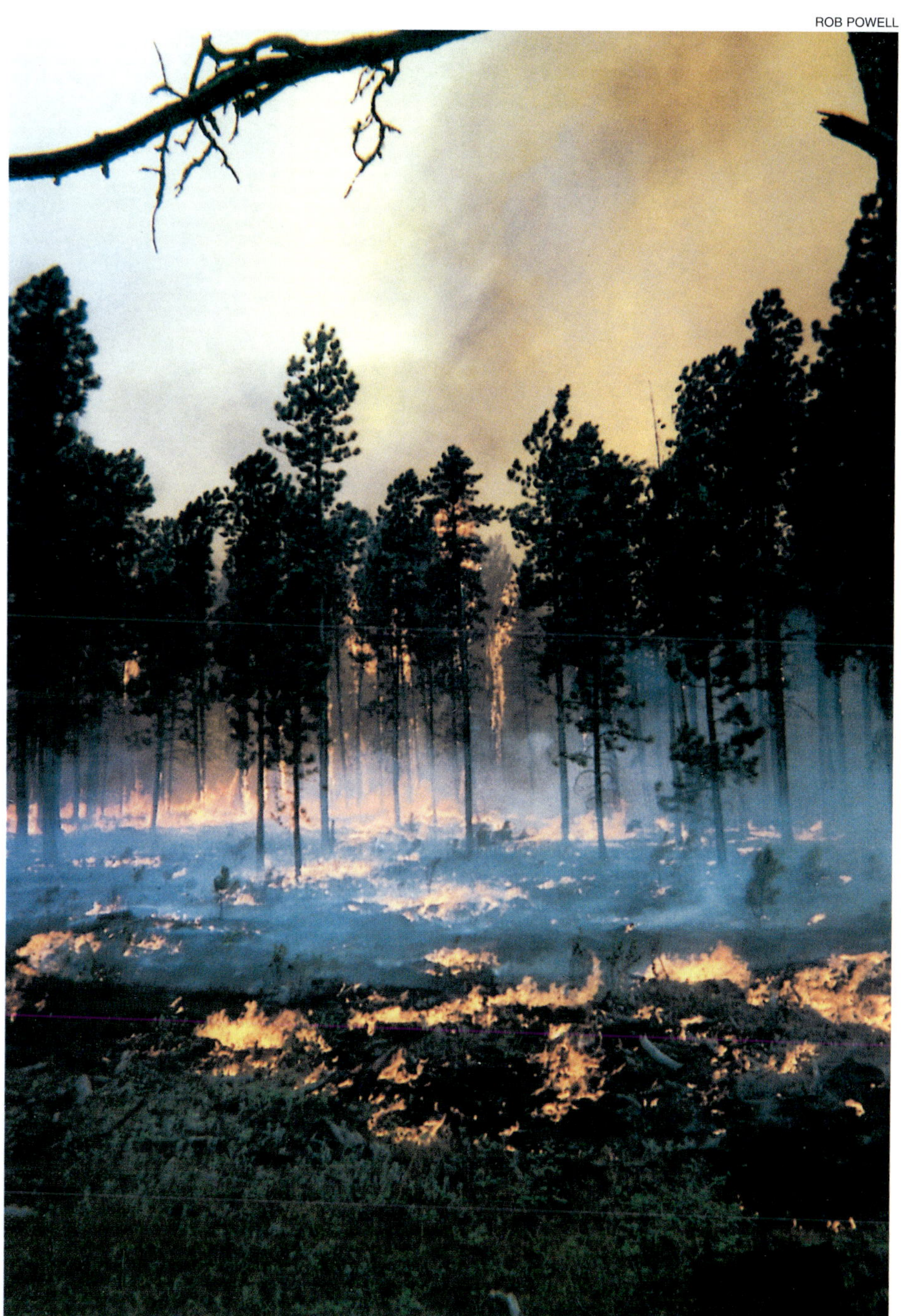

Forest fires are a summer hazard in the Black Hills. The infamous Jaspar Fire, perhaps the biggest in modern history, blackened 85,000 acres of the southern Hills in September of 2000.

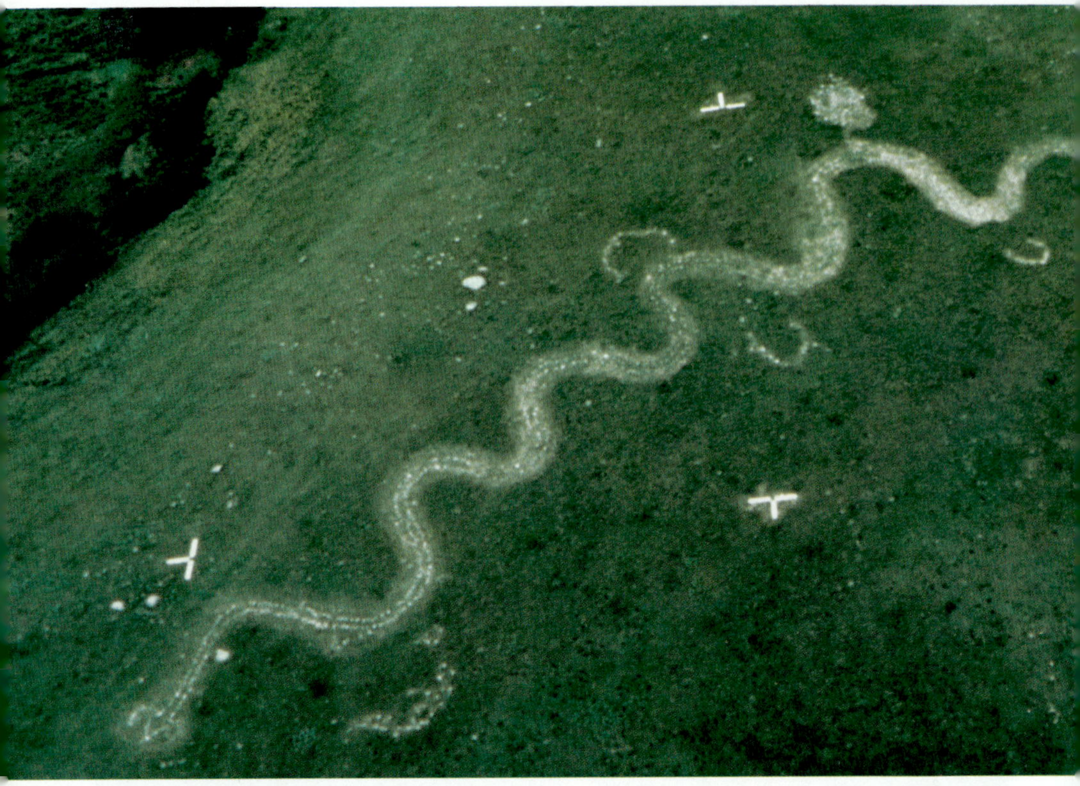

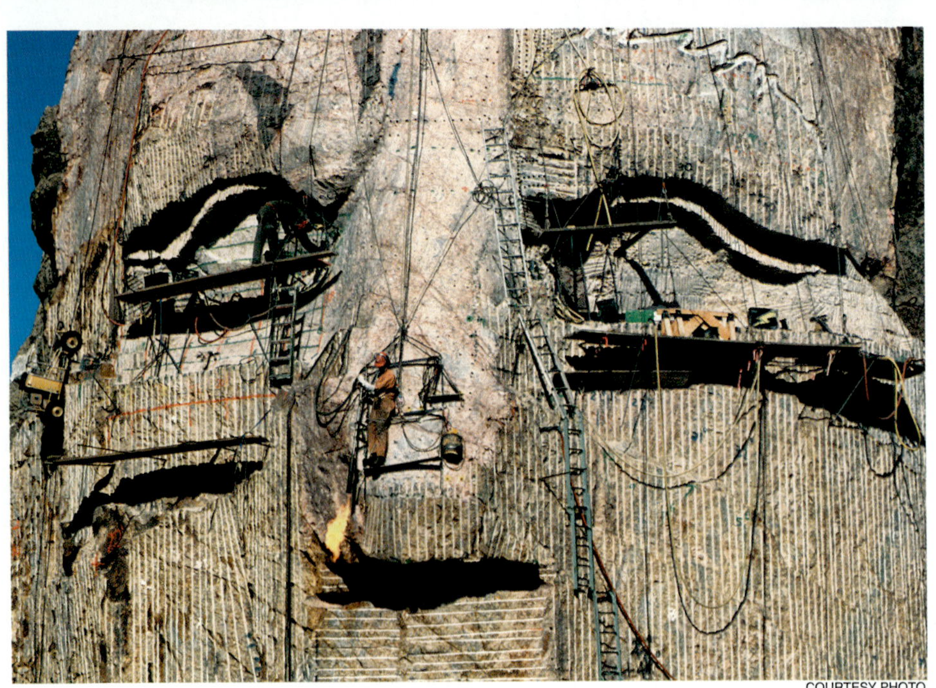

COURTESY PHOTO

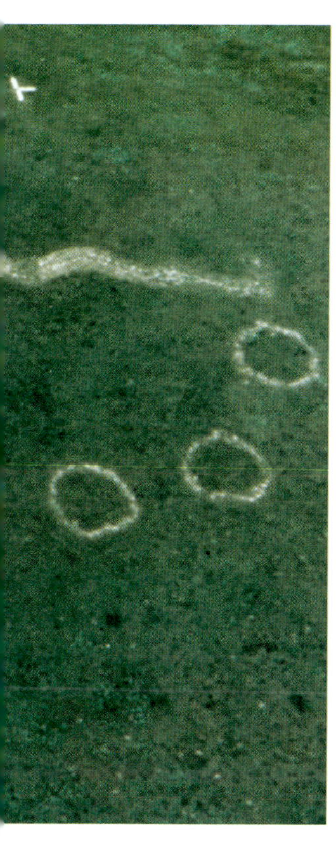

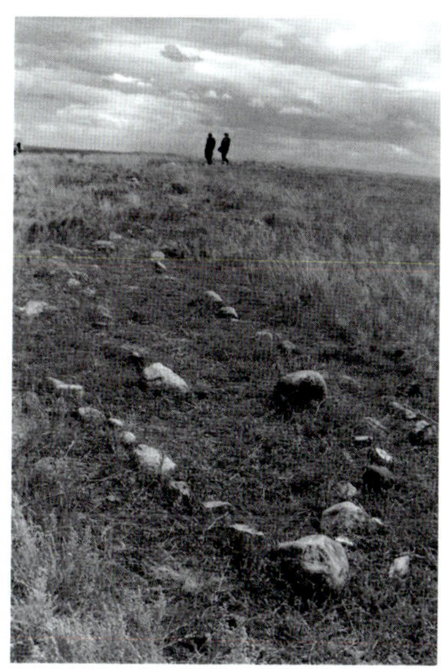

Stone art has a tradition in South Dakota. Hundreds of years ago, native people used stones to create the outlines of serpents and turtles. Such a design remains on Snake Butte south of Harrold. Baking powder was dusted on the rocks to distinguish the design for an aerial photo (above). Of course, the Crazy Horse sculpture (left and right) near Custer is better known — and the only powder used there is dynamite.

COURTESY PHOTO

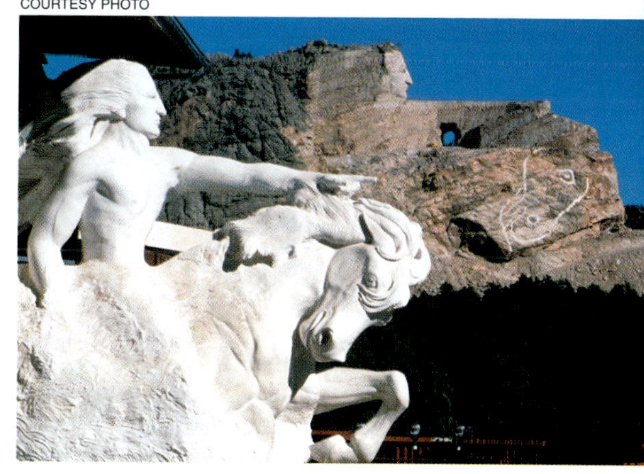

SD TOURISM

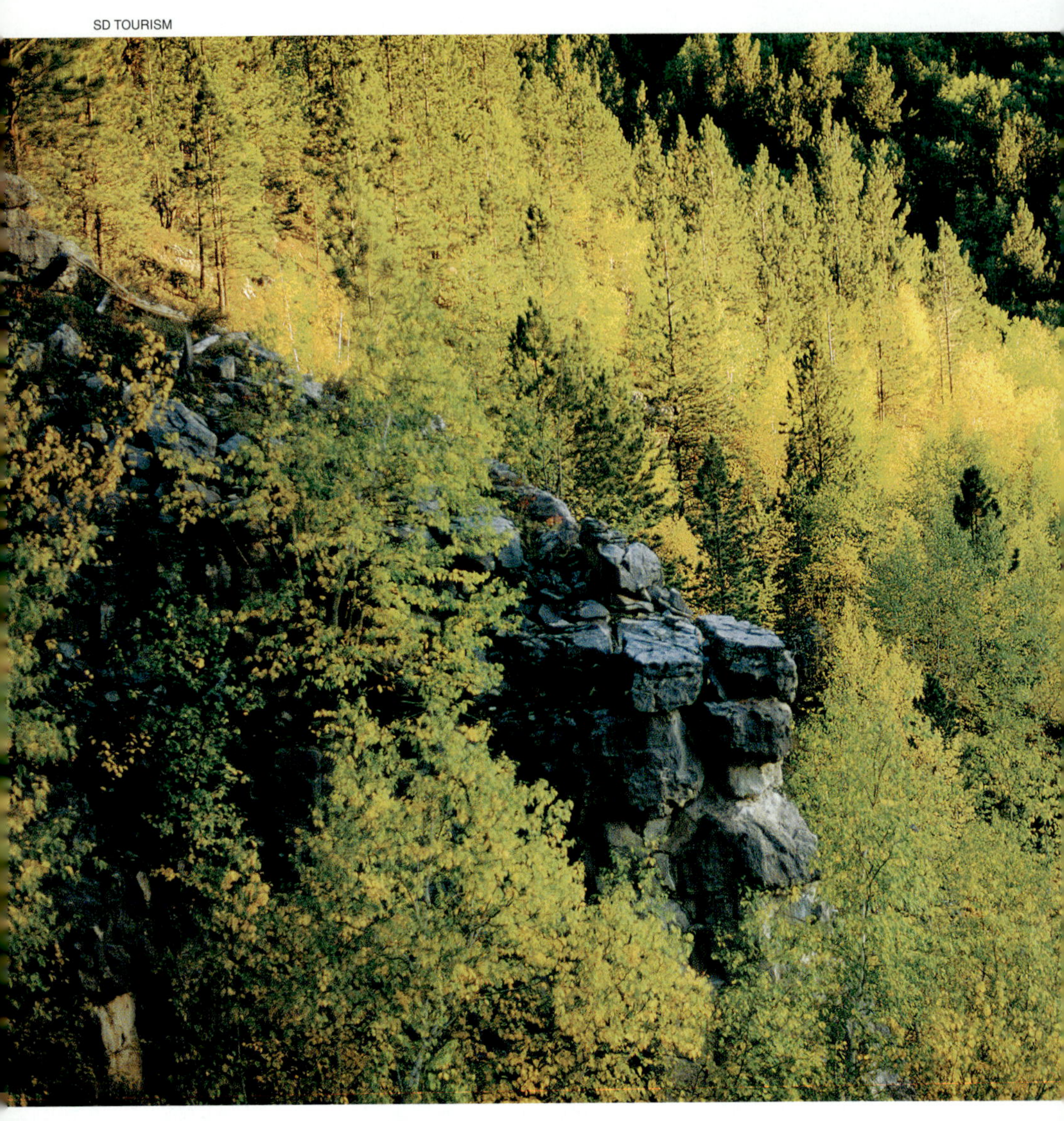

Scientists have counted 1,300 plant species in the Black Hills, but in autumn only two really matter — the aspen and birch, which account for most of the golden foliage in Spearfish Canyon, South Dakotans' favorite fall drive.

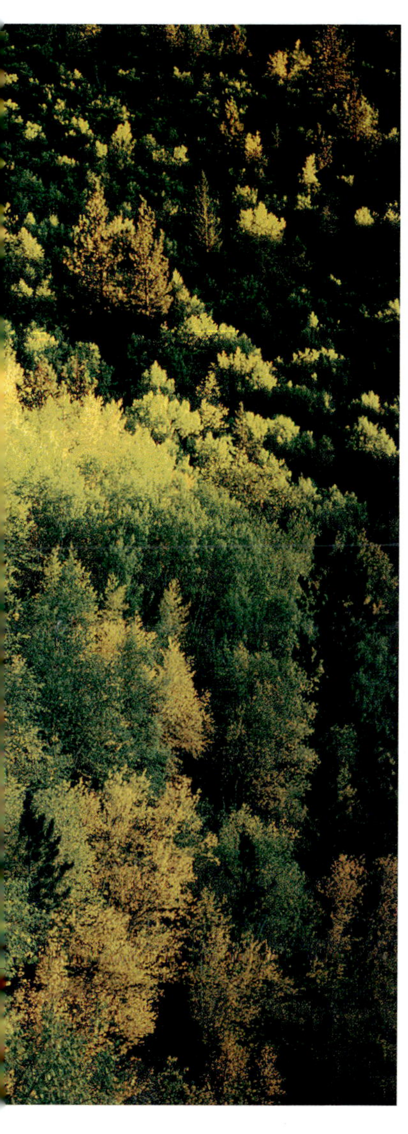

Autumn

Autumn in South Dakota is a return to normalcy. Spring comes full of promise, and then summer squeezes everything from us in a warm rush of long days.

When the corn can't grow another inch, when the dog can't take another all-day snooze in the shade, when we can't possibly fit in another ball game or cook-out, when we're finally ready for dinner after dark — that's when summer mercifully ends and autumn settles us down with a cooler pace.

The exception, of course, is the grain farmer, whose task it is to gather his annual income in a few hectic weeks.

Winter in October would be too sharp, but by then we're surely in need of autumn.

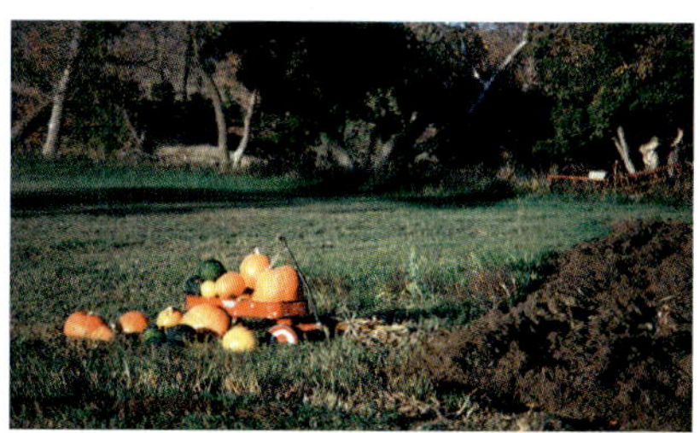

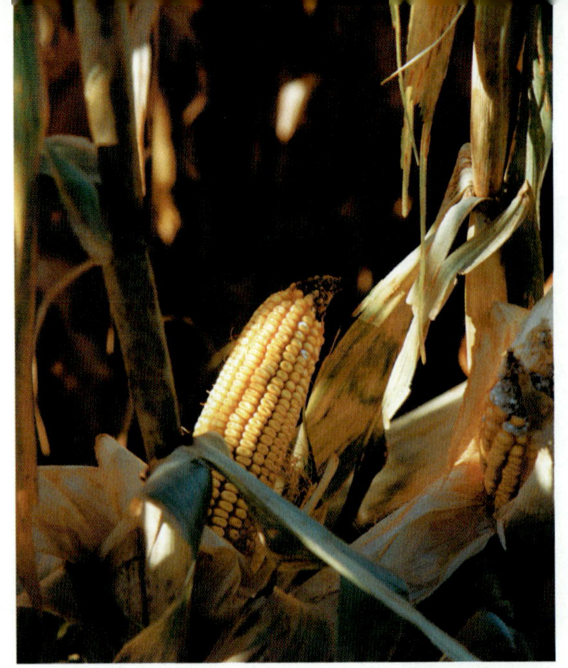

The harvest is significant in our agrarian culture, whether it involves corn (our top cash crop), or the pumpkins grown in Sanborn County, or the big wheat fields of West River (right).

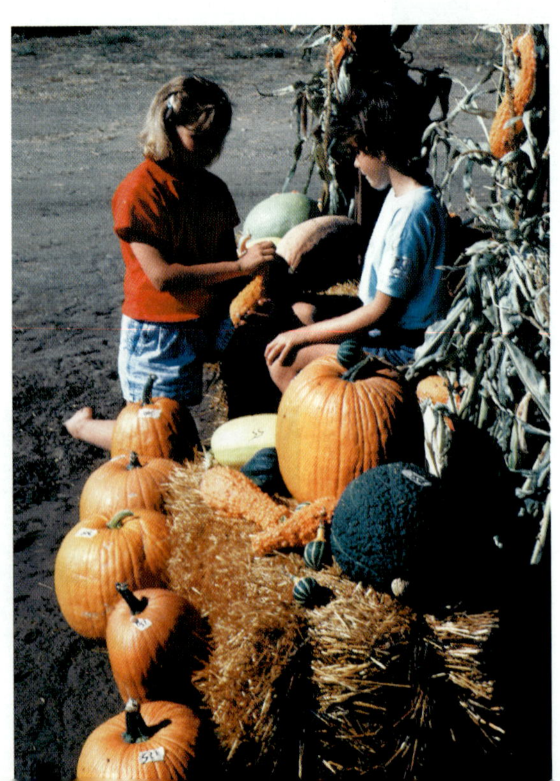

GREG LATZA

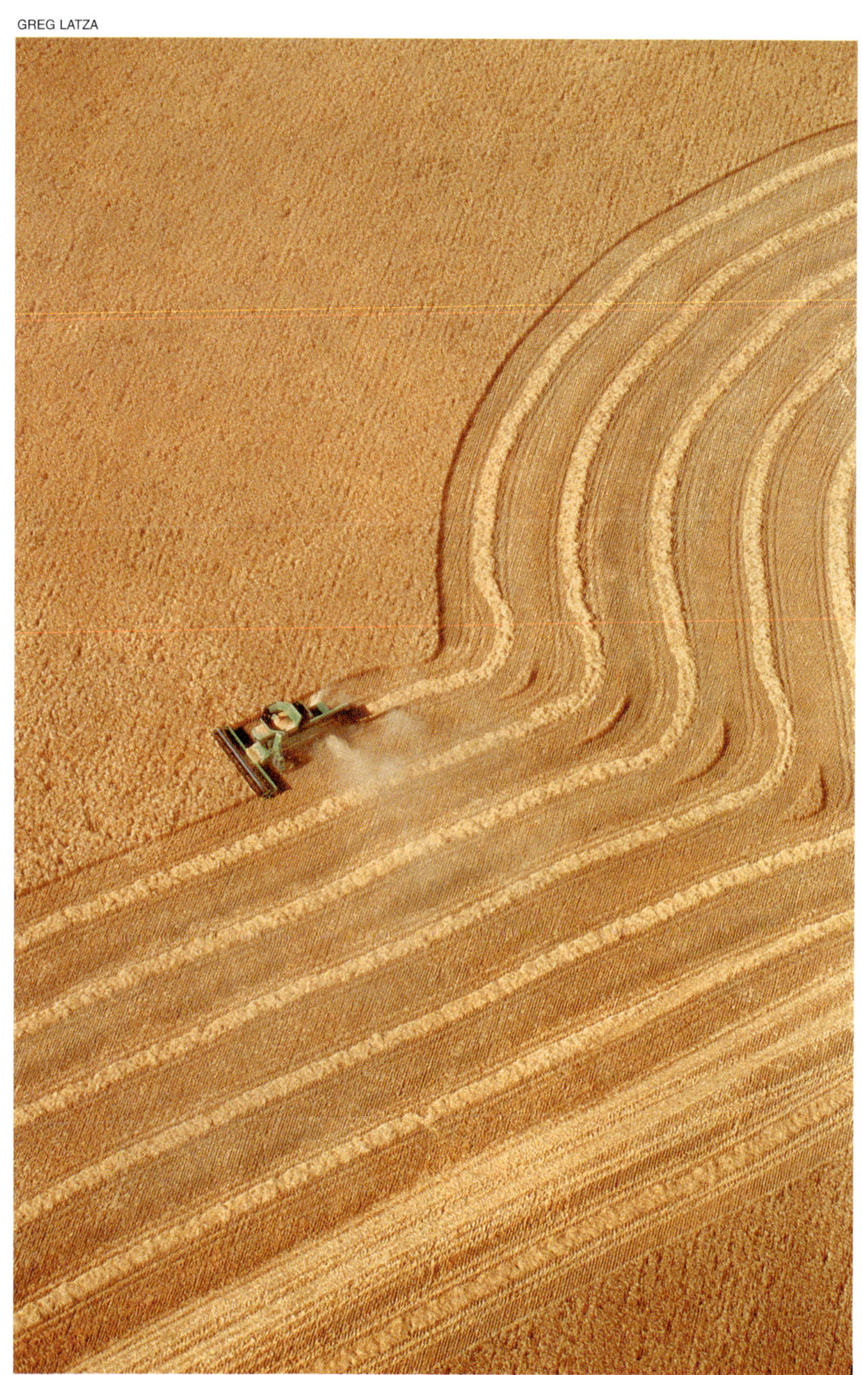

SD TOURISM

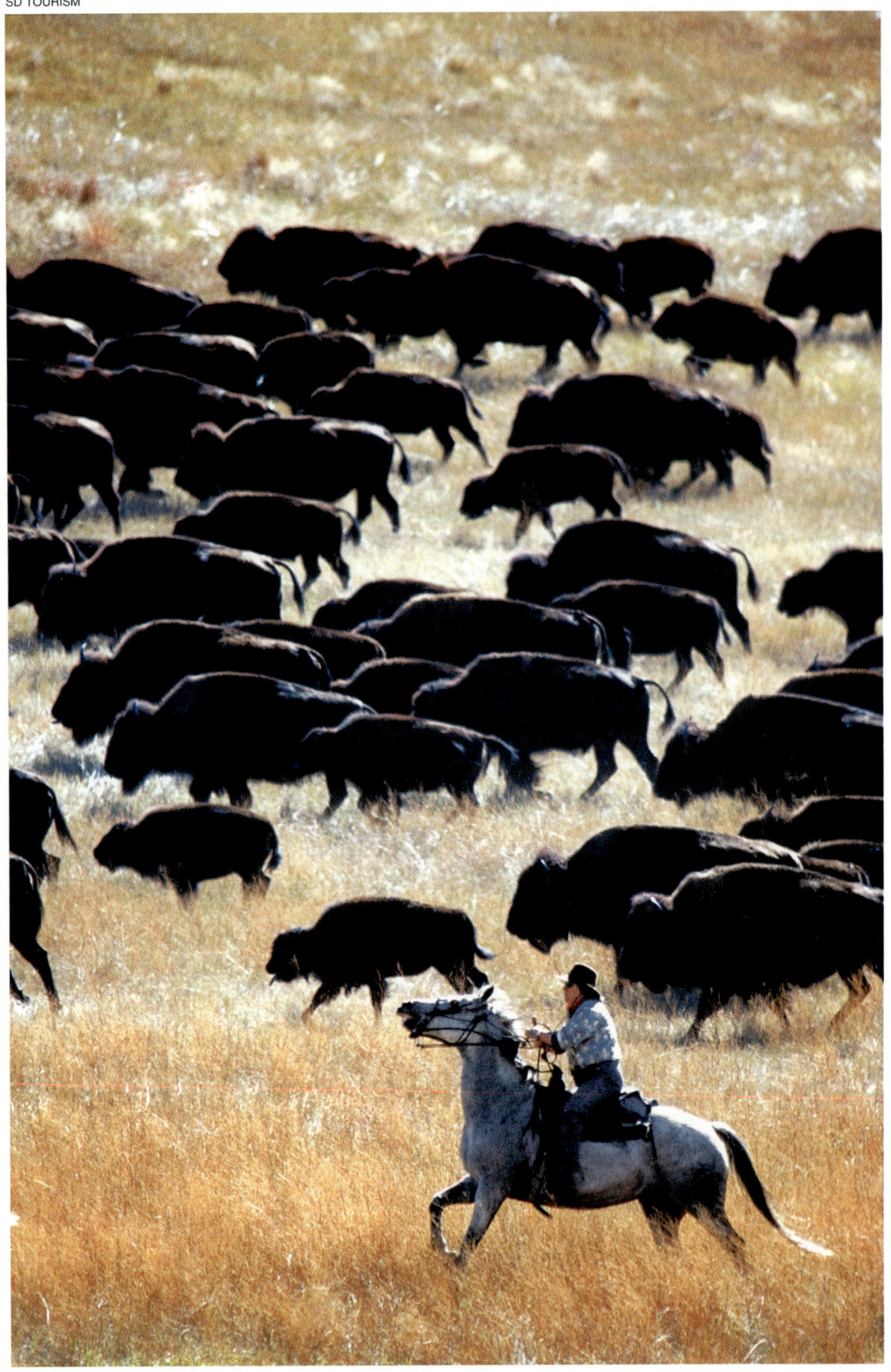

The annual buffalo roundup in Custer State Park (opposite page) has become one of South Dakota's great autumn adventures.

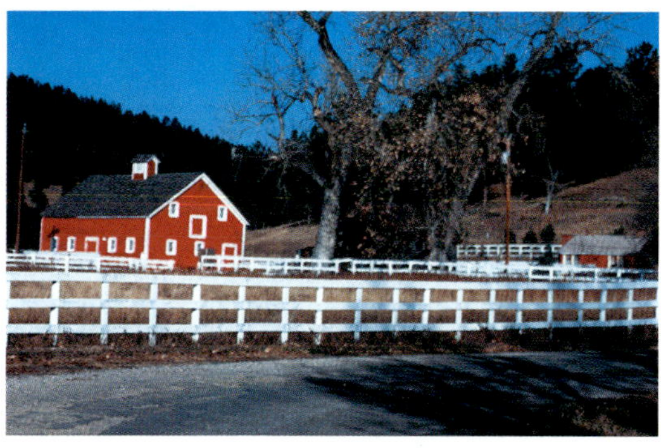

Small farms still exist in the Black Hills, despite pressure from both pine trees and developers.

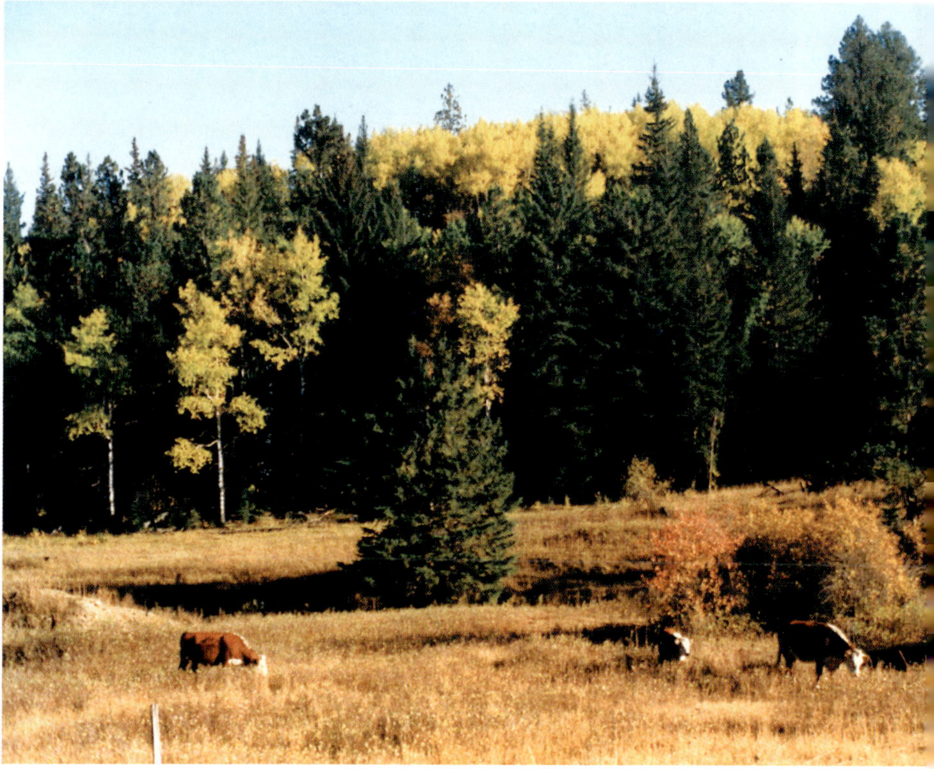

PHILLIP HENRY

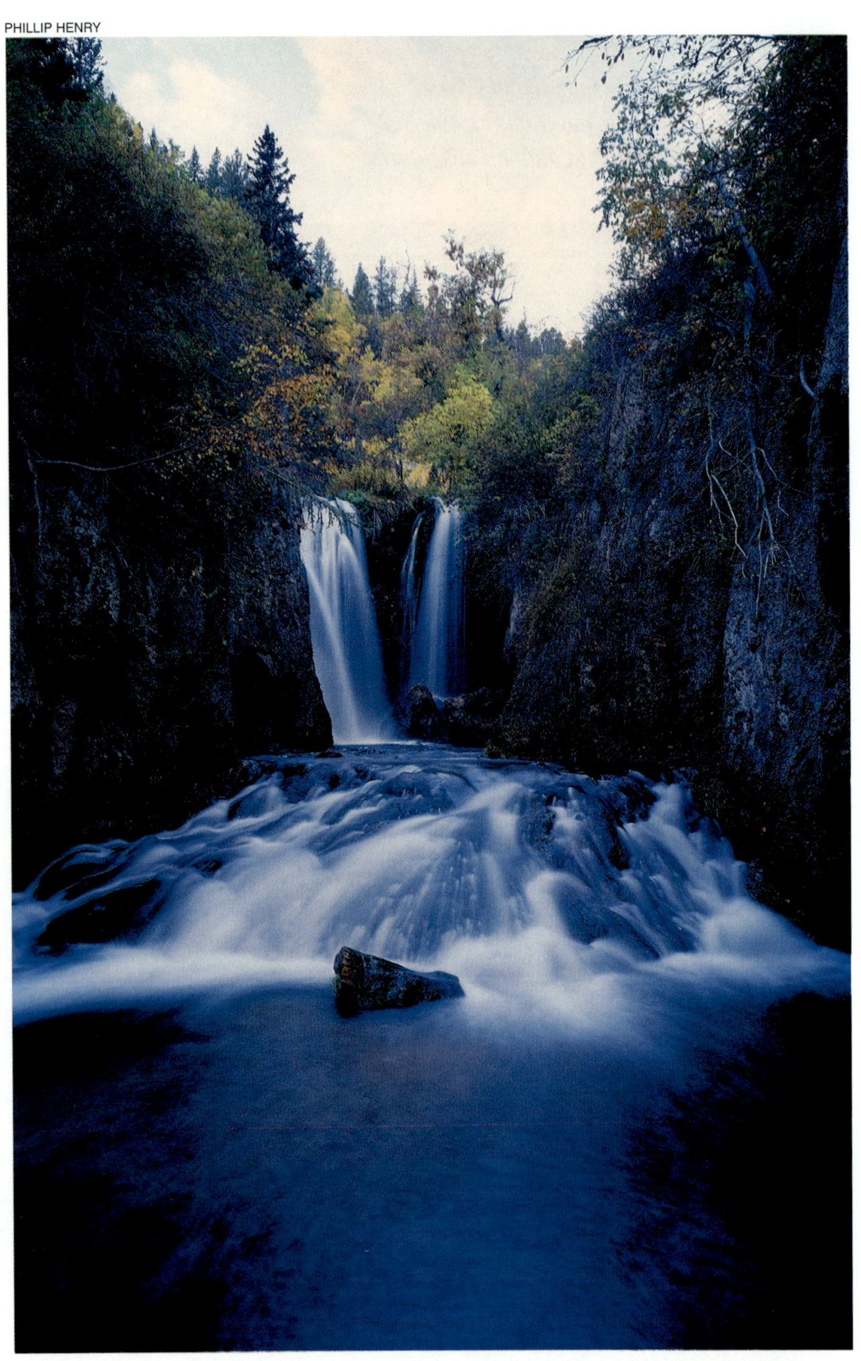

Roughlock Falls on Little Spearfish Creek is a restful place in the Northern Hills.

BILL HONERKAMP PHOTOS

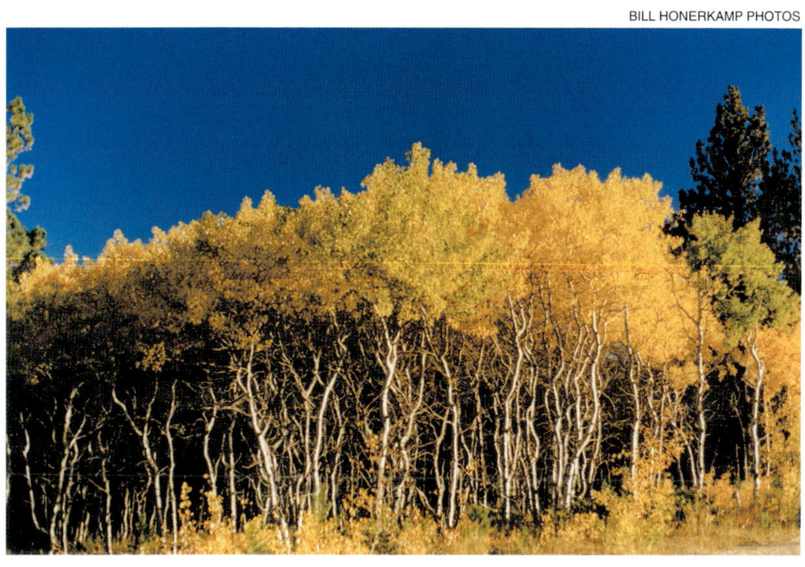

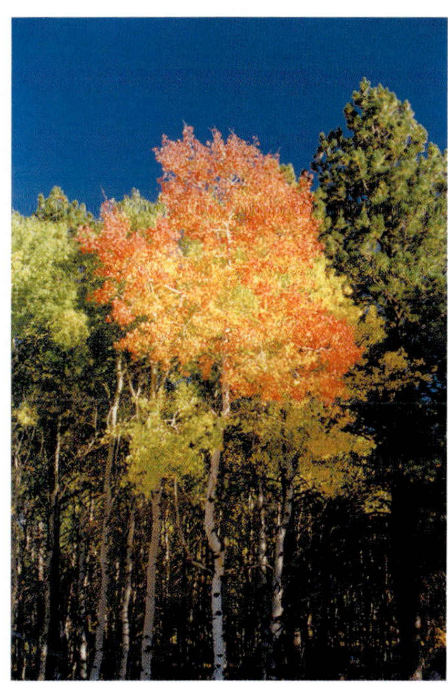

Iron Creek Road, lesser known than Spearfish Canyon, is a favorite foliage trip for local residents. Its thick stands of aspen were called "bow trees" by the Lakota because of the branches' flexibility. Loggers called them "weed trees" because they had no commercial value.

JOEL STRASSER

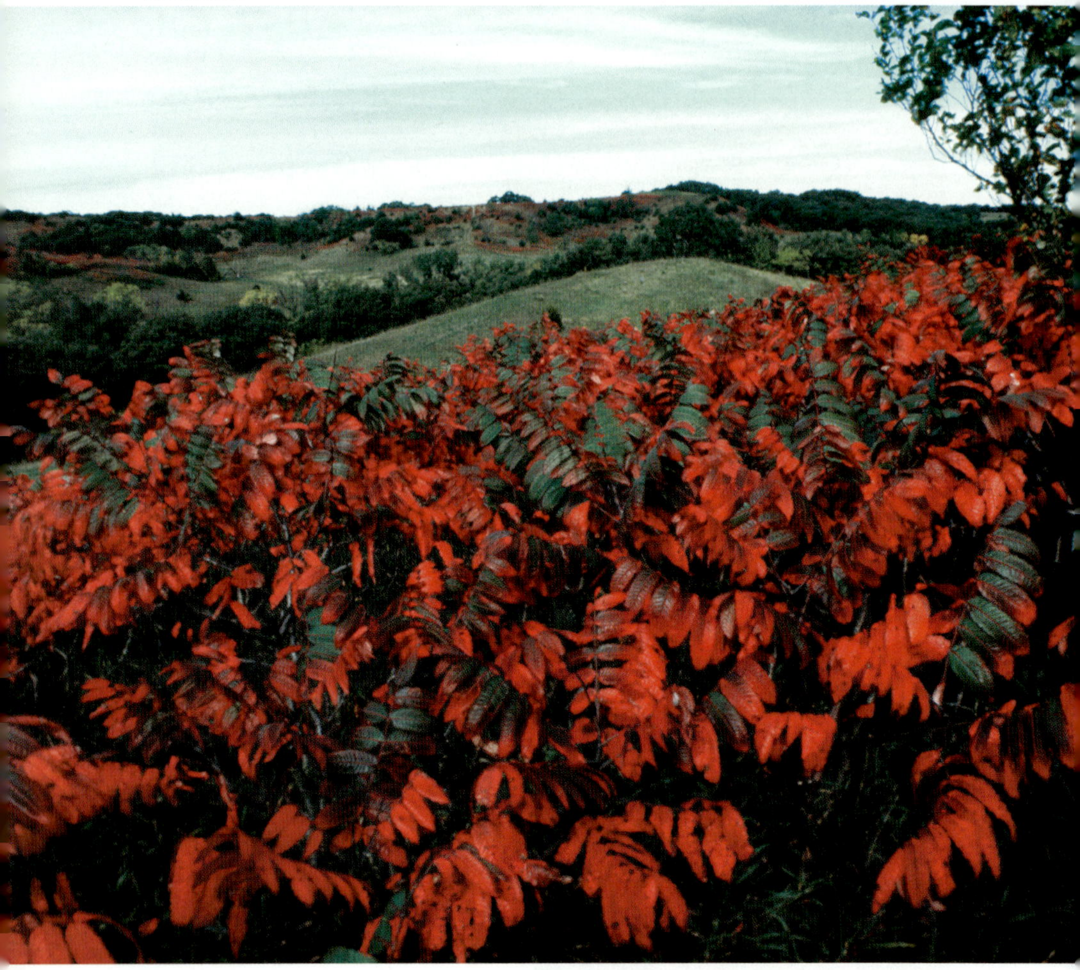

Whether growing wild, like the sumac of Newton Hills in Lincoln County (above) or in a Yankton garden (right), South Dakota plant life shows new glory at summer's end.

PAT HANSEN

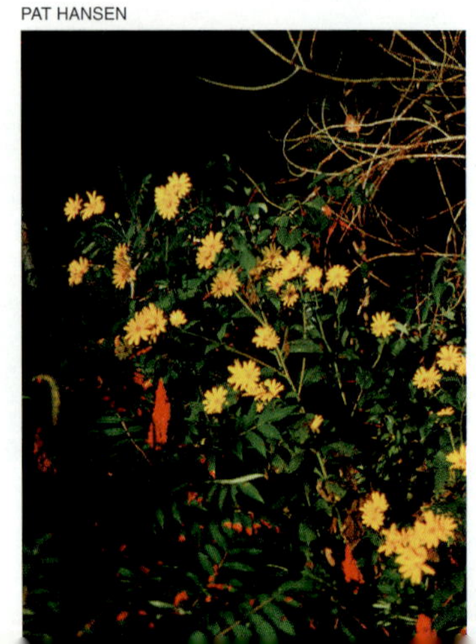

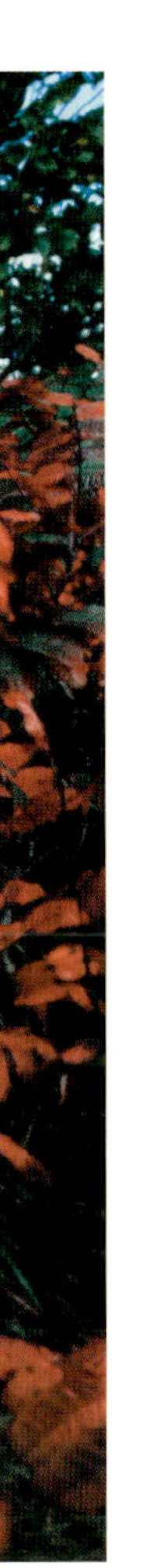

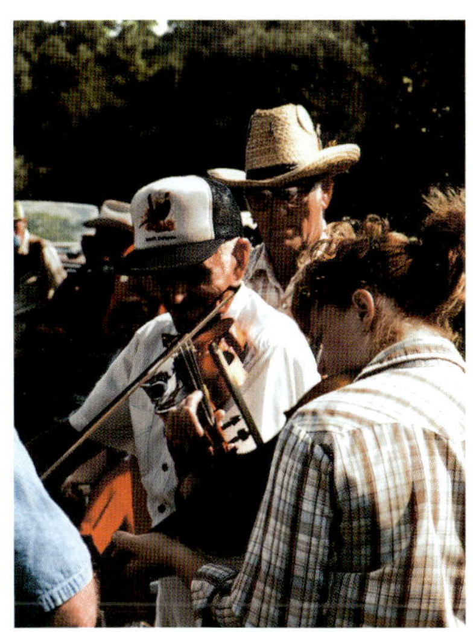

Old-time fiddlers preserve a pioneer music tradition with an annual contest in Yankton every September (above). Cottonwood trees near Interstate 29 lean with the wind (below).

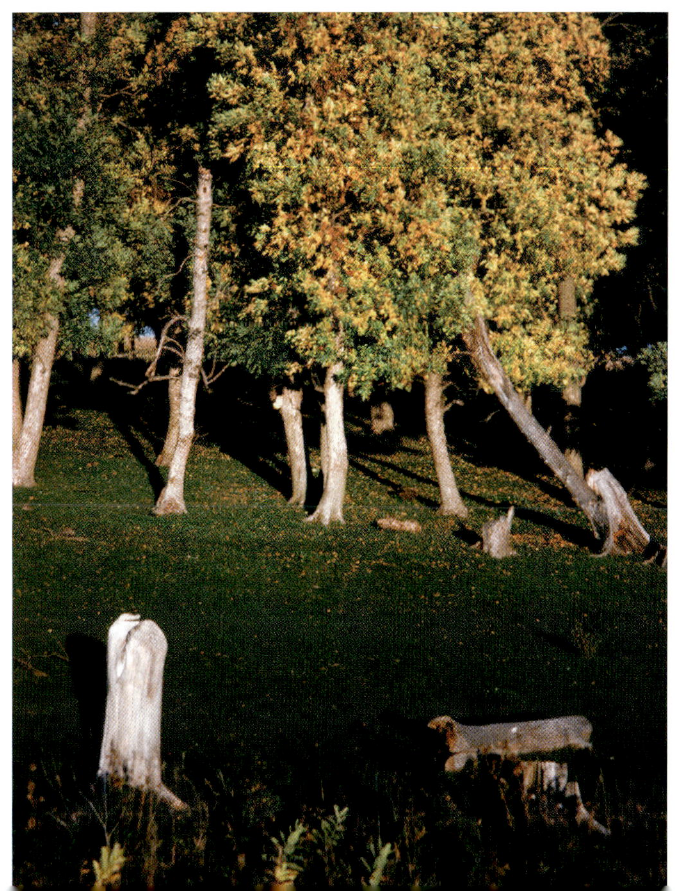

PAUL HORSTED

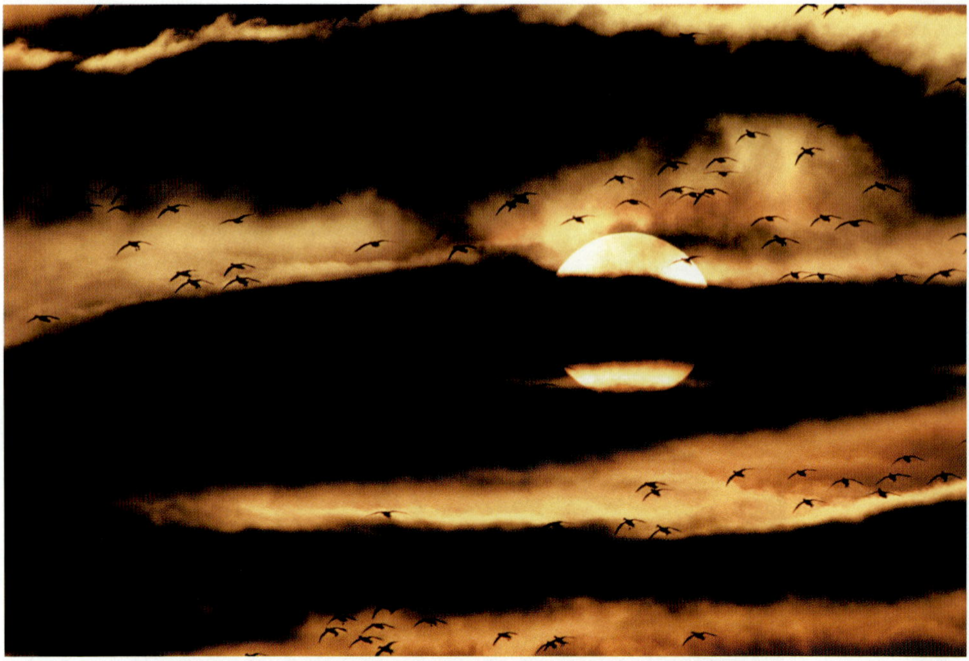

PAT HANSEN

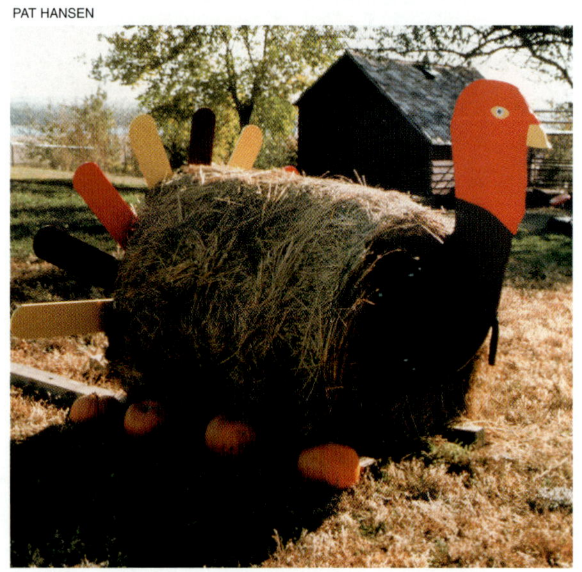

Migrating waterfowl, silhouetted by the sun, are one sure sign of autumn. Another is when rural people have time for hay bale humor (right), like this baled turkey.

STAFF PHOTOS

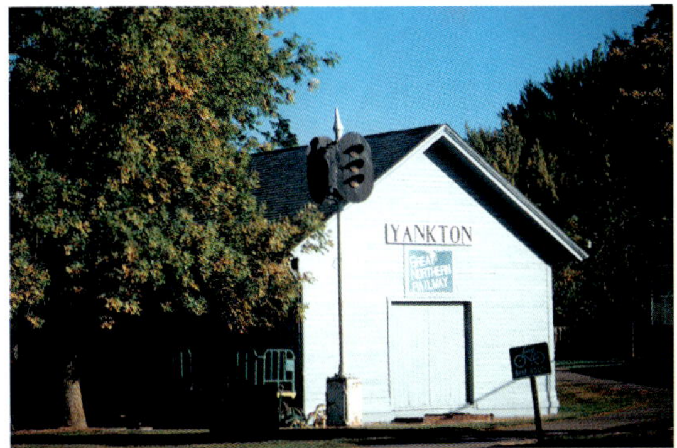

The Great Northern Railroad no longer goes through Yankton, but its wood depot houses train memorabilia at the city's Dakota Territorial Museum.

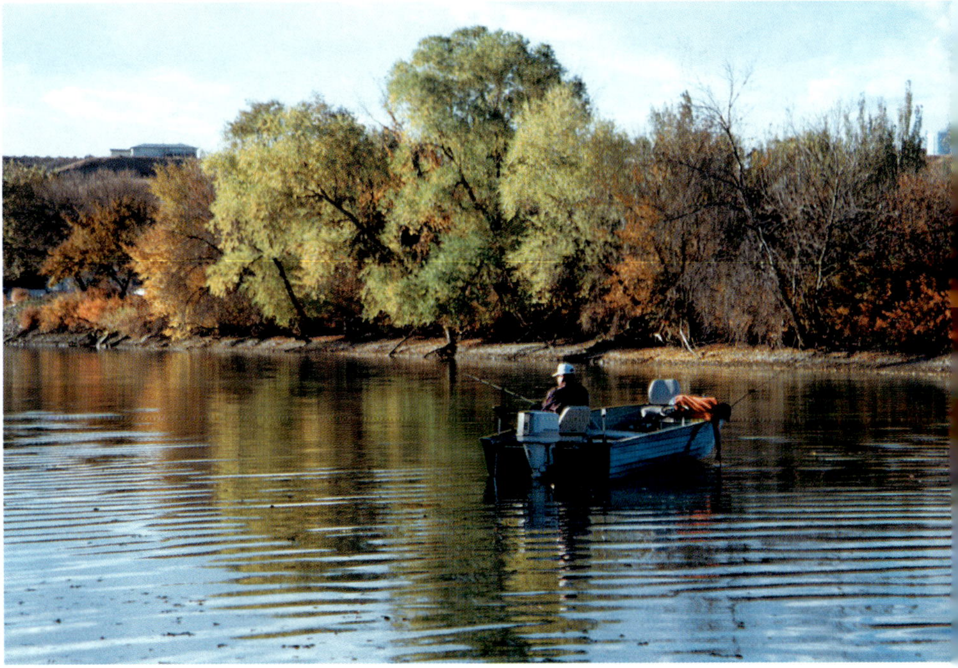

The Bad River has good fishing, especially in the cool and sunny days of September and October. The river runs northeasterly from Philip to Fort Pierre, where it empties into the Missouri.

SD TOURISM

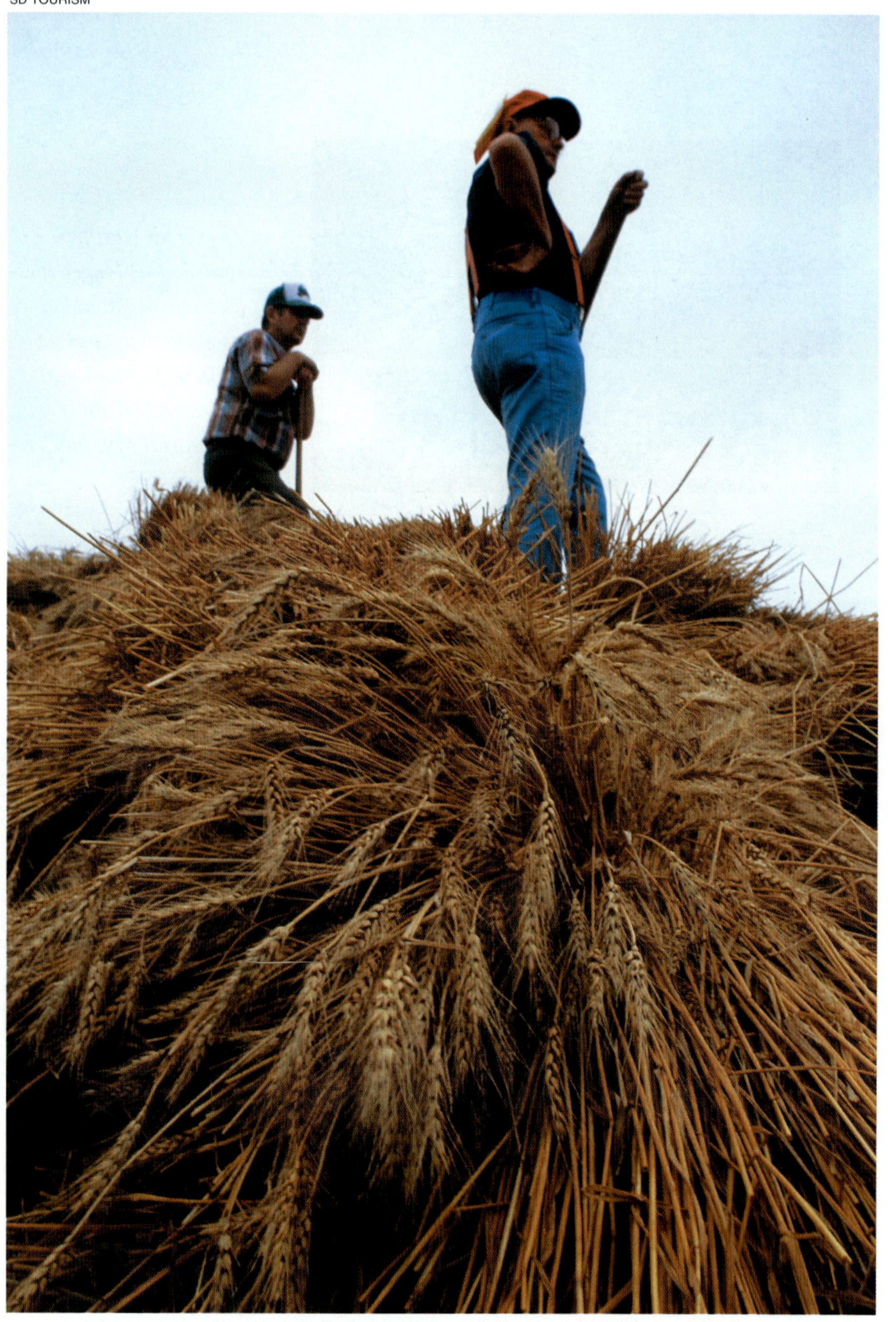

A dozen or more towns in South Dakota celebrate the fall harvest with threshing jamborees, where oldsters show younger generations how they gleaned wheat and oats from bundles with big metal separators.

PAT HANSEN

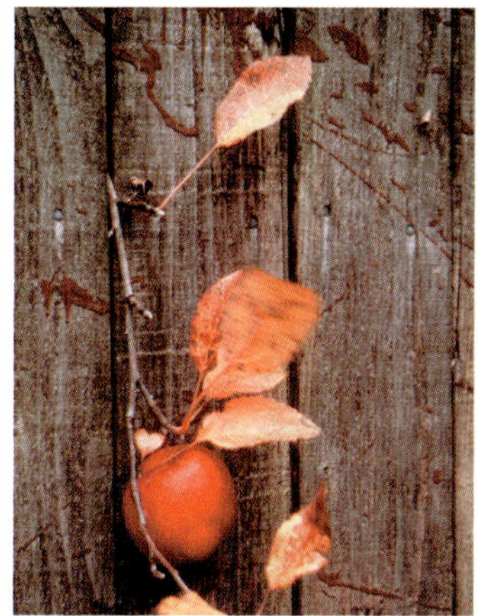

Often in autumn the colors of the day help to create melancholy moods, whether they be apple reds or yellowing leaves or the misty grays of the double-deck Meridian Bridge (below) that connects South Dakota and Nebraska at Yankton.

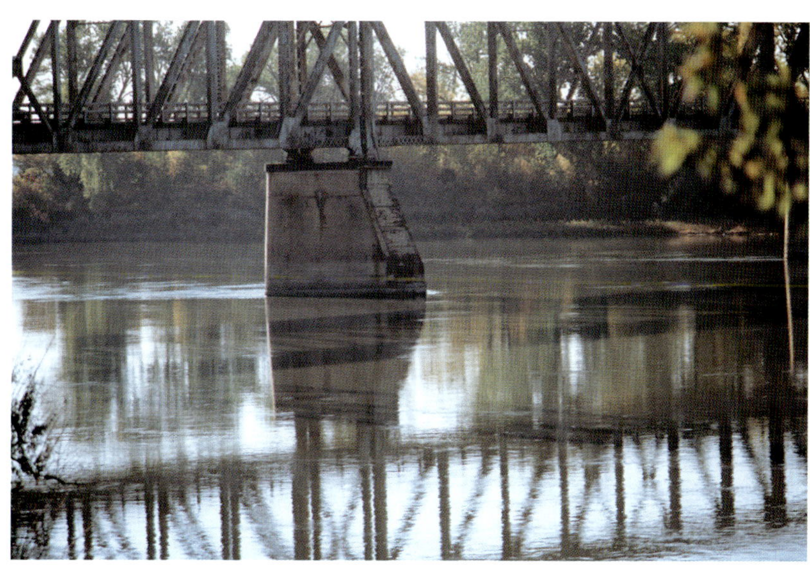

BERNIE HUNHOFF

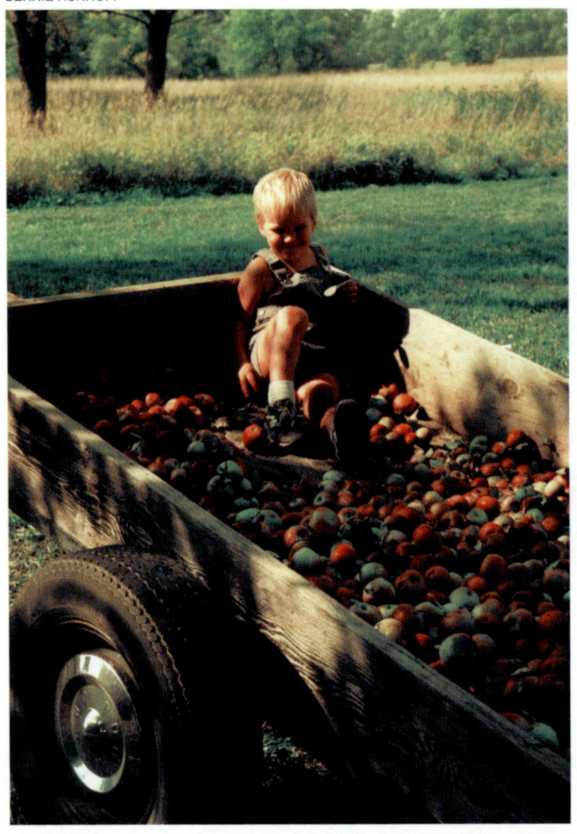

PAT HANSEN

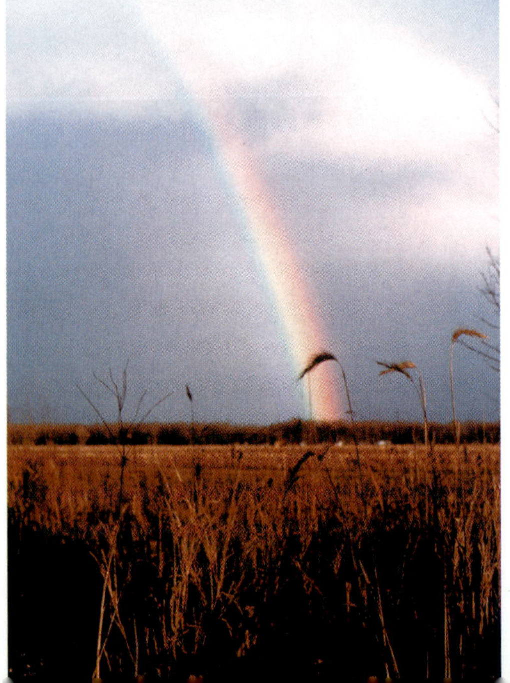

A boy enjoys the autumn apple harvest at the Big Sioux Recreation Area southwest of Brandon.

Rainbows are generally associated with spring rains, but they are just as spectacular over fields of golden grain.

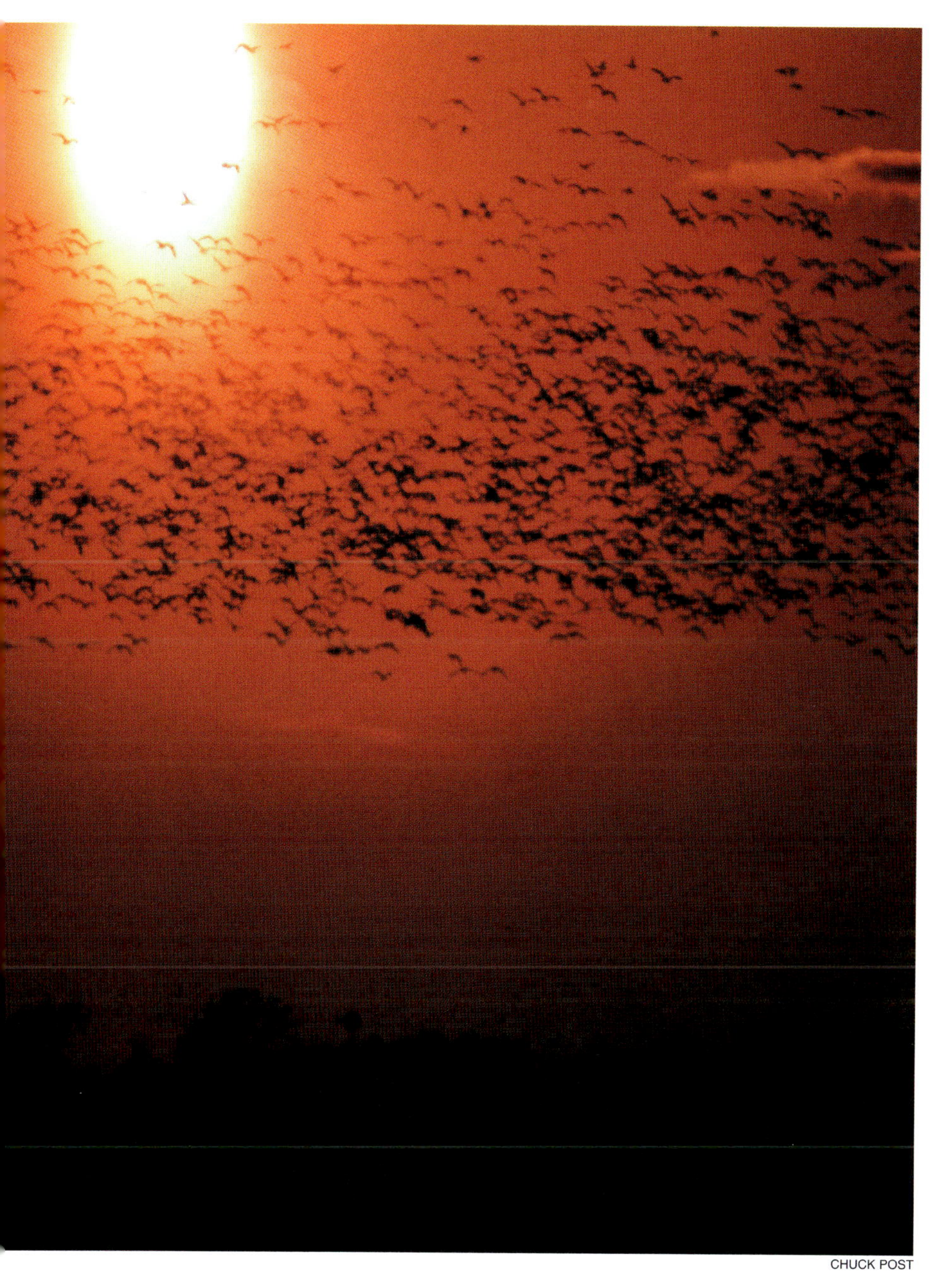

CHUCK POST

Fifteen million ducks migrate through South Dakota's prairie pothole region in the fall, along with nearly a million geese.

STAFF PHOTOS

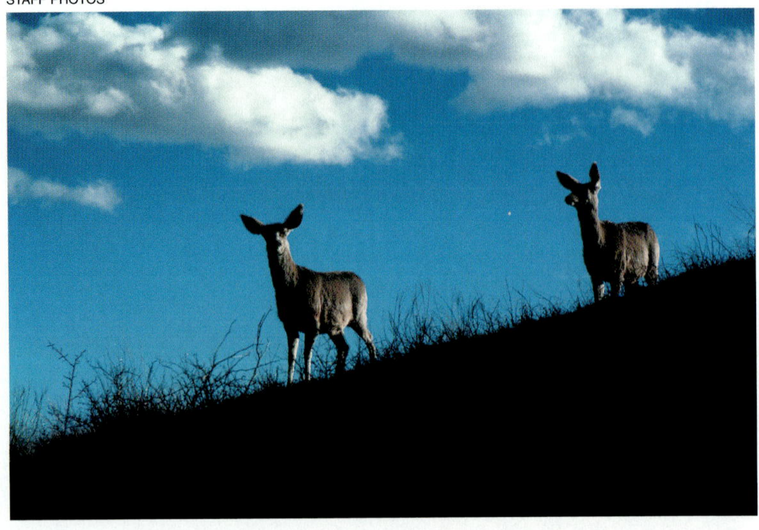

Whitetail deer can be found throughout South Dakota, but most of the state's mule deer population is West River.

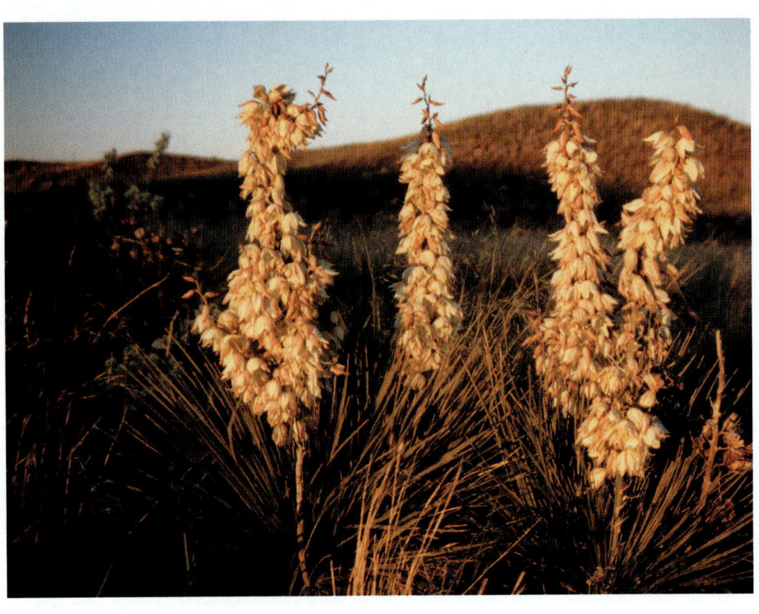

Long ago, Native Americans used the wild yucca plant for food and medicine. They also made a cleaning agent from the roots.

PAT HANSEN PHOTOS

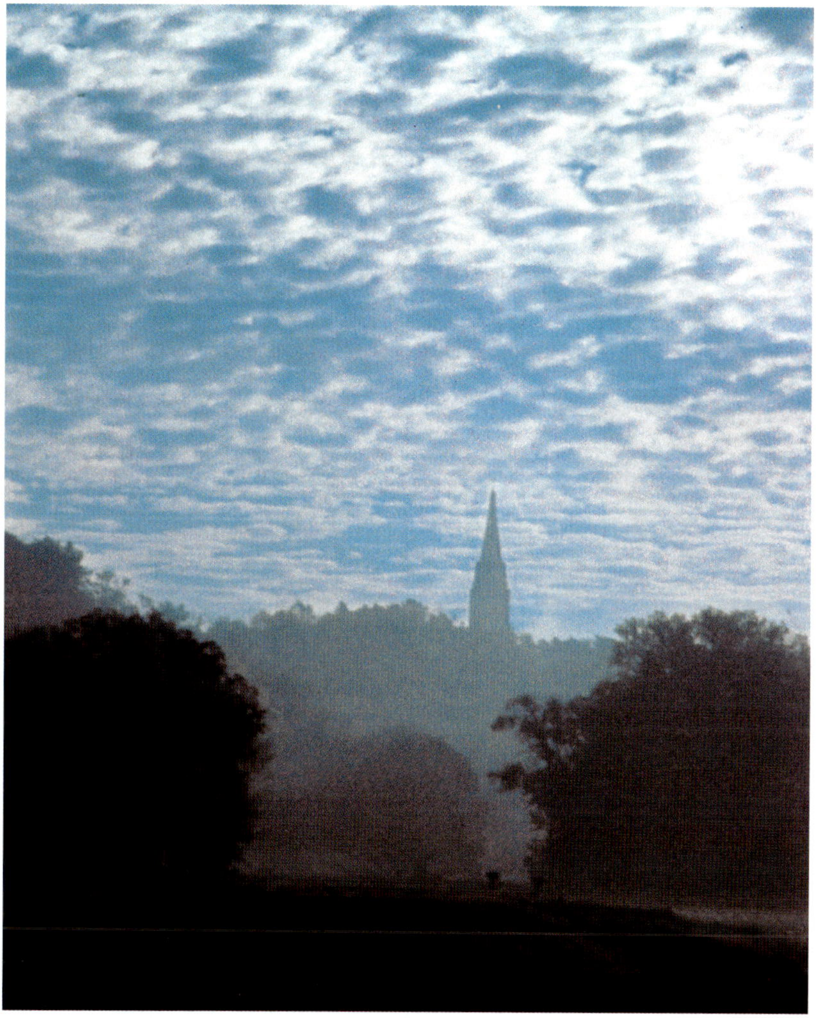

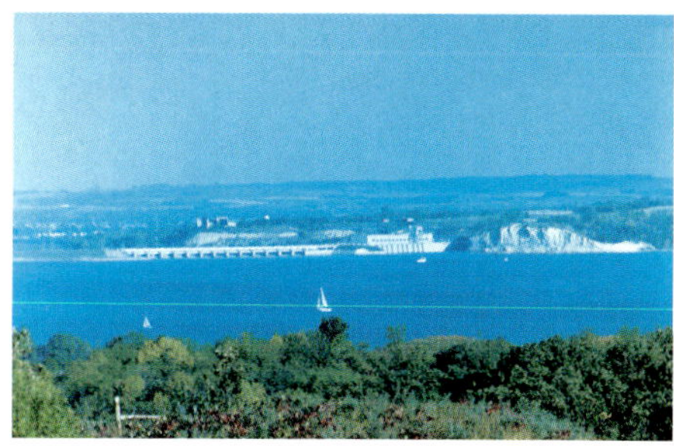

On some brisk autumn mornings, a mist rises from the Missouri River and envelopes Yankton's Mount Marty Chapel (above). As the sky clears, sails appear on Lewis and Clark Lake.

Four hundred mustangs live at the Wild Horse Sanctuary south of Hot Springs. Some young horses are sold every year to control the population and help meet expenses.

GREG LATZA PHOTO

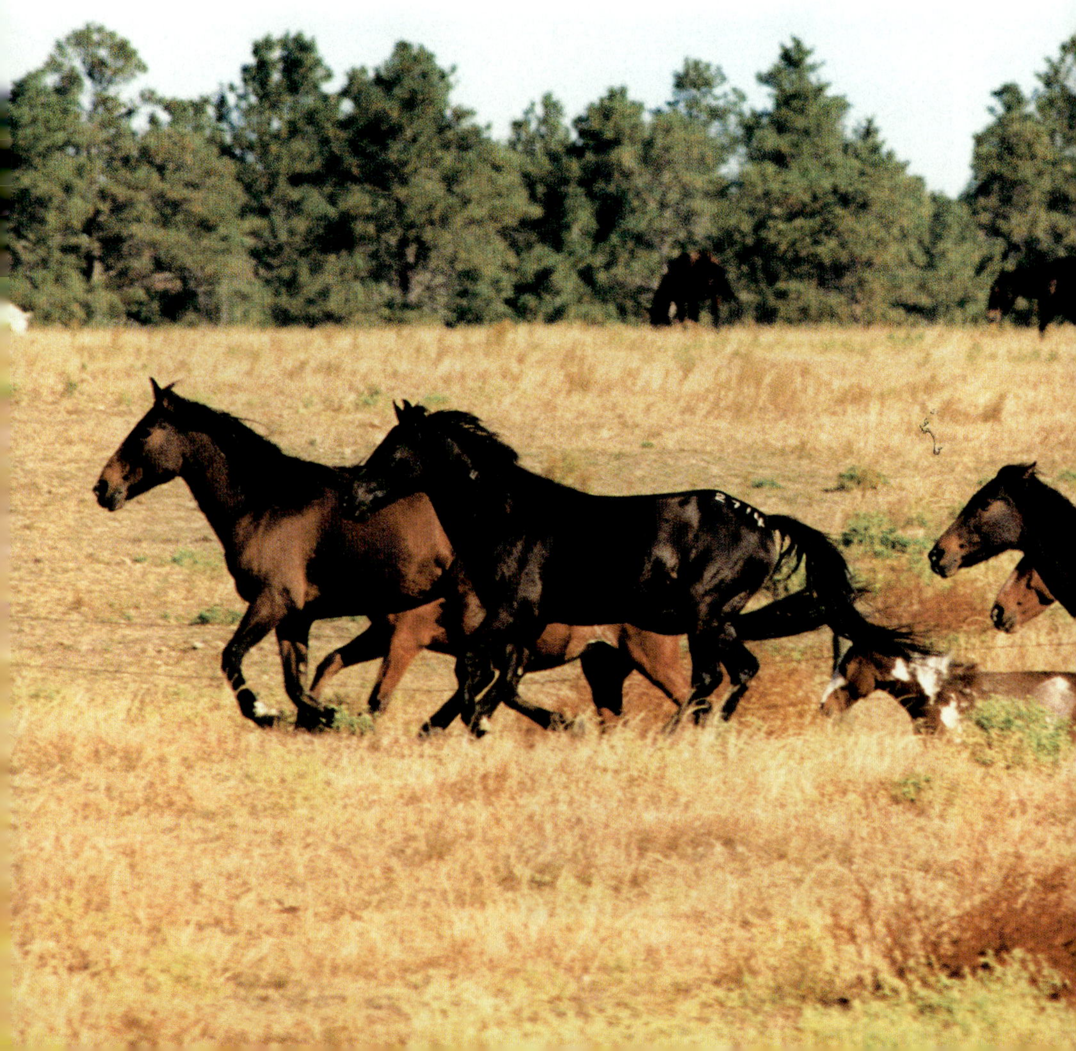

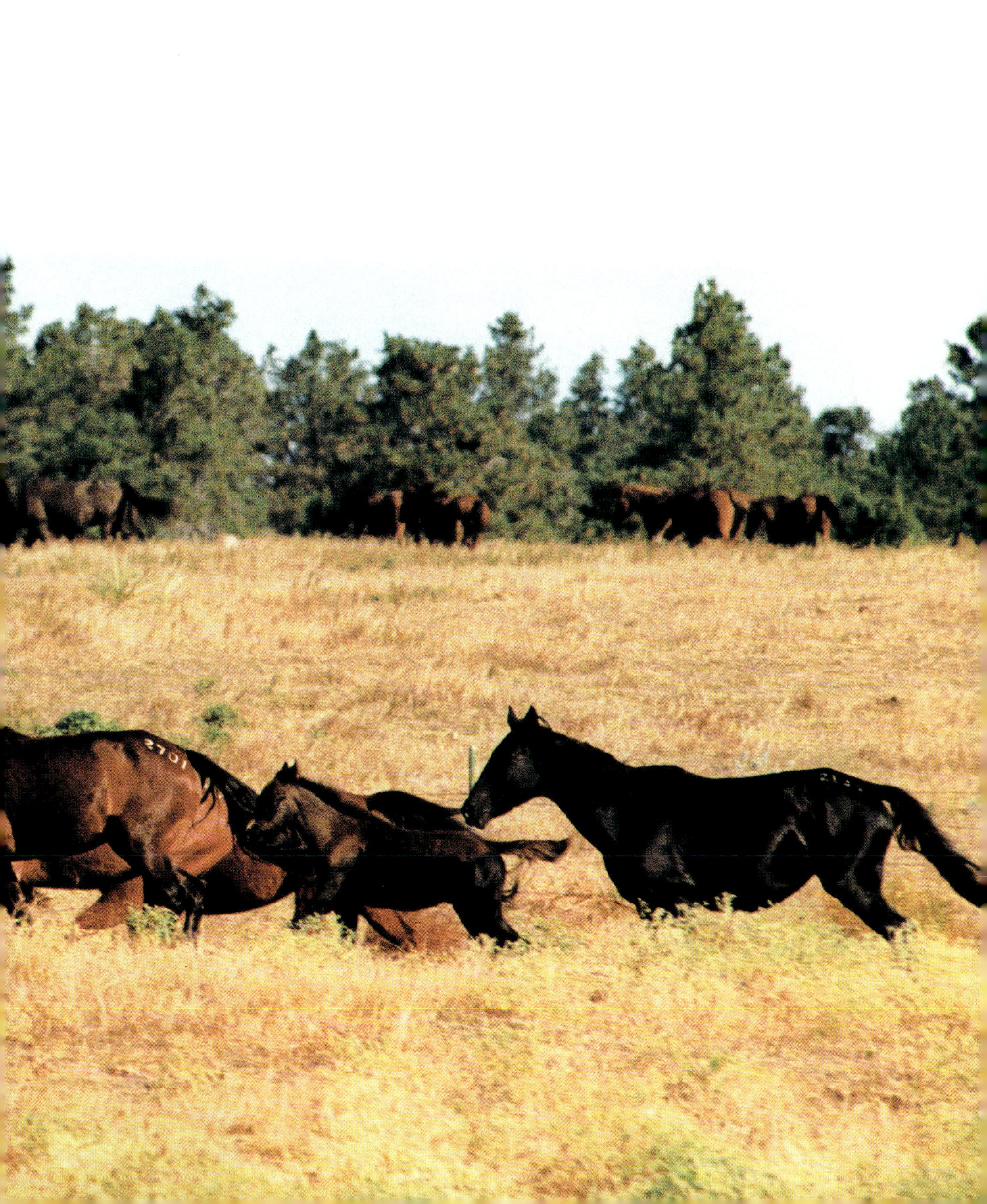

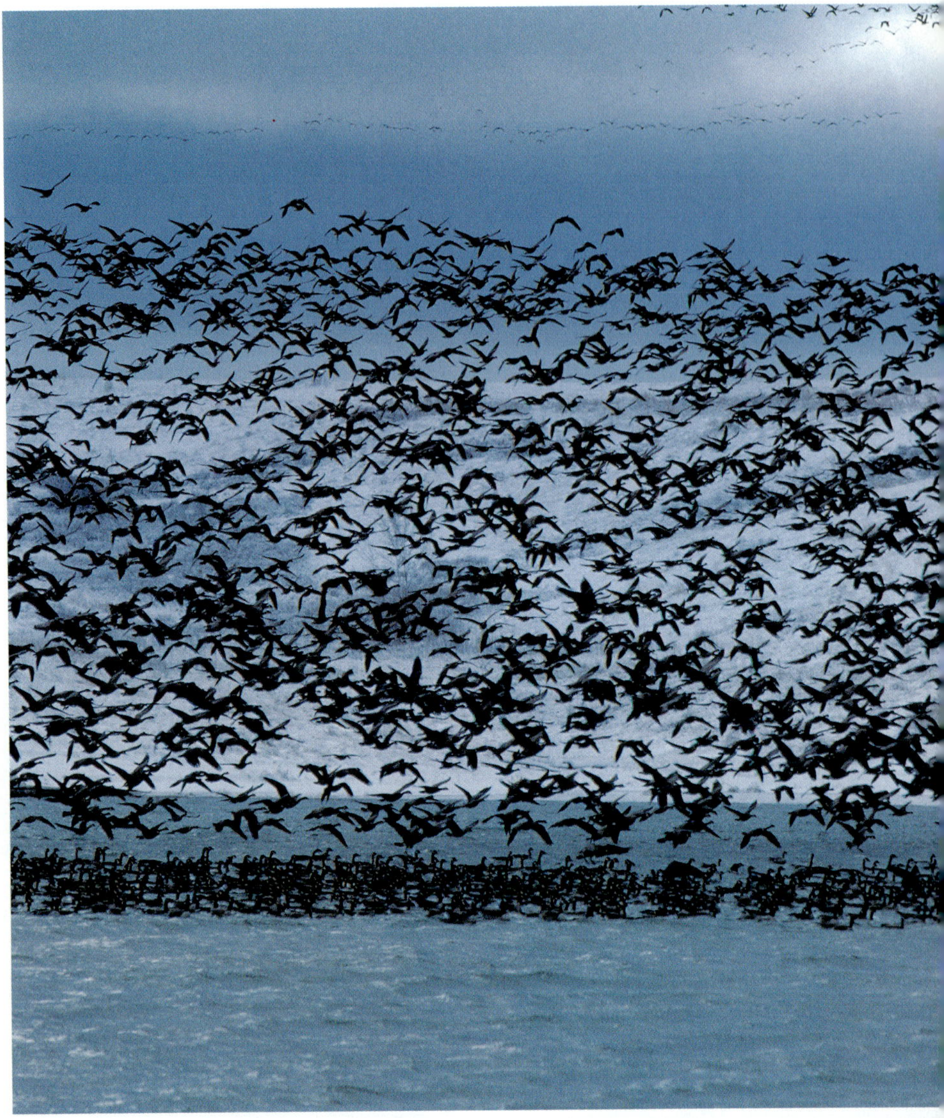

The sun sets on Pelican Island at LaCreek Wildlife Refuge near Martin. At right, a weed called mullen is silhouetted by a sunset over Sheep Mountain Table in the Badlands.

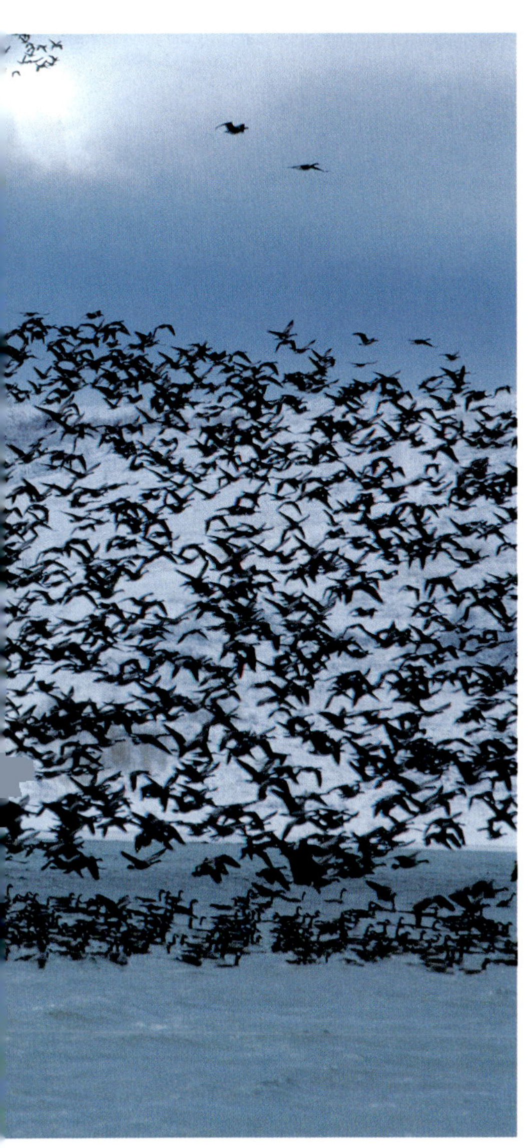

KATIE HUNHOFF

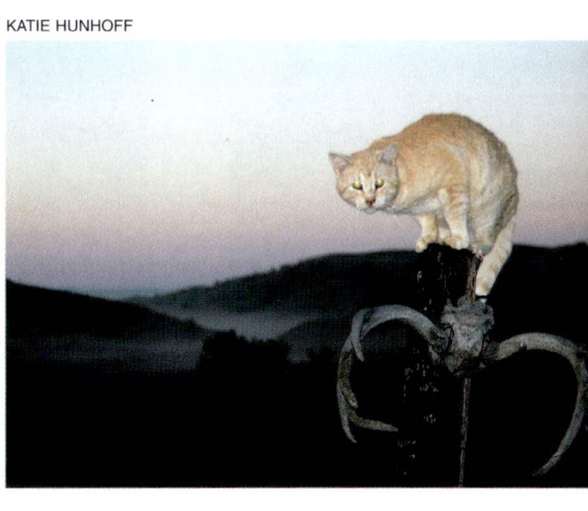

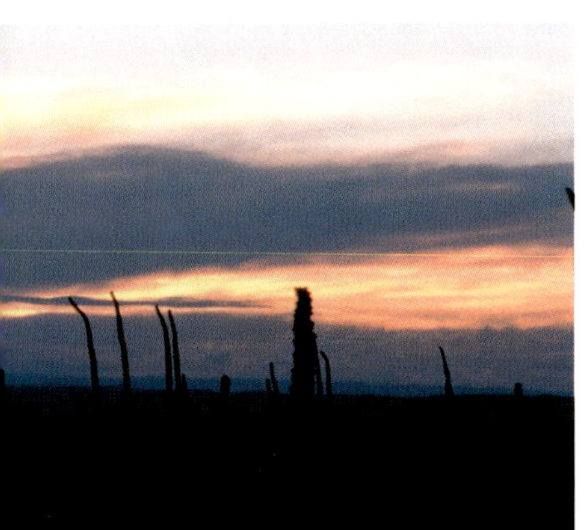

There's a West River joke that ranches are now so few and far apart that they all must have their own tomcat.

TROY MCQUILLEN

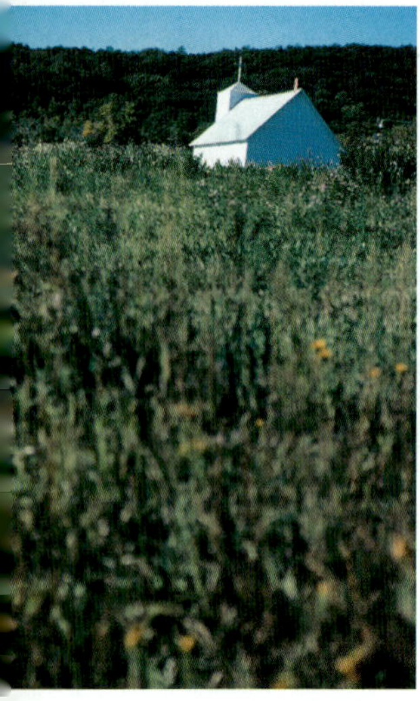

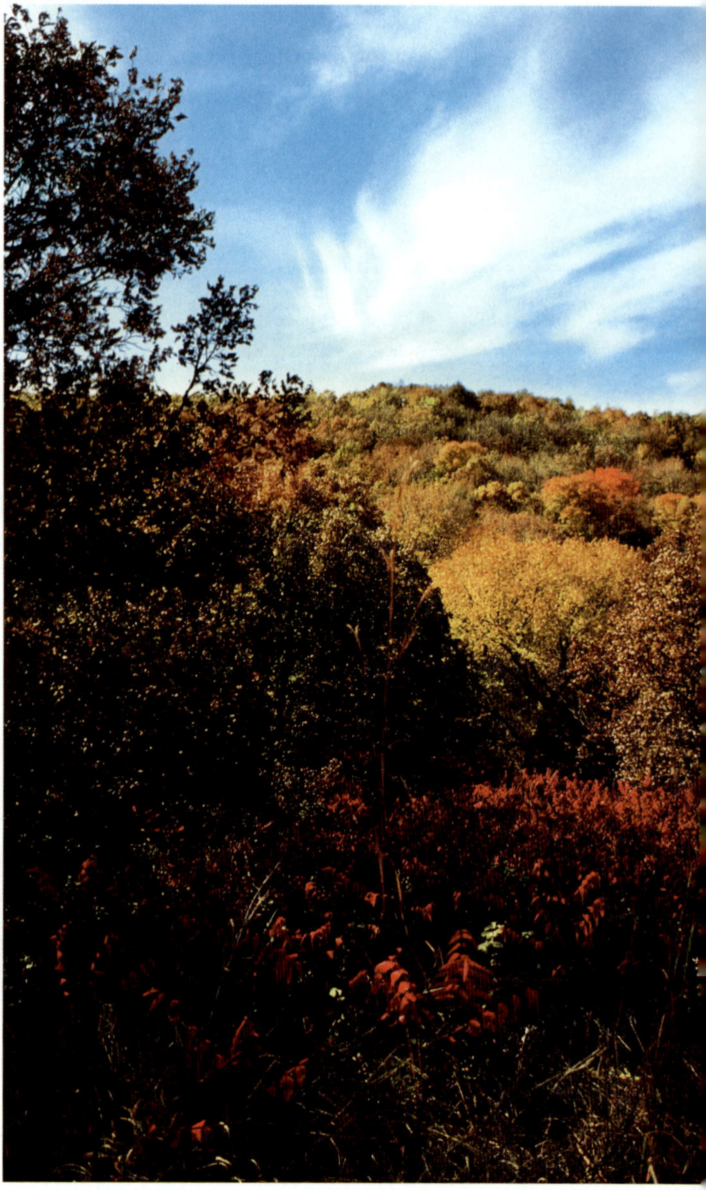

In northeast South Dakota, a forest called Sica Hollow is known for its fall colors. An old country church is buried among hills south of the main park.

TROY MCQUILLEN

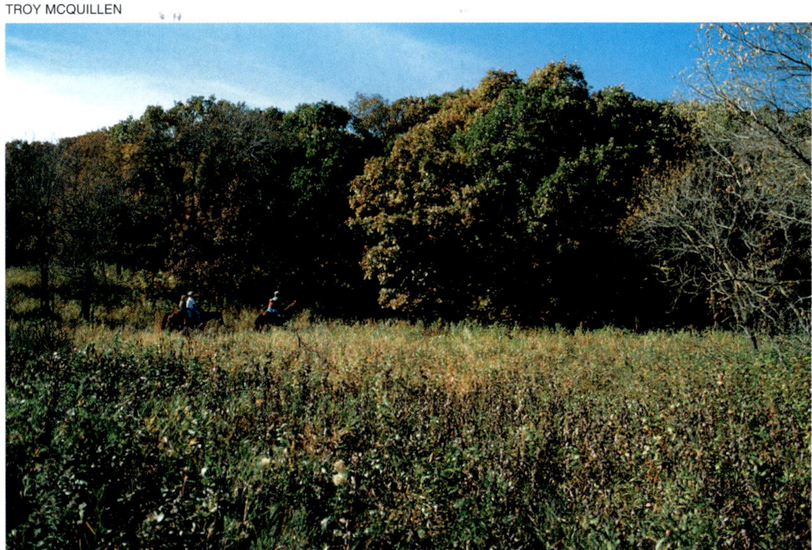

BERNIE HUNHOFF

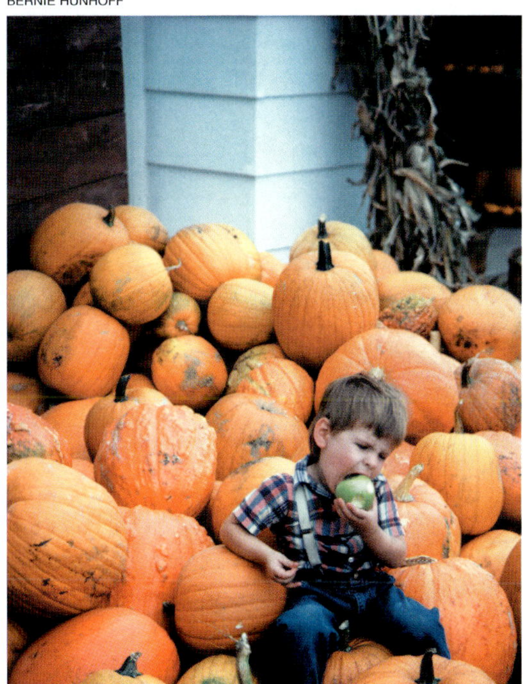

Horseback is one way of touring Sica Hollow (above). The "R" (below) stands for Ringer Ranch, west of the popular hollow.

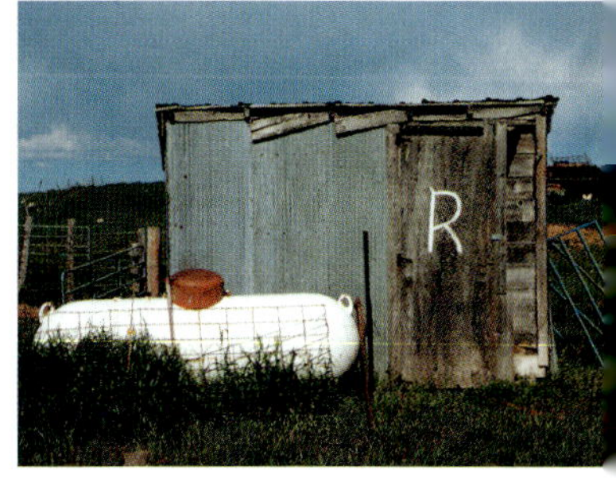

Garrity's Prairie Gardens near Mission Hill is famous for weekend festivals in autumn. Orchards and wineries have also started in other locales.

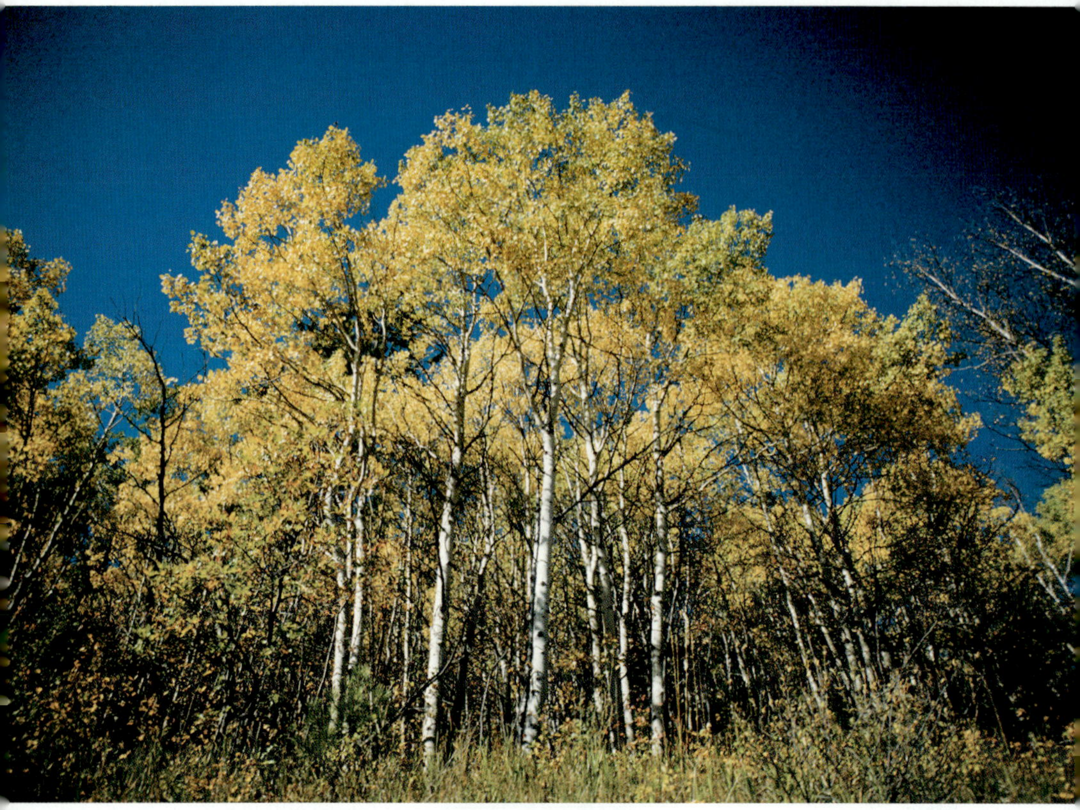

SD TOURISM

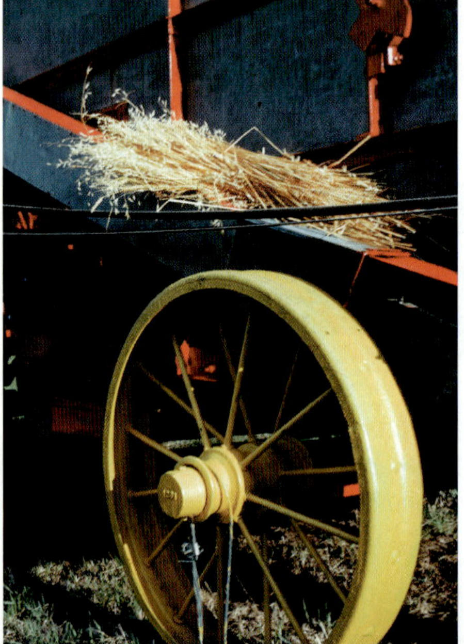

"Peak foliage" is a term heard often around the Black Hills in autumn. Radio commentators, coffee shop buddies and newspaper writers offer their best guesses on when to visit the canyons.

PAUL WASSERMAN

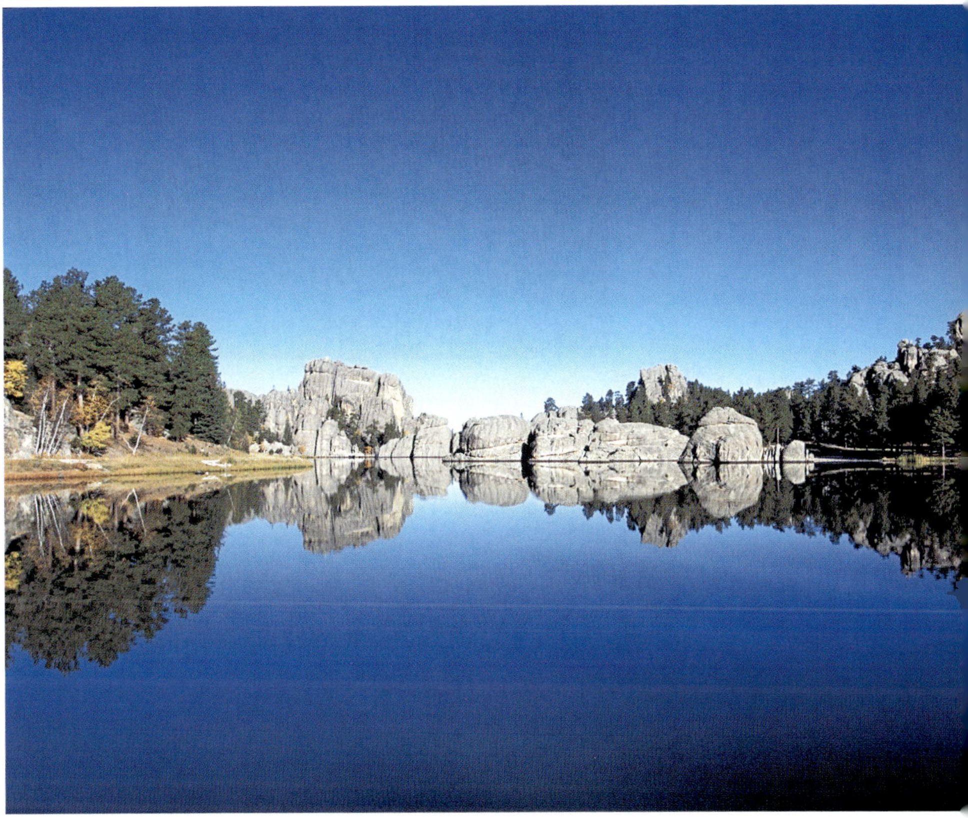

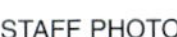

STAFF PHOTO

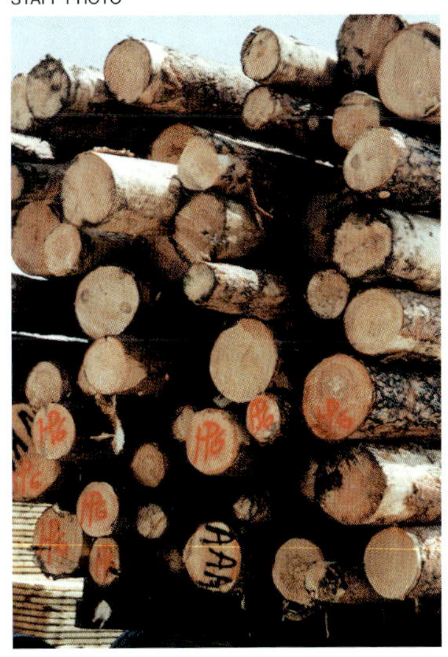

Sylvan Lake, in the northwest corner of Custer State Park, is surrounded by pine and spruce. Logging (left) has been a major part of the Black Hills economy for more than a century.

SD TOURISM

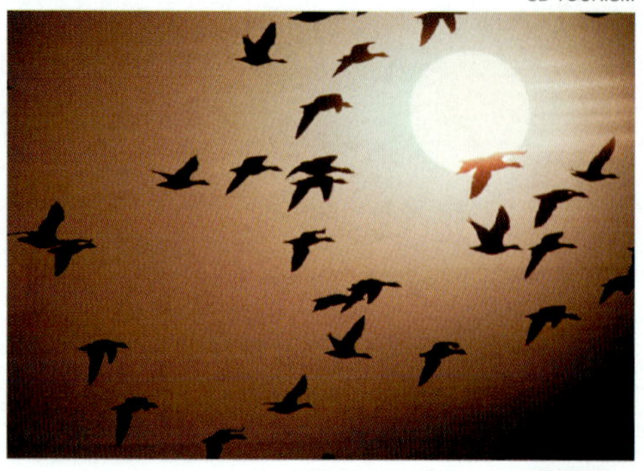

PAT HANSEN

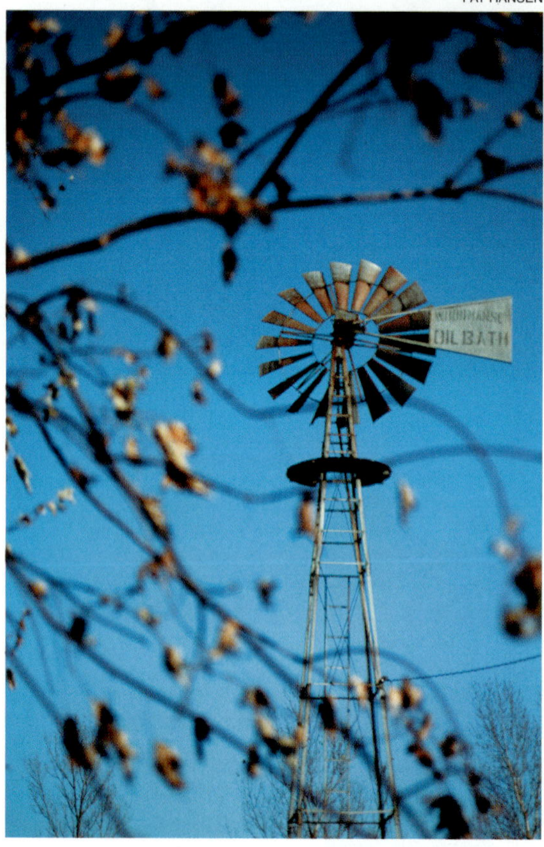

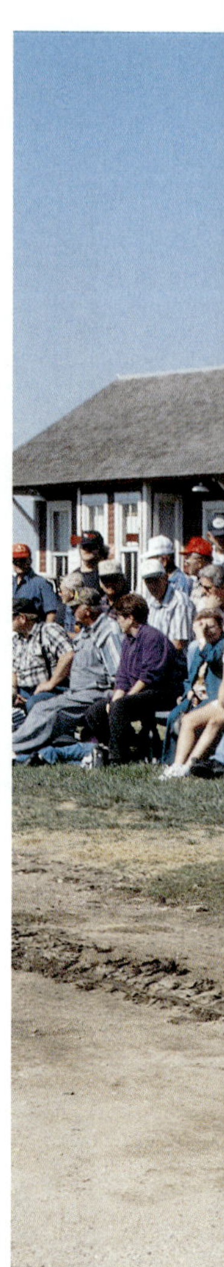

South Dakota is among the nation's most rural states; that heritage is proudly celebrated at autumn events like the Menno Power Show, where old farm equipment is paraded around and about historic buildings.

BERNIE HUNHOFF

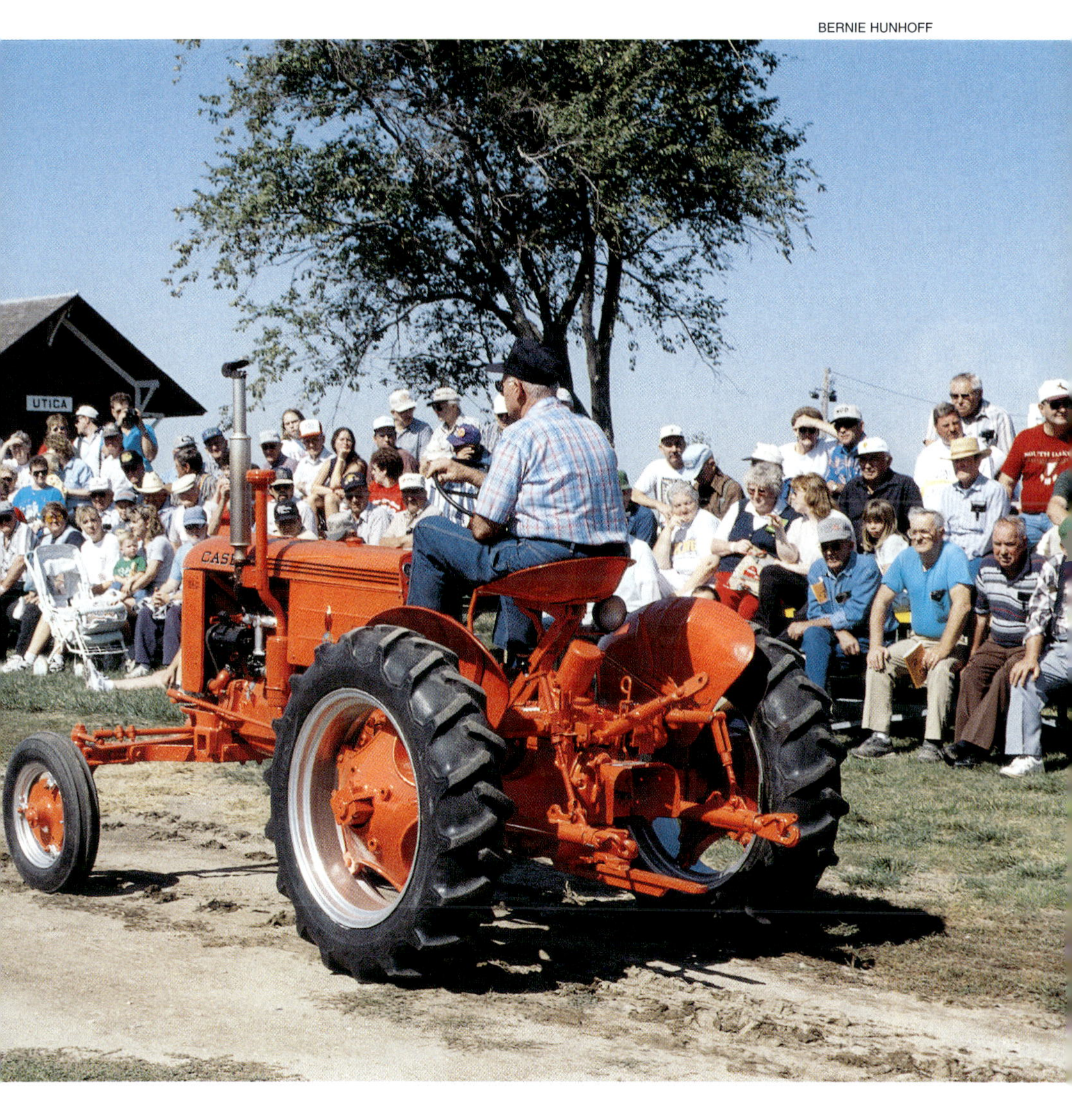

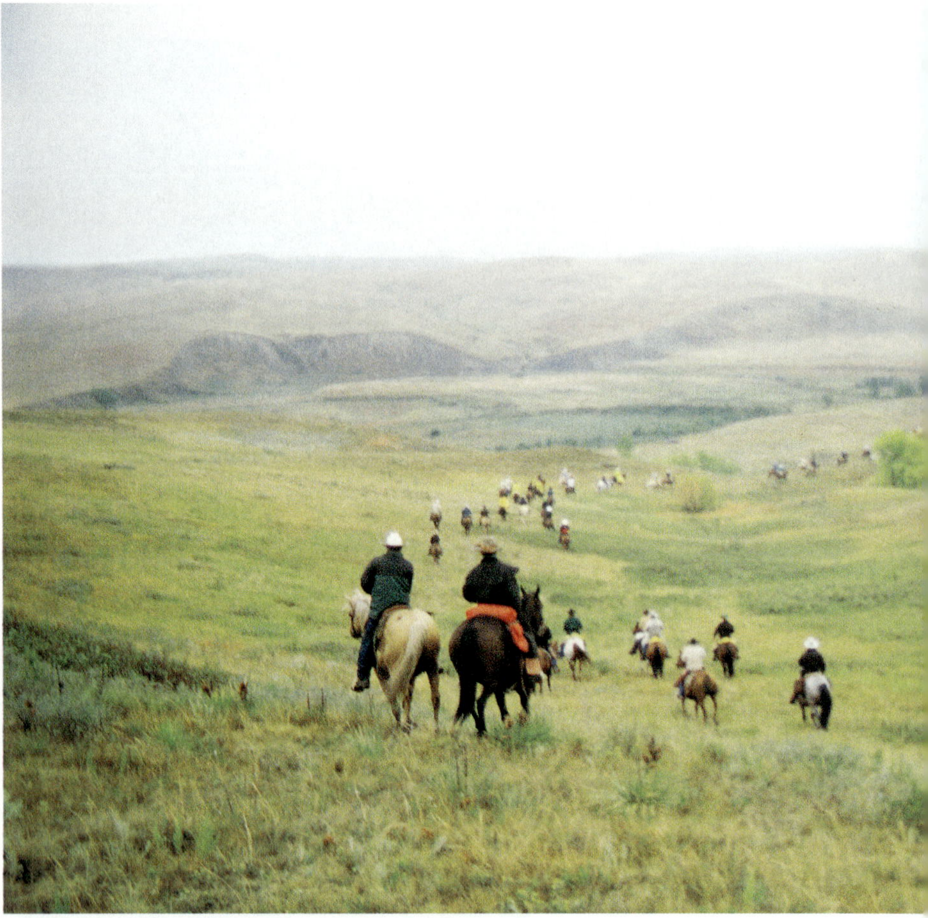

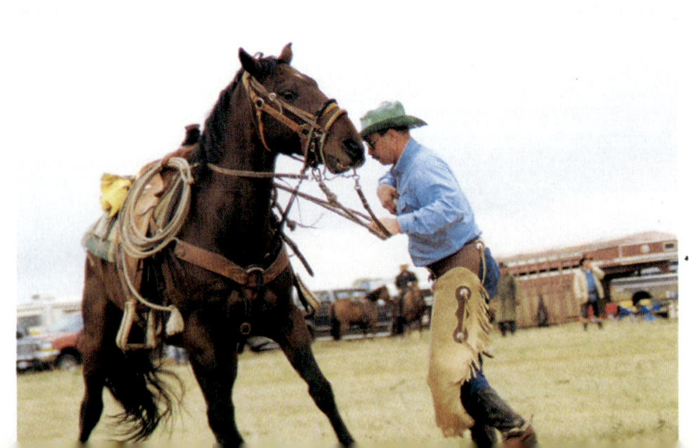

JERRY WILSON PHOTOS

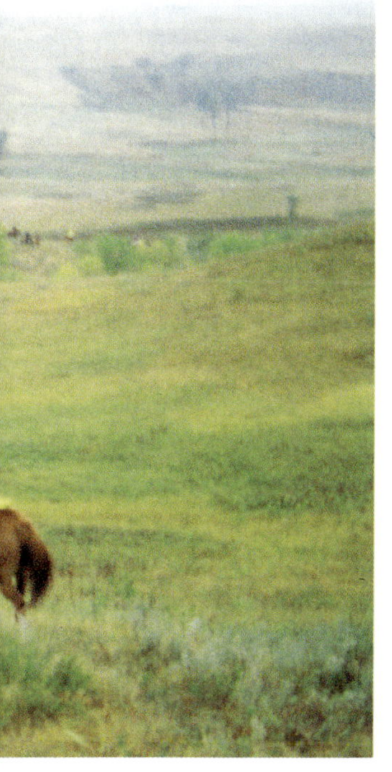

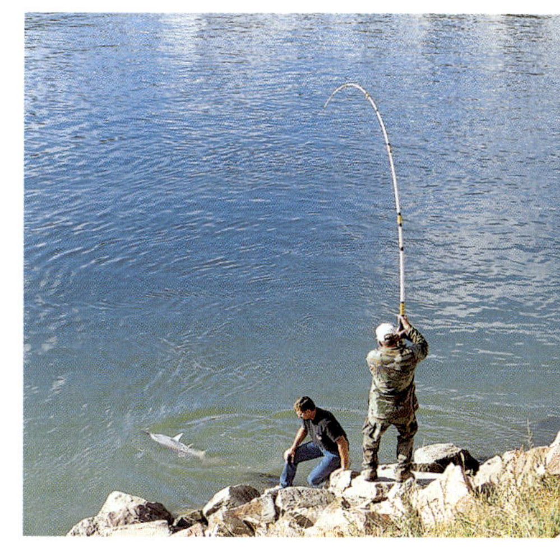

NORM BLAALID

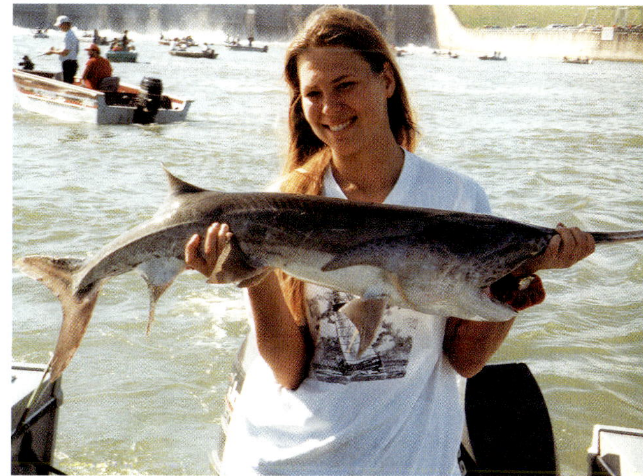

Cool nights and short days don't send South Dakotans indoors. A few hundred members of the Western South Dakota Buck-a-roos hold a trail ride when the grass goes brown (opposite page). At Lewis and Clark Lake, avid anglers (above) snag paddlefish, also known as freshwater whales. Scientists think paddlefish existed before dinosaurs.

STEPHEN GASSMAN

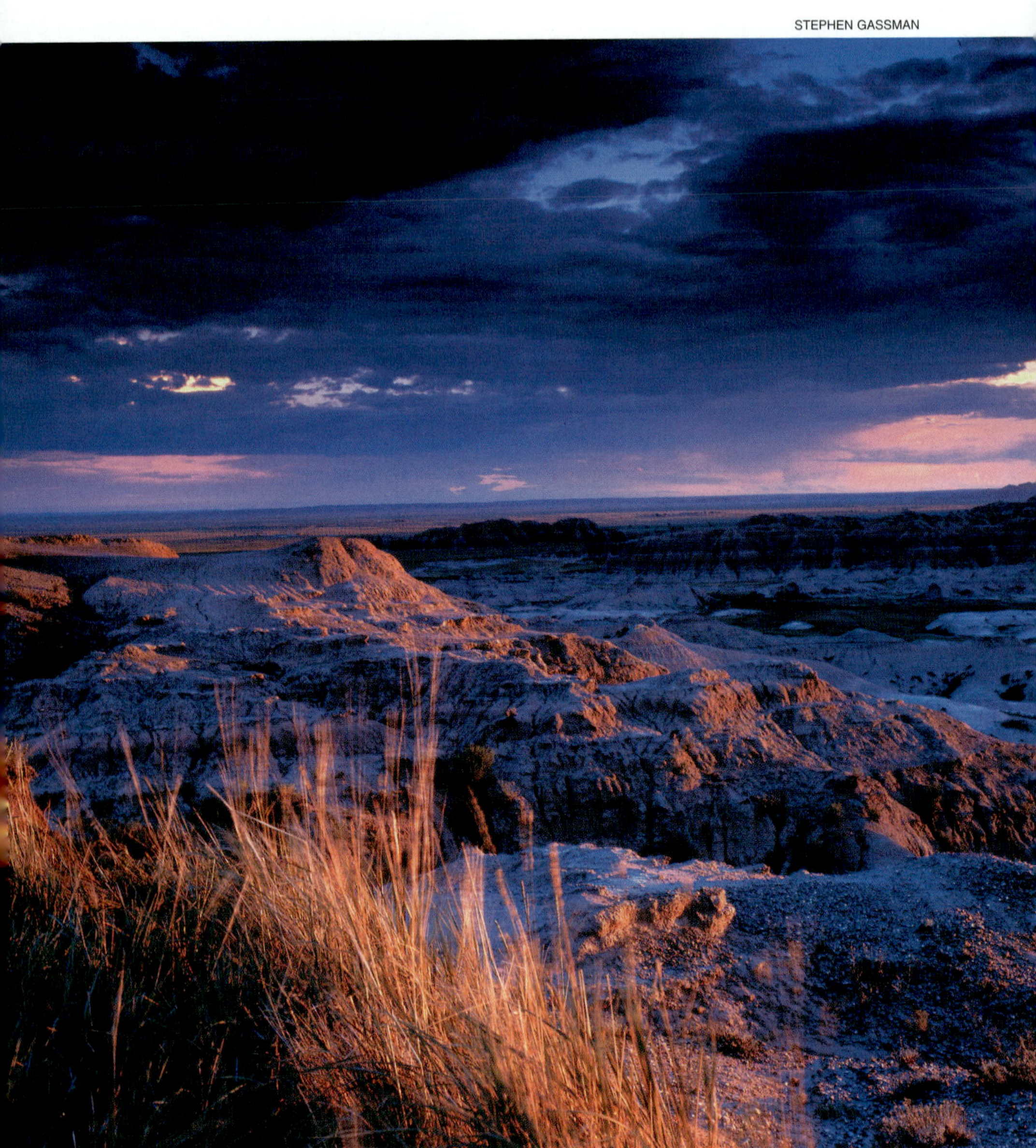

JULI WILCOX

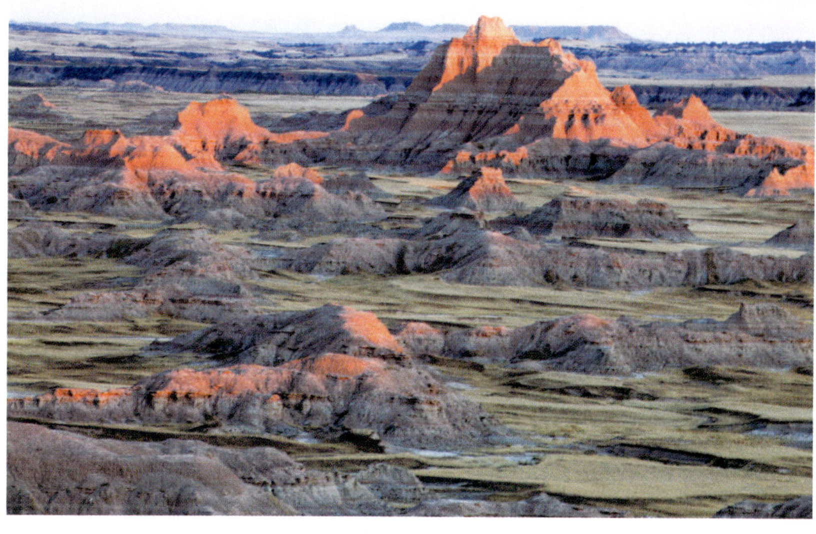

BERNIE HUNHOFF

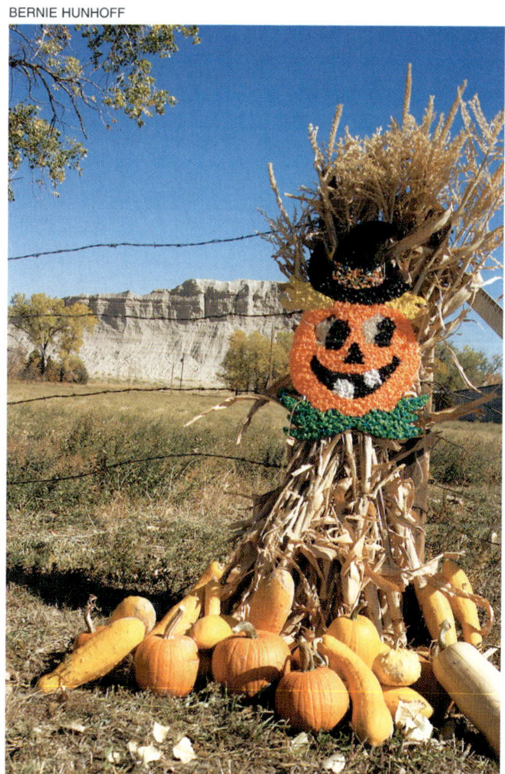

Travelers who enjoy subtlety will love the Badlands in autumn. It is one of the most unspoiled regions in the West. Serrated sand buttes look much as they did millions of years ago. Occasional trees, golden grasses and a ranch family's pumpkins and gourds add color to the landscape.

MARK KAYSER / SD TOURISM

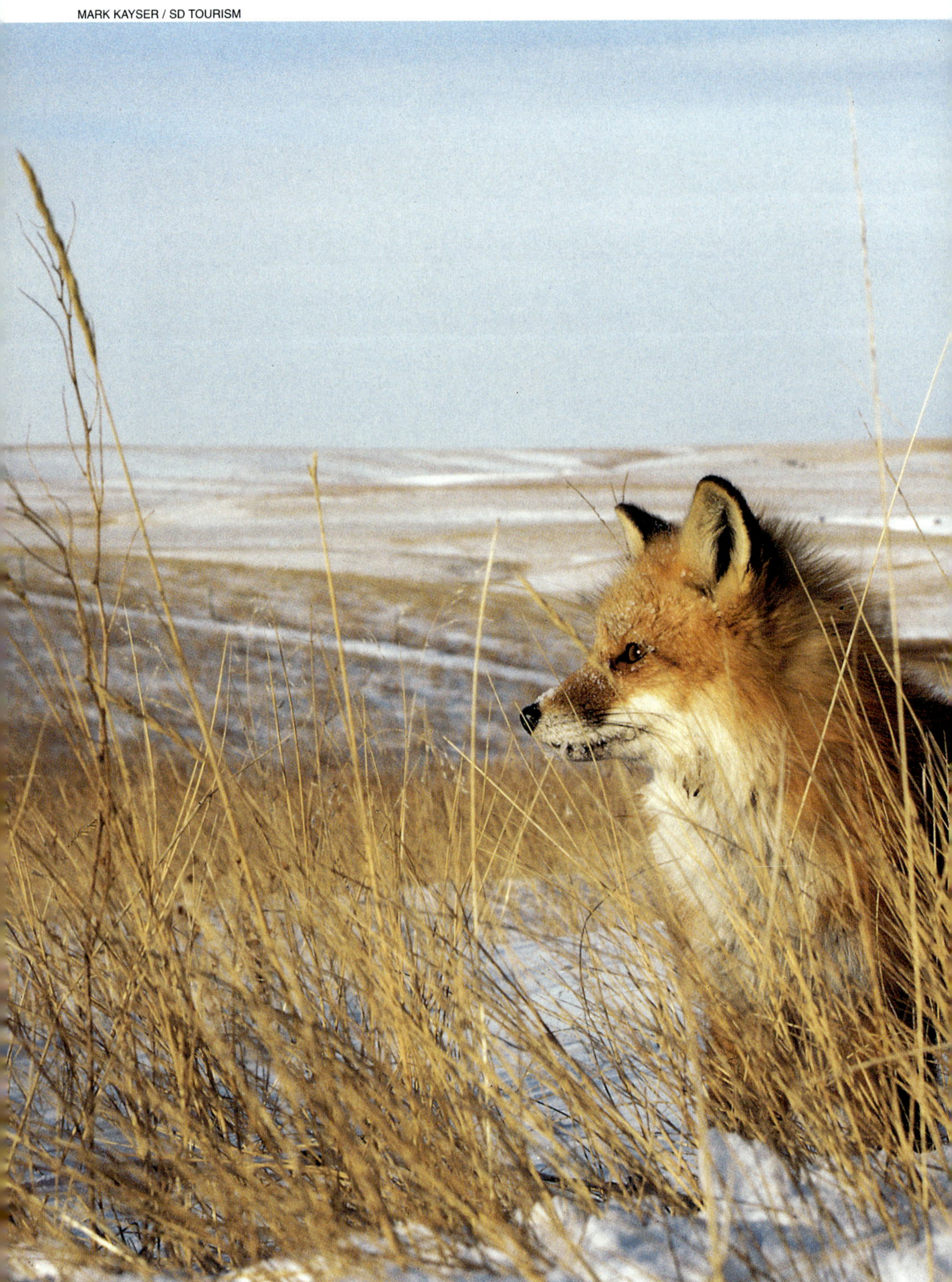

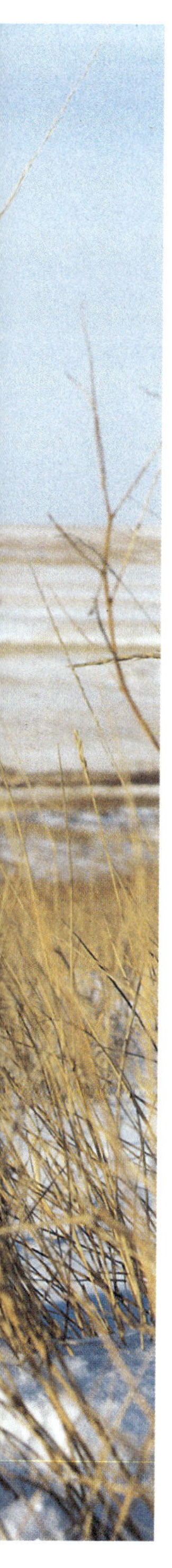

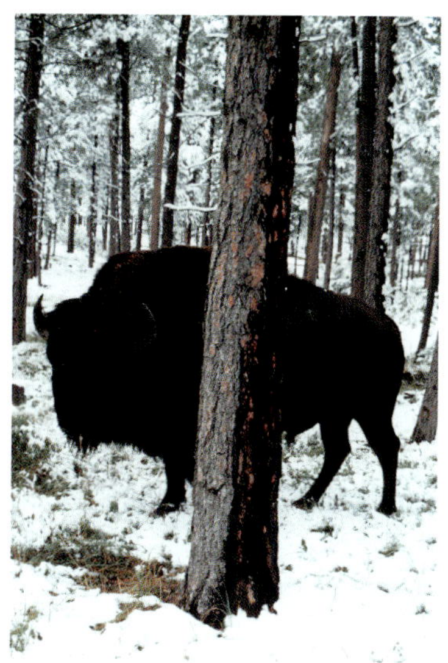

Winter

Remember. We are South Dakotans. We're of hardy stock. The weaklings have long since fled the territory, and the snowbirds have flown south. But the rest of us pride ourselves on our ability to clench winter in our teeth and face the snow and wind.

Properly conditioned by occasional Arctic blasts, we're well-prepared to truly enjoy the season. Yes, winter in our latitude is too long. But the quickest short-cut to spring is to indulge ourselves and our senses in all the freshness and toughness and beauty that winter can deal.

A medical doctor and his wife arrived in South Dakota in the 1970s so he could teach at the School of Medicine in Vermillion. Many years later, he and his wife were driving to Sioux Falls when he looked out at the frozen brown and gray landscape and said, "Isn't this beautiful!"

"Damn!" she said. "Now you'll never move." And they never did.

Winter makes you a true South Dakotan.

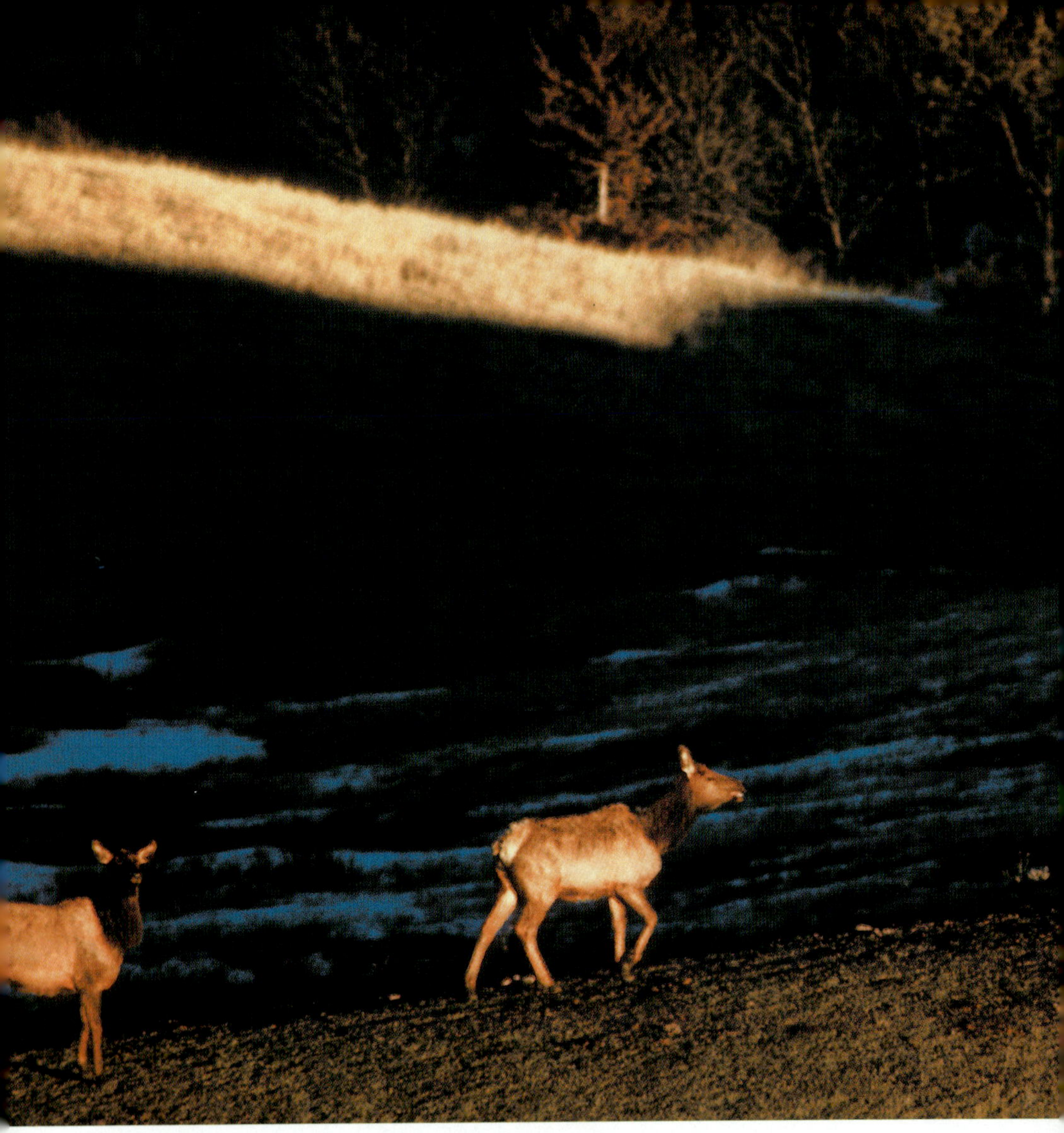

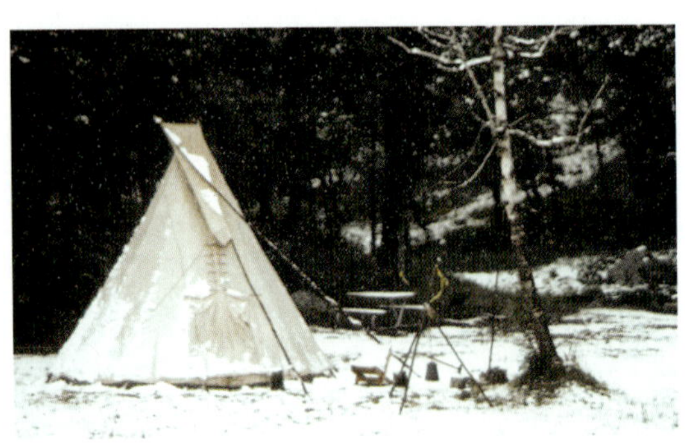

Elk once freely roamed all the prairies, but today their travels in South Dakota are limited to the Black Hills and Butte, Bennett and Gregory counties, where their range is generally restricted by wire. A limited hunting season is allowed. At left, a hunter established a winter camp before going afield.

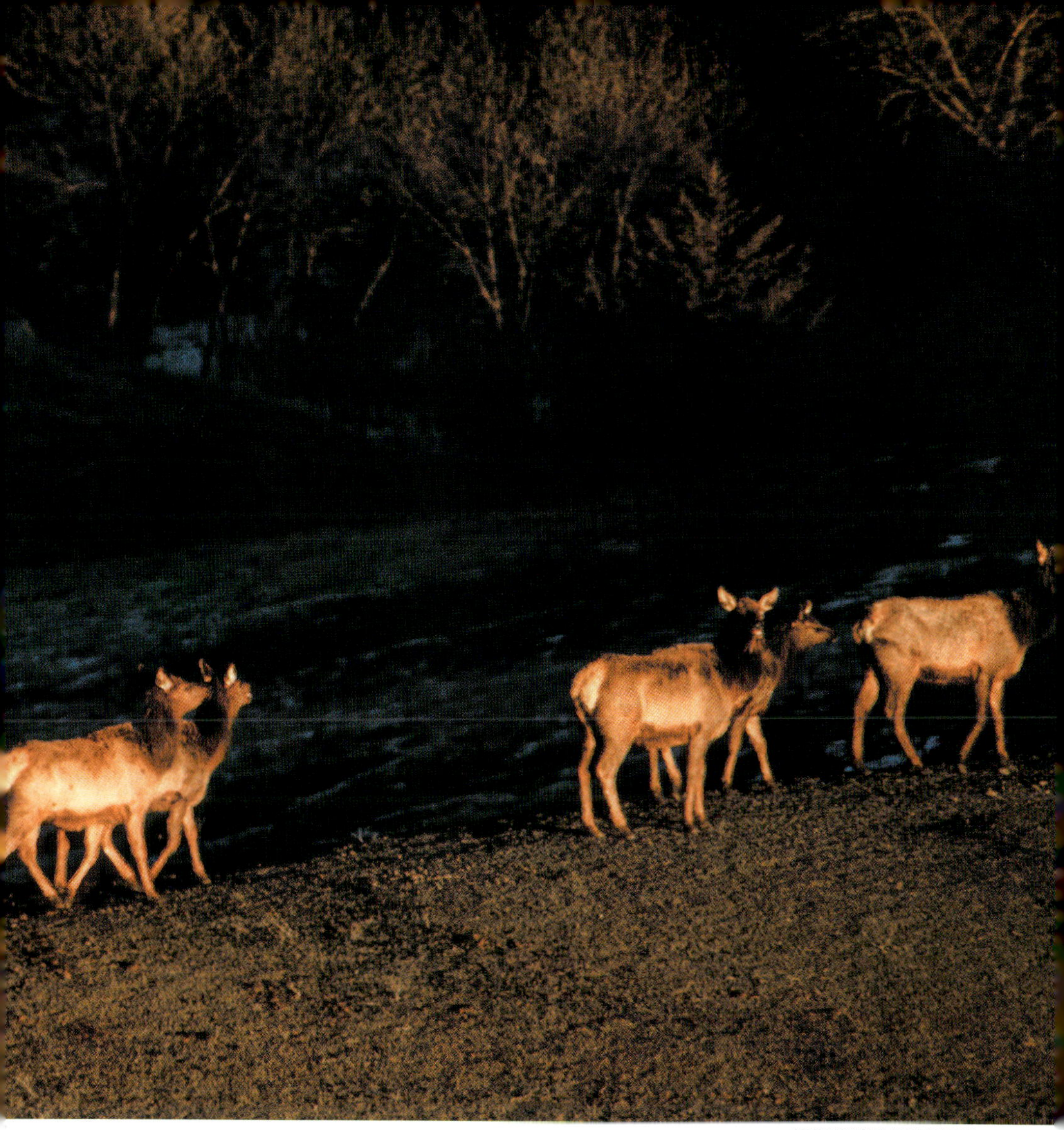

MARK KAYSER / SD TOURISM

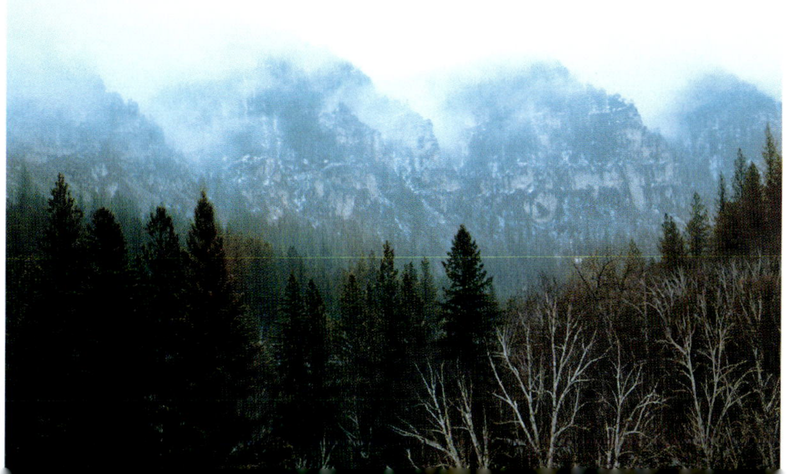

BERNIE HUNHOFF

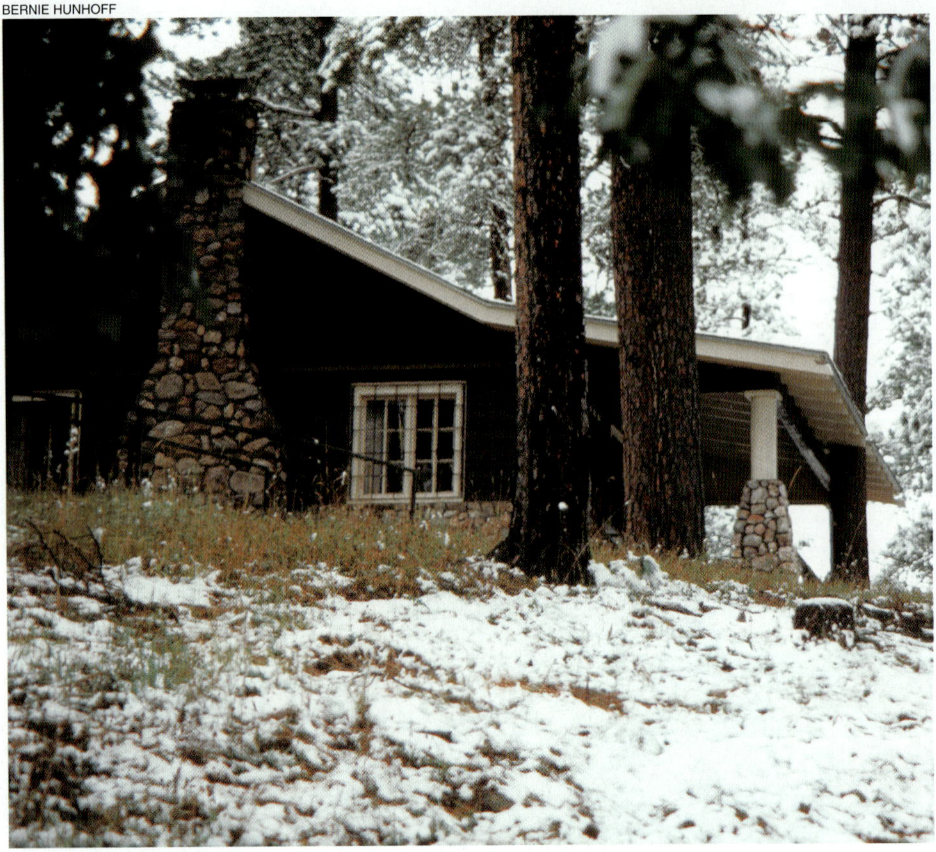

COURTESY DAKOTA WESLEYAN UNIV.

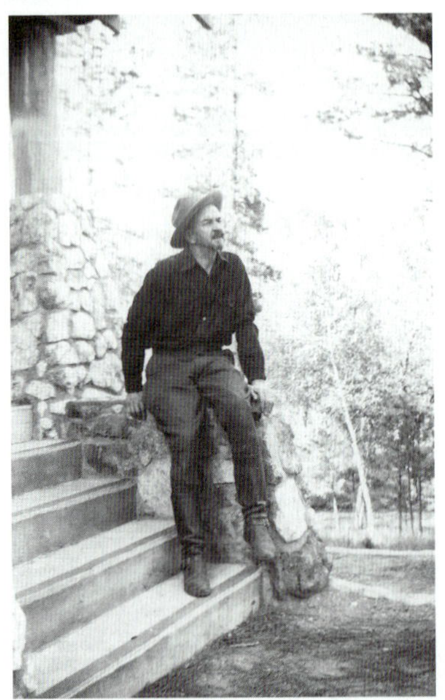

Witty and stylish, South Dakota's favorite poet, Badger Clark, could have been a favorite in any city but he chose the solitude of a small cabin near Legion Lake in Custer State Park. Clark wrote the timeless "Cowboy's Prayer" and many other verses extolling the virtues of the West. He died in 1957. His cabin (above) is open to visitors.

'Let cattle rub my tombstone down
And coyotes mourn their kin,
Let hawses paw and tromp the moun'
But don't you fence me in!'

—from Clark's
"The Old Cow Man"

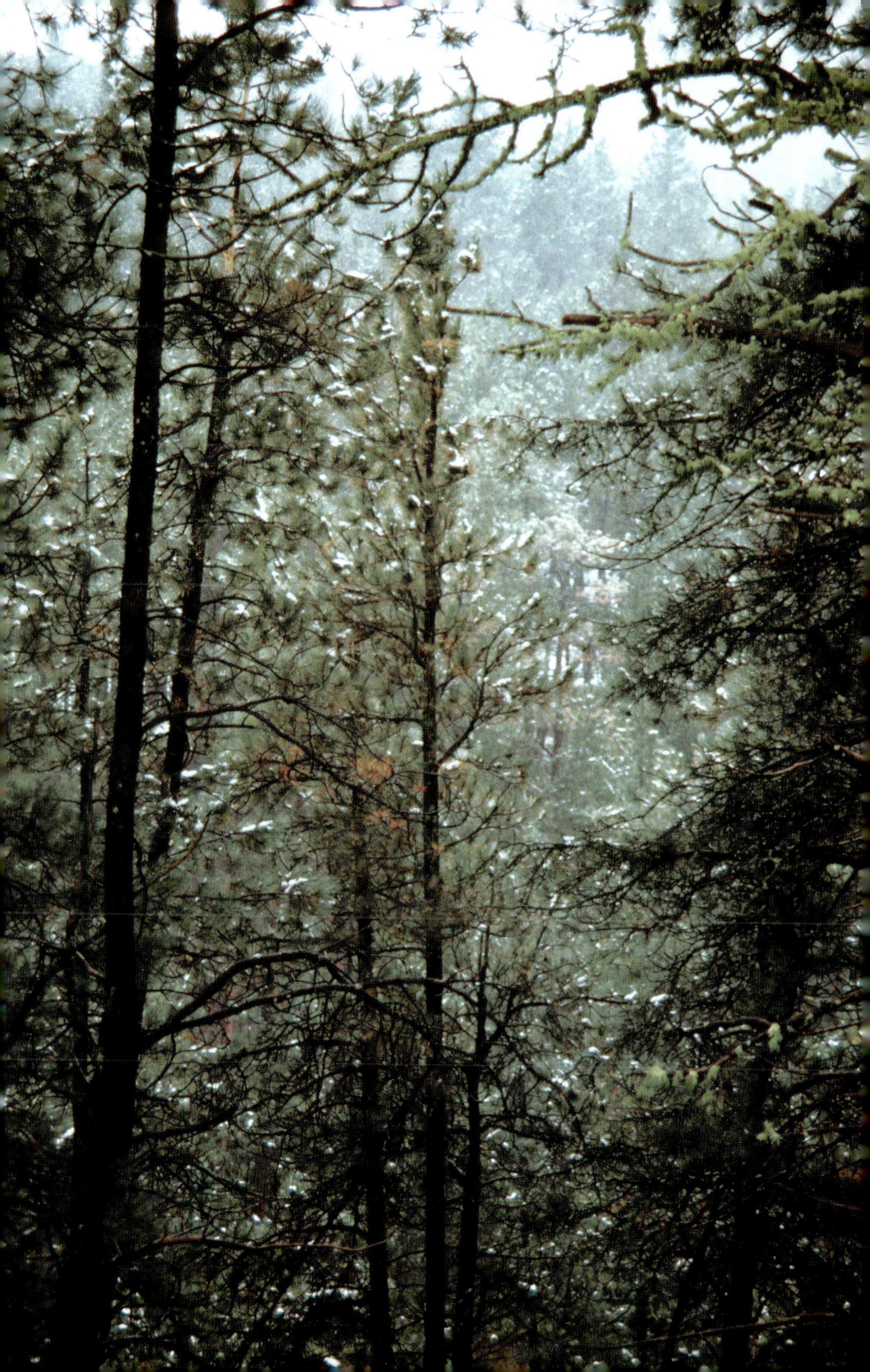

ARNOLD WOLD

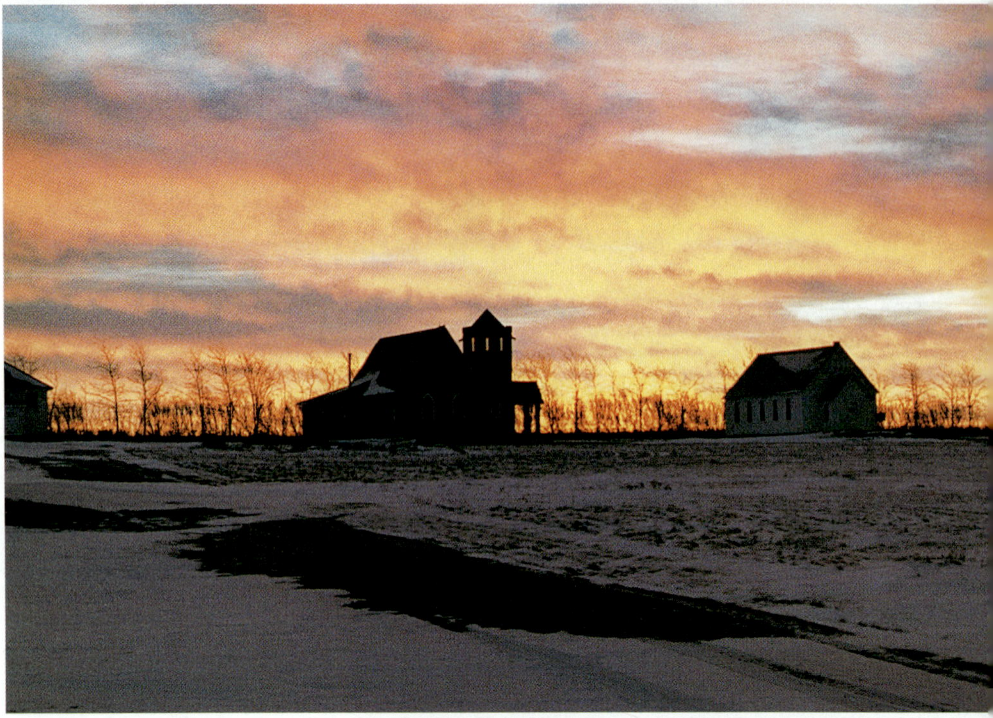

Winter's short and chilly days separate us from one another, and thus the season gets its reputation for loneliness. The Little Brown Church at Winner (above) is warmed by a winter sunrise. A flat Marshall County landscape (right) looks barren in snow.

JOHN FRONT

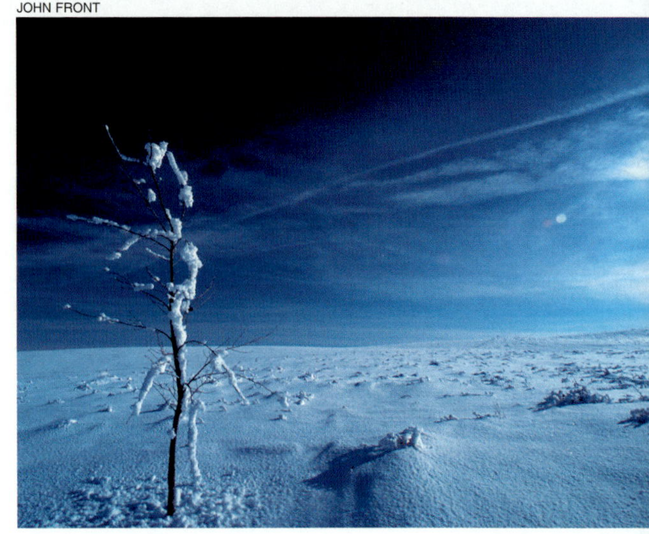

GREG LATZA

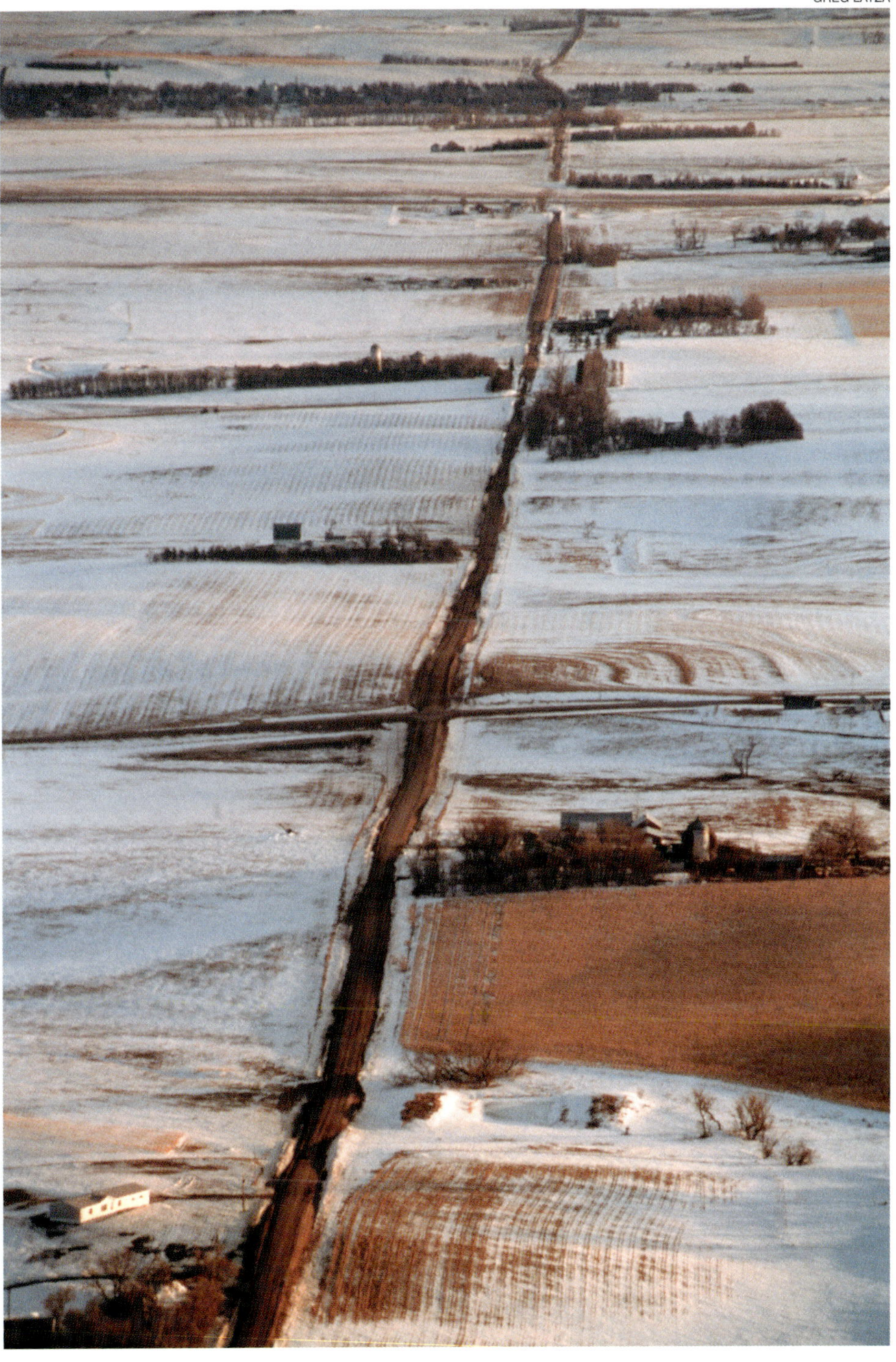

A country road in Minnehaha County is empty of traffic on a cold, clear day.

KATIE HUNHOFF

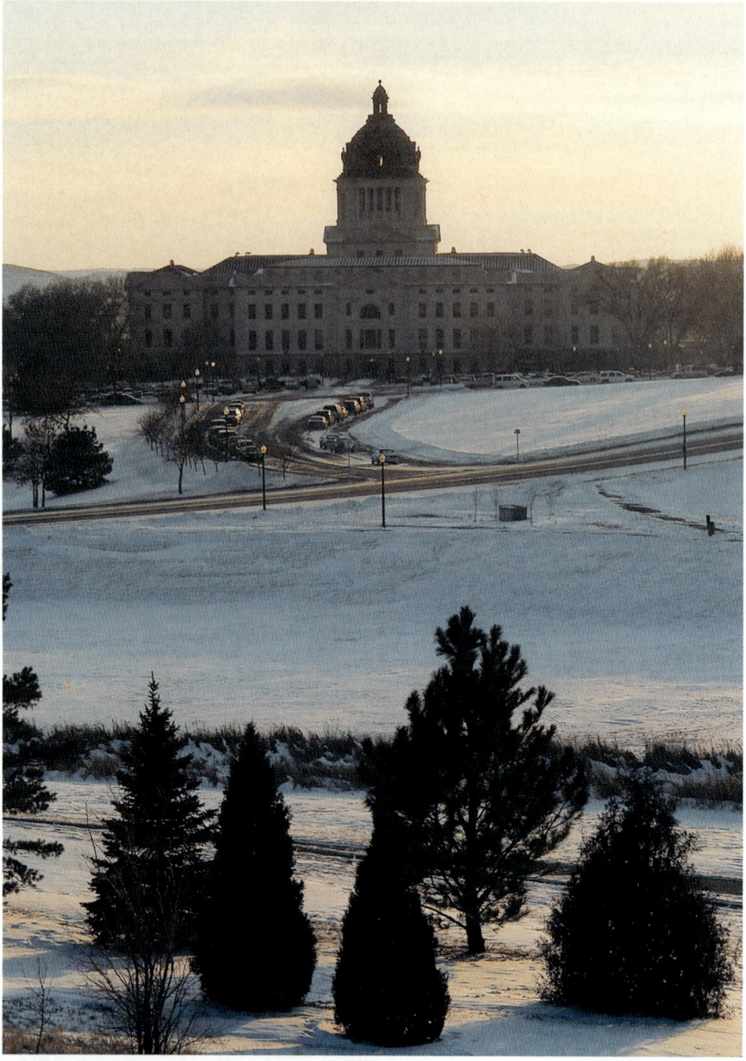

BEN HANTEN

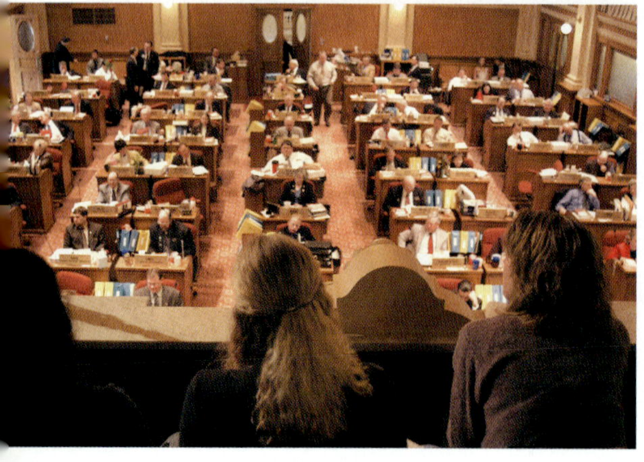

Some say South Dakota's favorite winter sport is the state legislature, which meets every January and February in Pierre. Most of the 105 lawmakers live out of suitcases in motel rooms for the duration. Lobbyists, news reporters, school children and concerned taxpayers come and go, depending on the weather and the issues.

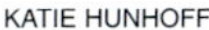

KATIE HUNHOFF

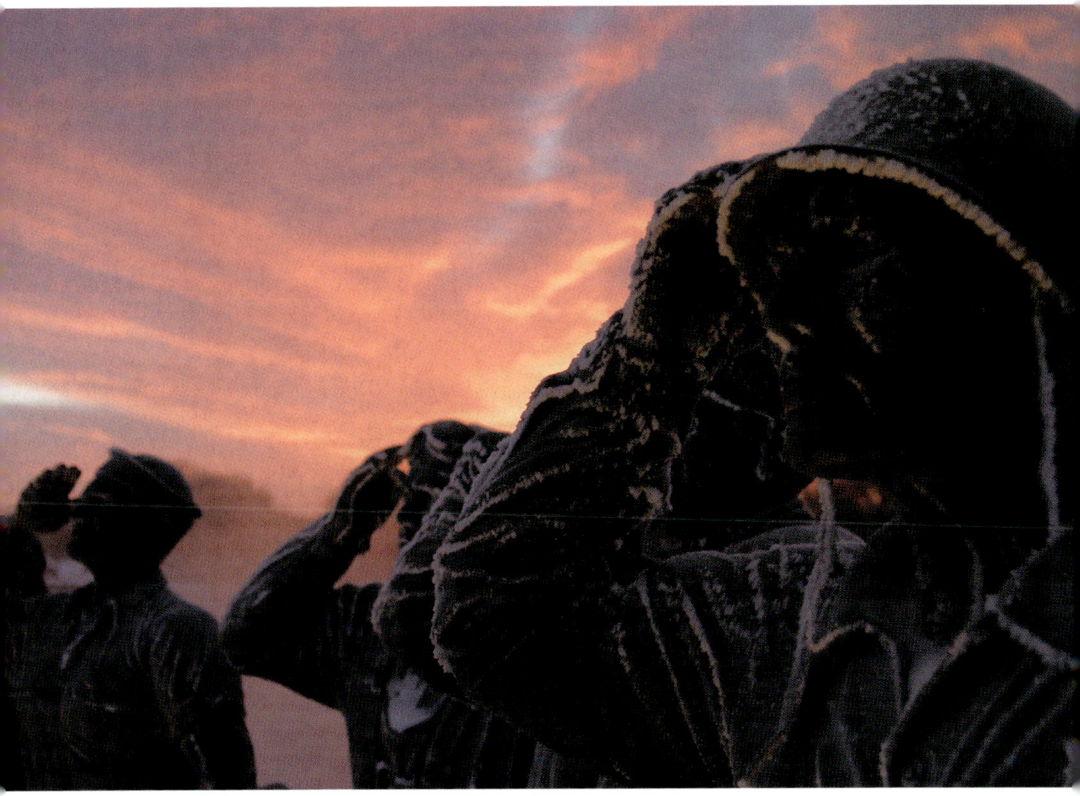

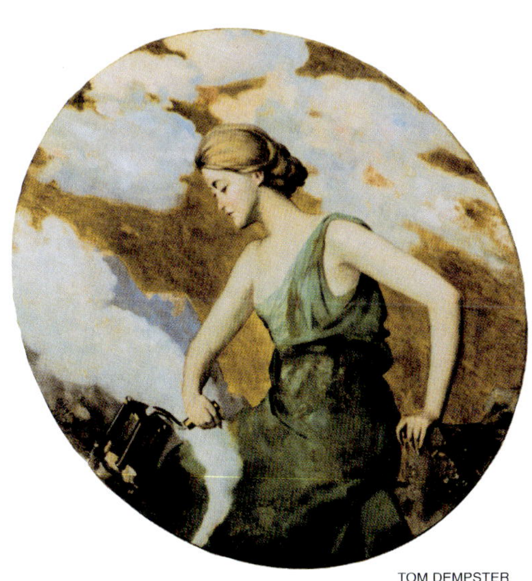

TOM DEMPSTER

The capitol grounds are rich with art, indoors and out. A memorial to WWII veterans (above) was dedicated in 2001. Paintings of Greek goddesses, including Minerva, proprietress of wisdom, adorn capitol walls.

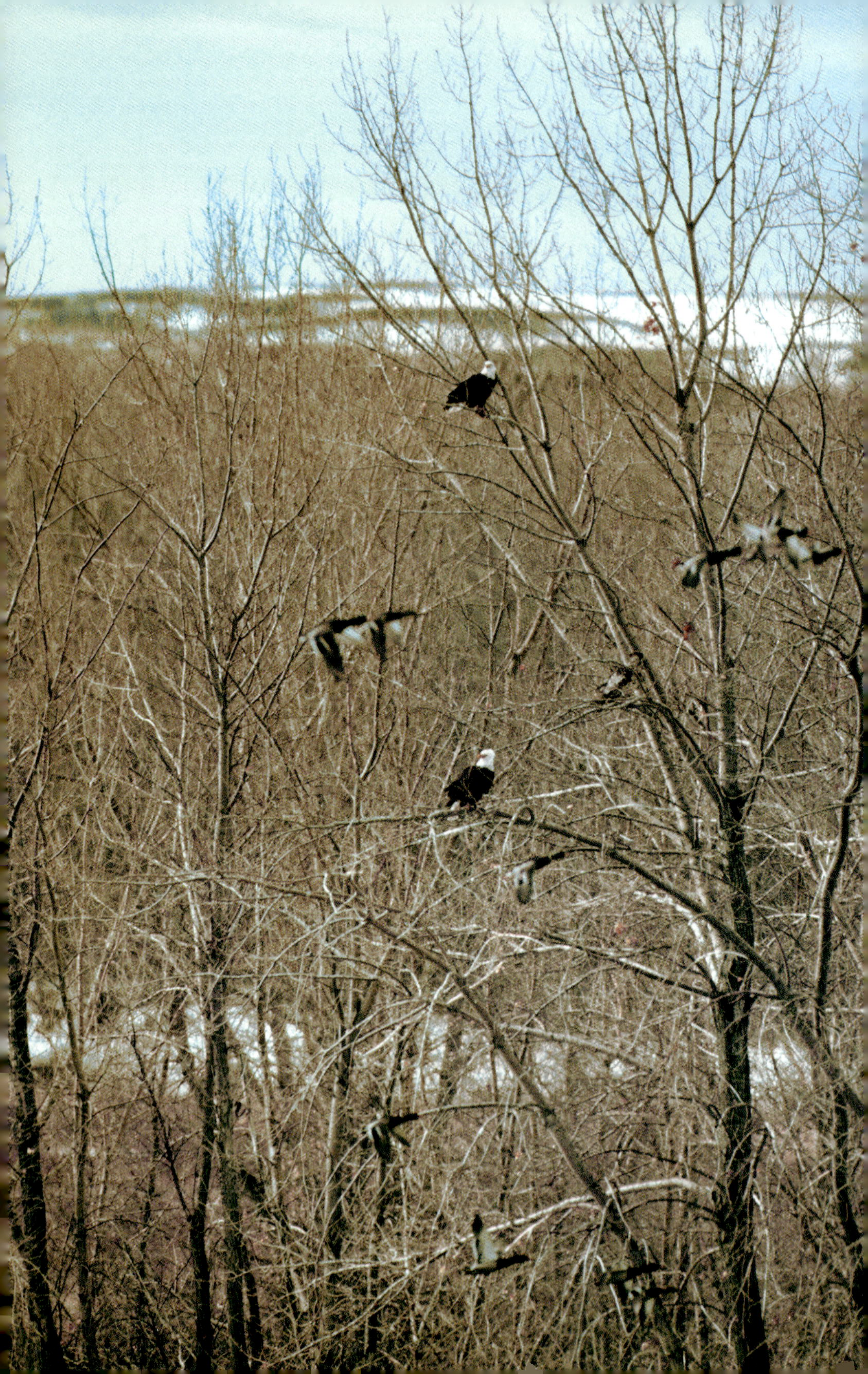

DAVE DRINGMAN

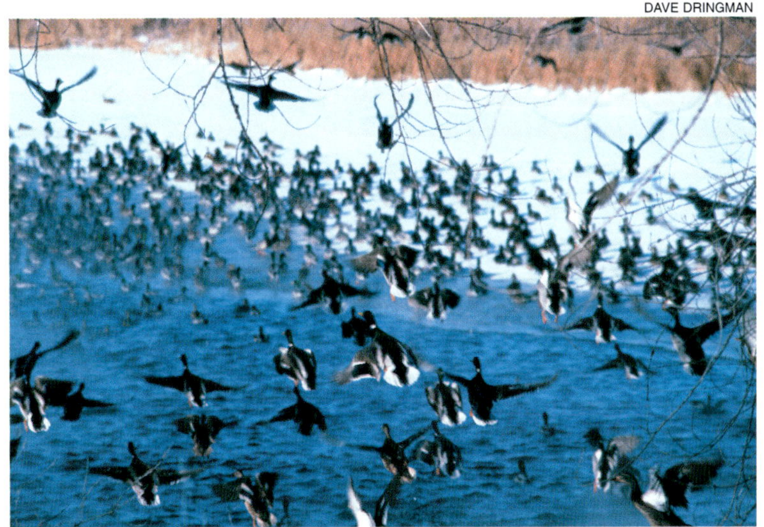

Open water along the Missouri River attracts bald eagles (left) and mallards in winter. Youngsters have a road to themselves (below) after a snowfall in hills along the river south of Tabor.

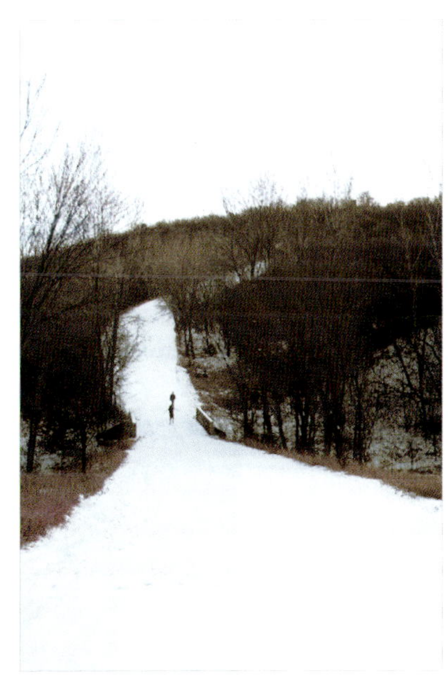

BERNIE HUNHOFF

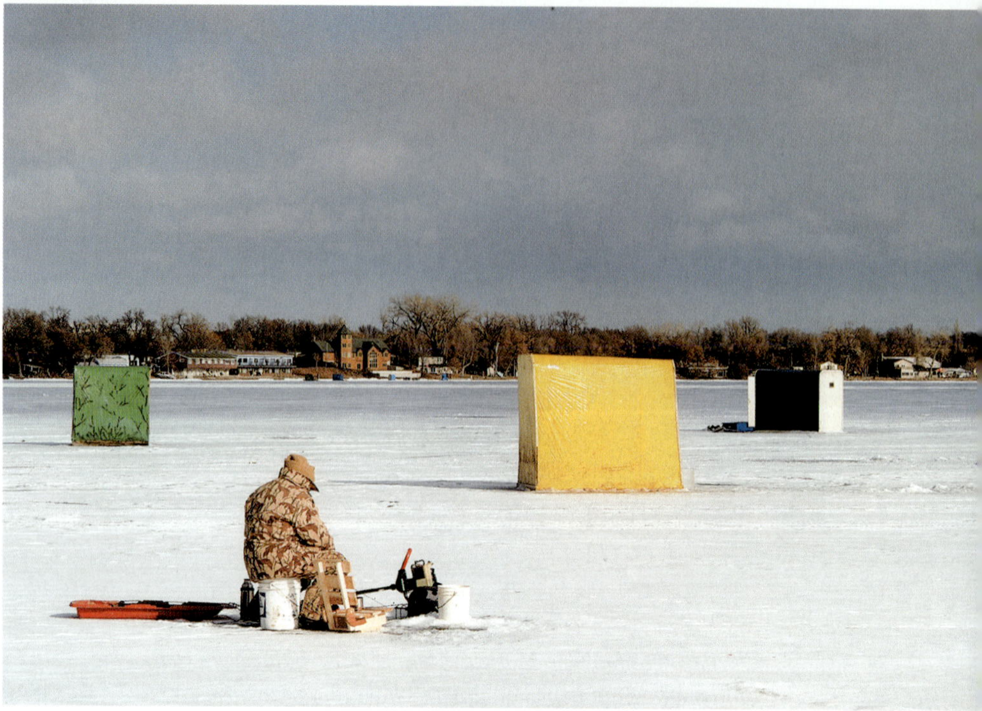

CHRIS HUNHOFF

Fishing shacks color Lake Madison. The glacial lakes typically have 30 inches of ice, though anglers feel safe with far less than that. Chalkstone bluffs border Lake Yankton in southeast South Dakota. The chalkstone was once mined as a building material.

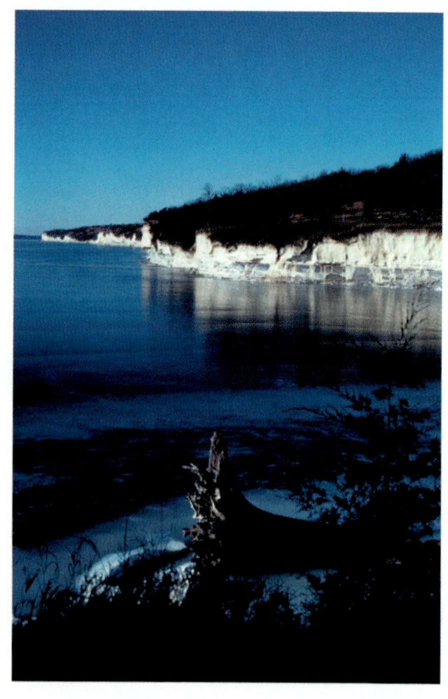

GREG LATZA

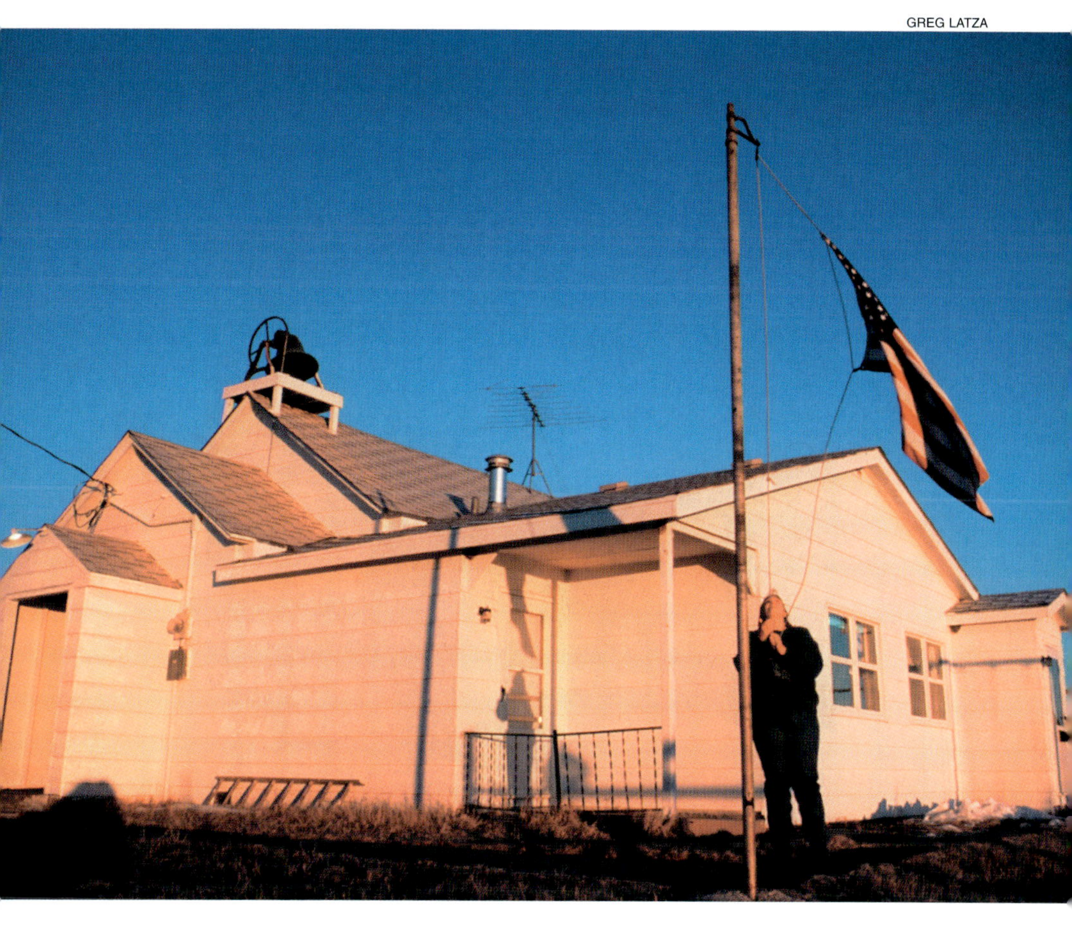

Orton Country School is both an education center and a rural gathering place for ranch families around Mission Ridge.

BERNIE HUNHOFF

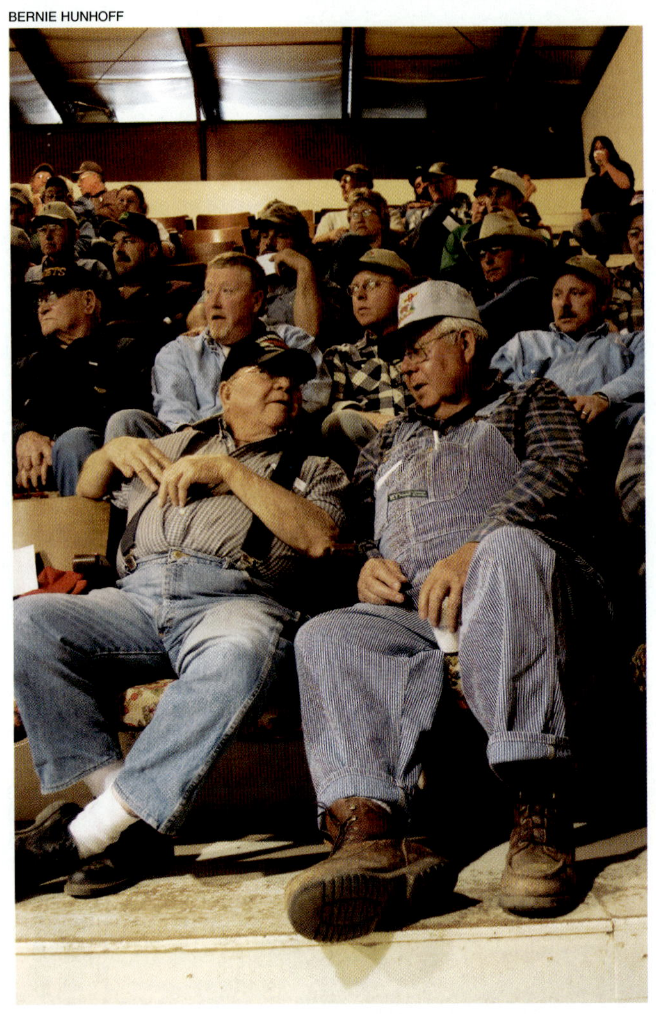

South Dakota's livestock auction barns are busiest in the winter months. Buyers and sellers, like this pair at the Platte Livestock Auction, fill bleacher seats to watch the cattle. A sprinkling of snow doesn't bother the white-faced calves (opposite page) being moved to winter quarters near Fort Pierre. They are among a herd of 1,700, in a part of the state where most cattle don't get indoors until sale day.

GREG LATZA

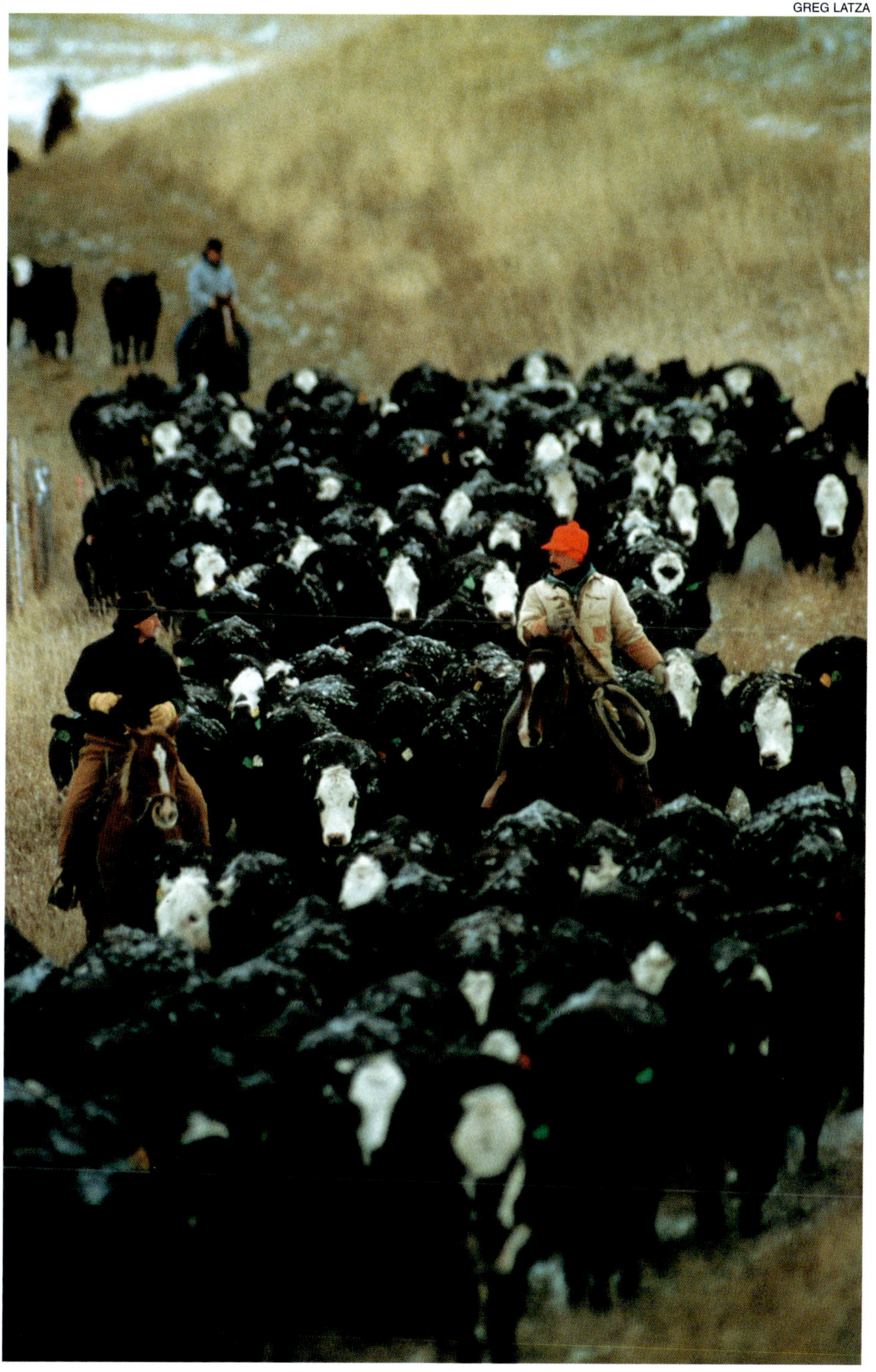

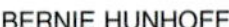

BERNIE HUNHOFF

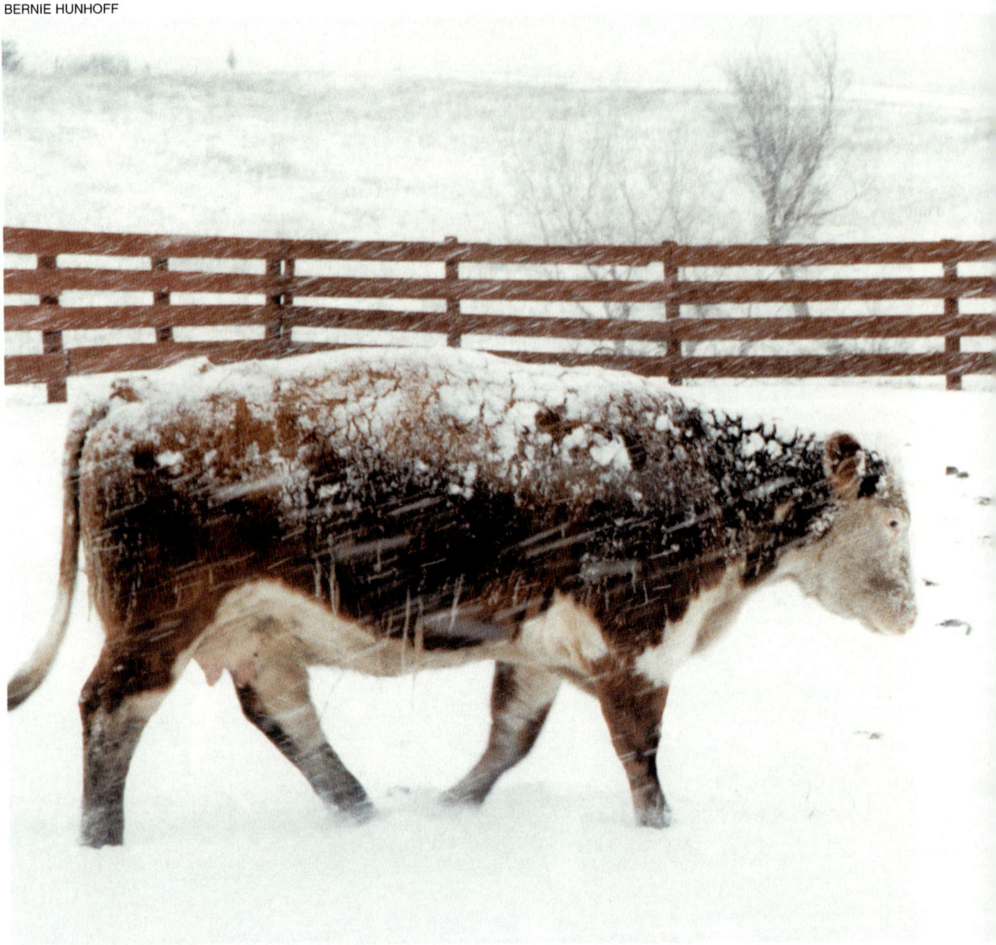

JOHN FRONT

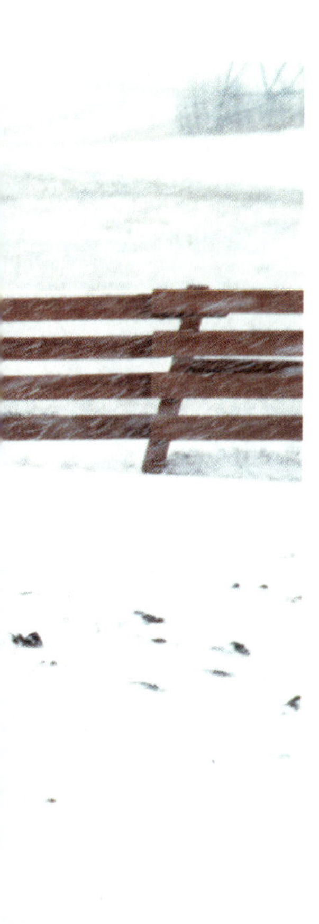

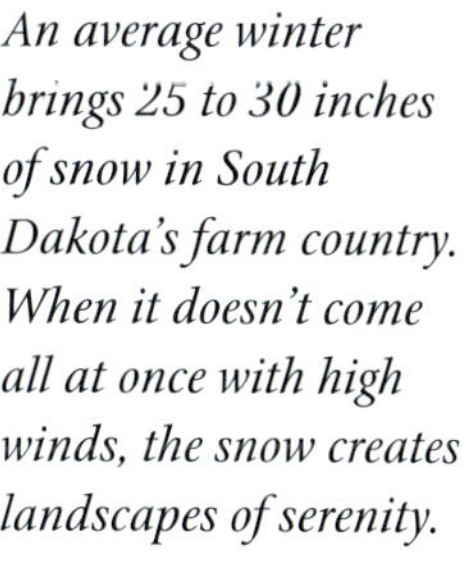

An average winter brings 25 to 30 inches of snow in South Dakota's farm country. When it doesn't come all at once with high winds, the snow creates landscapes of serenity.

GREG LATZA

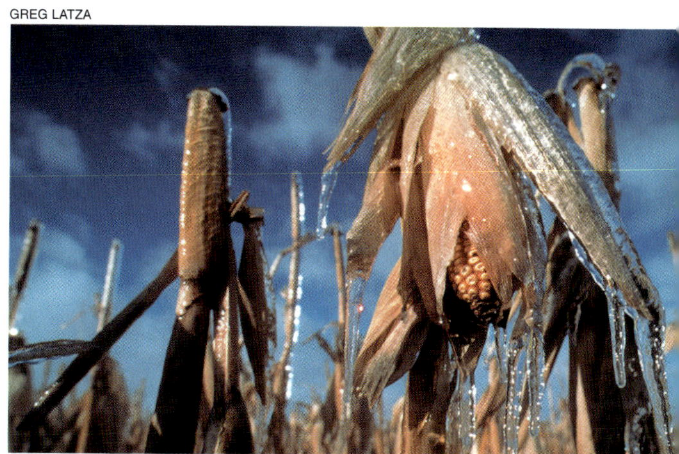

STAFF PHOTO

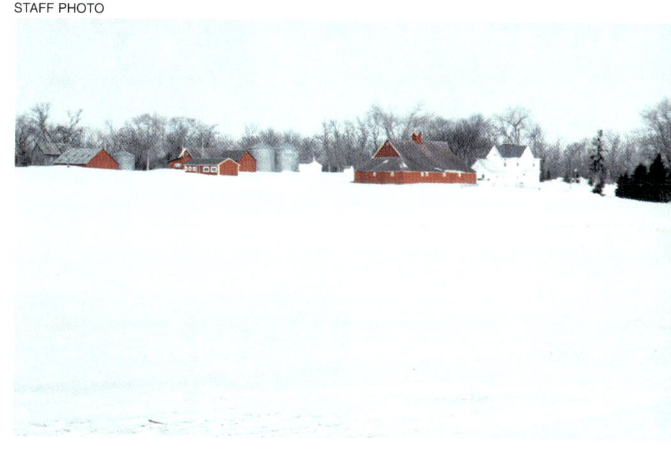

BERNIE HUNHOFF

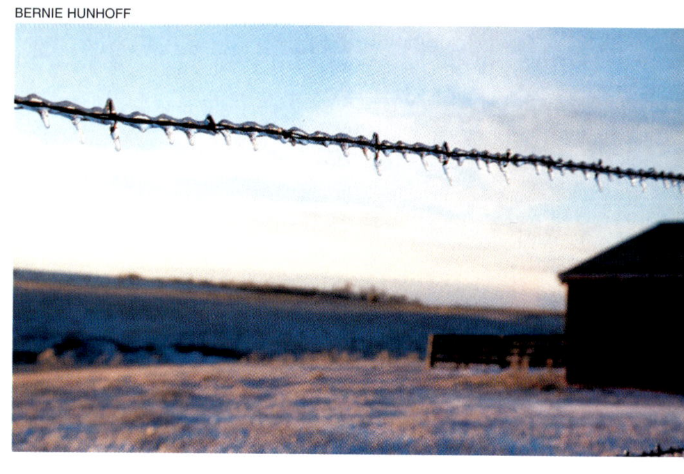

GREG LATZA

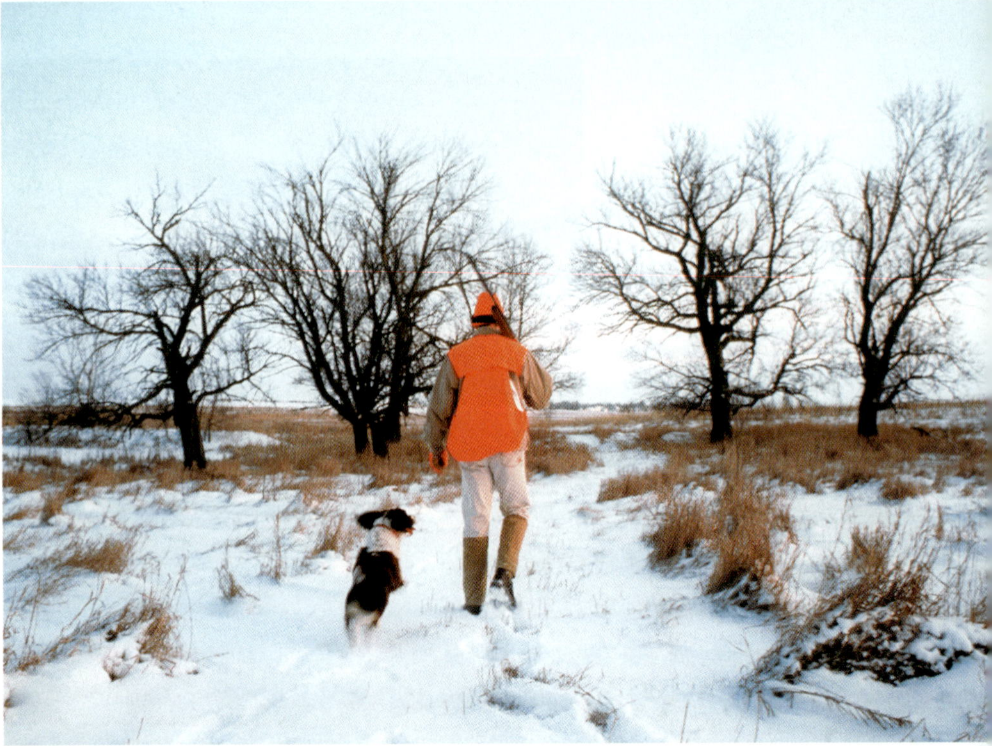

JOHN FRONT

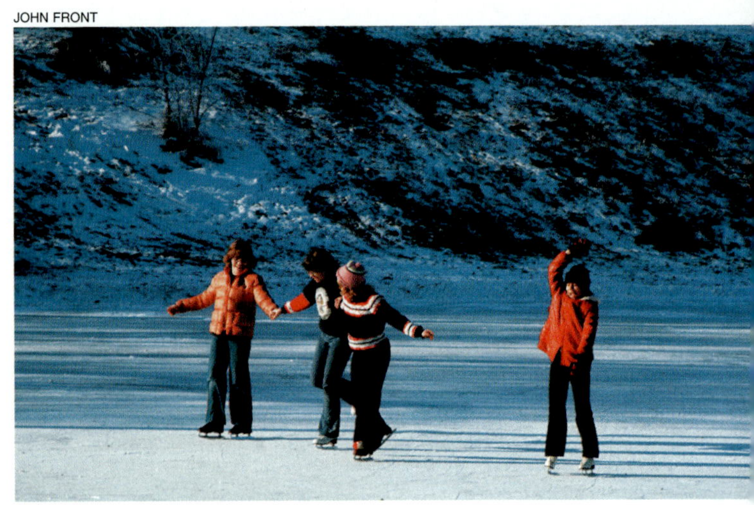

Sportsmen and women, dogs and children are the least likely to object to a snowy forecast.

STAFF PHOTO

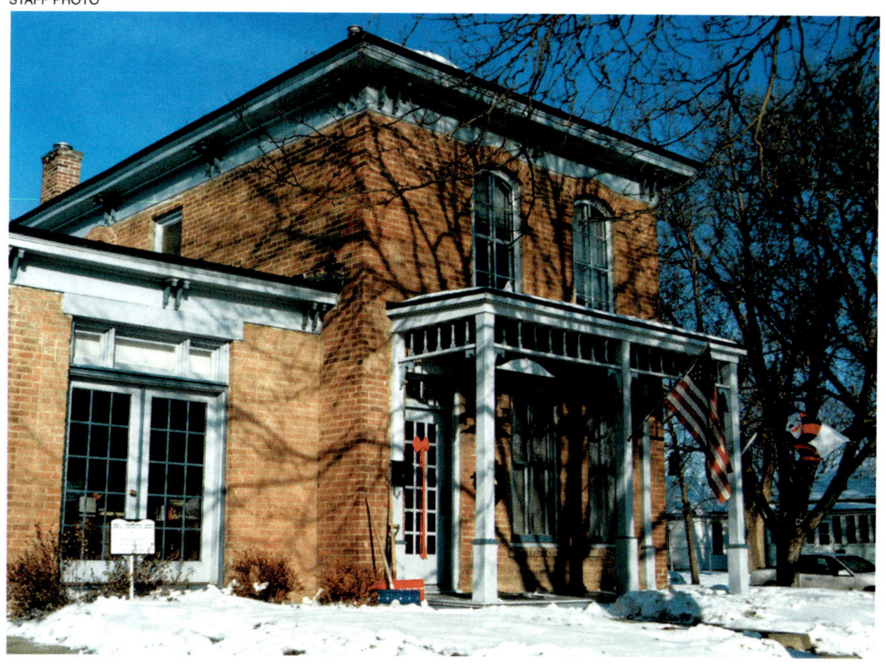

Yankton's Pennington House (above), home to South Dakota Magazine since 1987, has a red bow for the holidays. Pennington was a territorial governor in the 1870s when Yankton was the capital city. In Pierre, the current capital city, the capitol rotunda glimmers with tinseled trees decorated by organizations from across the state.

SD TOURISM

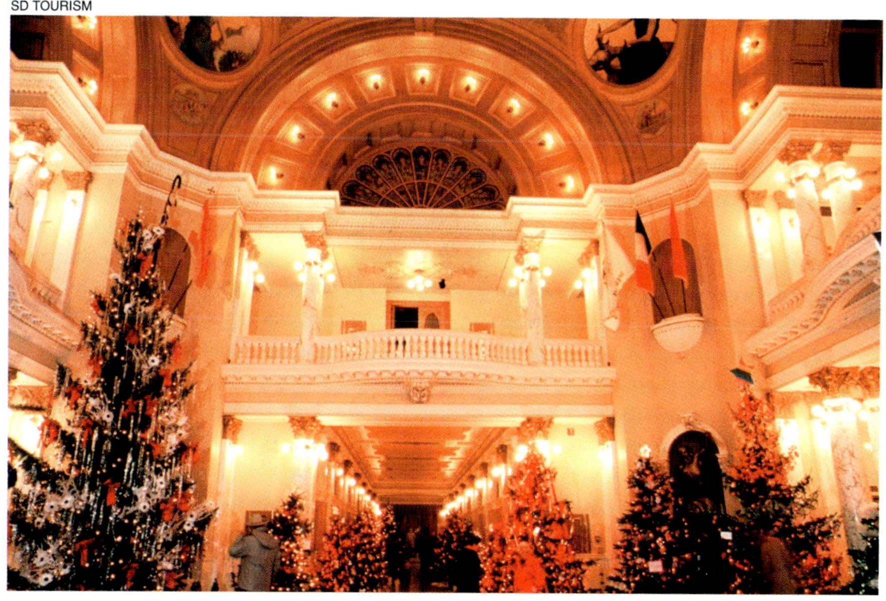

BERNIE HUNHOFF

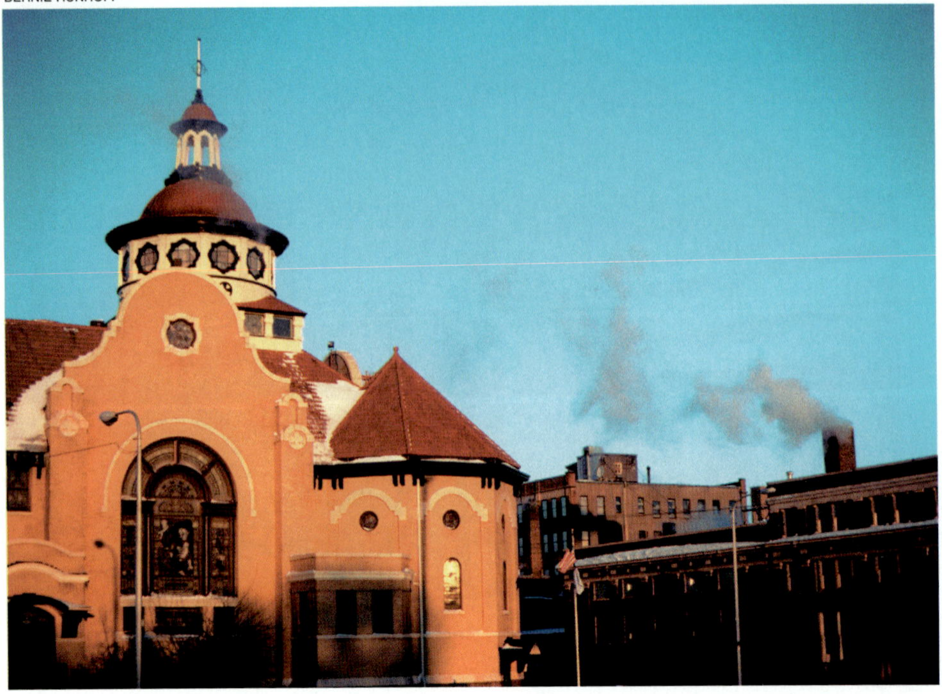

Clear and cold mornings have one effect on Aberdeen's towering First Methodist Church, and quite another on Mother Nature's hibernating trees in Britton.

JOHN FRONT

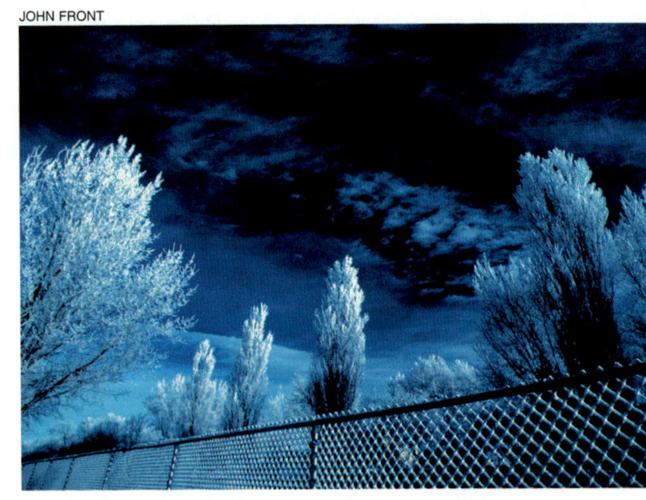

BERNIE HUNHOFF

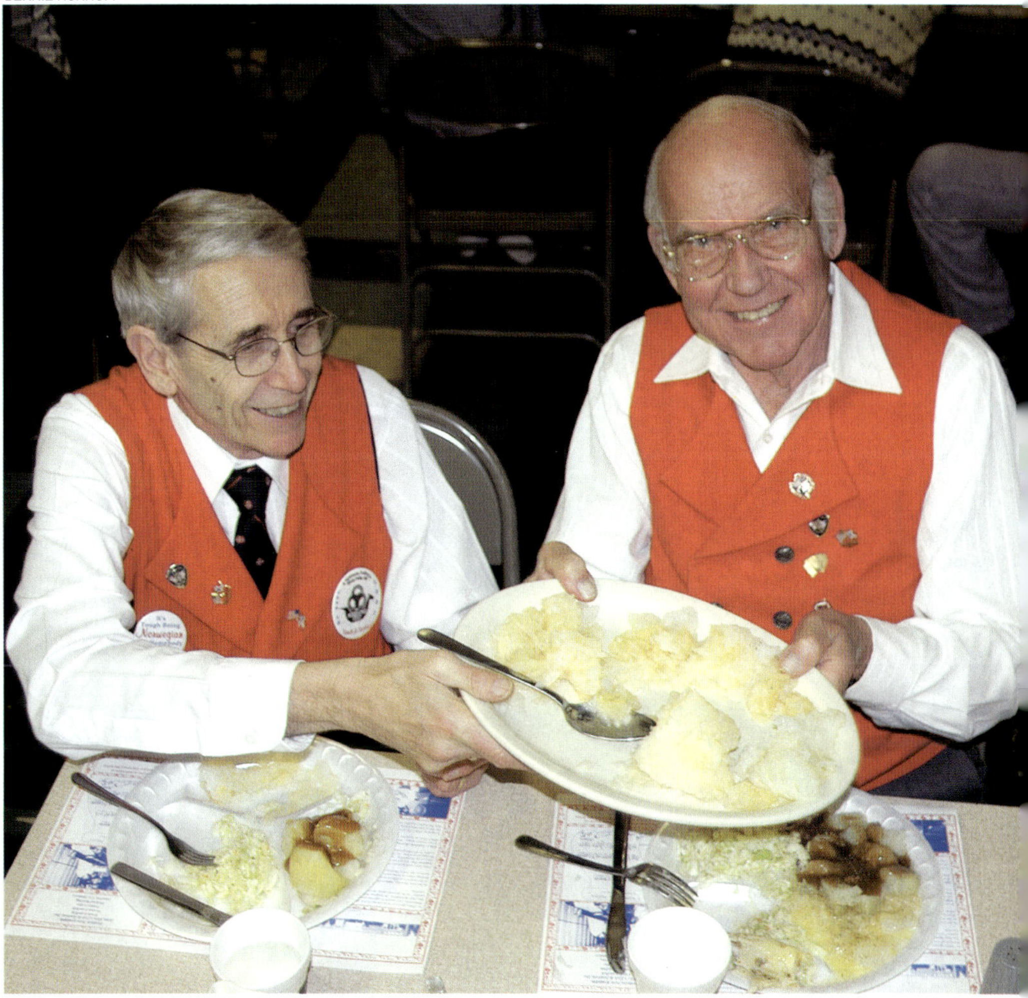

Lutefisk feeds are winter traditions in South Dakota's Norwegian communities. Sons of Norway members (above) pass a plate of the much-harangued codfish at their annual dinner in Nordic Hall in Sioux Falls. Below, chefs bring the main dish to a boil. Diners like to joke about the edibility of lutefisk, but potsful of the fish disappear as the night goes on, along with lots of hot butter and lefse.

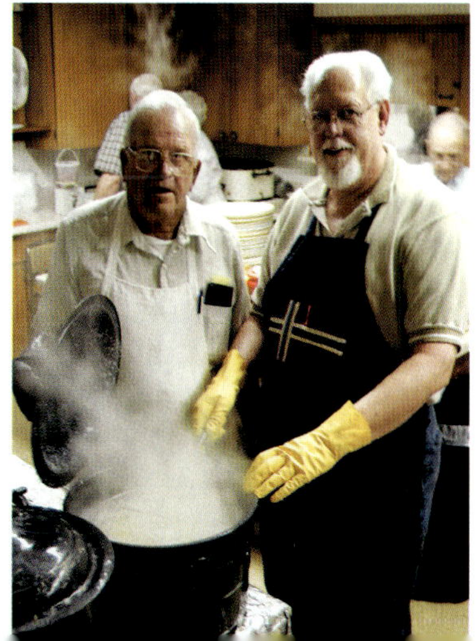

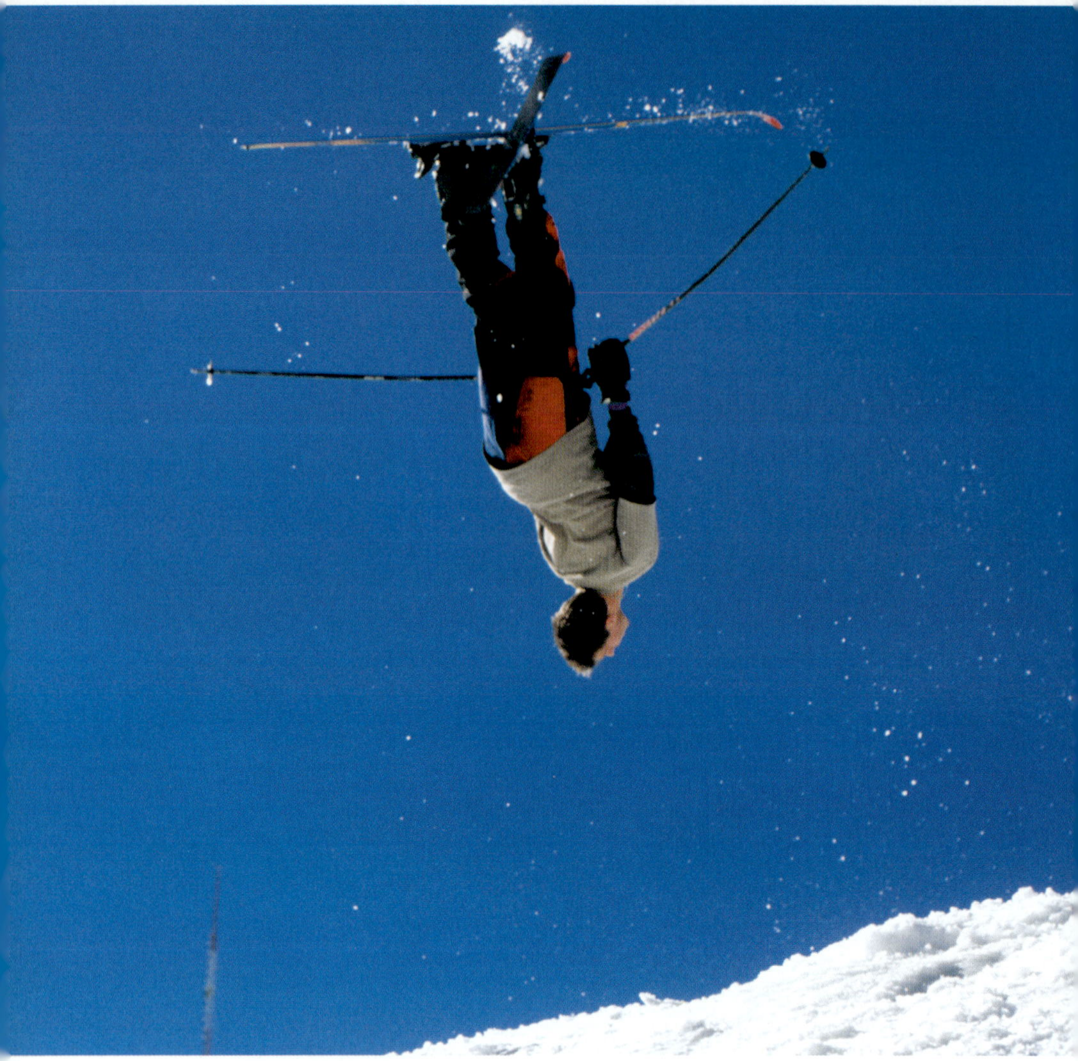

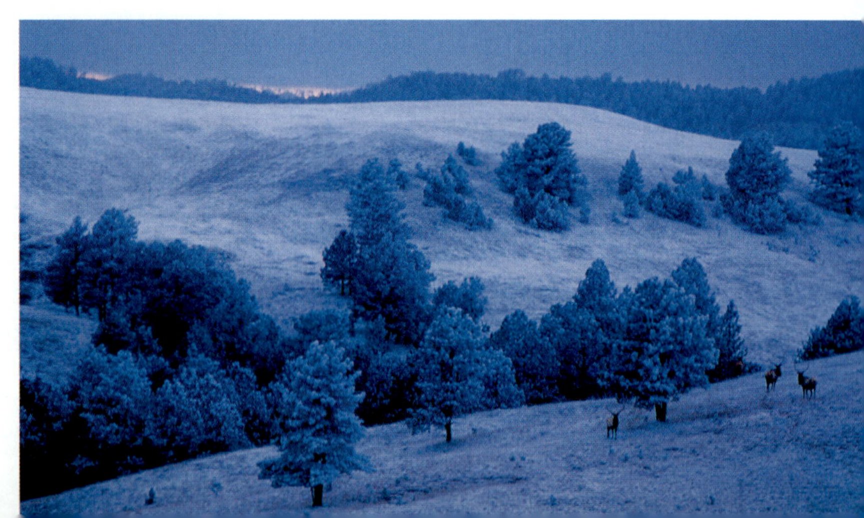

South Dakotans are at risk of cabin fever, but there is relief: skiing, sledding, hiking, camping, hunting, fishing, snowmobiling and a host of other activities. The cure is like granddaddy's liquid cough medicine — it makes the affliction seem quite tolerable.

PHOTOS BY JOHNNY SUNDBY

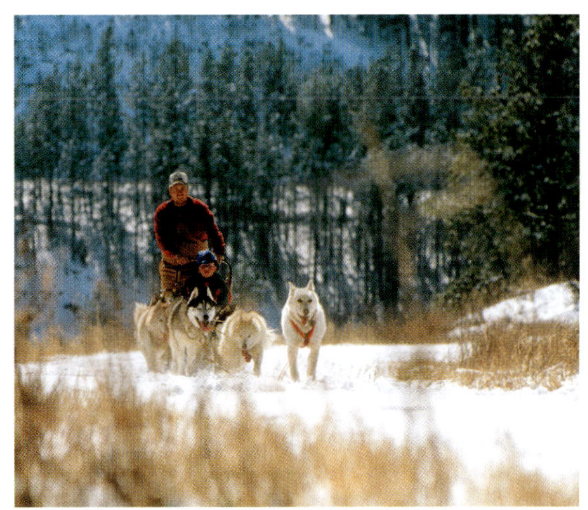

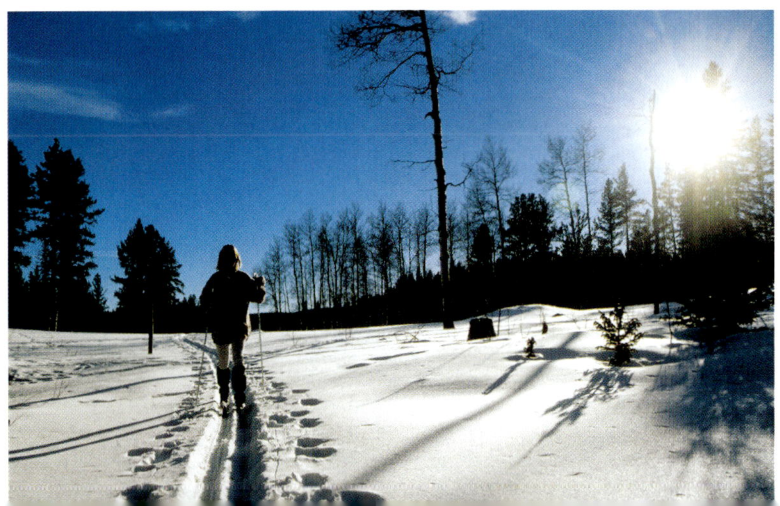

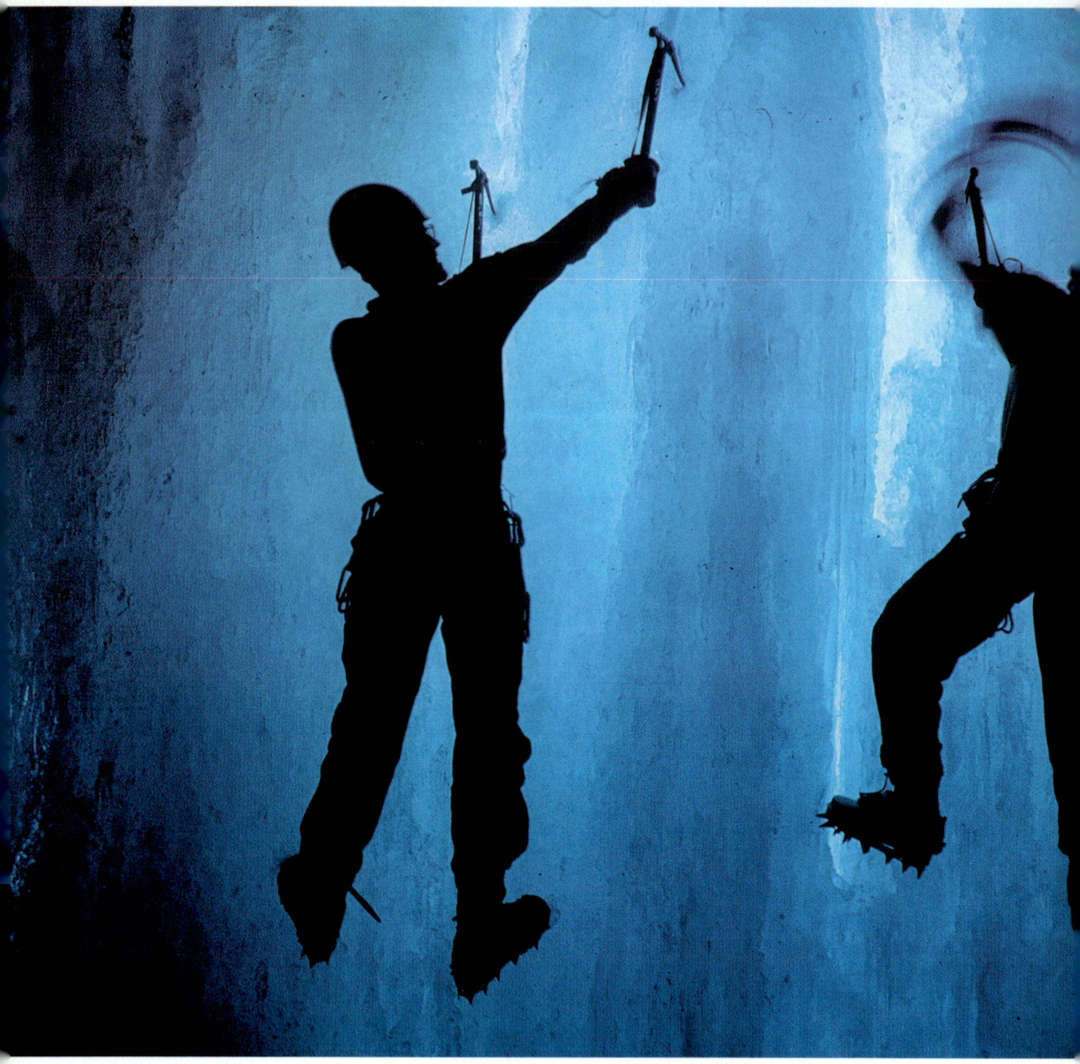

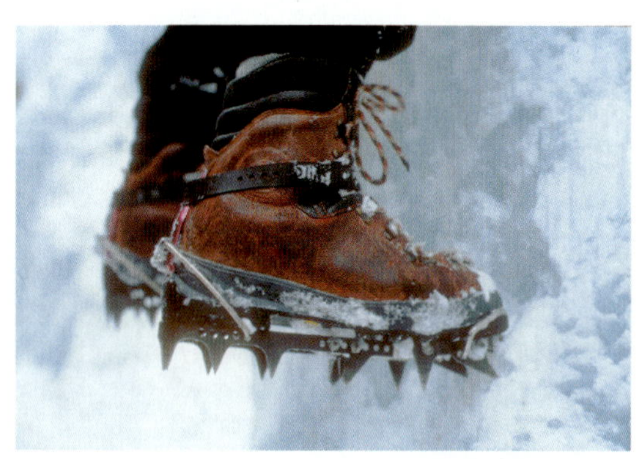

Ice climbing the frozen waterfalls and icy cliffs of the Black Hills has become a winter variation of mountain climbing for some outdoorsmen. At left, climbers work their way up a pillar of ice in Spearfish Canyon's Swallow Cliff. At right, a climber scales Bridal Veil Falls.

PHOTOS BY JOHNNY SUNDBY

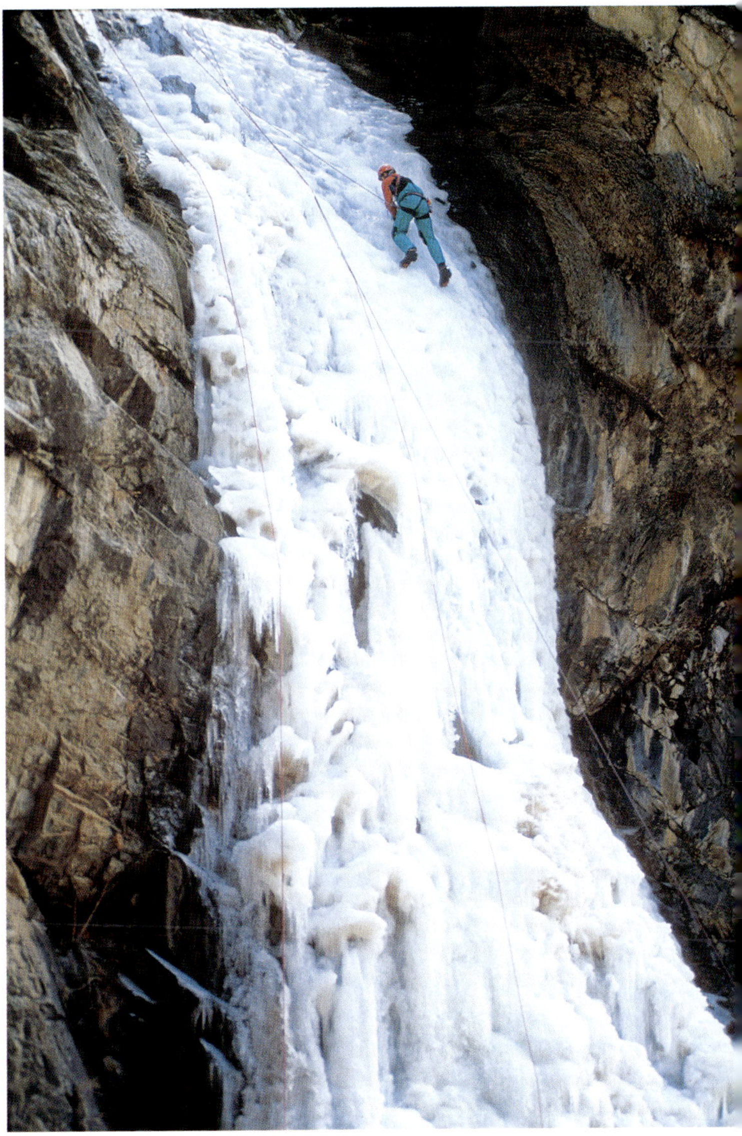

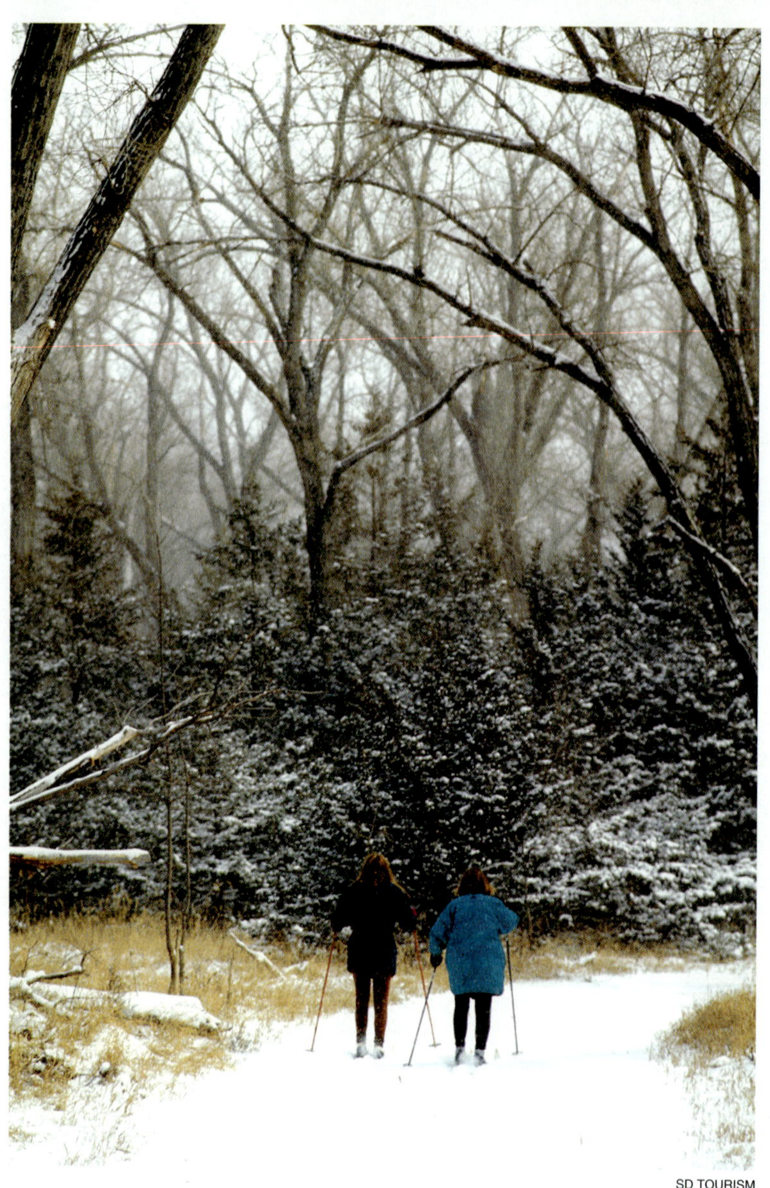

SD TOURISM

Cross-country skiers enjoy LaFramboise Island in Pierre. The island on the Missouri was referred to by Lewis and Clark as "Bad Humor" because of their tense encounter nearby with the Teton Sioux. It is named for Joseph LaFramboise, a Frenchman who had a trading post west of the island at the mouth of the Bad River.

JOHN FRONT

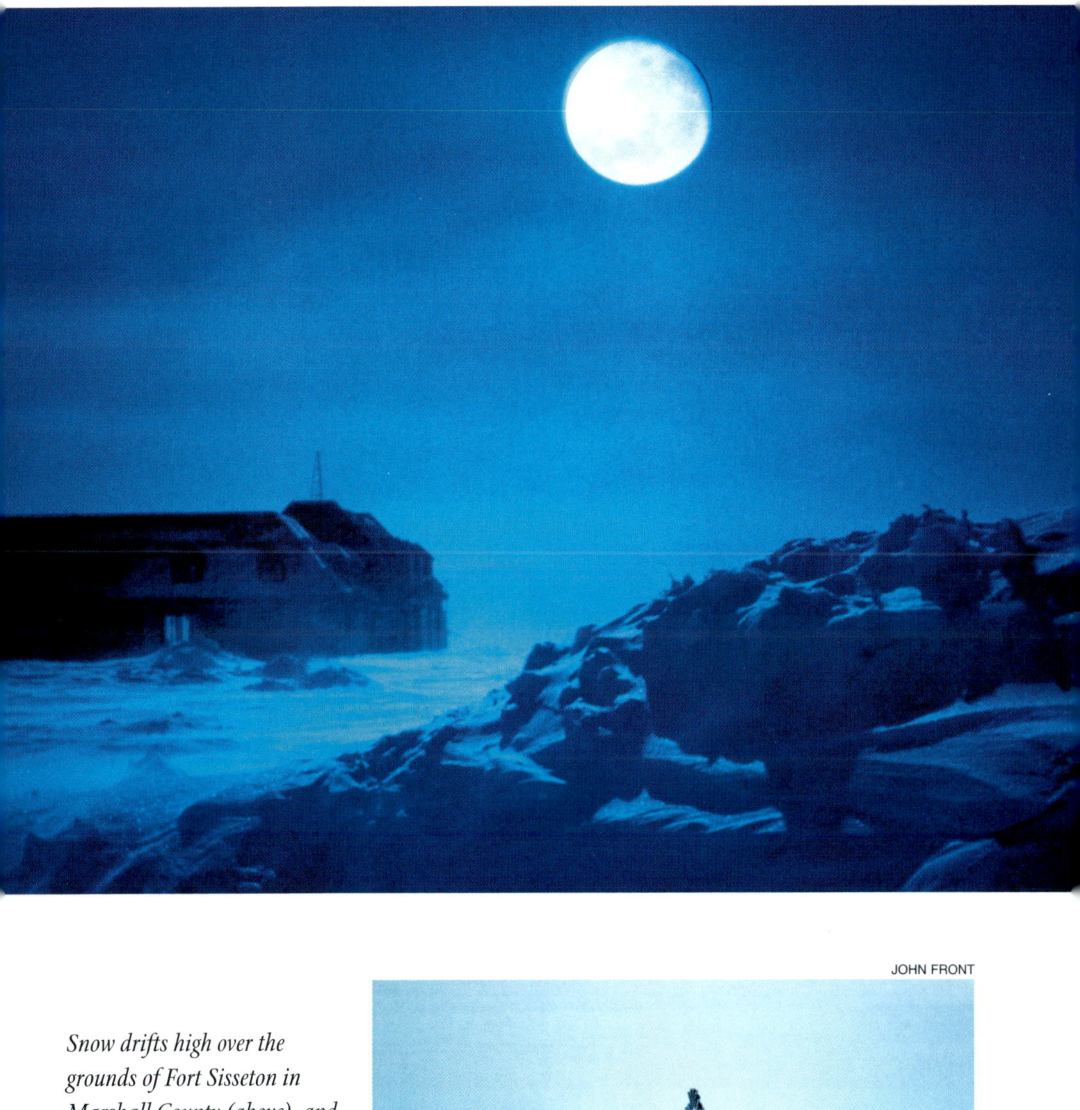

JOHN FRONT

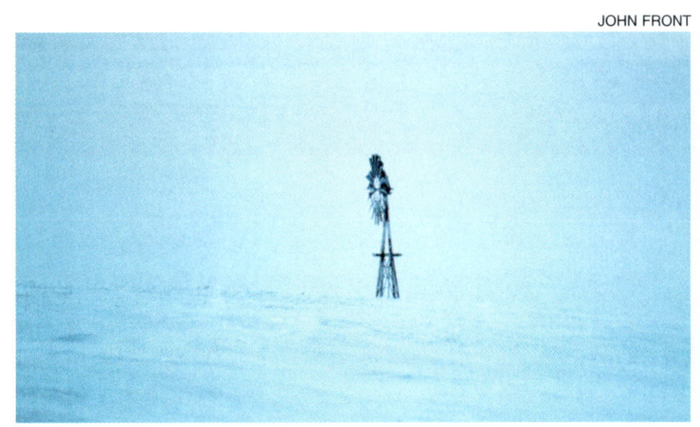

Snow drifts high over the grounds of Fort Sisseton in Marshall County (above), and it strands a windmill in a sea of white.

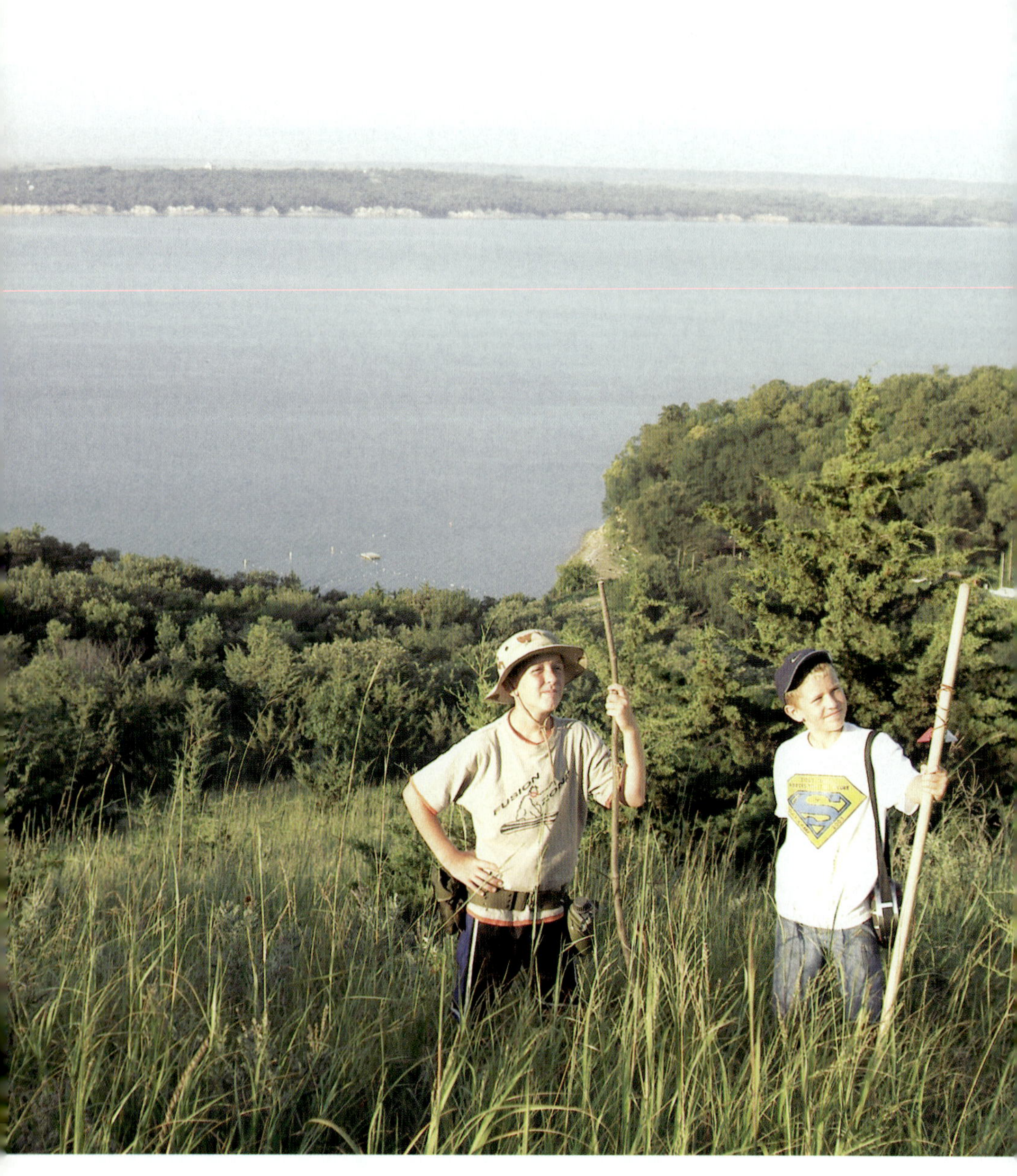

Famed explorers Lewis and Clark were not the first to explore the Missouri River valley, and they were not the last. The river attracts adventure seekers, like these boy scouts at camp on Lewis and Clark Lake. The bicentennial of the 1804-1806 expedition prompted older "boys" to build replicas of 19th century keel boats (opposite page).

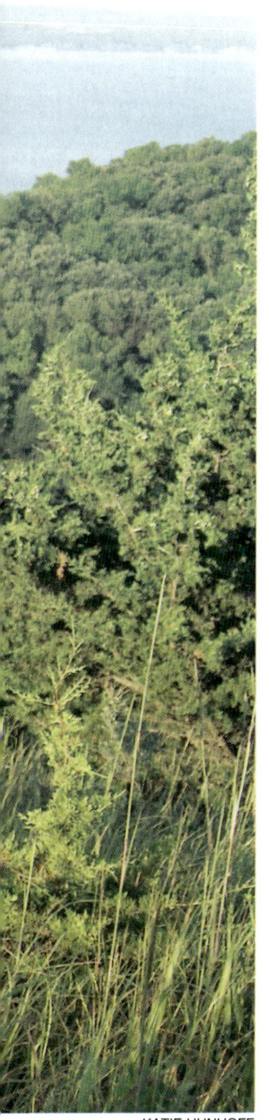
KATIE HUNHOFF

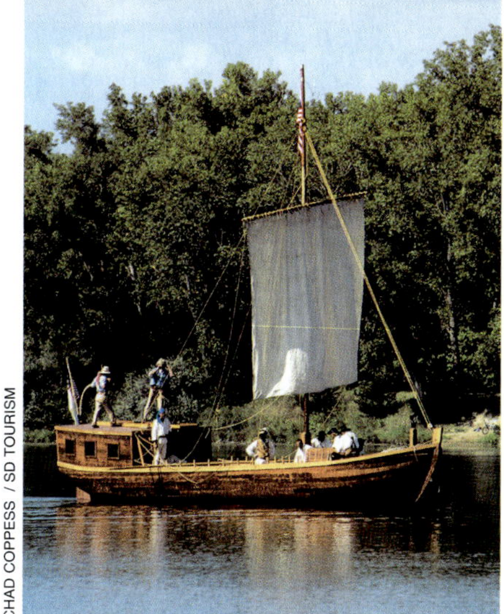
CHAD COPPESS / SD TOURISM

Our Mighty Missouri

SHE UNITES AND DIVIDES US

By Roger Holtzmann

The Missouri River has cachet — if we dare use such a word in South Dakota. Homes within sight of the river bring more money. Golf courses seem more fun when the river forms a natural hazard. Hunting lodges and hotels get higher rates when they are within shotgun range. Even farmland is now thought of as more valuable when it's near the Missouri.

The river has economic, agricultural, recreational and social implications for all South Dakotans. It unites us because it splits the middle, like a main road in a town that everyone recognizes as common ground. It divides us because of political issues and the geo-social differences that have sprung up between East River and West River. Because of its importance, the Missouri has become part of our soul, our history, our everyday lives, and it has always been so.

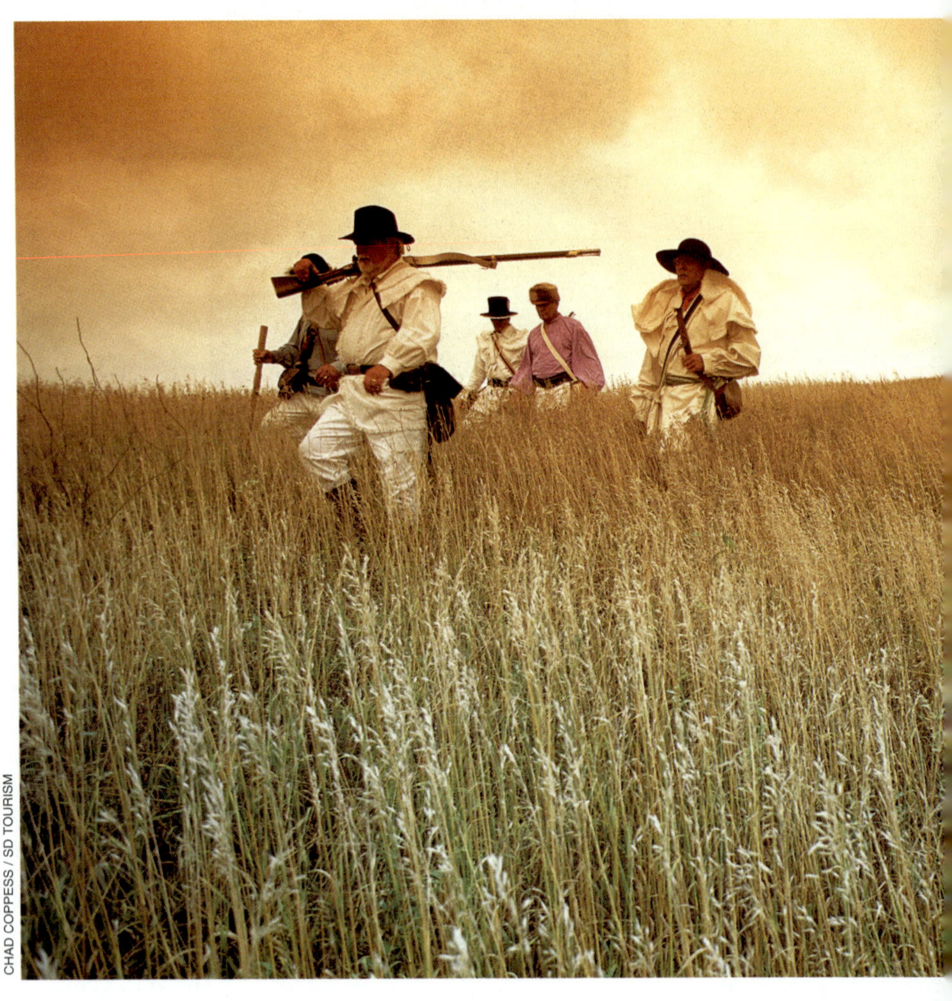
CHAD COPPESS / SD TOURISM

Man has doubtless lived along the Missouri since he first came to this region, but the first we can trace definitively are the Arikara. Their connection was forged by the heat of a searing summer sun. When decades of drought turned lesser streams to dust in their ancestral home on the southern plains, the Arikara migrated northward, always clinging to the river, a life-giving oasis. They arrived in what is now South Dakota just as Columbus appeared on these shores, and by the time of their first contact with Europeans they were living along the Missouri from Big Bend to the mouth of the Cheyenne River.

Though they ventured as far as the Black Hills to hunt, the Arikara always returned to their river home, an environment that provided

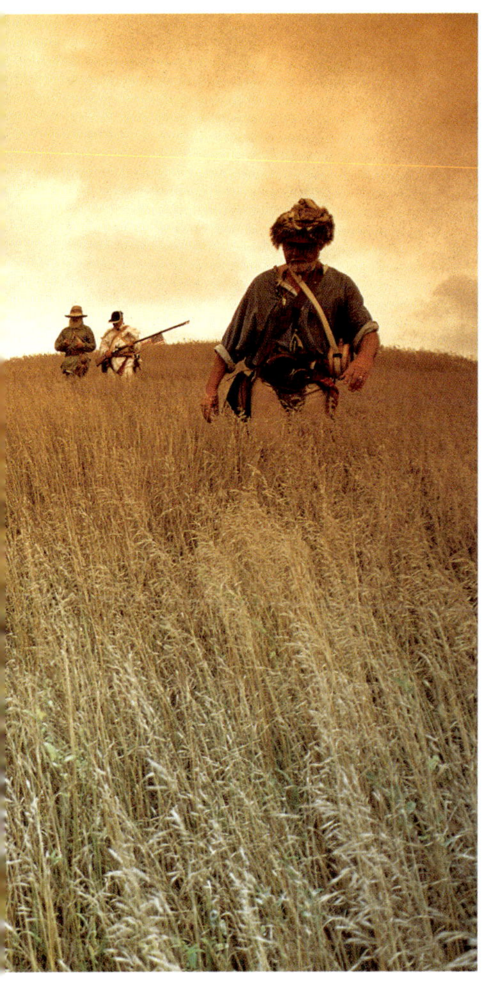

Reenactors commemorated people and places from the Lewis and Clark expedition, such as Spirit Mound near Vermillion (left) and the experiences of York, a black slave who made the journey (below).

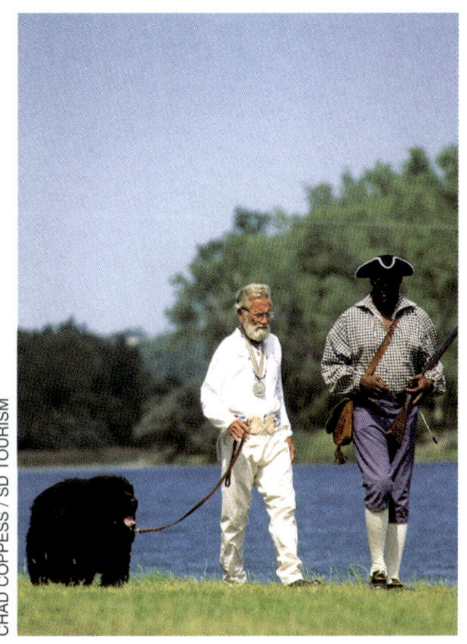

CHAD COPPESS / SD TOURISM

life's necessities. From the Missouri's depths came bass, paddlefish and catfish; her banks yielded clams and mussels. There was timber in the valley for building and fuel. Chokecherries, wild grapes and all manner of useful plants grew in profusion. Game was drawn to the river and its many tributary streams, as were men. Nature's bounty was supplemented by the Arikara's industry. They raised corn, beans, squash and pumpkins in terraced fields, and made pottery from clay mined at the river's edge.

The Arikara lived in fortified villages situated above the flood line and tucked into the valley's scalloped ravines for shelter from winter winds, but their palisades were of no use against what proved to be the most devastating enemy of all. Their presence in settlements beside the river

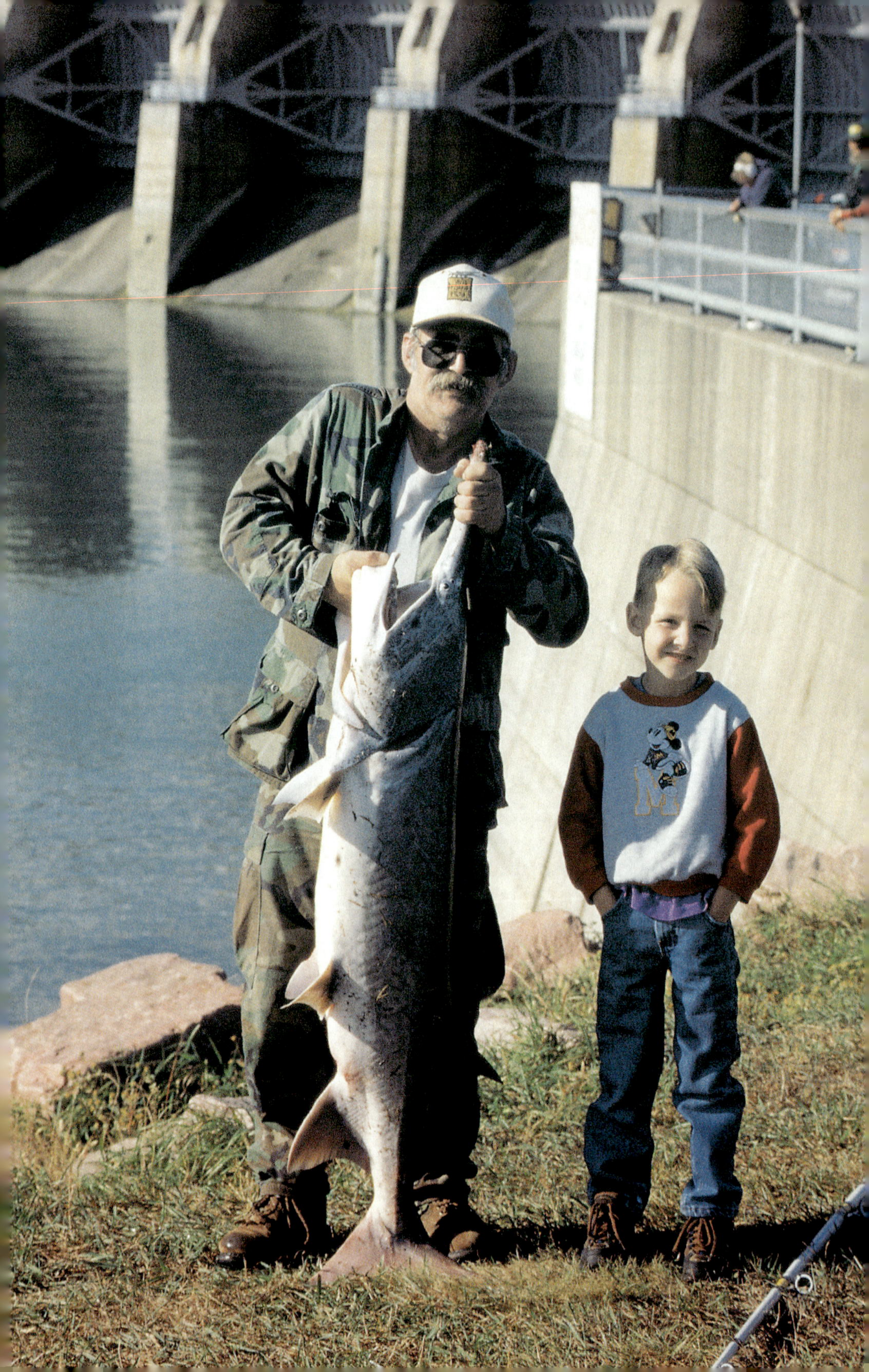

SD TOURISM

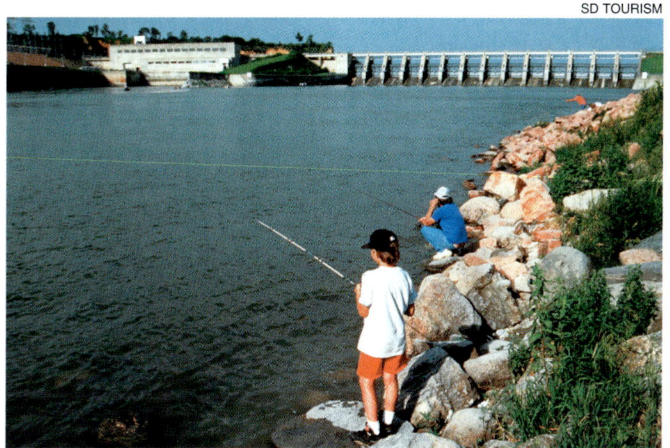

Gavins Point Dam's tailwaters attract fish and fishermen. In October, anglers snag paddlefish (opposite page) that can grow to 100 pounds. The species co-existed with dinosaurs 75 million years ago and adapted with time.

exposed them to white traders, and white diseases, long before nomadic tribes like the Oglala. A ruinous smallpox epidemic occurred in 1780-81, one of several outbreaks that brought them to ruin. At the height of their prosperity, in the late 17th Century, the Arikara counted 4,000 warriors among 32 villages; by the time of Lewis and Clark they were huddled in three villages near the Grand River, vulnerable to the much stronger Lakota. Soon they could not even maintain an independent existence. Diminished by warfare and disease, they were forced to combine with the Mandan during the 1830s. Thus did the tribe pass into history.

Like the Arikara before them, whites followed the Missouri into this country. Lewis and Clark were not the first, but they were the best-funded and most prominent. They were sent by President Thomas Jefferson to find a water route to the Pacific Ocean. But the inquisitive Jefferson also assigned them a long list of scientific tasks, asking for documentation of the land, wildlife, native peoples, vegetation, climate and commerce.

They began their 7,000-mile trip in May of 1804 and returned to St. Louis in September of 1806. In their months on the Missouri, they experienced one of the greatest adventures in American history. Two hundred years later, tens of thousands of Americans try to retrace the route by cars, busses, motorboats, and bikes.

Of course, there's no shame in following another's footsteps. Lewis and

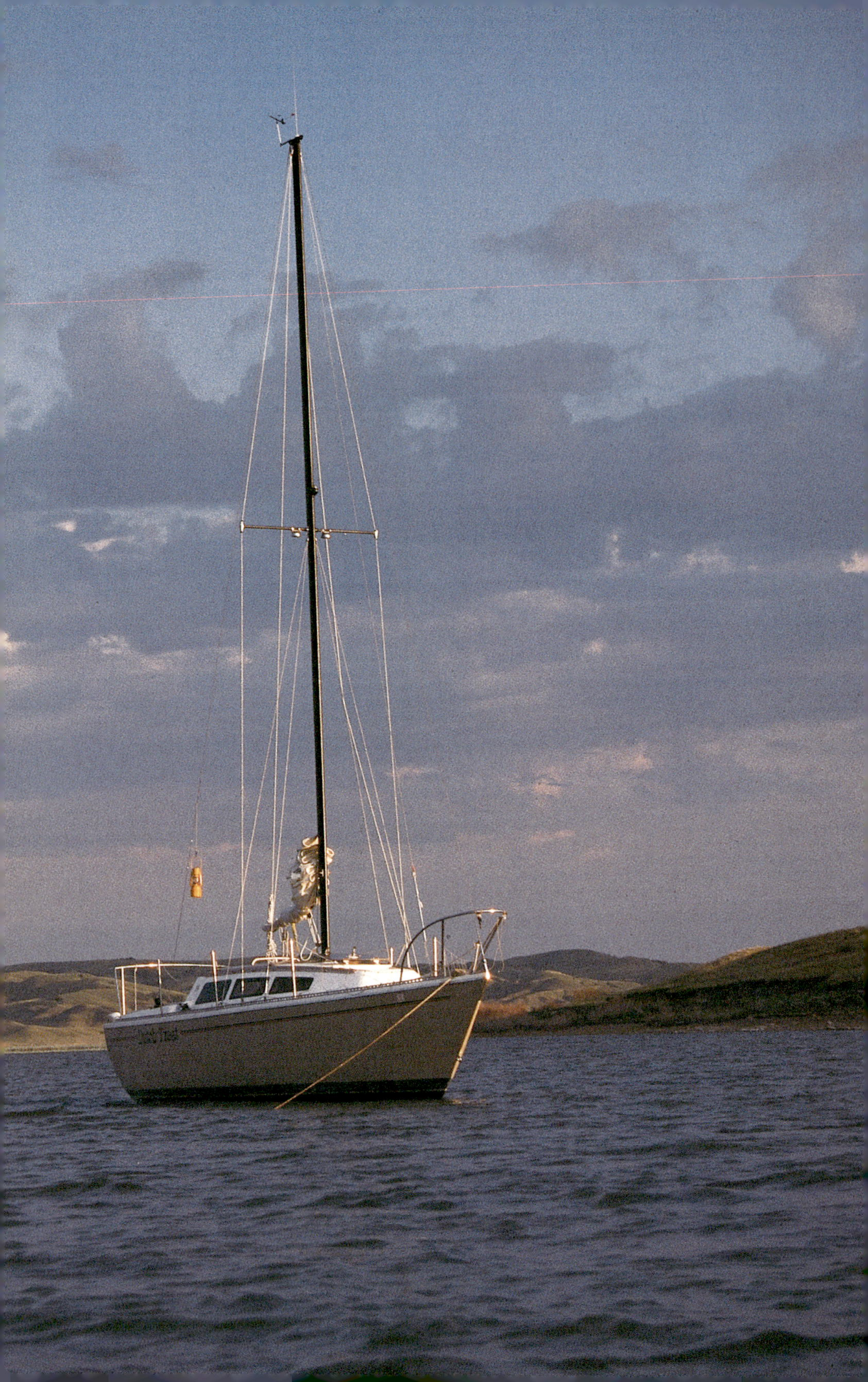

Lake Francis Case's 80 miles of navigable water between Pickstown and Chamberlain has spawned a small sailboating community at Dock 44, west of Platte.

Clark did the same. Fur traders were well ahead of them, drawn by the region's beaver, mink, muskrat and buffalo. This commerce was limited initially by the amount of cargo men could muscle upriver in keel boats, but in 1831 a new era dawned. The stern-wheeler Yellowstone departed St. Louis laden with trade goods, bound for Fort Tecumseh, near the mouth of the Bad River. After a brief layover it returned, loaded with pelts and 10,000 pounds of buffalo tongues – the last a newly-fashionable taste sensation back east, the satisfaction of which left thousands of buffalo carcasses rotting on the prairie, unused but for their tongues.

When the Yellowstone returned the following season, it carried Pierre Choteau Jr., scion of a family that made a fortune in the western fur trade. Fort Pierre, at the confluence of the Bad and Missouri rivers, was named in his honor. During the following decade it developed into one of the most important posts in the West, shipping tens of thousands of pelts every year, but even this bountiful region could not sustain such a pace indefinitely. Before another 10 years went by the fur trade was past its peak, and another new day arrived along the river.

In 1858 the Yankton tribe was prevailed upon to cede a huge tract of land in what is now eastern South Dakota. Thousands of land-hungry whites flooded into the area at the earliest possible moment, and town sites were established along the Missouri at Bon Homme, Vermillion and Yankton. Of these three, the last proved most adept at political maneuvering. When Dakota Territory was organized three years later, Yankton was designated the territorial capital – a grand title indeed for the mud-street, log and clapboard town.

Until the railroad's arrival in the 1870s, steamboats on the Missouri continued to be the easiest way into and out of Dakota Territory. Yankton's position as the busiest port on the river contributed greatly to its growth and prosperity, but what the river gave, it could also take away. The winter of 1880-81 was the

TOM DEMPSTER

SD TOURISM

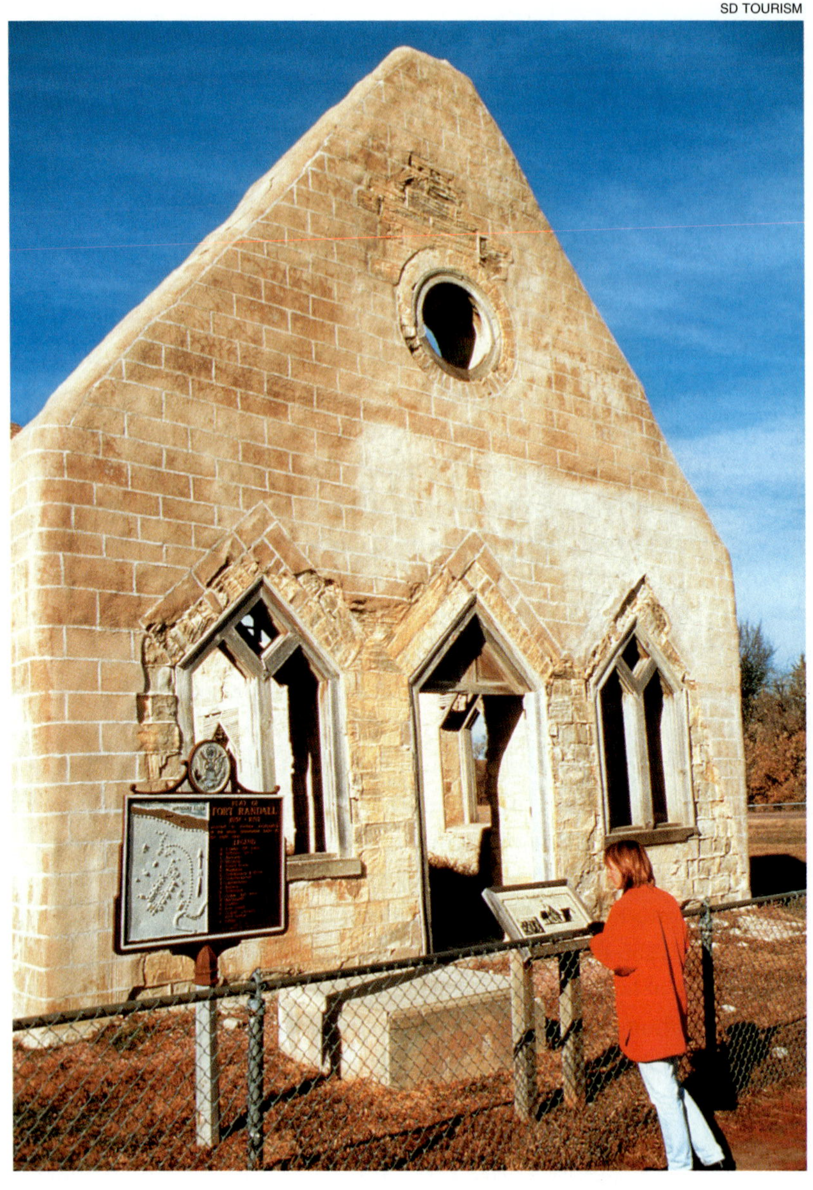

Built of native chalkstone in 1875 by cavalry and homesteaders, the chapel at Fort Randall on the Missouri was abandoned a scant 17 years later. Visitors to the nearby dam still visit the chapel and the post cemetery (opposite page).

worst anyone in Dakota Territory could remember. Blizzard followed blizzard for months on end, and when the accumulated snow began to melt, there was hell to pay. A fearful ice jam built up from Yankton to Springfield, a distance of 30 miles. When it broke loose, the city's proud fleet of riverboats, pulled up on shore for the winter, was reduced to driftwood in a matter of hours. They were never rebuilt.

Some of the boats still lie beneath the water. The wood skeleton of the *Western* sometimes shows up when the river is low by Yankton. Altogether, about 30 such ships are buried between Yankton and Omaha. They were not primitive, over-size rafts, but finely built ships that measured over 200 feet in length and carried hundreds of tons of cargo. According to local legend, the *North Alabama* sank near Vermillion with treasure of some sort.

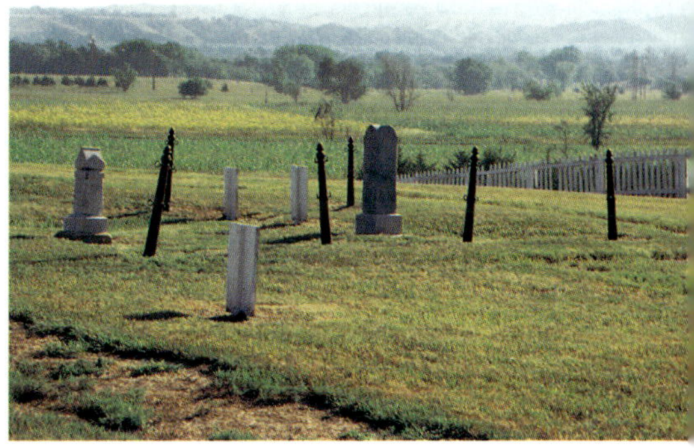

Ironically, once it was no longer a vital avenue of transportation, the river was seen as an impediment to travel. The Missouri could only be crossed by ferry boats, on rickety pontoon bridges, or if it was the right time of year and you were stout-hearted, on the ice. With some justification, it could be argued that the river divided South Dakota into two states, East River and West River. What in later years became a punch line for jokes and fodder for sociological study had a basis in fact.

Permanent spans across the river weren't completed until 1907, at Chamberlain and Pierre, and they carried rail traffic only. Nearly two decades would pass before an automobile bridge was built at Yankton, but even then, it connected that city to Nebraska. Knitting the eastern and western halves of South Dakota together had to wait until Peter Norbeck arrived on the scene. Governor Norbeck, one of the most dynamic leaders in state history, claimed he could build five bridges across the Missouri for $2.1 million. His detractors scoffed and said he couldn't even finish one for that amount. John Kirkham, a five-foot-two-inch bundle of energy, was the engineer Norbeck called upon to make good his boast.

TOM DEMPSTER

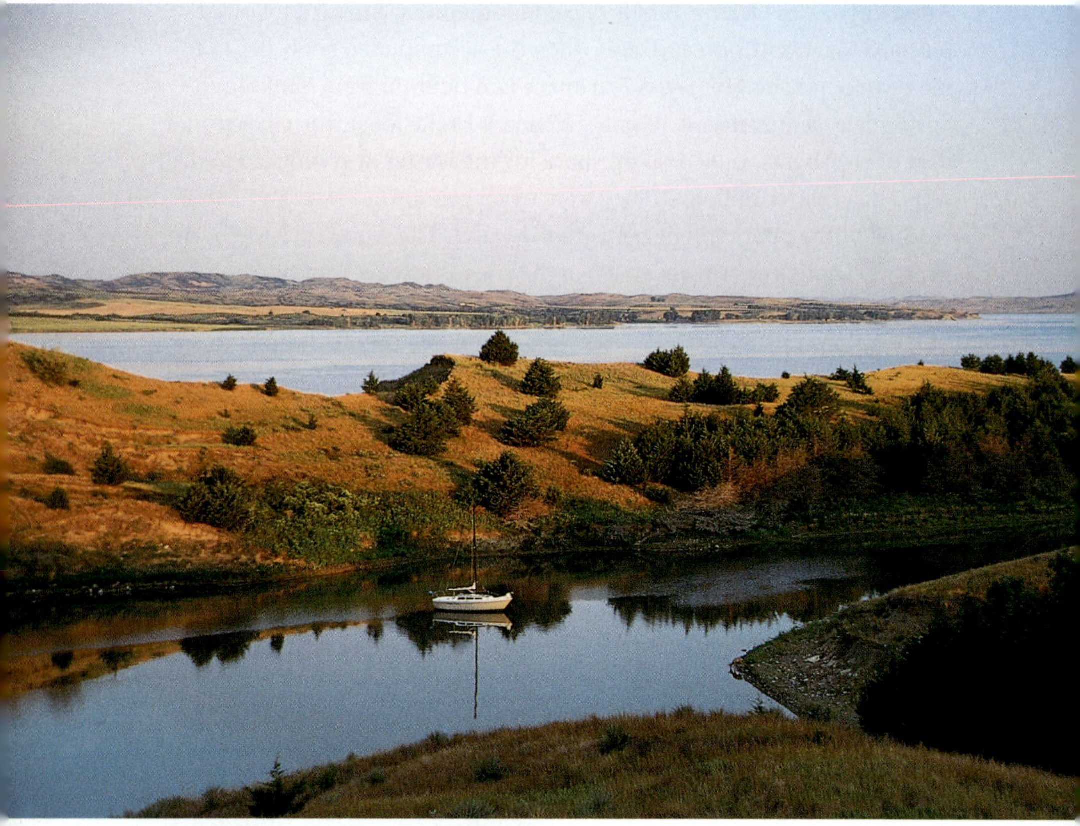

SD TOURISM

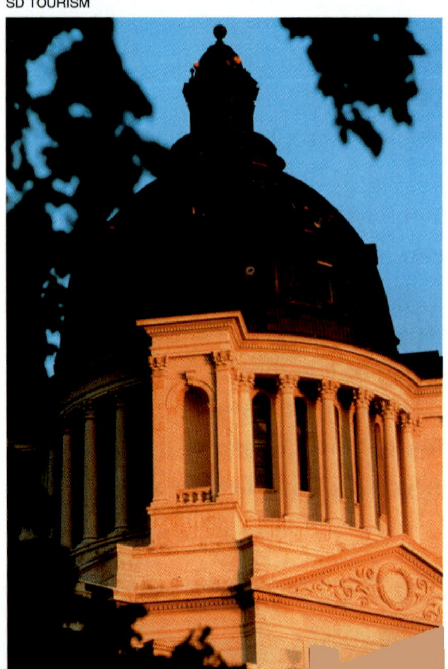

The damming of the Missouri in the 1940s and 1950s created countless bays and inlets. Boaters have their favorites, and seldom have to share. The Missouri stretches 2,341 miles across America's heartland and through many cities, including South Dakota's capital, Pierre (left).

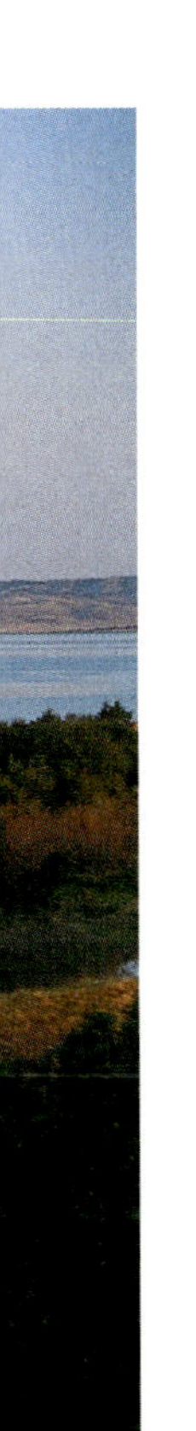

To call Kirkham eccentric would be a considerable understatement: he routinely wore a gun belt and twin six-shooters to work, and strutted around job sites barking orders like a drill sergeant. Whatever his quirks, John Kirkham delivered the goods. South Dakota got five solidly-built highway bridges — at Mobridge, Forest City, Pierre, Chamberlain and Wheeler — for just a hair over Norbeck's estimate. Though the river was bridged and its banks well-settled, nothing about the Missouri had changed much. It behaved as it had for millennia, devouring islands and banks without apology, and occasionally flooding the valley from bluff to bluff. What had changed was the attitude of those who lived on the Missouri's shores. These were not the Arikara, who placed their villages above the flood line and were content to deal with the river on its terms. The new Americans planted farms and cities in the path of those waters, and when they were inundated, resolved to mold the river in ways more to their liking.

Lt. Gen. Lewis A. Pick, of the Army Corps of Engineers, wanted to control the Missouri's floods and provide for navigation downstream. W.G. Sloan, of the Bureau of Reclamation, saw water to irrigate the arid West and untapped hydroelectric potential when he looked at the river. Their visions came together as the Flood Control Act of 1944, whose key components in South Dakota were four massive, earth-filled dams: Oahe, Big Bend, Fort Randall and Gavins Point.

Pick-Sloan ended floods along the Missouri in South Dakota, and diminished their severity downstream, saving lives and billions of dollars in property damage. Each year the dams generate millions of kilowatts of clean electric power for an energy-hungry nation. Though the irrigation promises of Pick-Sloan have been mostly unfulfilled, recreational opportunities on the reservoirs, almost an afterthought in 1944, have proven an important draw for the state's tourism industry.

In exchange, the untamed, bountiful stream that drew the Arikara into this country — the river that carried trappers and soldiers and settlers — now lies beneath the placid waters of South Dakota's great lakes. Yet the Missouri lives on, part of our daily lives and part of South Dakota's very soul. It will always be so.

Roger Holtzmann has been a writer and contributing editor at South Dakota Magazine *since 1990.*

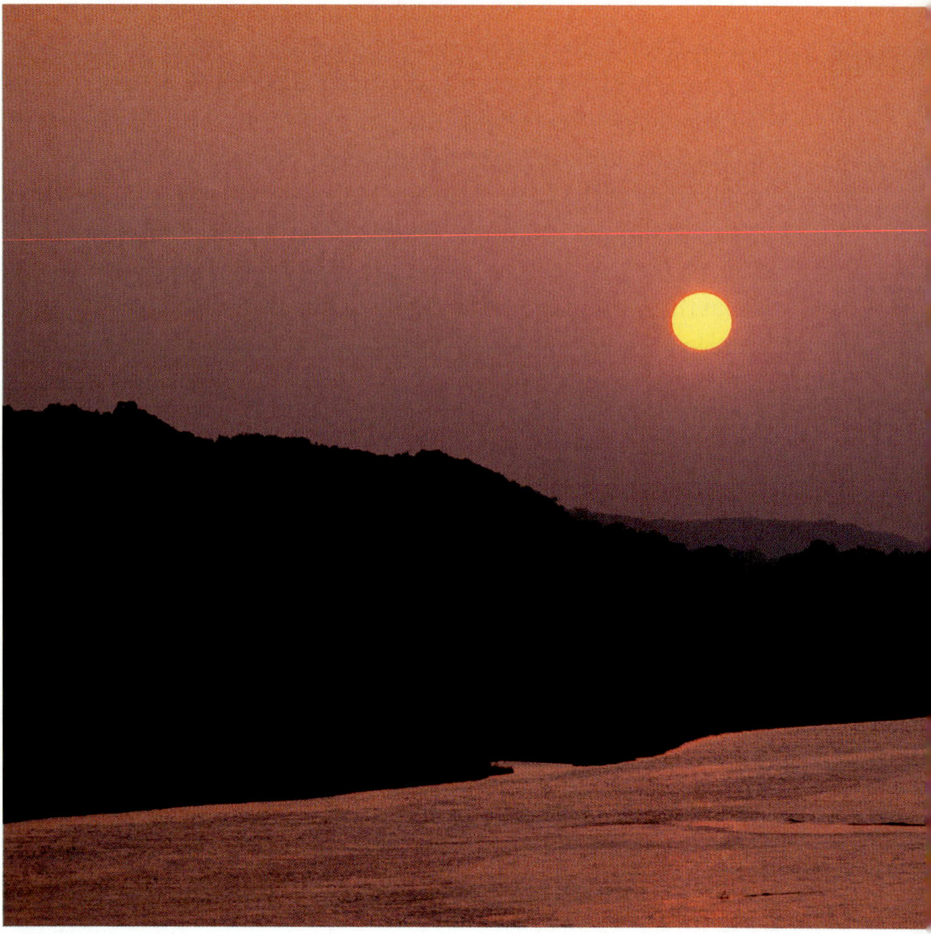

Boat ownership in South Dakota boomed upon completion of the four "great lakes" on the Missouri — Lewis and Clark, Francis Case, Sharpe and Oahe. Together, they meander for 443 miles and have 566,000 surface acres of water. Below the dams, Mulberry Bend (above) near Vermillion is in the middle of the last natural stretch of the Missouri River. Hobie Cat Beach and Lewis and Clark Marina provide docks for sailors (bottom photos), while huge Lake Oahe (top right) is a favorite of walleye fishermen.

PAT HANSEN

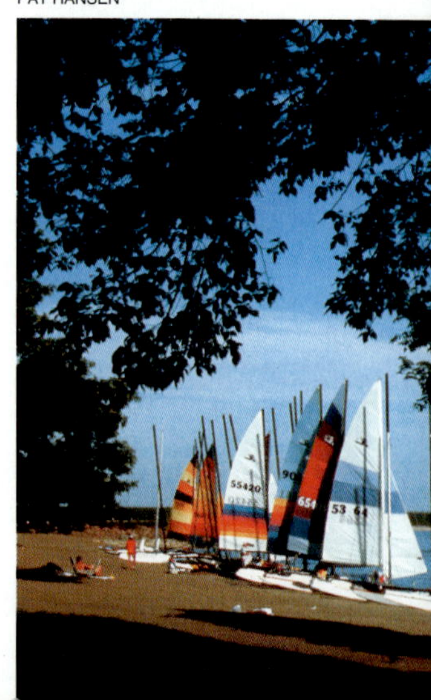

JIM PETERSON

CHUCK POST

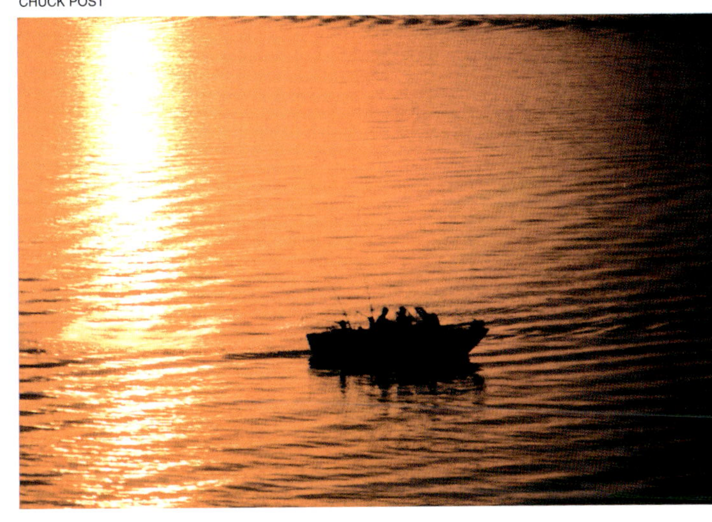

BERNIE HUNHOFF

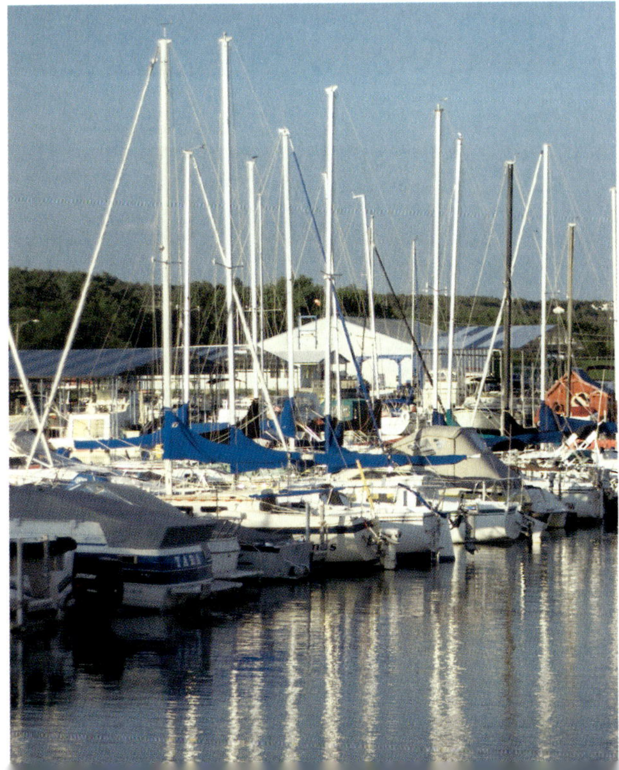

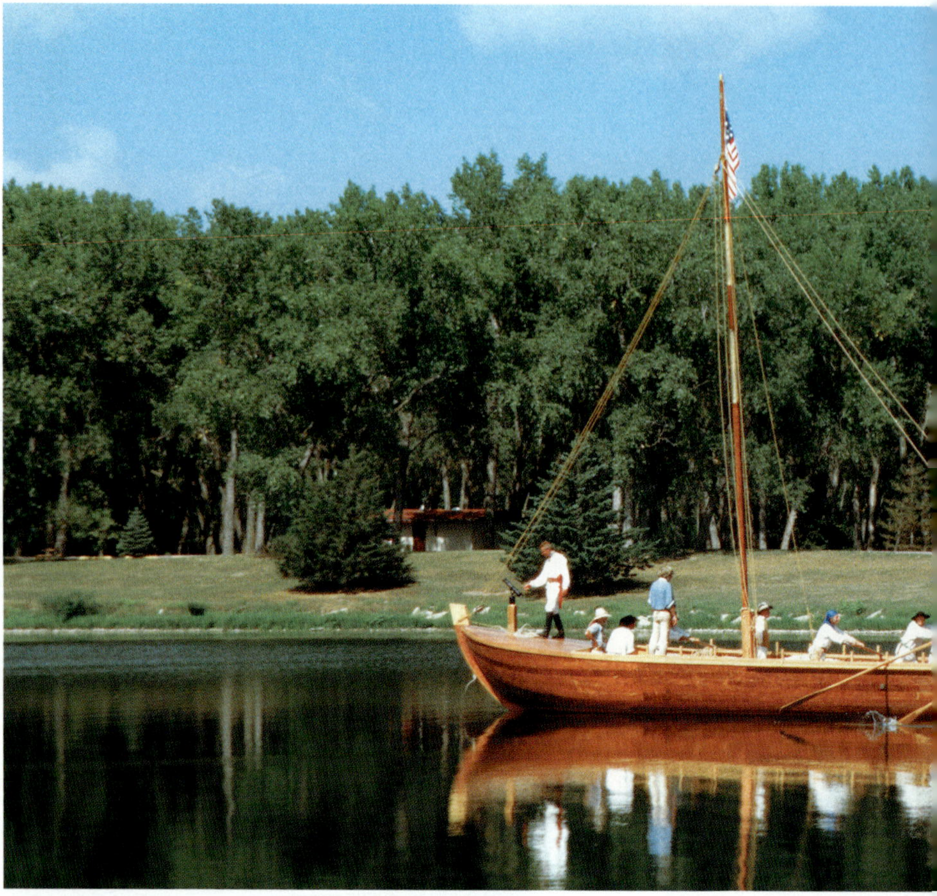

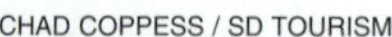

CHAD COPPESS / SD TOURISM

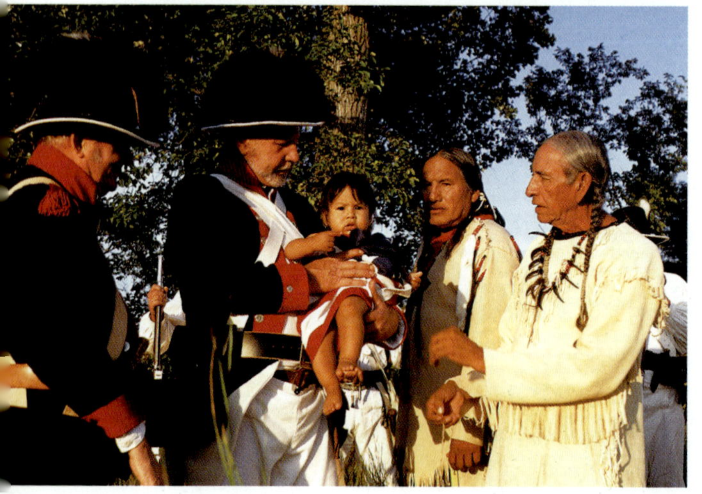

Reenactments have become common summer entertainment in river cities like Yankton, Fort Pierre, Chamberlain and Mobridge — thanks to a resurgence of interest in Lewis and Clark's journey, which was called the Corps of Discovery.

BERNIE HUNHOFF

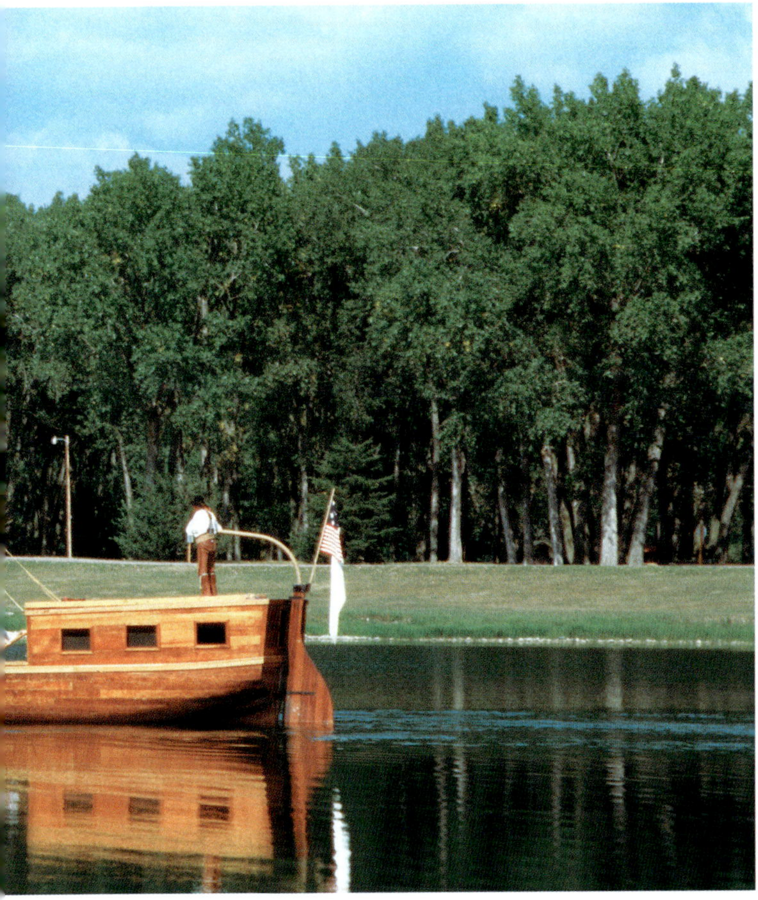

CHAD COPPESS / SD TOURISM

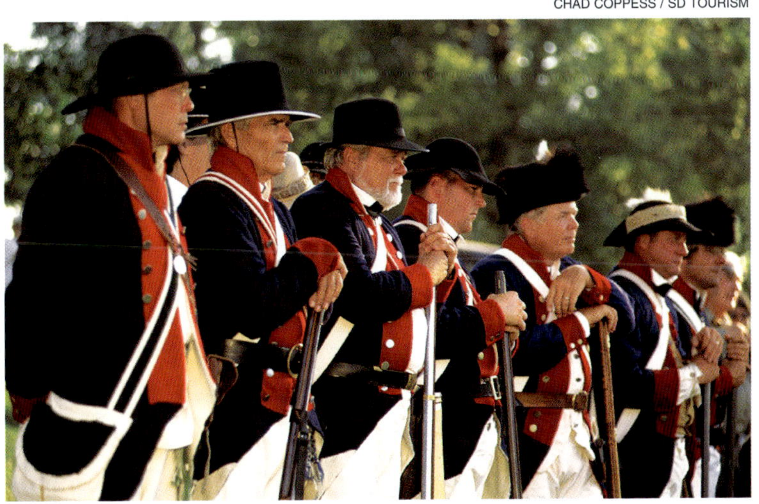

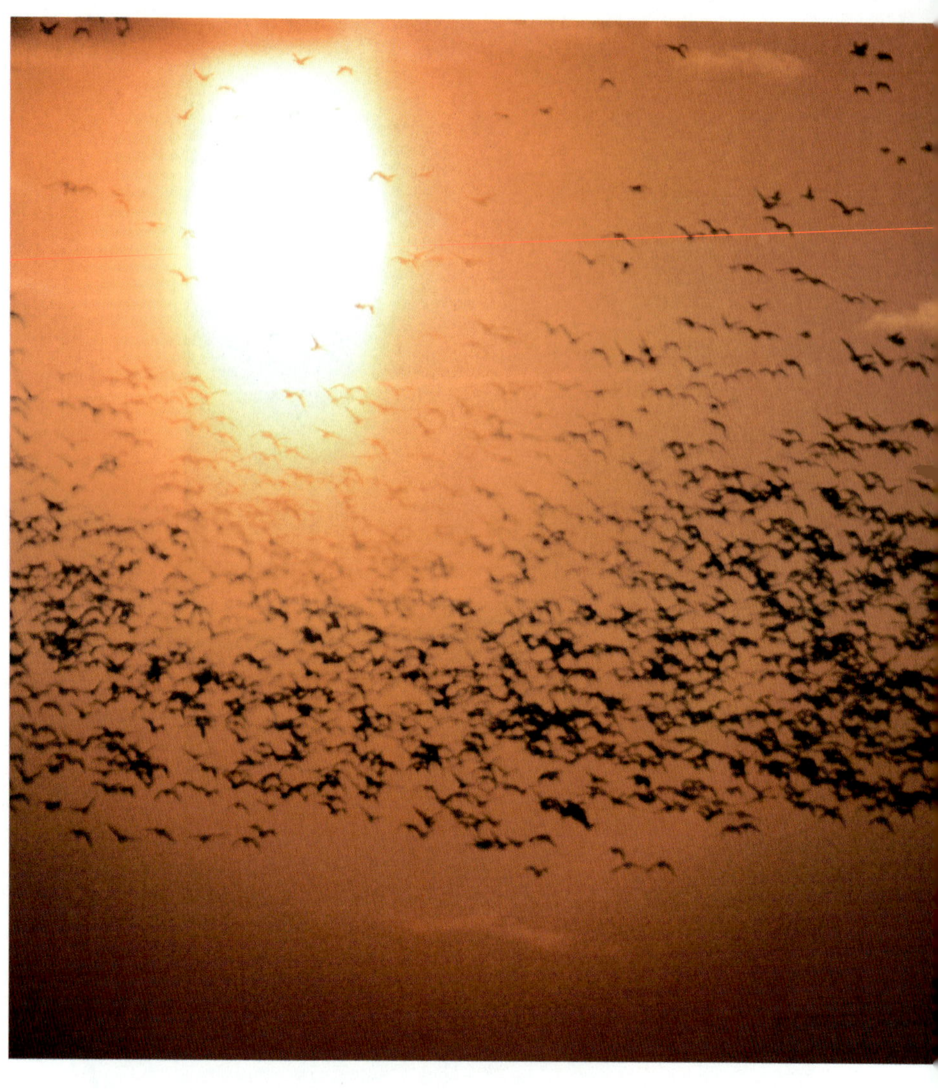

Five of South Dakota's nine Indian reservations abut the Missouri River, and many Native Americans have mixed feelings about celebrating the arrival of Lewis and Clark — an event that hastened white settlement. Some prefer to call the bi-centennial an observance rather than a celebration. Two hundred years ago, the explorers and Indians exchanged kindnesses and hostilities, generosities and diseases.

SD TOURISM

SD TOURISM

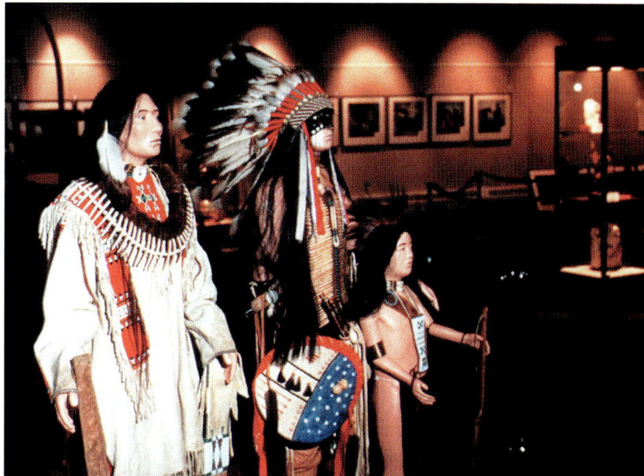

SD TOURISM

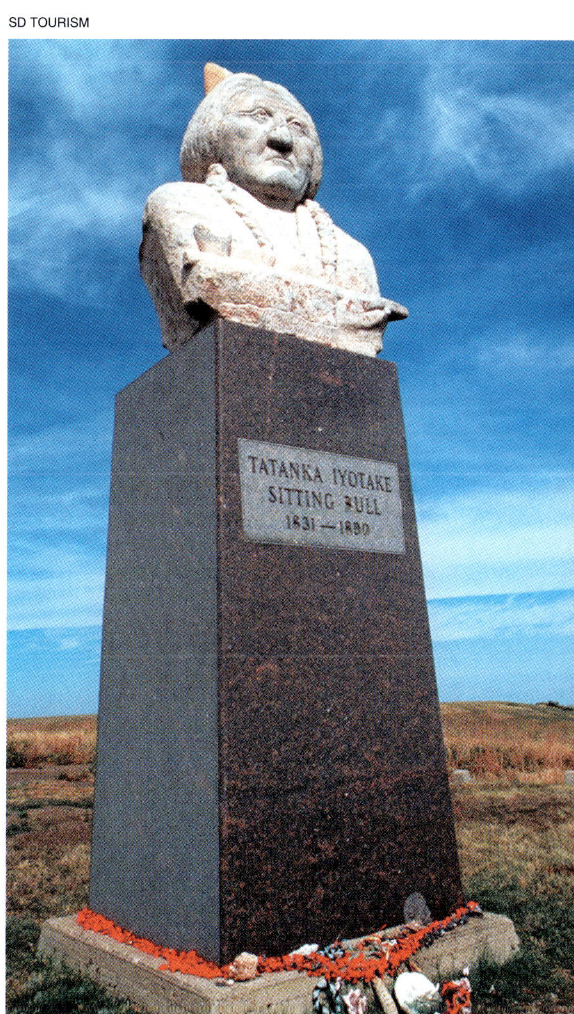

Native American heritage is exhibited at the state's Cultural Heritage Center (top) in Pierre. Sitting Bull, a powerful Sioux leader, is buried and memorialized on a hill overlooking the Missouri, west of Mobridge.

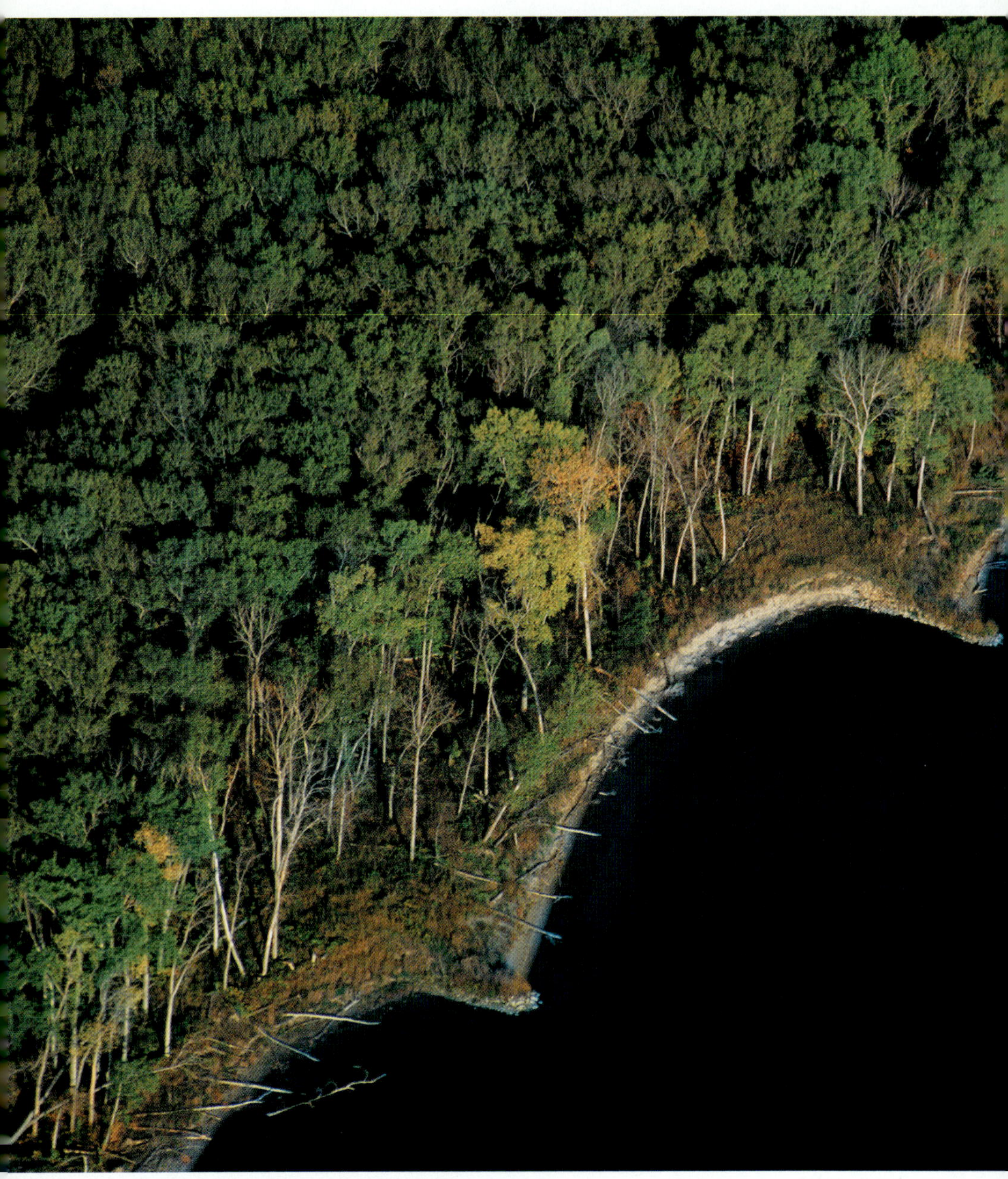

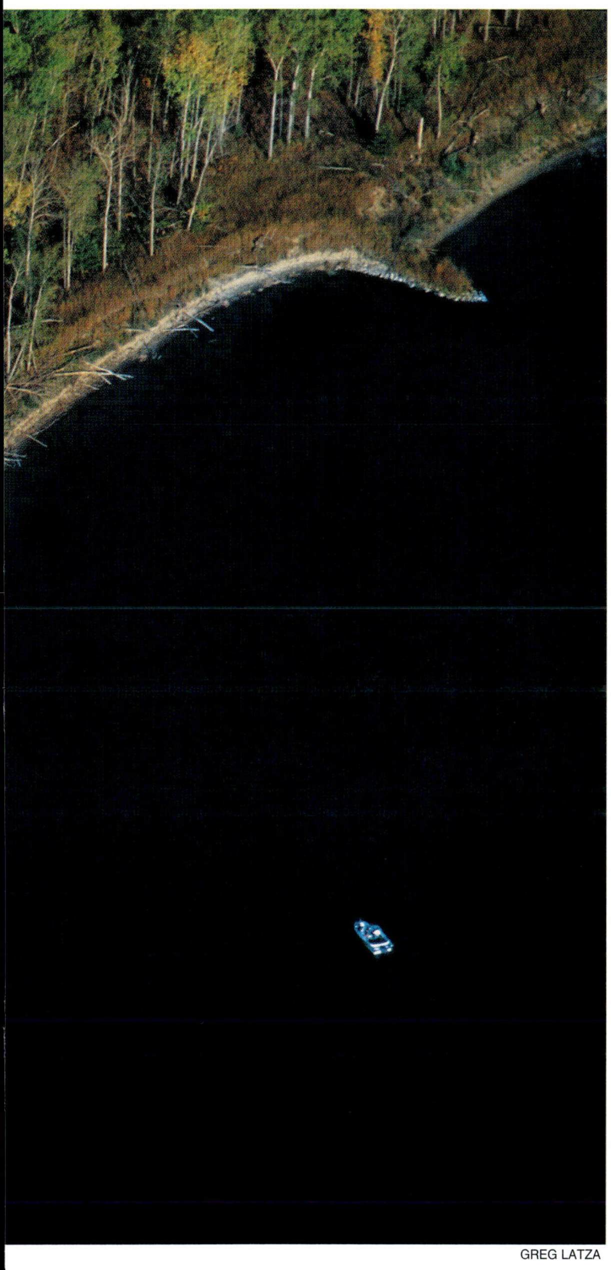

GREG LATZA

Erosion has always been a problem along the Missouri, which is prone to spring flooding. The problem is exacerbated downstream from the dams, because heavy releases of clean, fast-moving water eat at tree-covered shores. The cottonwood forest at the Karl Mundt National Wildlife Refuge below Fort Randall Dam at Pickstown is protected by an "armored" shore.

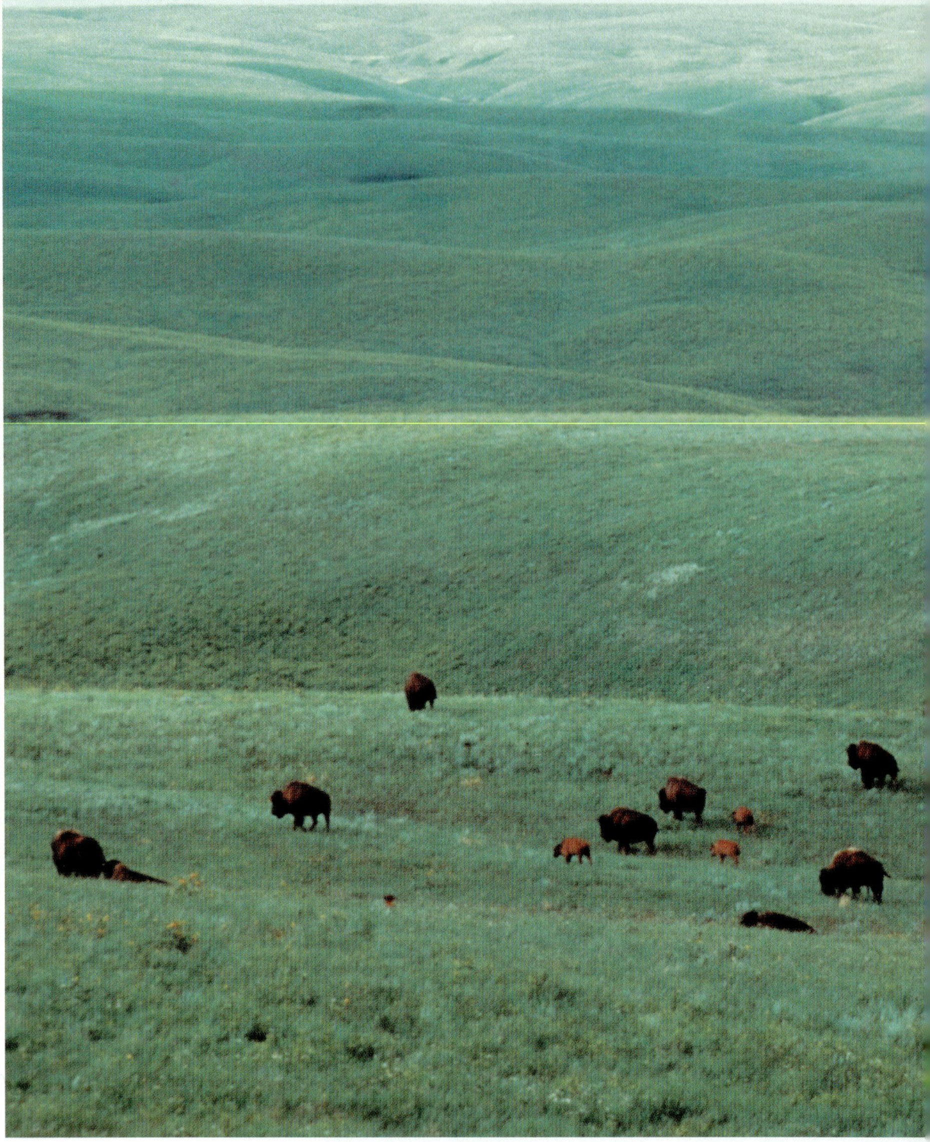

SD TO

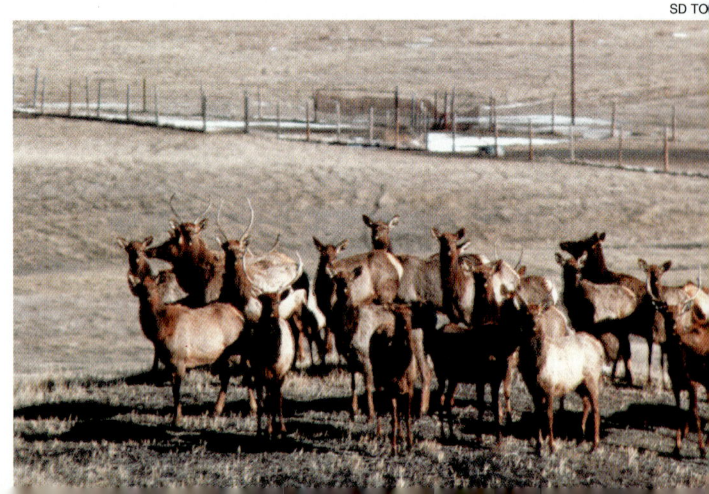

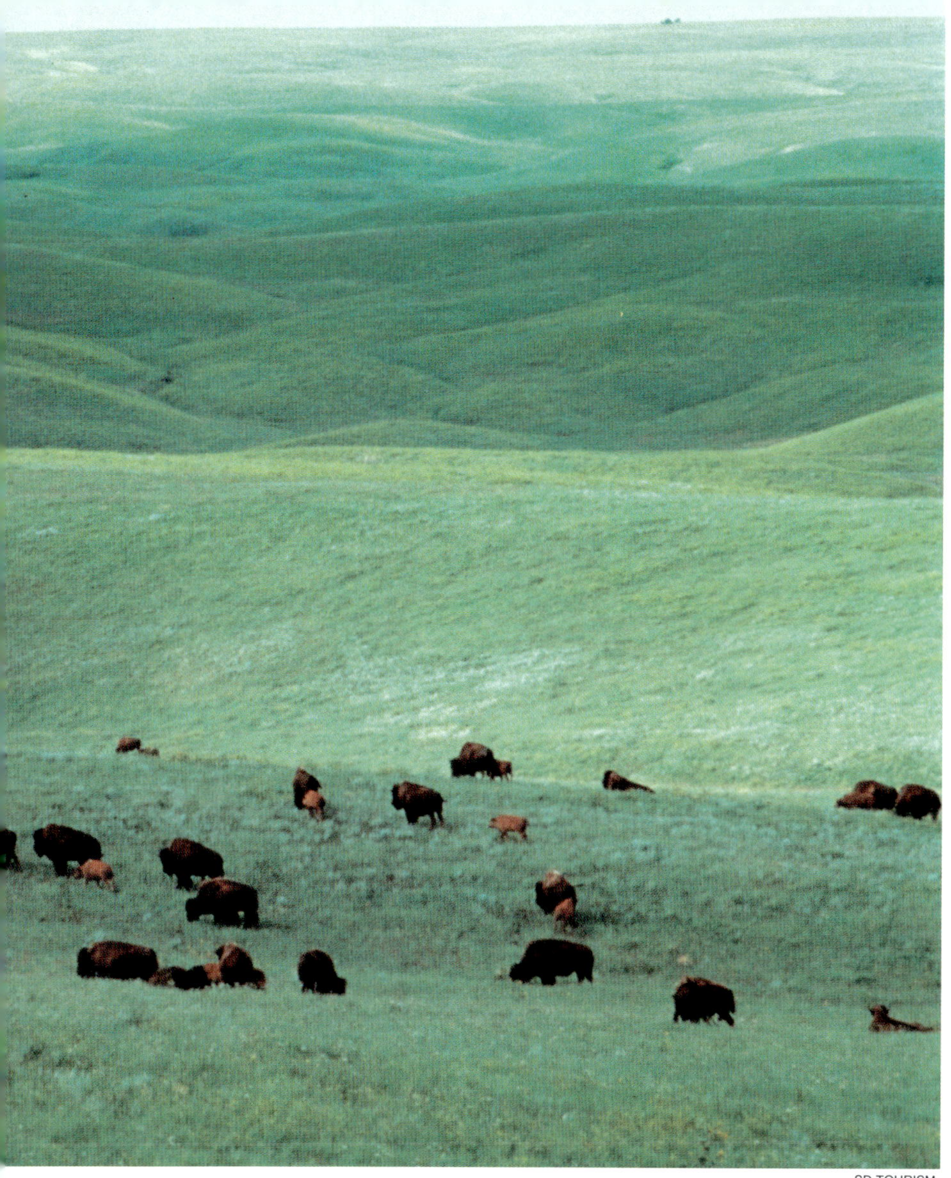

SD TOURISM

Elk and buffalo — once common to the Missouri valley — are returning, thanks in no small part to Indian reservations and private ranches. An elk herd roams the Lower Brule reservation north of Chamberlain (left). A big buffalo herd (above) grazes the hills east of Eagle Butte on the Cheyenne River Reservation, just west of the Missouri River.

SD TOURISM

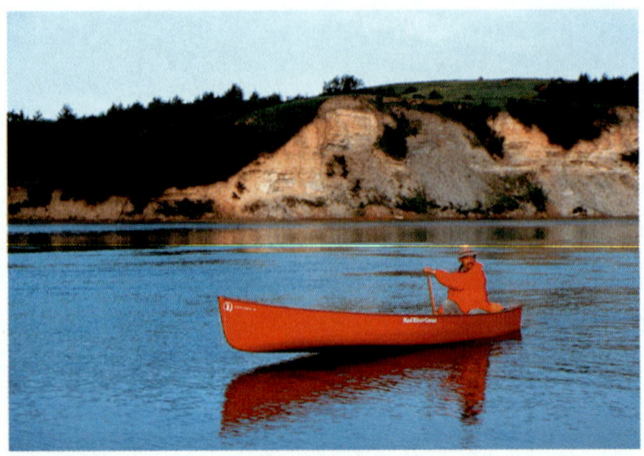

Paddling has become an increasingly popular way of traversing the Missouri. Outfitters are located in many cities. Stone Outdoor Adventures in Yankton (opposite page, bottom) provides river outings in a 29-foot canoe patterned after birch bark boats used by fur traders for 300 years. But most "river rats" use standard canoes and kayaks. The best part of canoeing the Missouri? Long expanses of water and prairie without people. The worst part? Long expanses of water and prairie without amenities.

JERRY WILSON

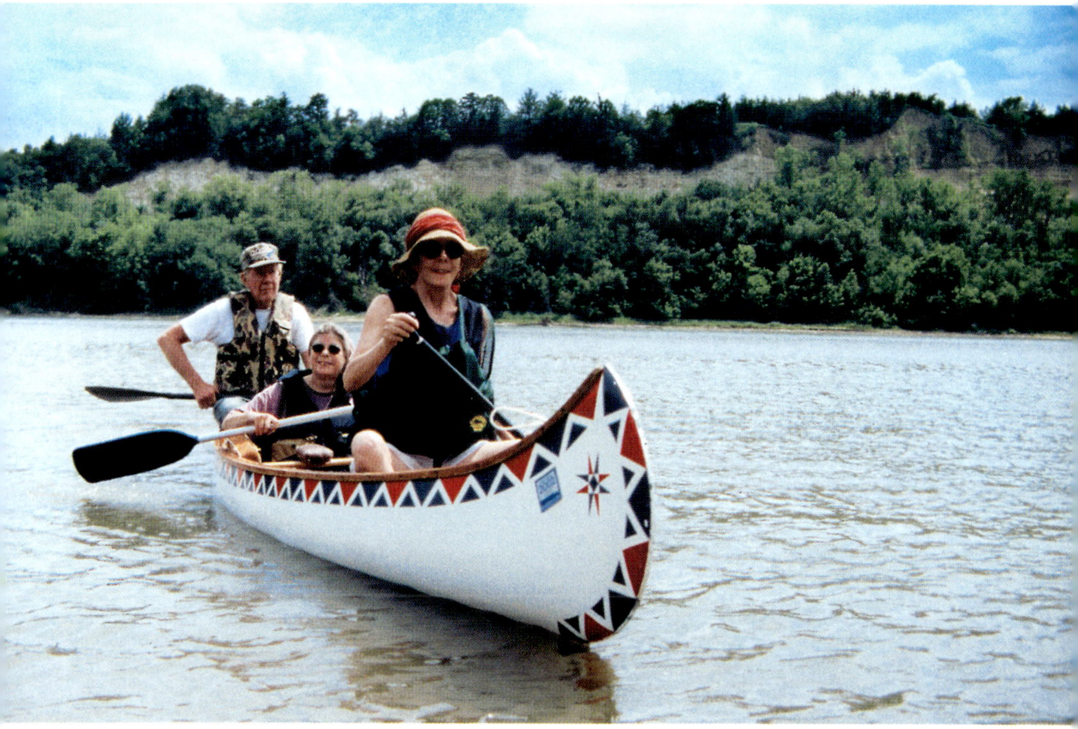

BERNIE HUNHOFF

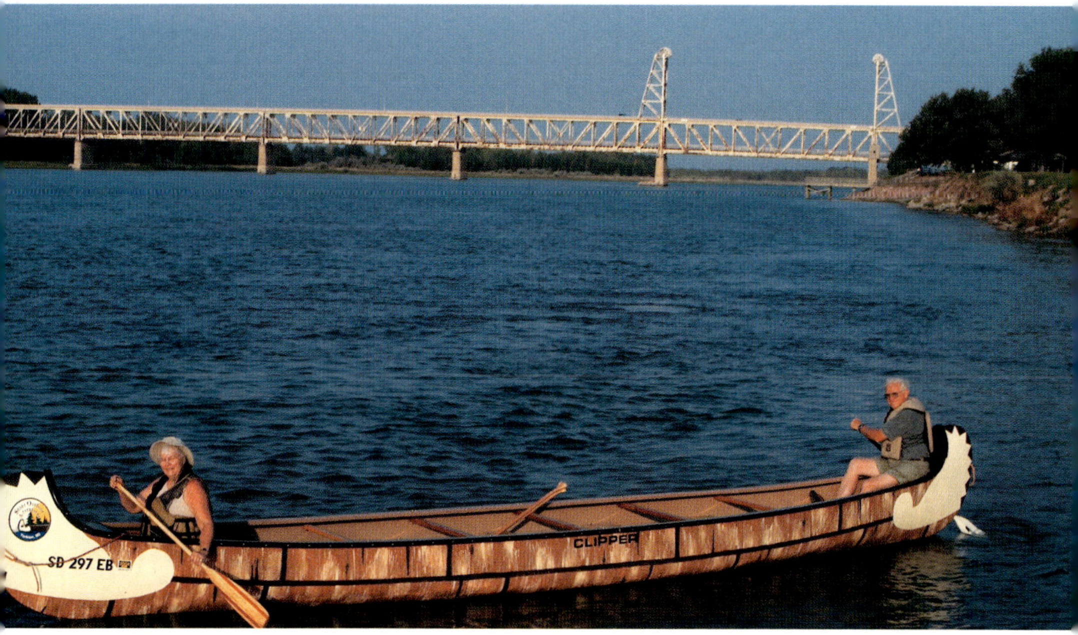

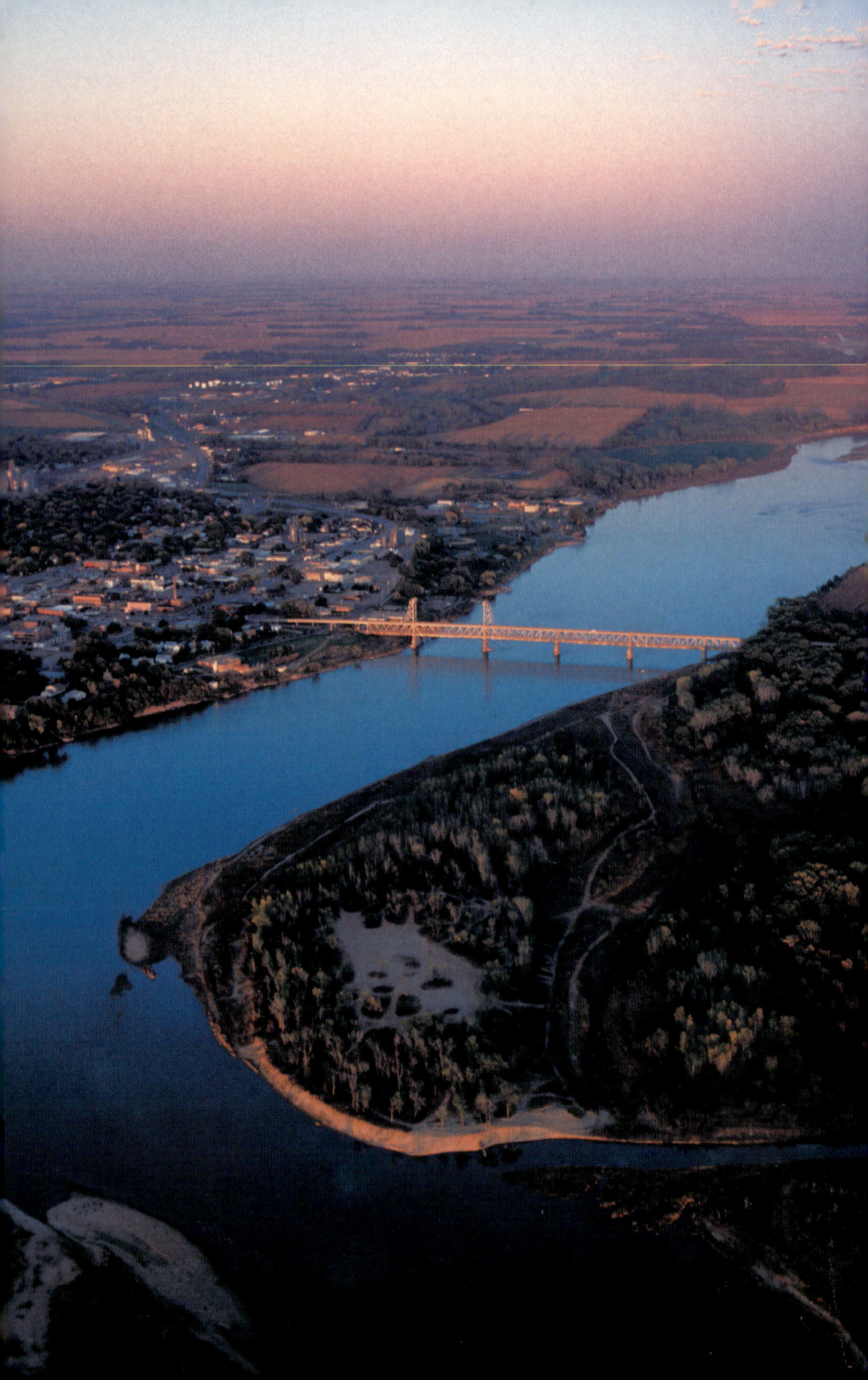

SD TOURISM

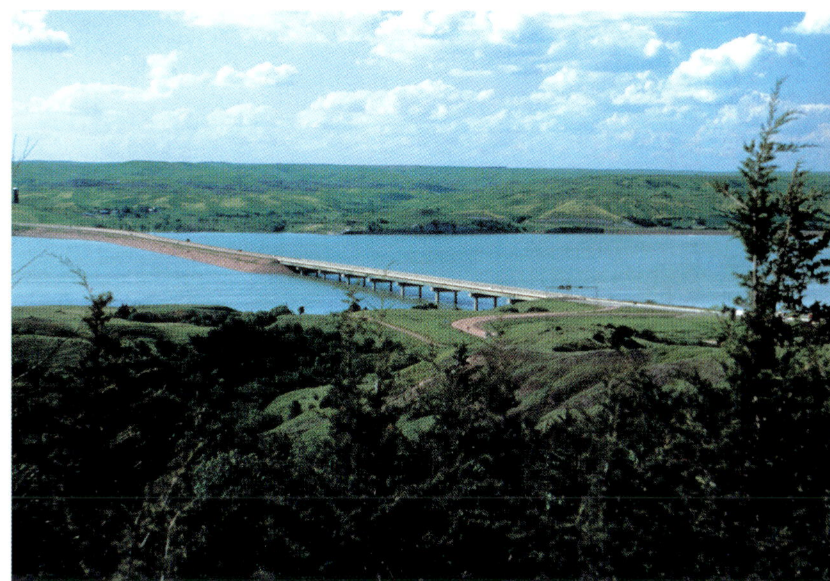

Bridges built at Springfield and Vermillion brought the total number of Missouri River car/truck crossings to 13 in South Dakota. The others are at Mobridge, Highway 212 near Gettysburg, Oahe Dam, Pierre/ Fort Pierre, Fort Thompson, Chamberlain (two), Platte-Winner, Highway 44 (above), Fort Randall, Gavins Point Dam and Yankton (left). The metal and concrete ribbons unite the state's West River and East River cultures, as bridges are wont to do.

GREG LATZA

SD TOURISM

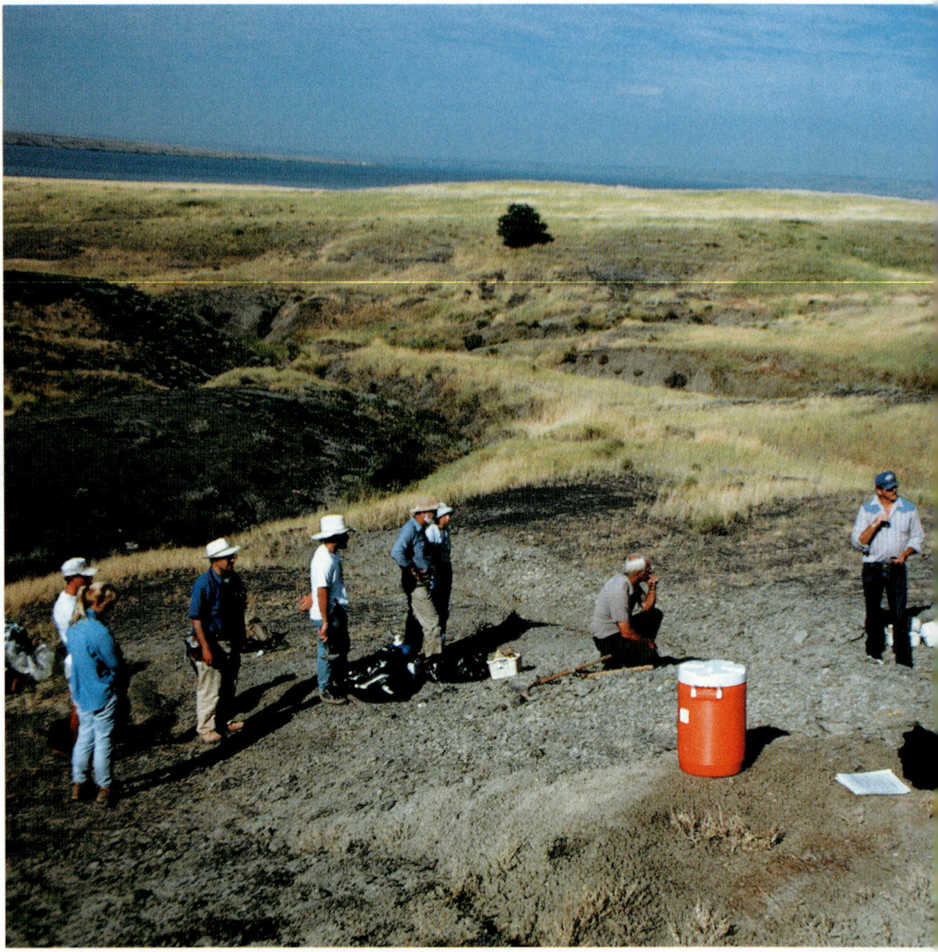

SD TOURISM

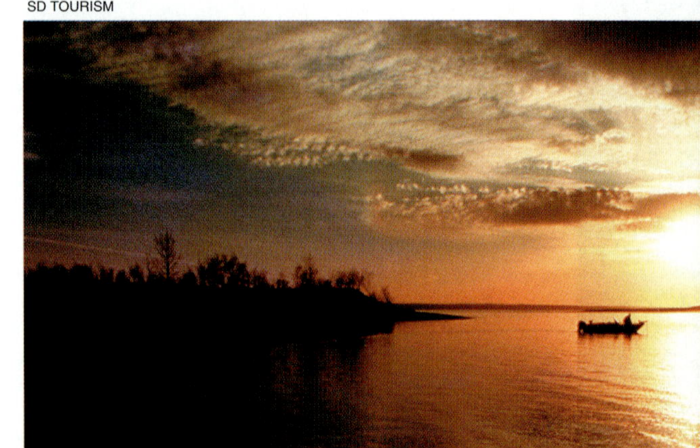

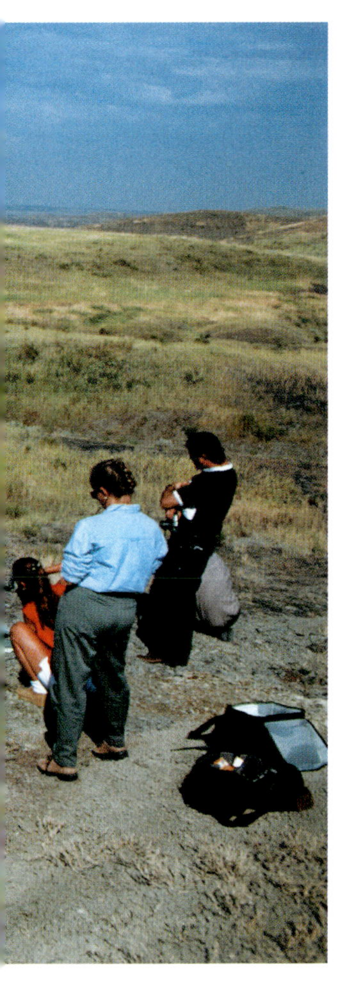

SD TOURISM

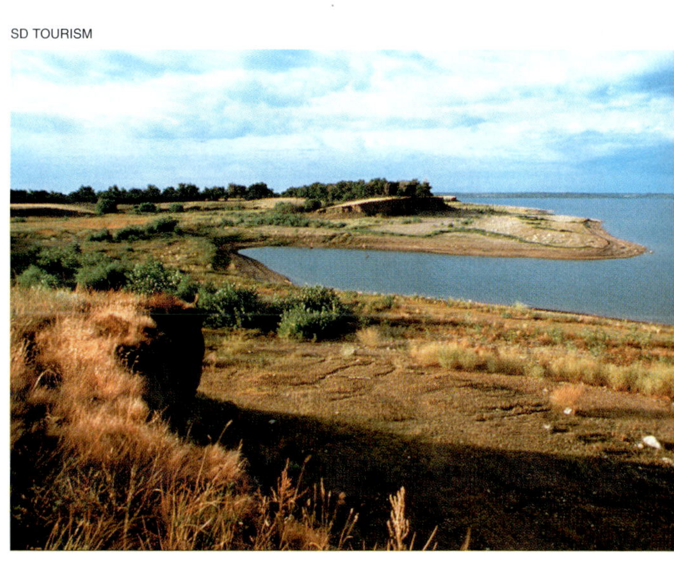

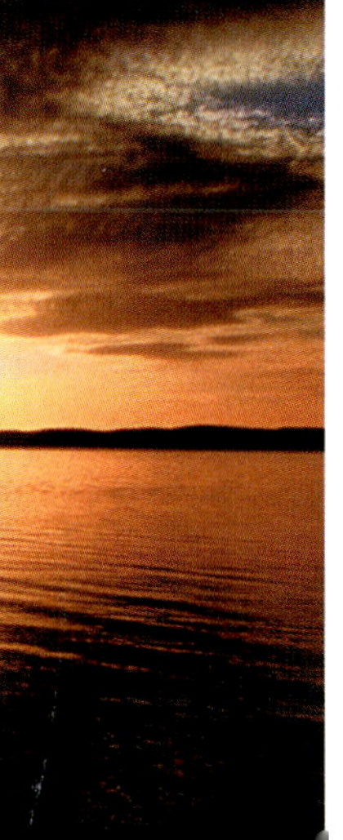

There are 156 fish species in the Missouri River system today. That does not include mosasaurs or plesiosaurs, ancient sea monsters that swam here 75 million years ago when present-day South Dakota was an inland sea. Paleontology teams from S.D. School of Mines and Technology (above, left) have unearthed fossils of the lizard-like creatures from the Missouri breaks on the Crow Creek Reservation.

BERNIE HUNHOFF

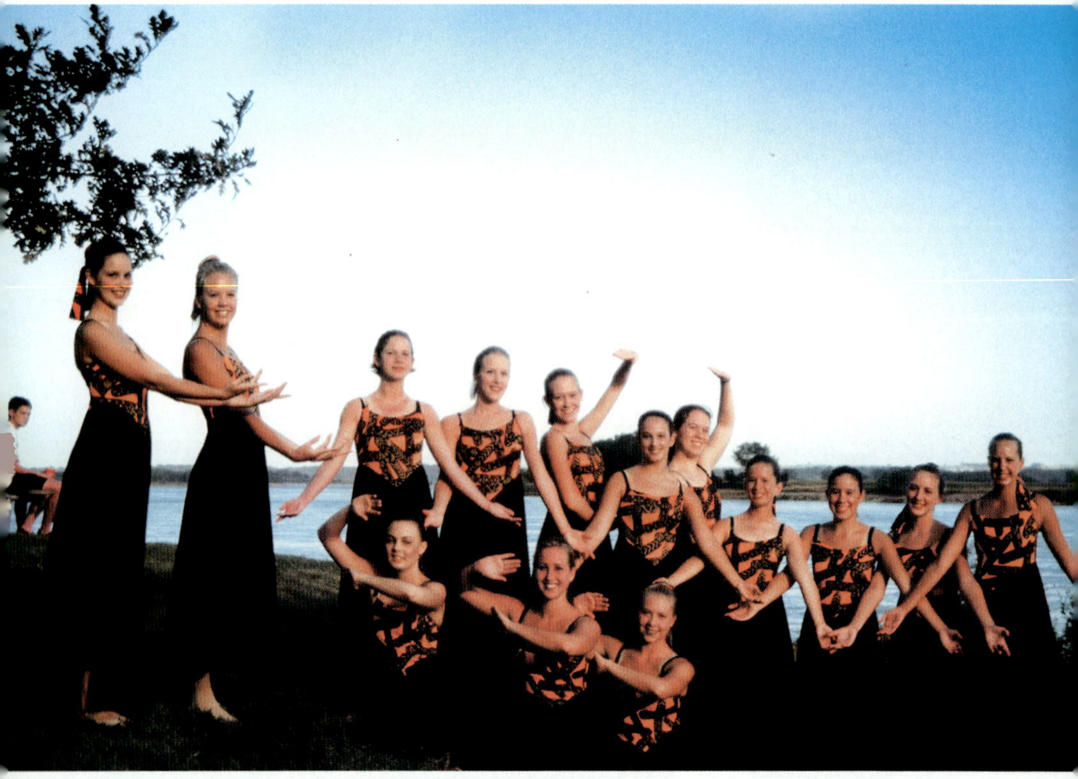

SD TOURISM

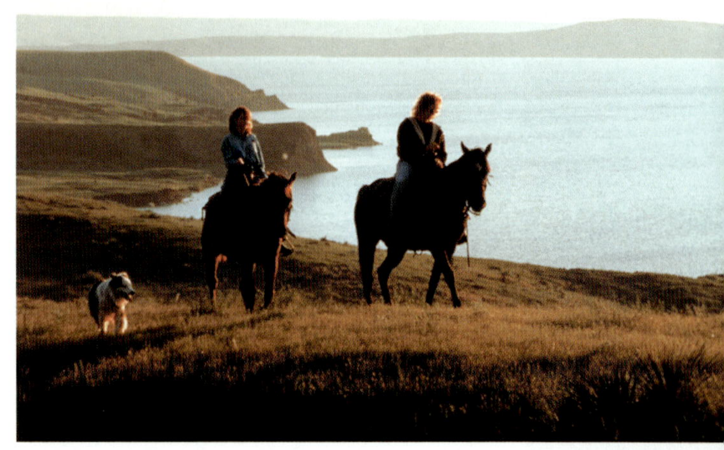

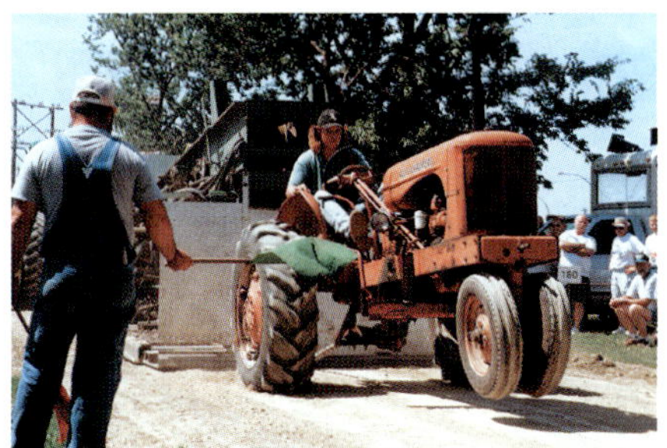

Fishing on Lake Oahe (below) requires water, but dry land activities like dancing and tractor pulls at Yankton's Riverboat Days, horseback riding, arts festivals, pow wows and foodfests are held as near as possible to the Missouri, North America's longest river.

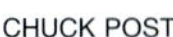

CHUCK POST

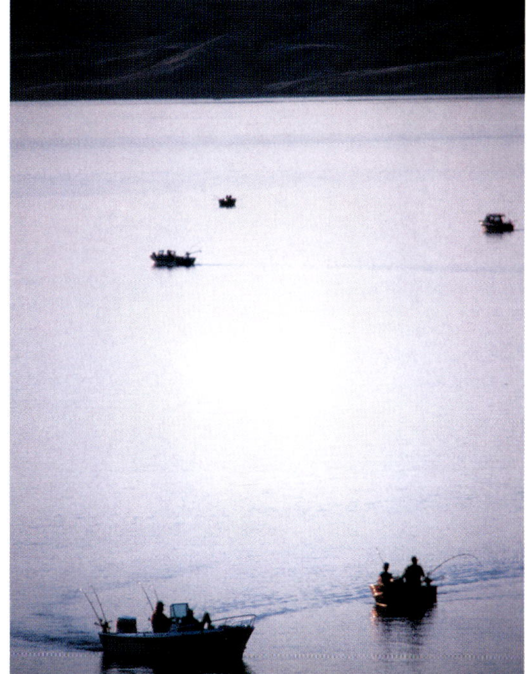

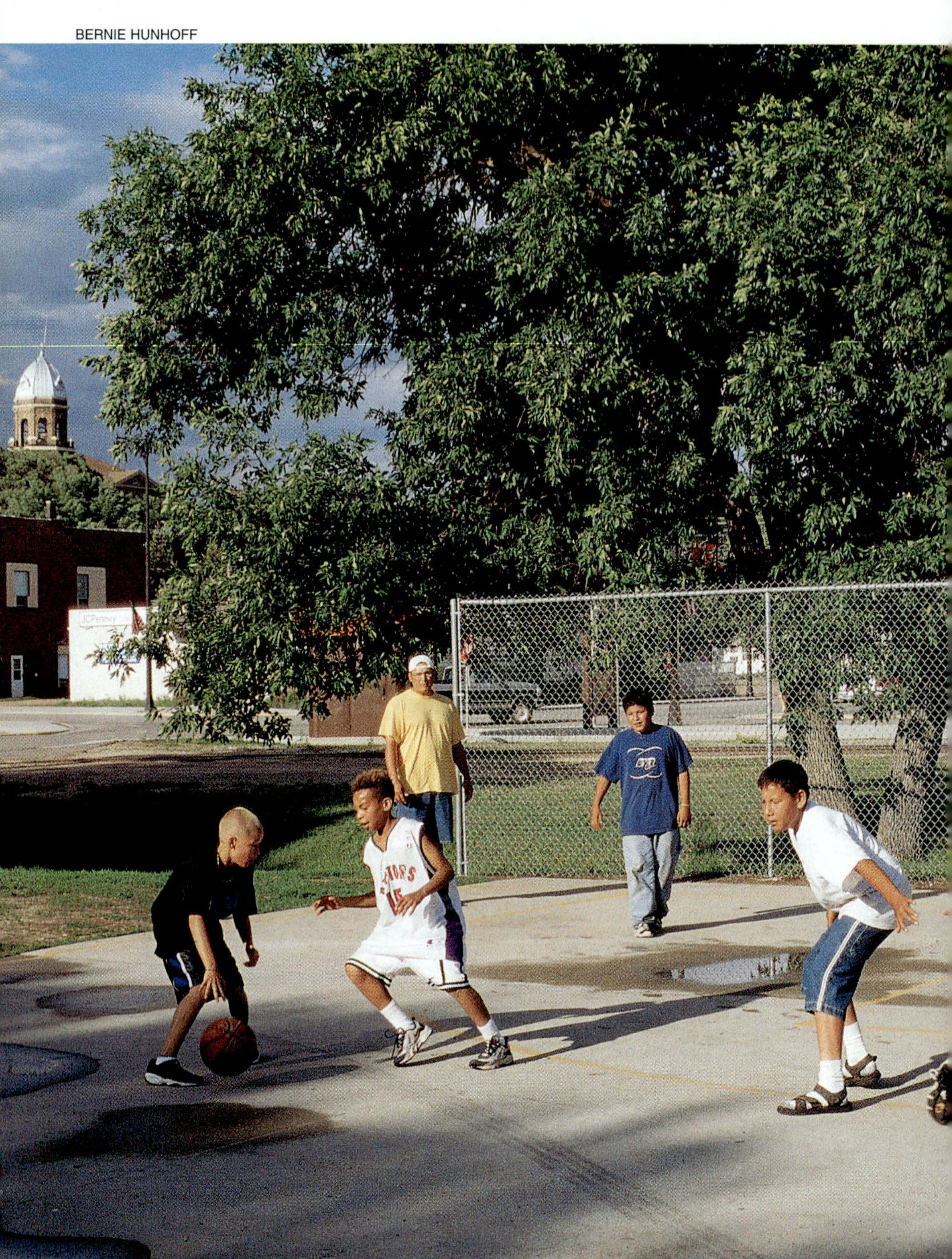

A pick-up basketball game in Sisseton's downtown city park.

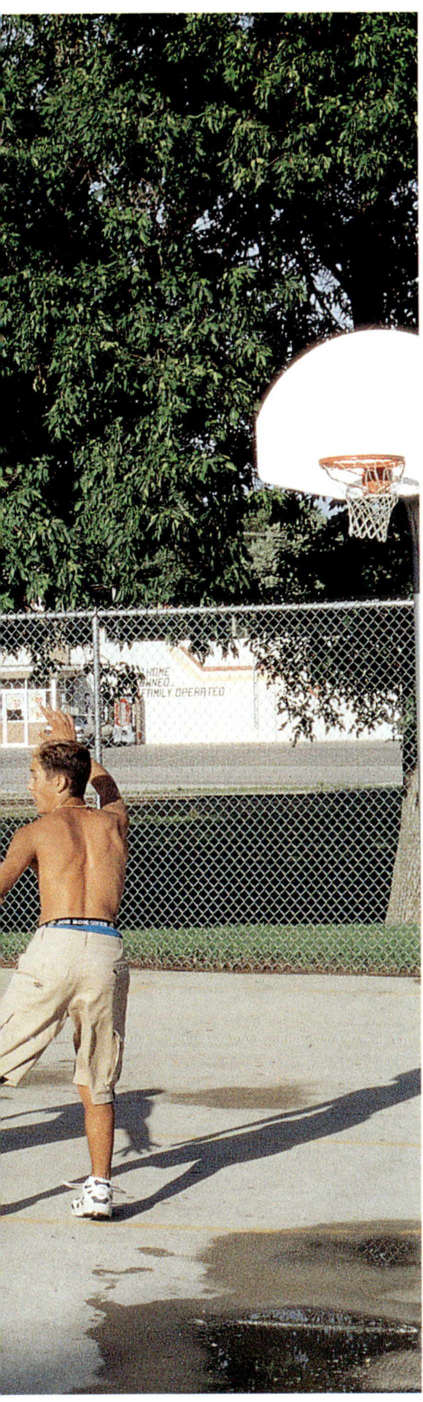

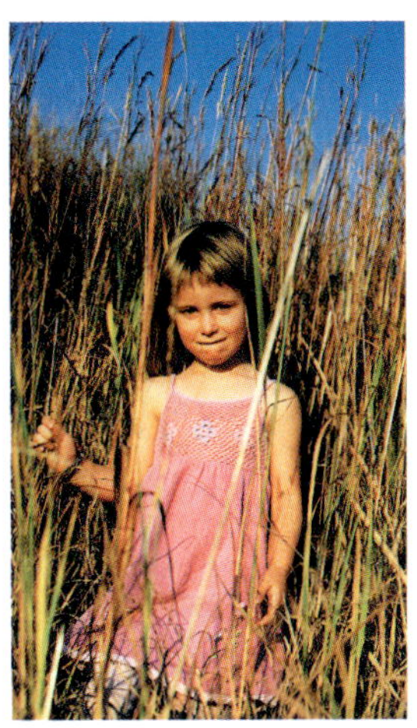

JERRY WILSON

Our Youth

Why, you might ask, did the editors devote an entire chapter of a photography book to children? What is the point? That our youth are better? No. That they are smarter, or more adventurous, or better cared for? Probably those are untrue statements, so we don't even imply them.

We do figure that as our youth go, so goes South Dakota. What else do we have? What else do we live for? I suppose we all, to some degree, try to preserve our own youthfulness, but before many decades pass it becomes obvious we're playing a losing game. With that realization, an unselfish person might turn his or her attention to making this a better

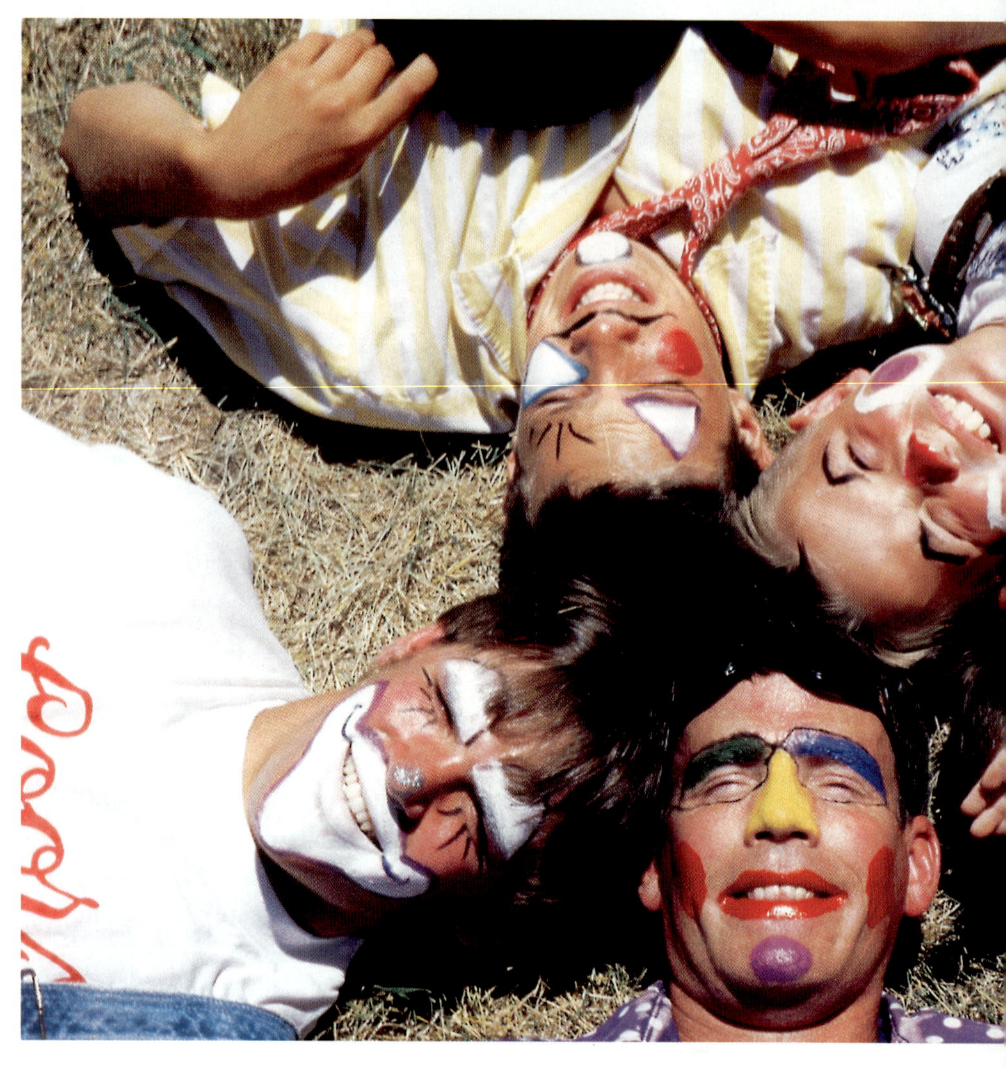

Kids and clowns are a fun-loving combination. The Crouse family and their friends have painted their faces and entertained at parades and community celebrations around Watertown for several decades. At right, a young girl dresses in period clothing for the Oscar Micheaux film festival in Gregory.

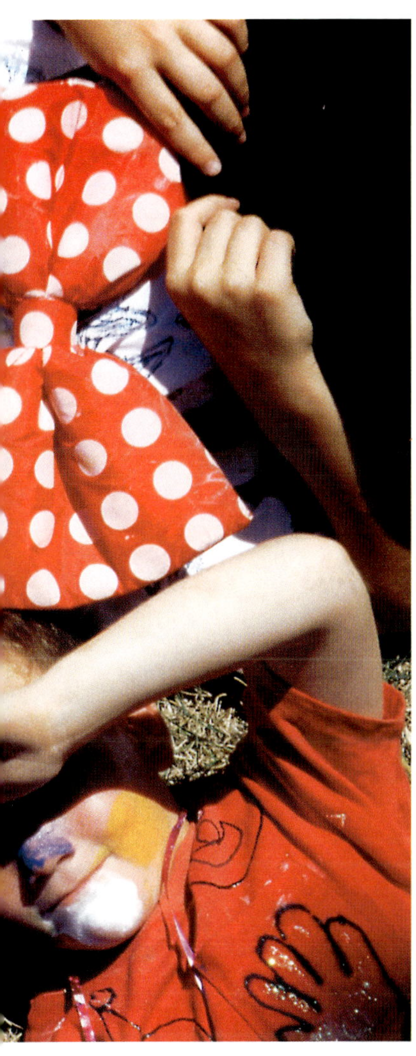

place for the young people around us.

A certain few communities seem to put more thought and pride in their cemeteries than their town centers, and then decry that their children seem bored and eager to leave at age 18. We build elaborate senior citizen centers, and the town's best gathering spots are "21 and older" liquor establishments, where we go to lament our dwindling populations.

Fortunately, however, the majority of South Dakotans — like any civilized people worth a nickel — live for their youth. An absence of children empties the energy from a house or a town. How a town looks and feels and sounds depends on whether the town has embraced and welcomed and nurtured the youth. In our travels, we visited places bursting with young people, and other places quiet and resting, with few or no children. The latter seem only slightly more active than those well-manicured

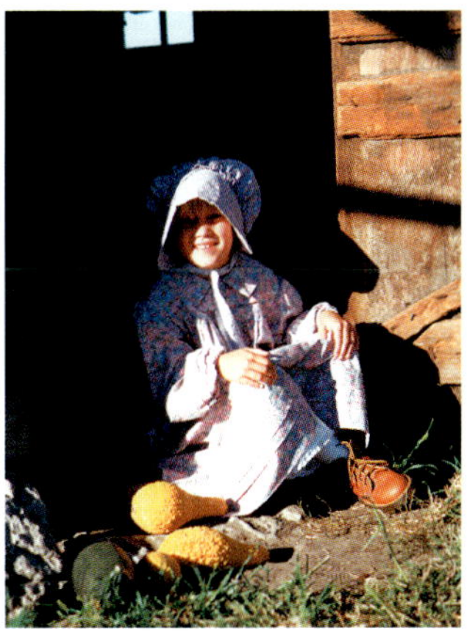

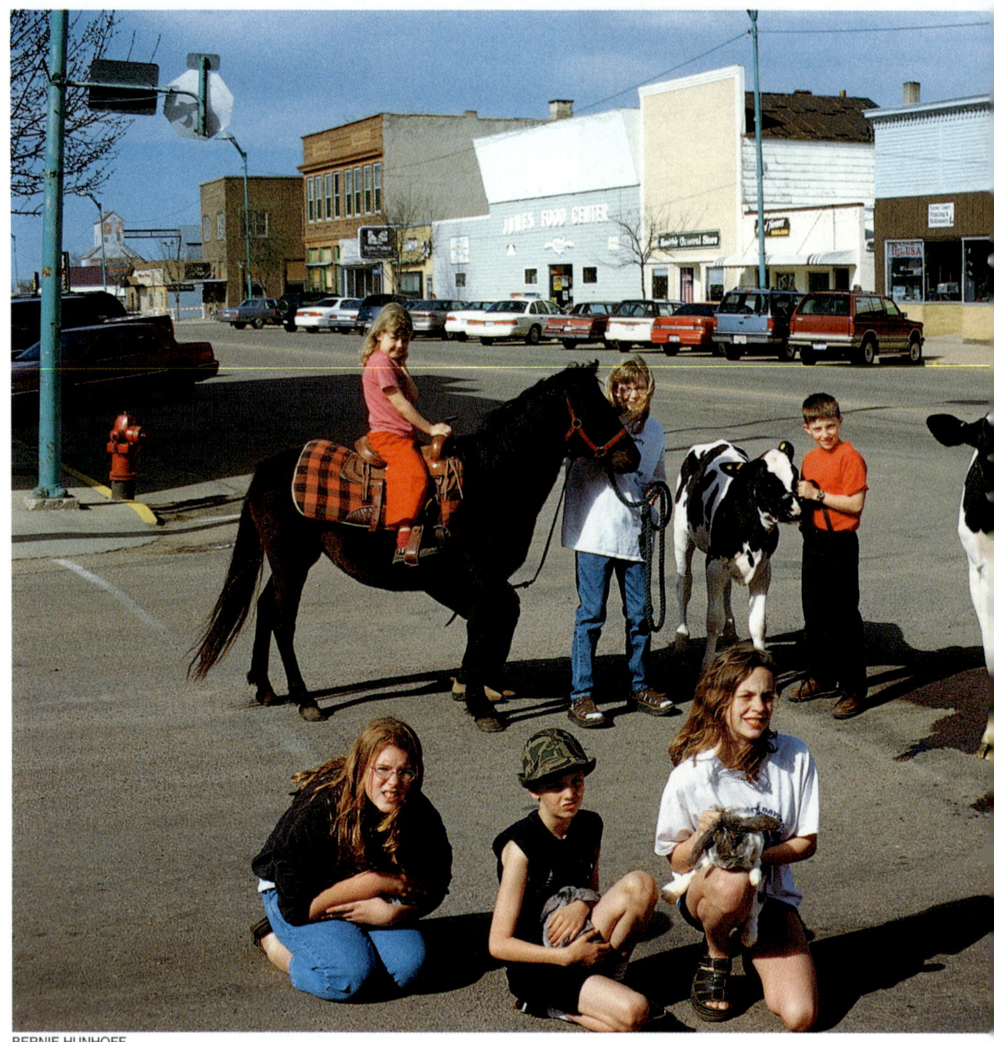

BERNIE HUNHOFF

One of South Dakota's most popular local fairs, the Turner County Fair at Parker, is oriented to 4-H. Youth from the farms and cities bring animals ranging from rabbits to Shetland ponies and Holstein milk cows.

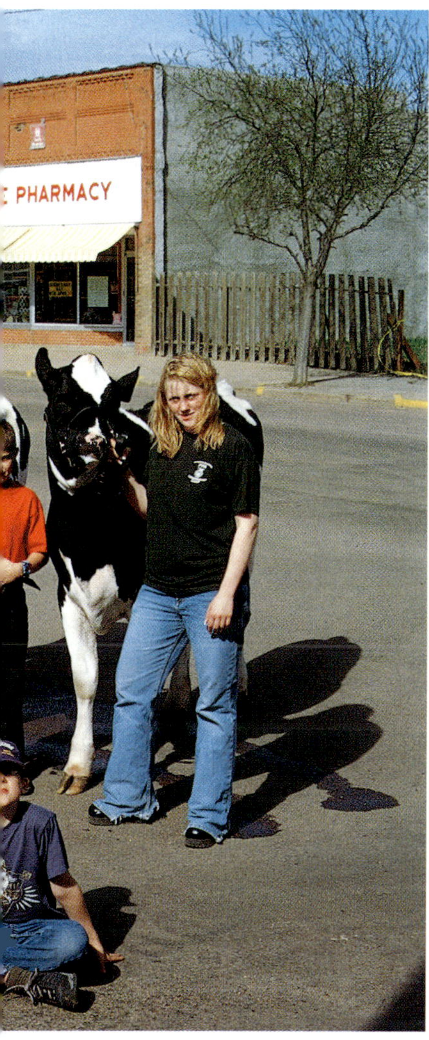

STEPHEN GASSMAN

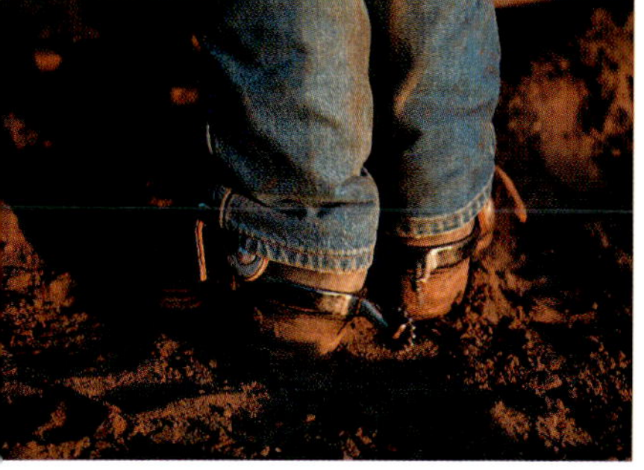

cemeteries.

Believing that to be true, we dedicated this chapter to our children. This is a photographic view of South Dakota at its absolute best — a state of wonder and beauty and freedom and creativity and hopefulness.

What adult wouldn't — if unshackled from our inhibitions, prohibitions and physical conditions — climb the rocky shoreline of Sylvan Lake, row across the glacial lakes, run through a windblown prairie wheat field, have a shootout in the haymow, or play basketball in the park?

Ralph Waldo Emerson said children are all foreigners. He meant, we assume, that they find surprises in life's littlest experiences: every hour, every plant, every animal, every view is new and interesting. We can bask in their joy over happenings we'd otherwise mistake as common.

Photographs of South Dakota children in this chapter show the freshness of South Dakota, full of hope and wonder and absent the limitations that age us.

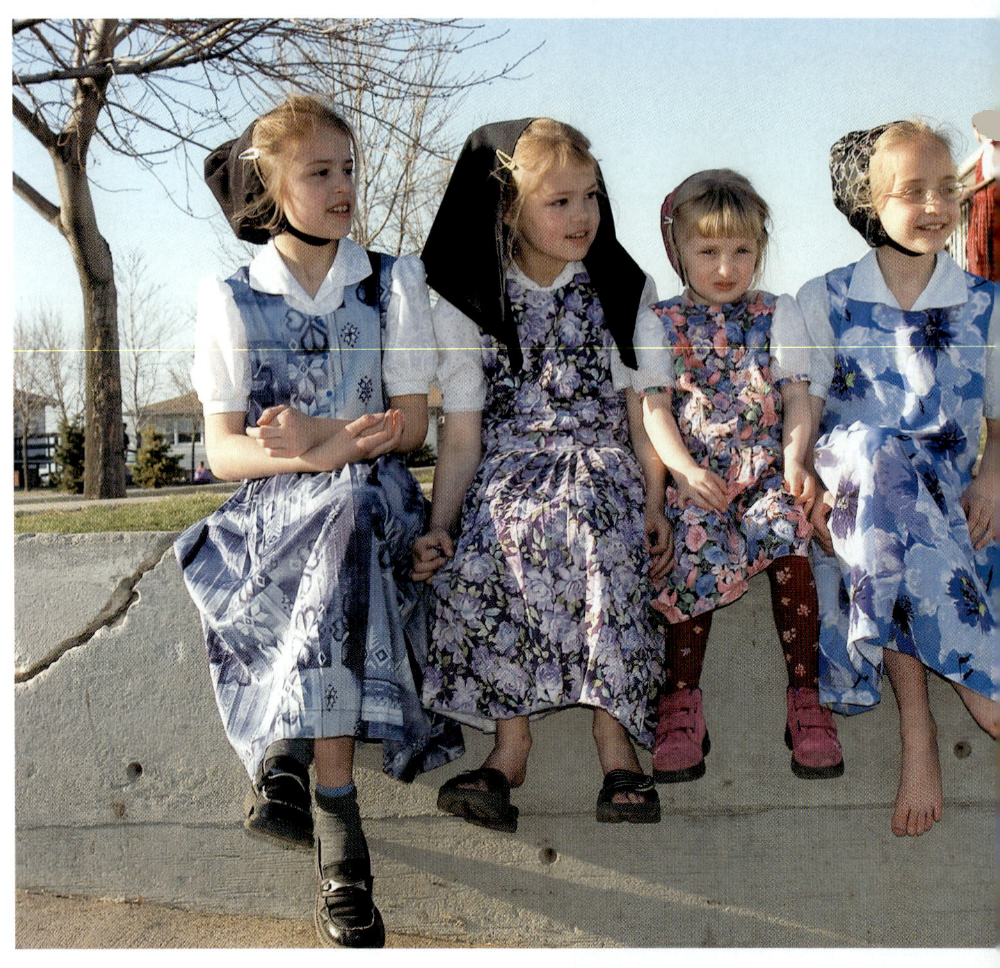

Their outward appearance hasn't changed, but globalization and modernization does affect the 6,000 Hutterites who live on 53 rural colonies in South Dakota. Their ancestors left Germany in the 16th century, seeking freedom of religion and a life of pacifism. At Old Elm Colony near Bridgewater, young girls welcome visitors to the annual spring bake sale. A boy shows off a smoked turkey at Hillcrest Colony near Clark (top right). The baseball bat-toting lad is from Bon Homme Colony south of Tabor.

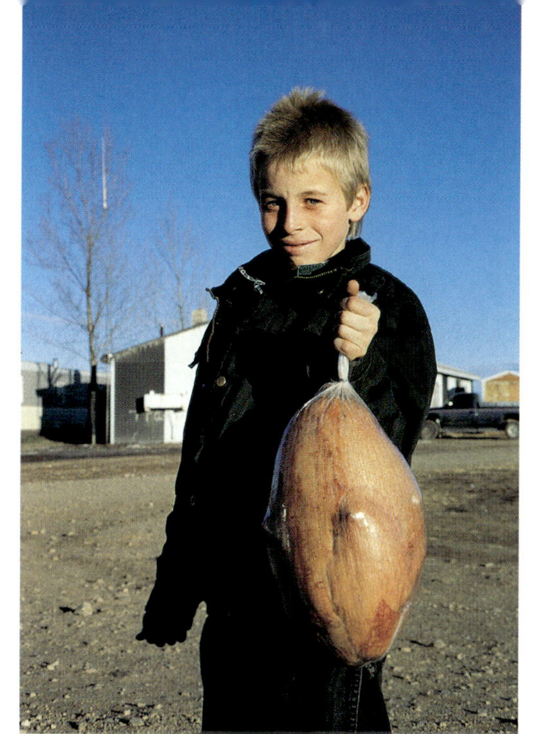

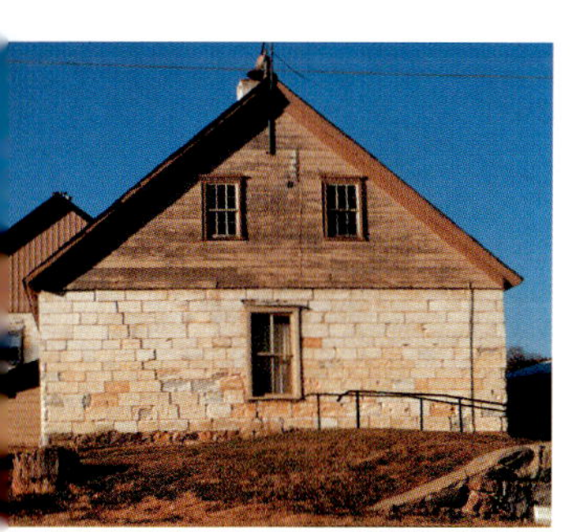

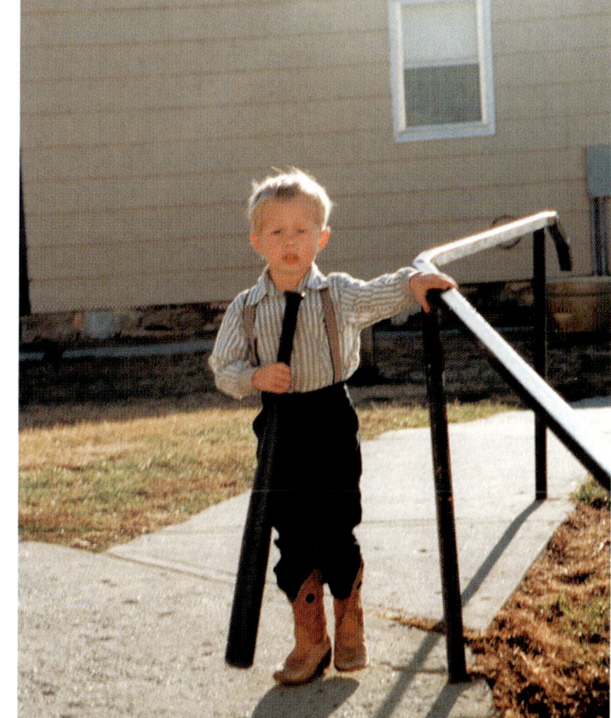

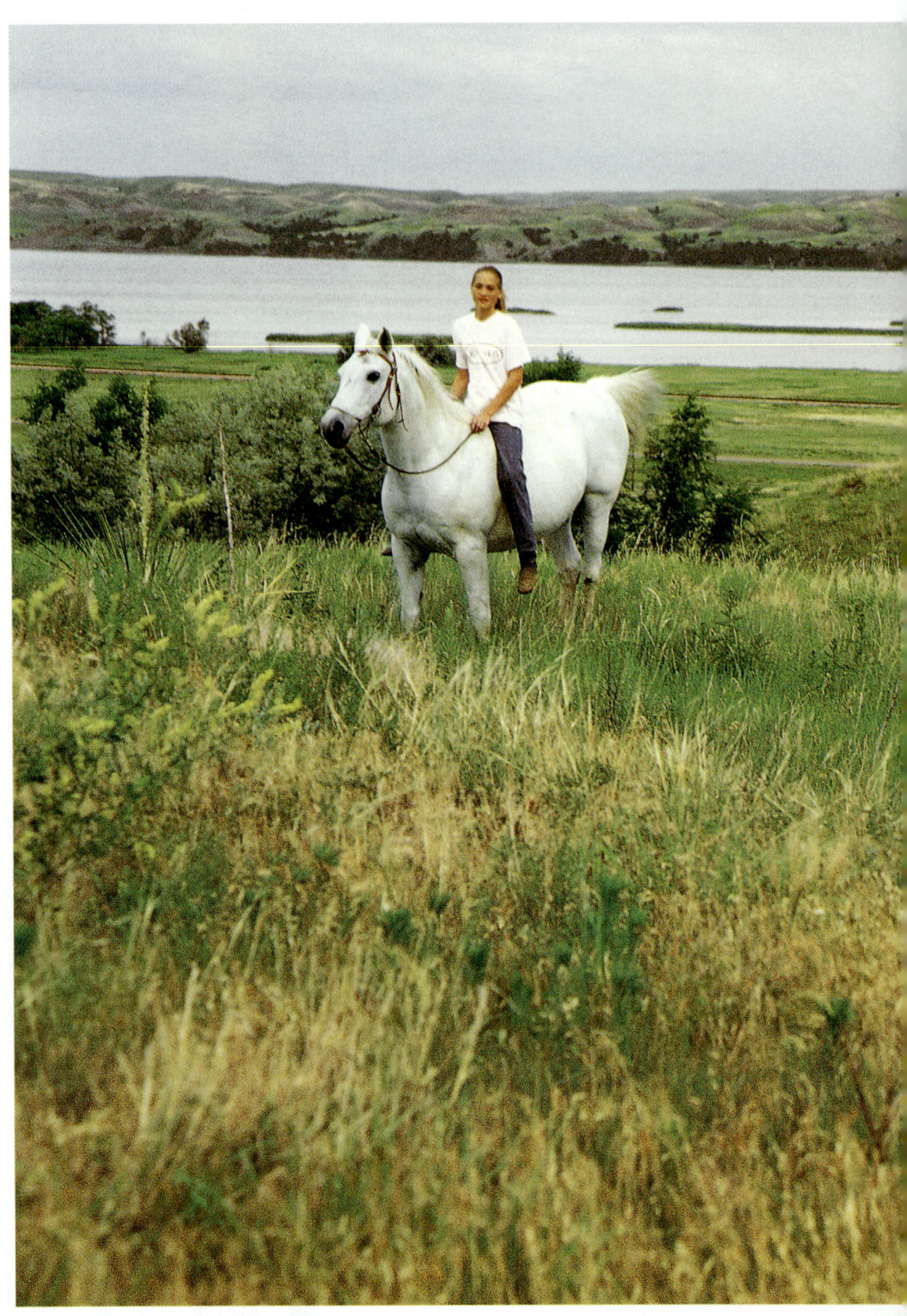

MacKenzie Kusser grew up riding her horse, Smokey, on Missouri River bluffs in Hughes County where an Arikara city existed 600 years ago. The 44-acre site is on her grandfather's ranch.

BERNIE HUNHOFF

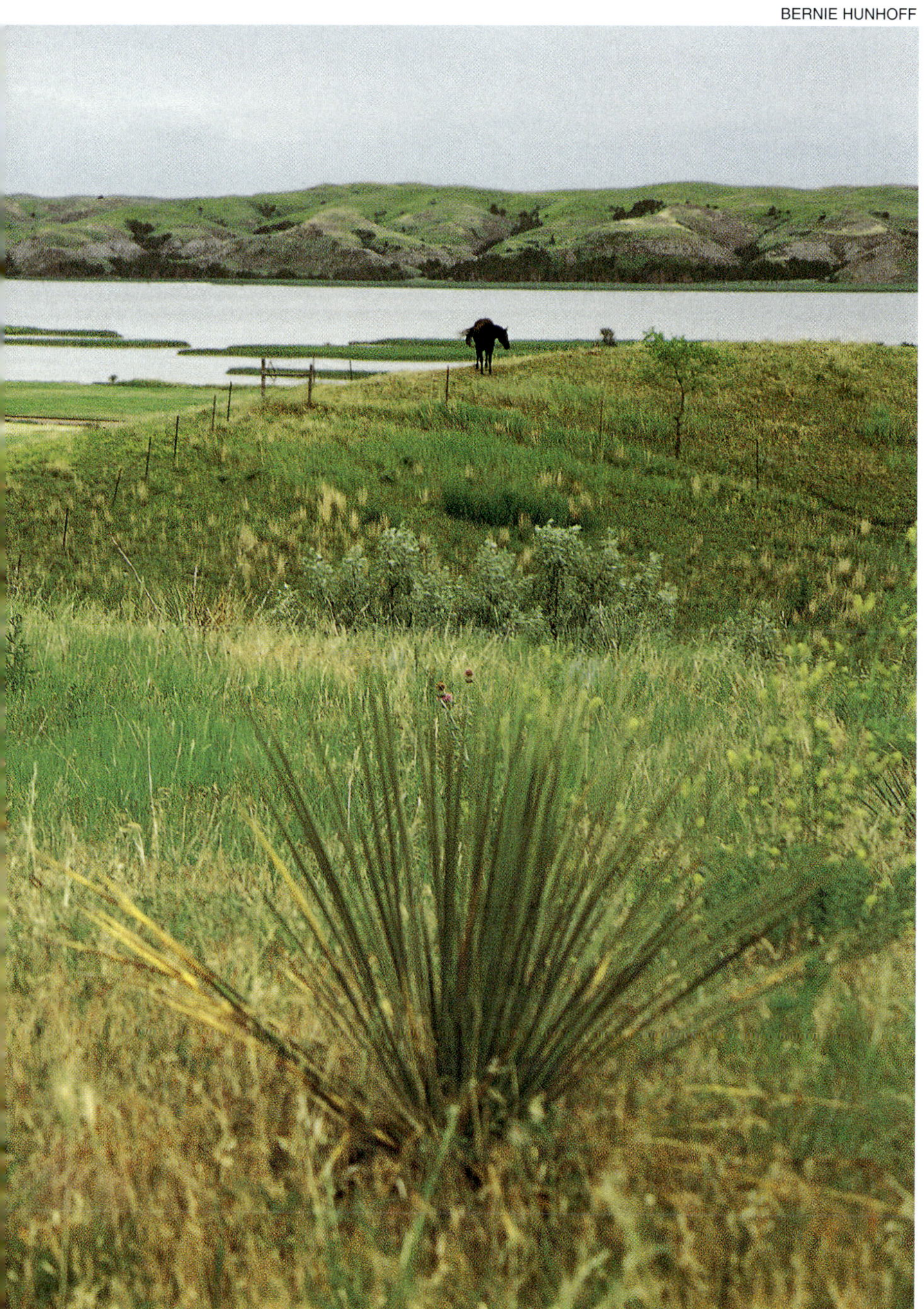

KATIE HUNHOFF

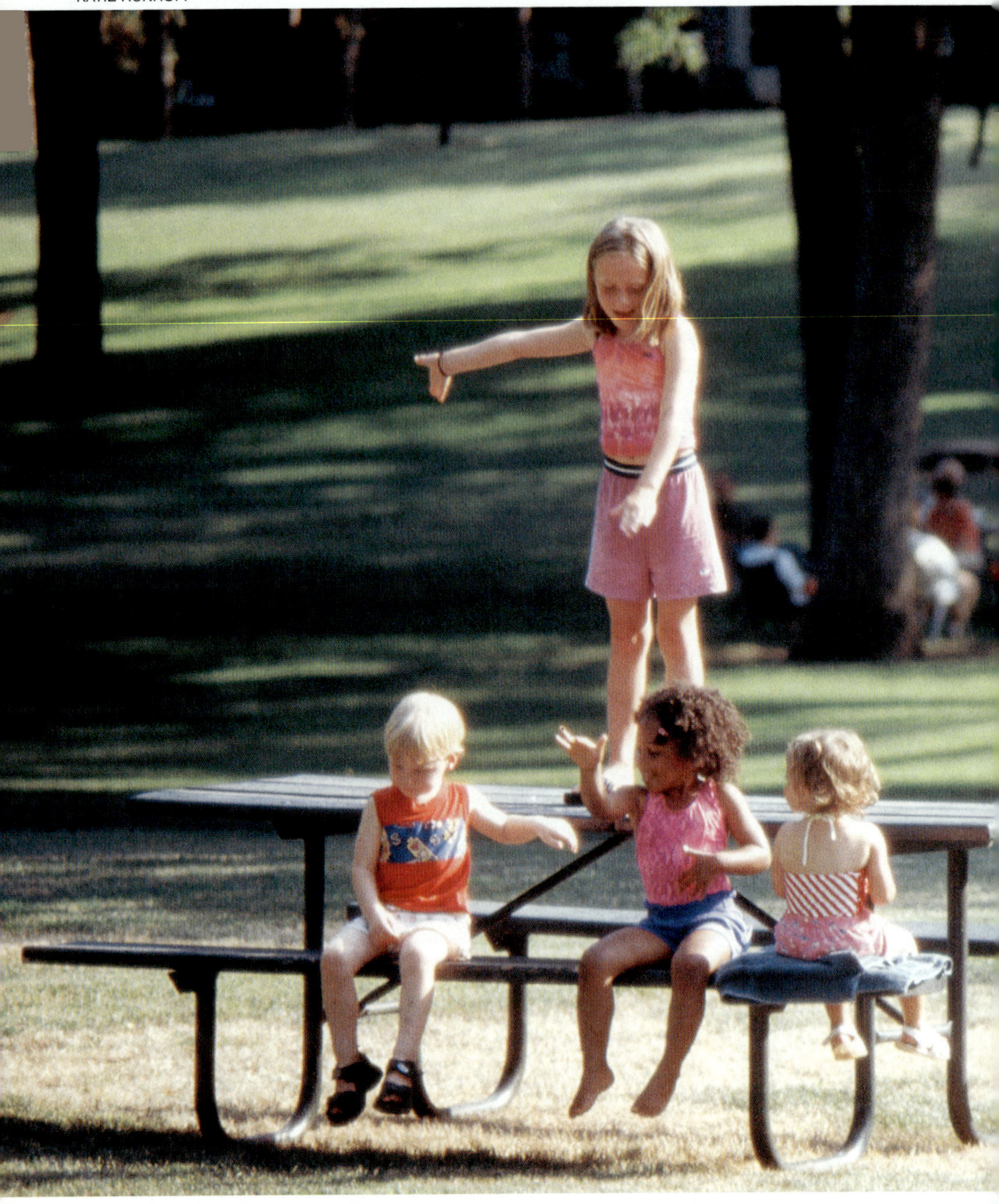

McKennan Park in Sioux Falls has much to offer kids, but for a true extrovert, nothing more than a picnic table stage is needed. The beautiful park is surrounded by some of the city's most historic homes.

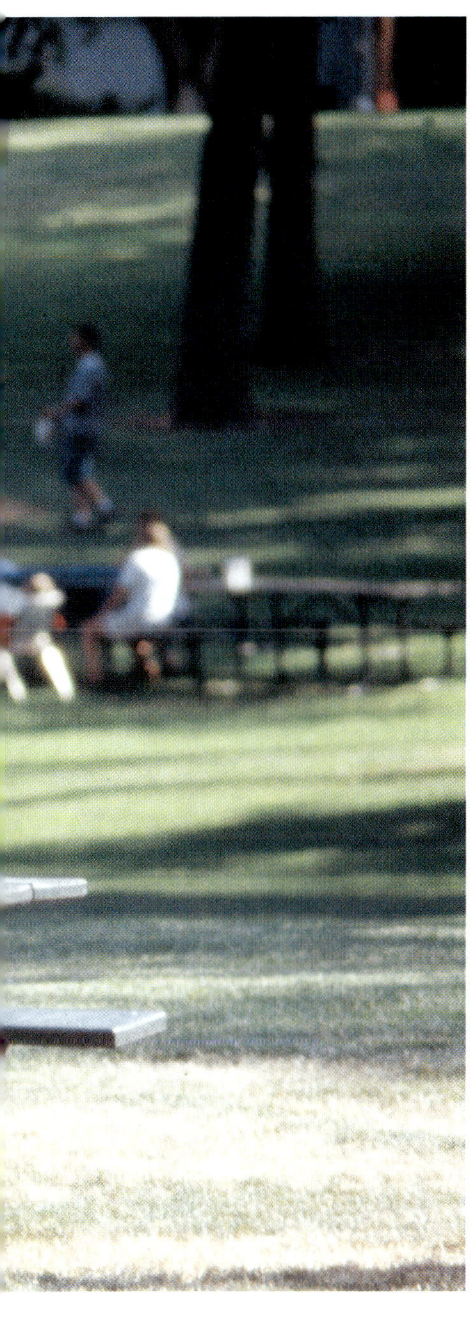

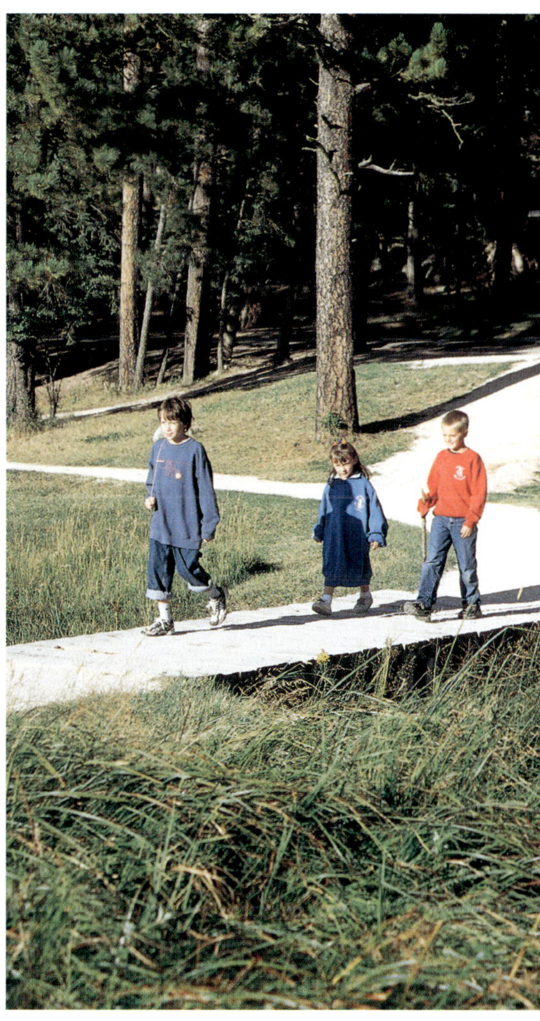

Three youth from Rapid City explore a walking trail that circles Sylvan Lake, at the foot of Harney Peak in the Black Hills. Sylvan means "in the woods."

The romance of the Old West is still alive among South Dakota's youth. The long-running Crystal Springs Rodeo at Clear Lake drew the young roper (right). The tug-a-war (far right) occurred at the junior stock-show in Rapid City. Below, young-sters lined up for a potluck lunch at a Yankton 4-H horse show.

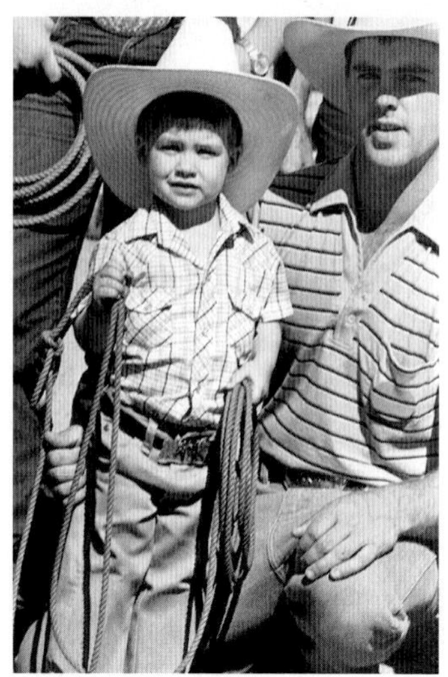

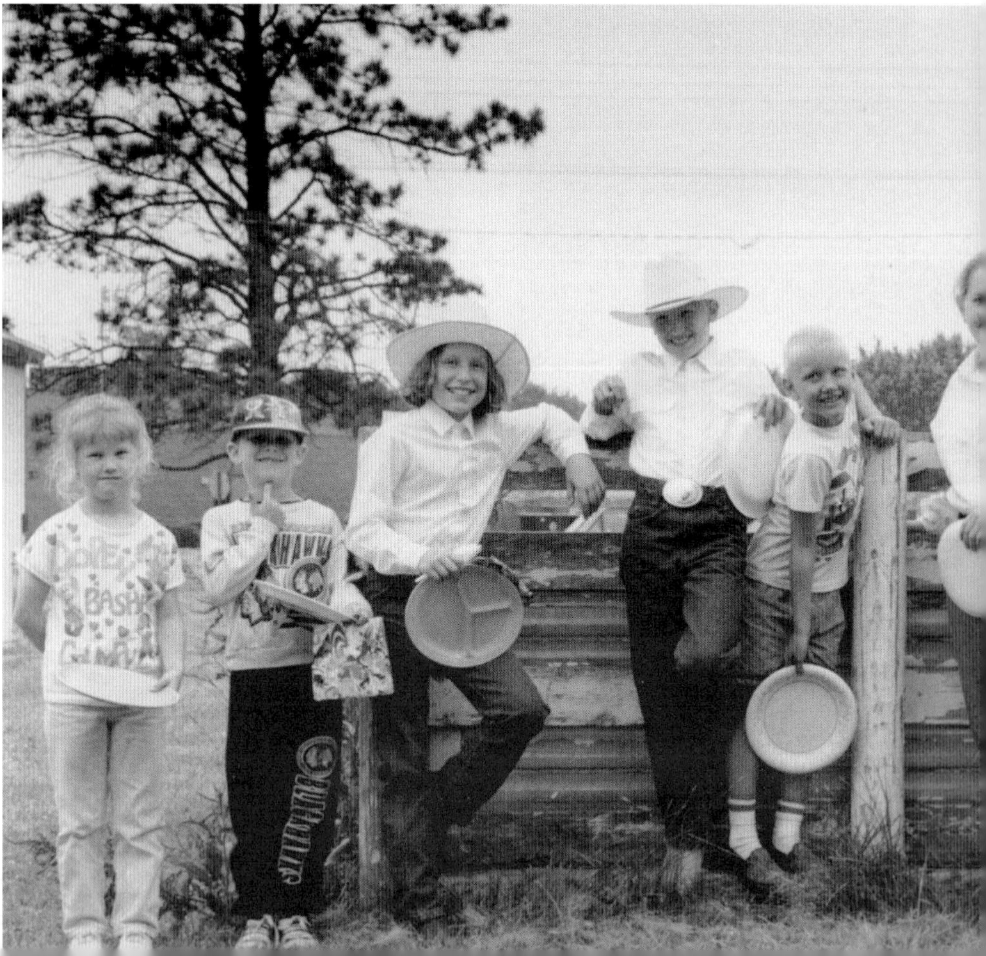

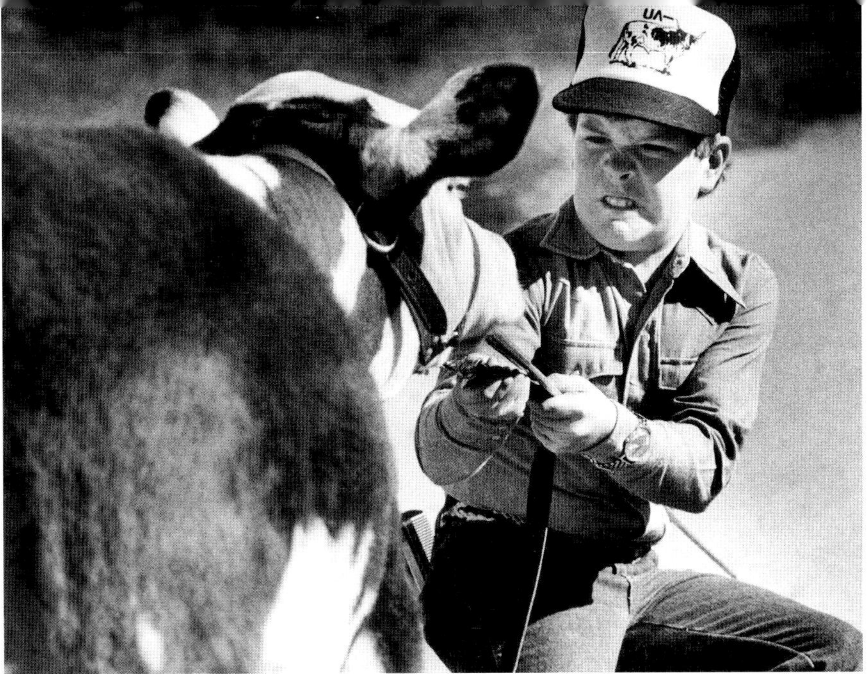

DON POLOVICH

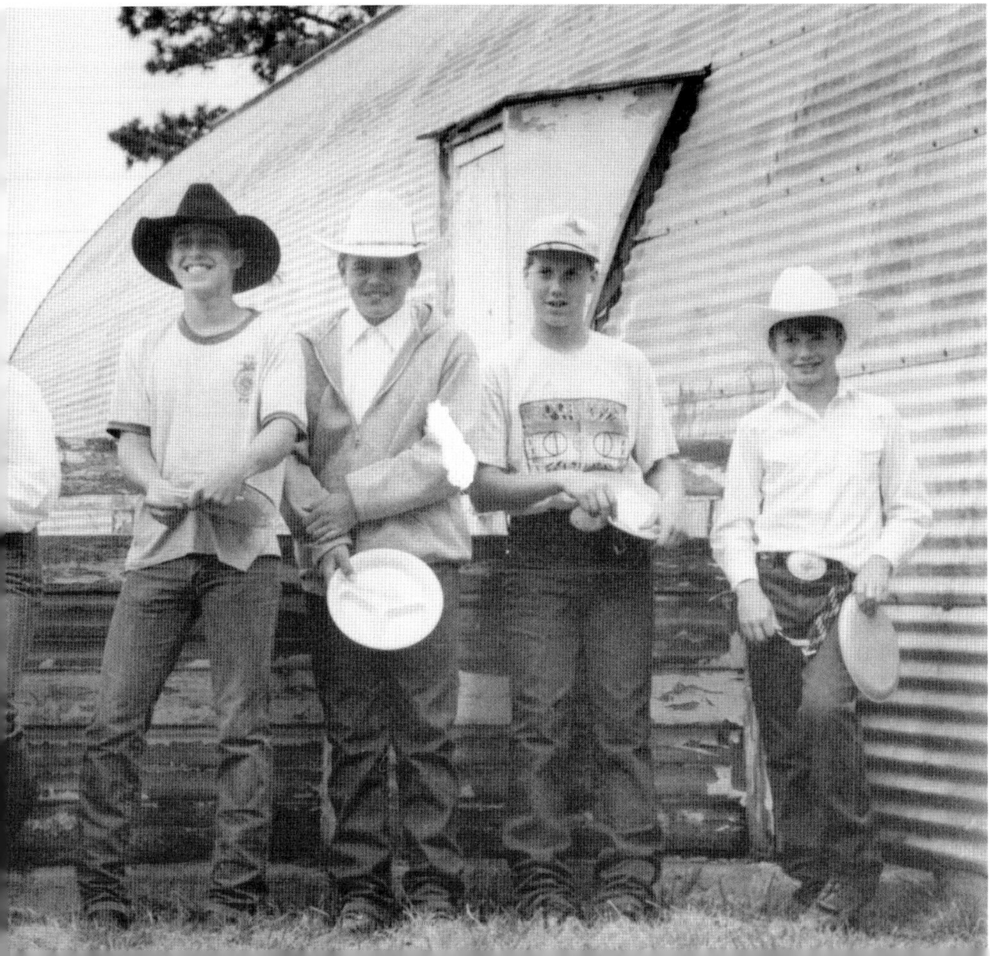

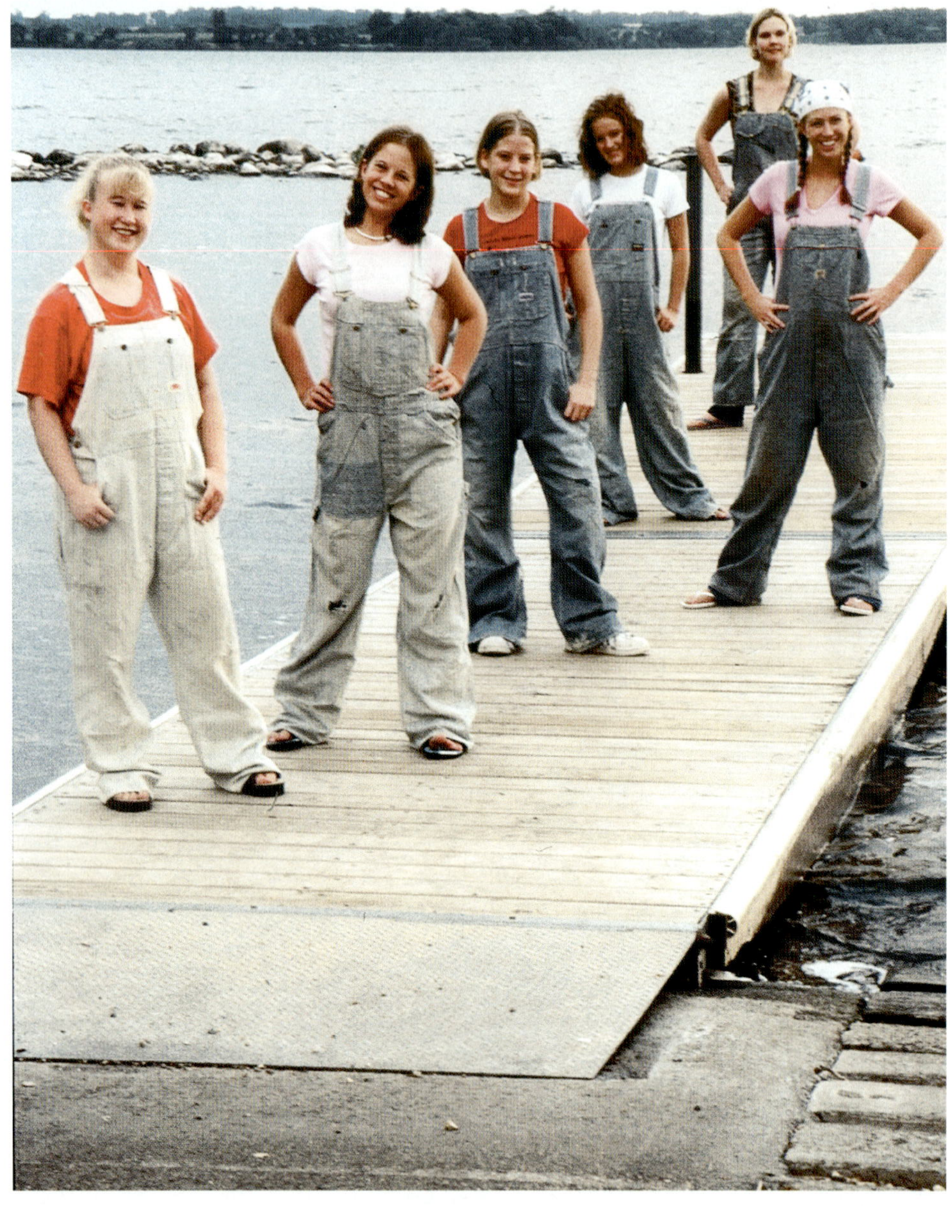

Brookings County farmer Trygvie Trooien's collection of overalls has been modeled at various hometown celebrations by local youth.

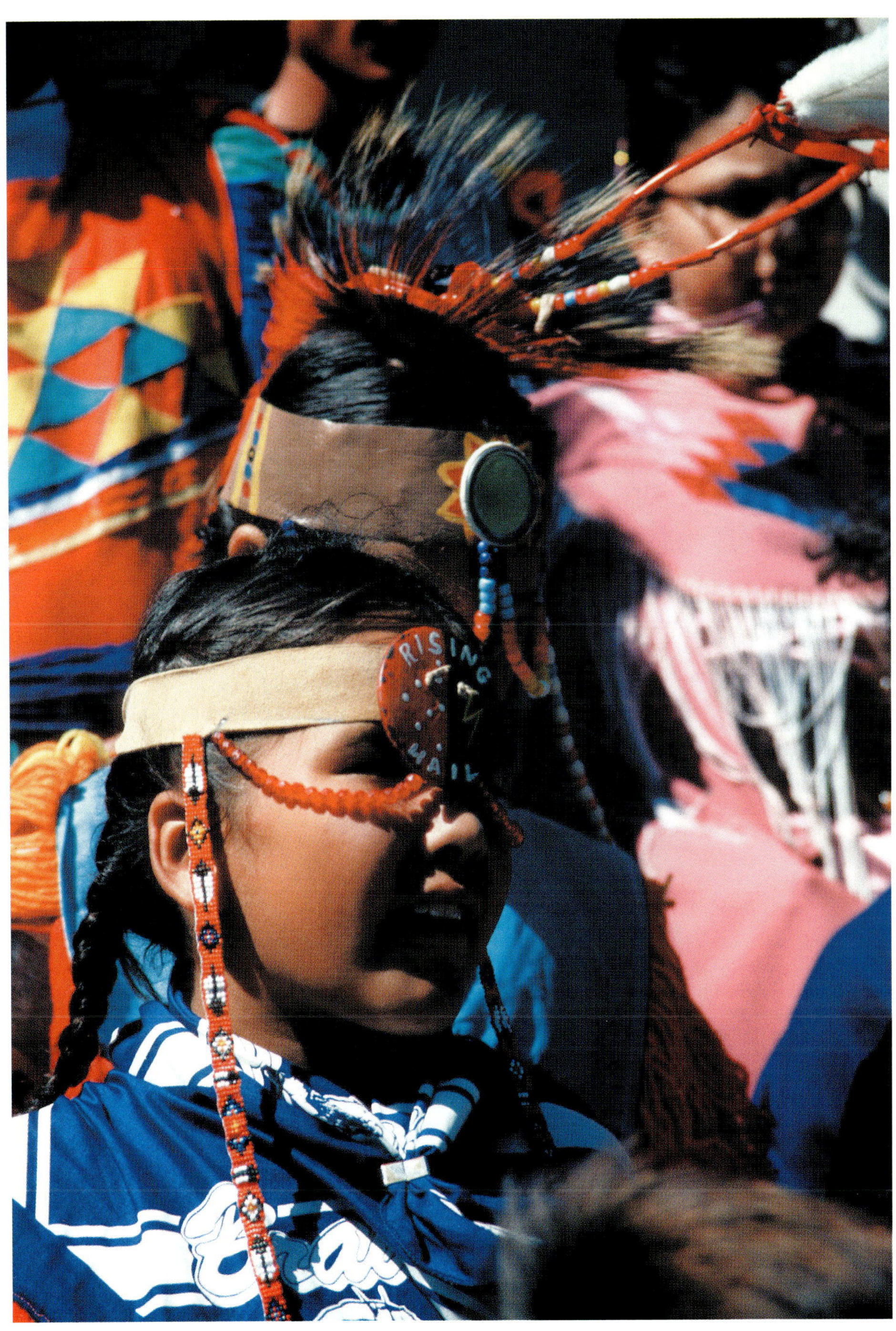

Youngsters from the Yankton Sioux Reservation dressed in colorful regalia for a unity mass at the church in Marty.

TOM DEMPSTER

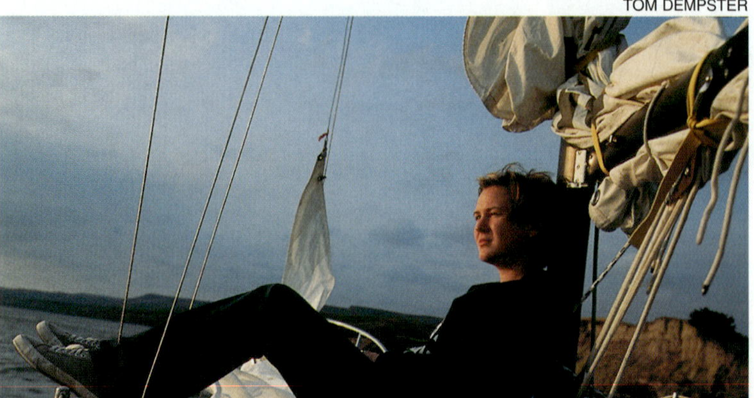

There's a wildness to water that attracts people, especially the youth, whether the water surrounds your sailboat on Lake Francis Case (above) or fills a community pool in Wessington Springs (below).

JERRY WILSON

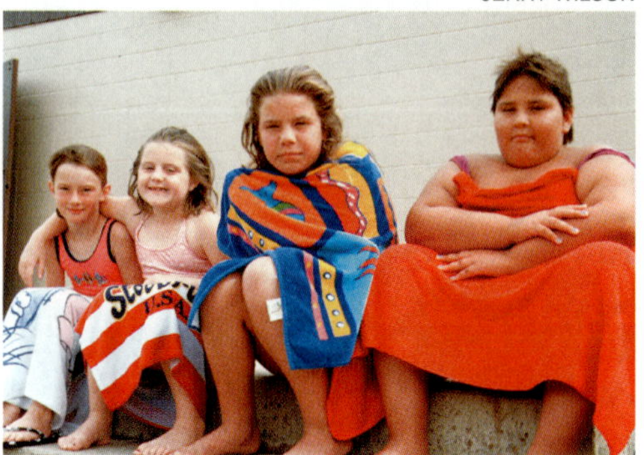

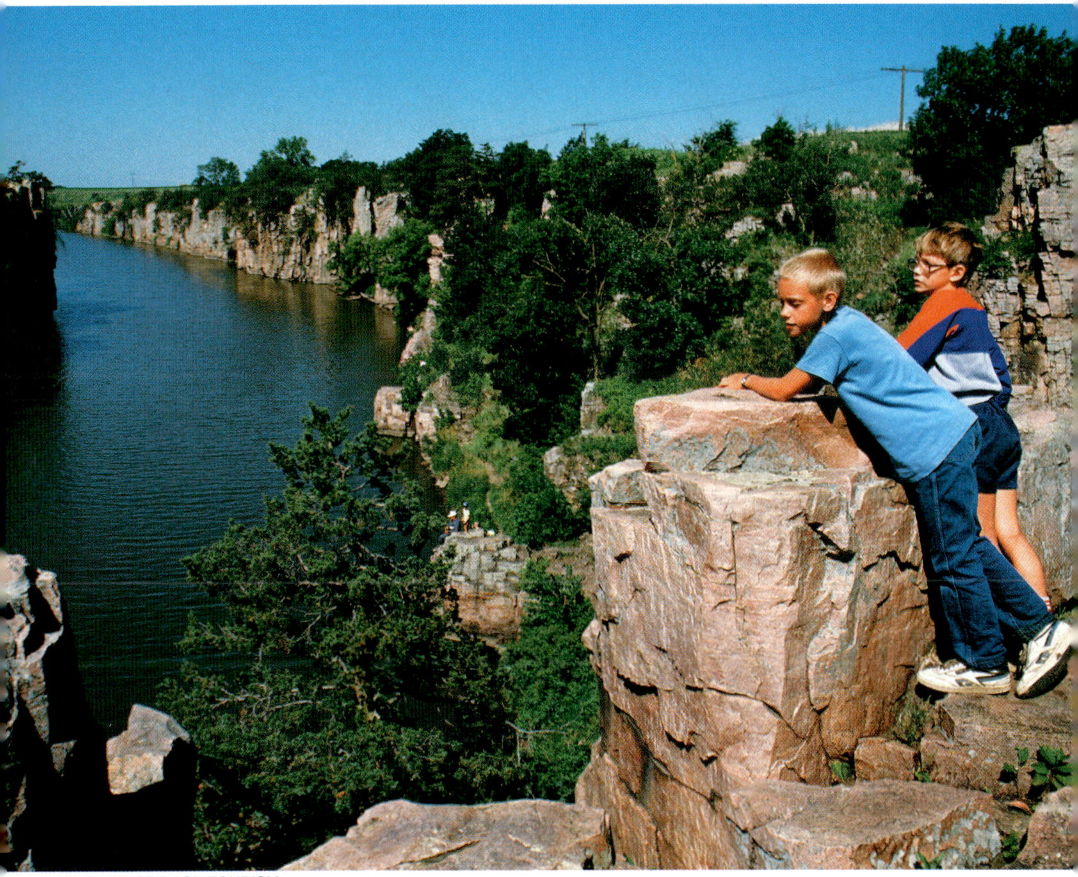

MARK KAYSER / SD TOURISM

The 50-foot quartzite cliffs (above) of Split Rock Creek near Garretson are tempting climbs. Below, a lone angler tries his luck in a Codington County pond.

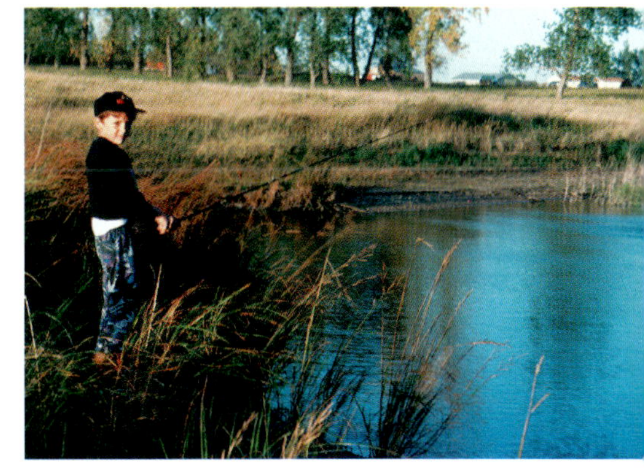

ROBIN REINHOLD

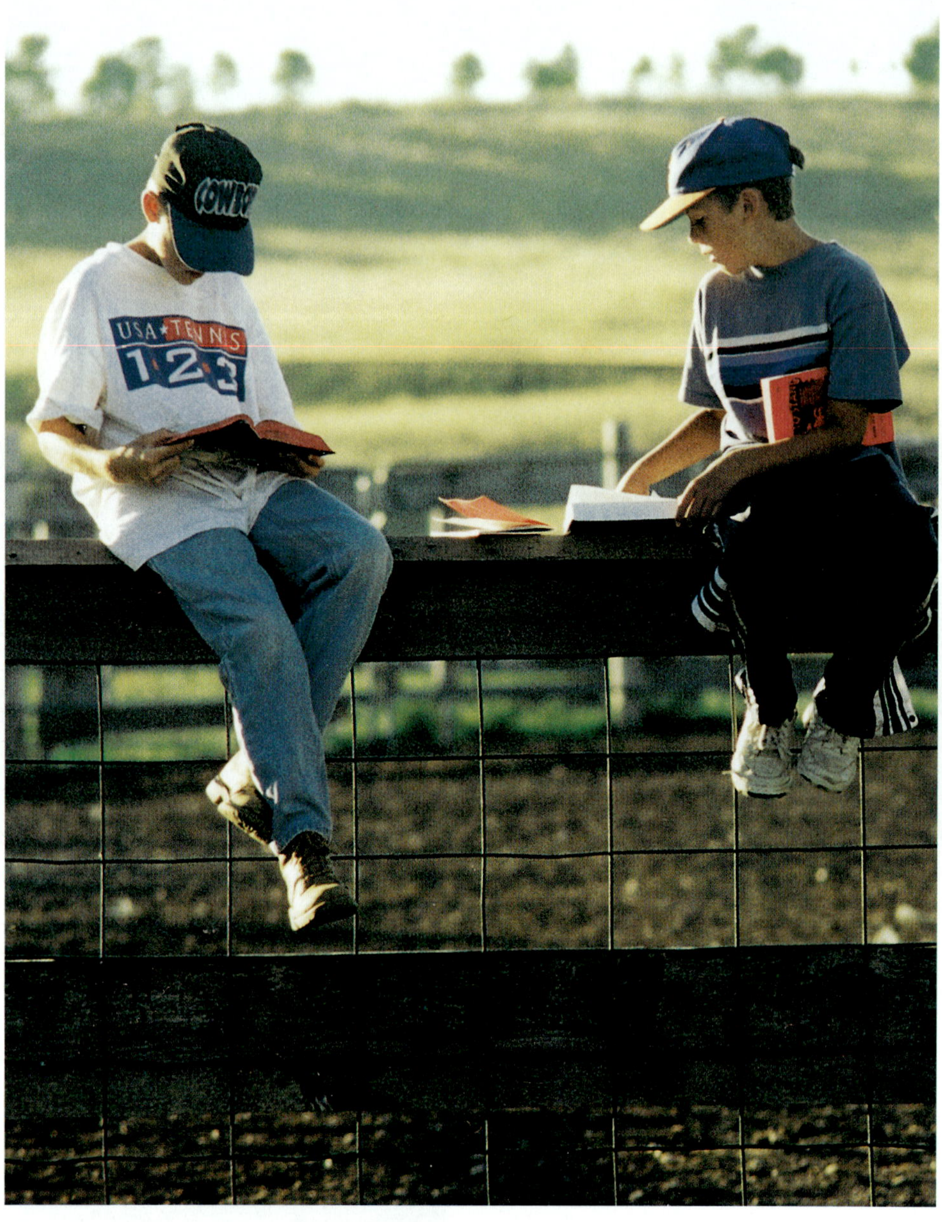

South Dakota's kids attend camps in the forest and at the lakes and at the Reinhold family ranch near Sturgis called Rainbow Bible Ranch, where some Bible study is part of the regimen.

BERNIE HUNHOFF

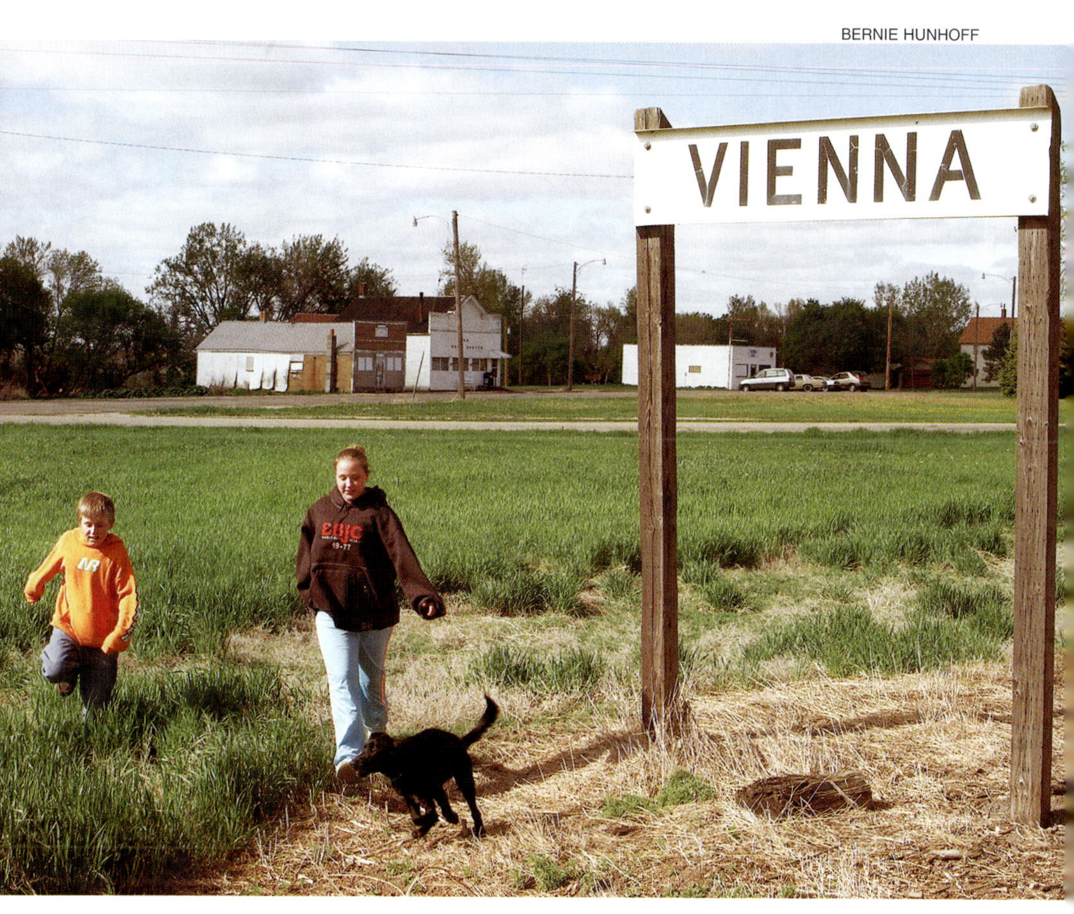

The joys of growing up in small towns like Vienna in Clark County, population 78, are impossible to measure. There's space to run free, security and a culture that emphasizes children. Vienna (pronounced Vy-anna, and named by settlers from Austria), will consider itself alive and well as long as it has a child living there.

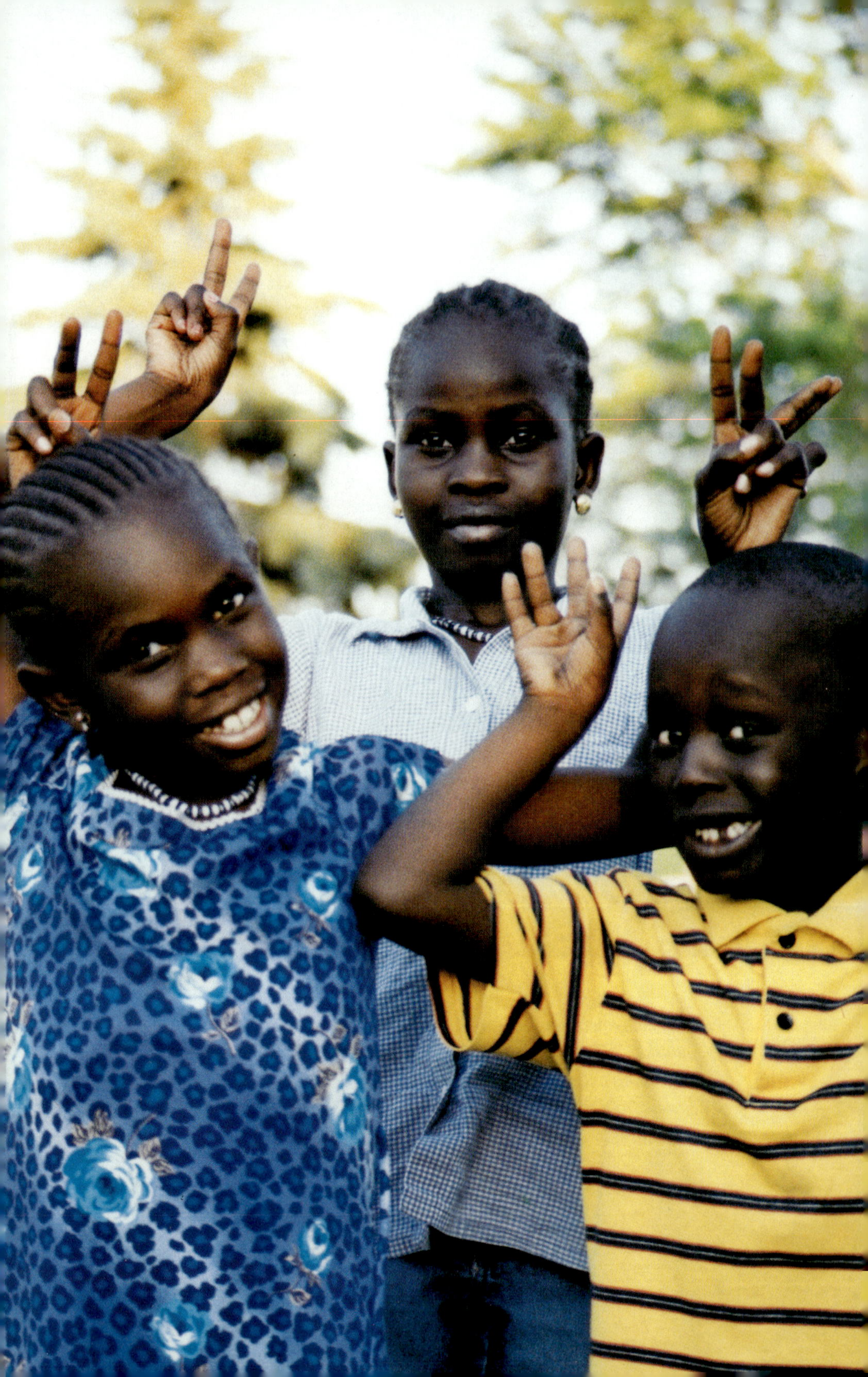

SD TOURISM

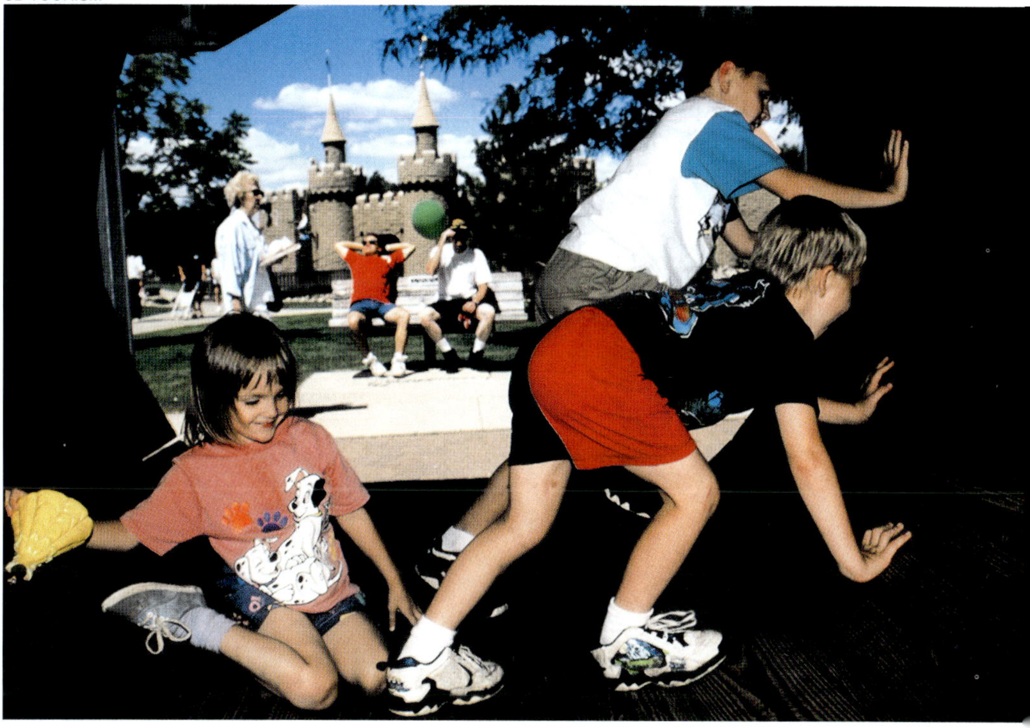

Youth play starring roles in many town celebrations. Three children from Sudan greet visitors to the Festival of Cultures in Sioux Falls (opposite page). Adults are allowed when accompanied by children at the Wizard of Oz festival in Aberdeen (above). Yankton youth stand at attention for a patriotic start to their school's homecoming parade.

BEN HANTEN

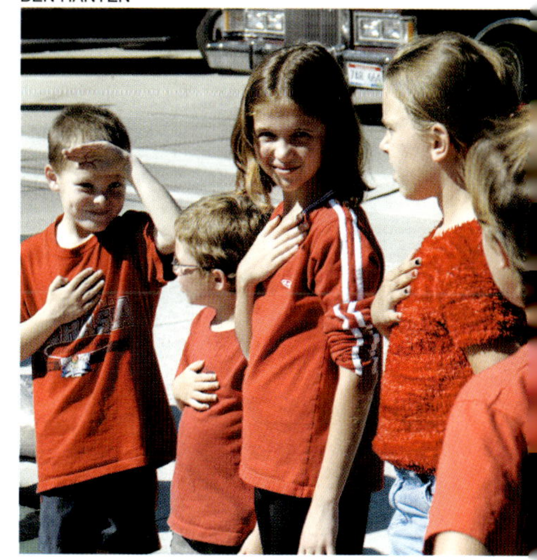

JERRY WILSON

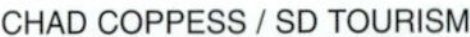
CHAD COPPESS / SD TOURISM

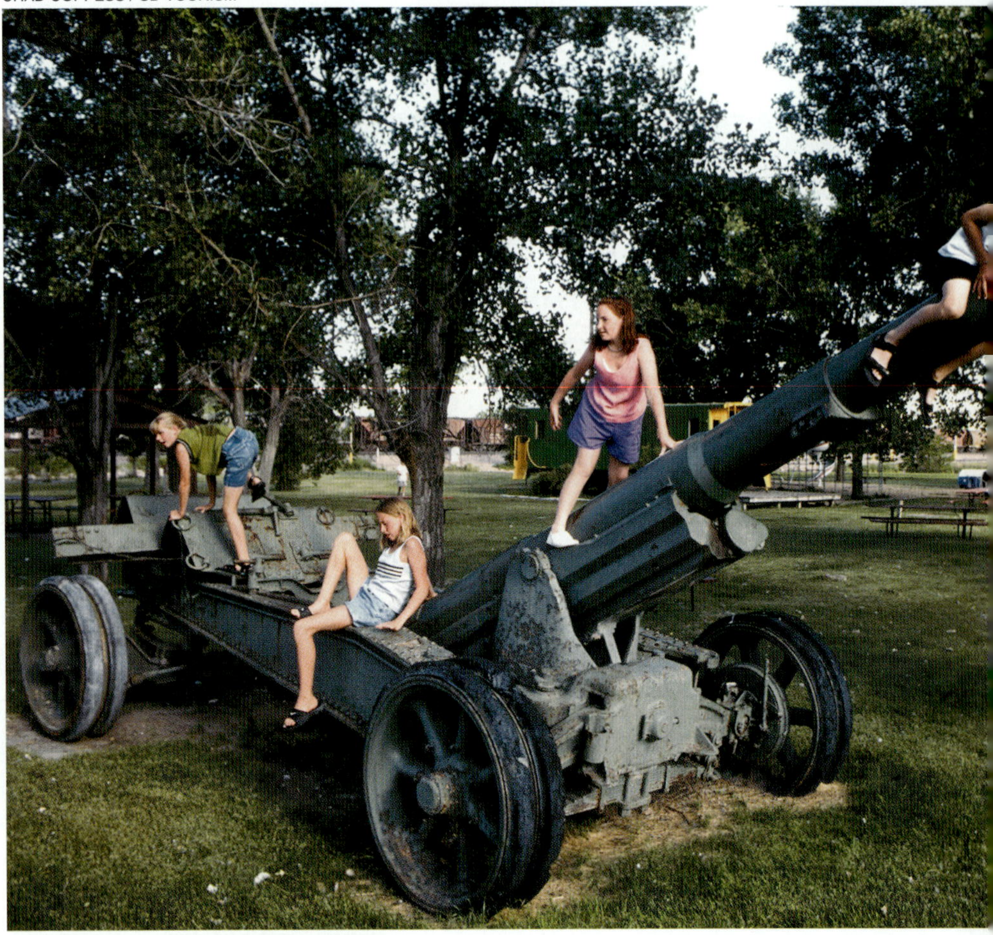

Growing up with guns and other weaponry is part of South Dakota life. Youngsters play on an old cannon at the Edgemont city park (above). Boys brandish toy pistols on a Dewey County farm (right); a girl and her muzzleloader at Mitchell (bottom right).

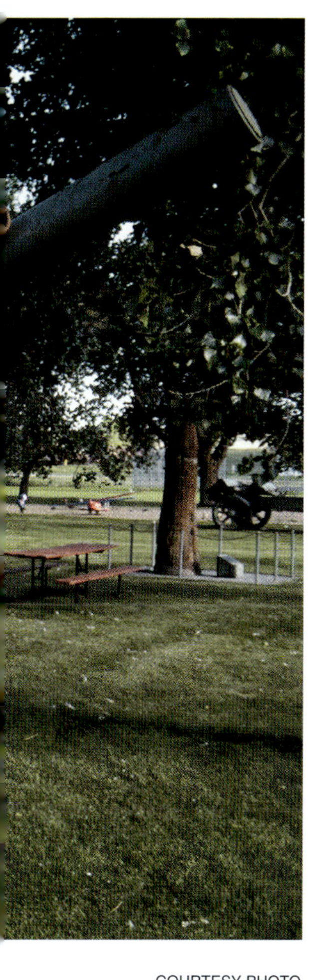

BERNIE HUNHOFF

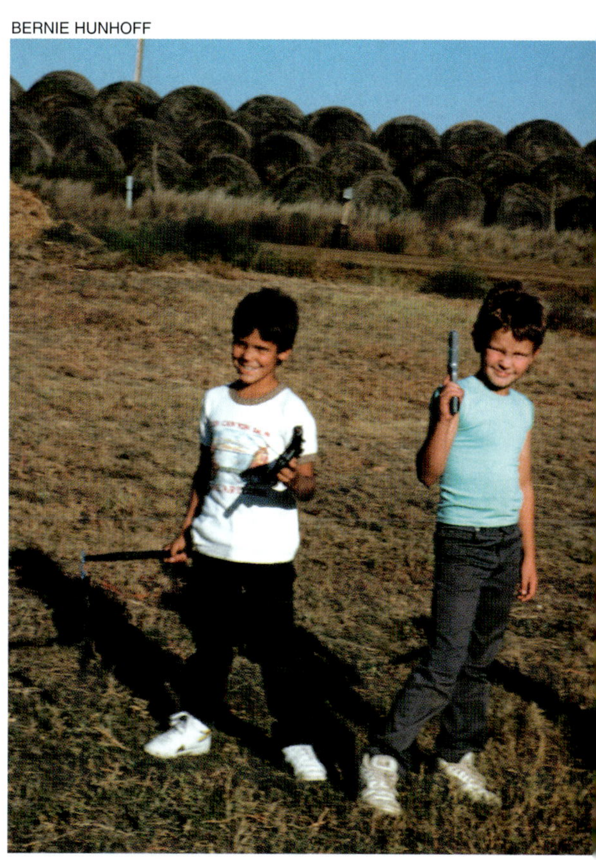

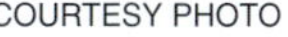

COURTESY PHOTO

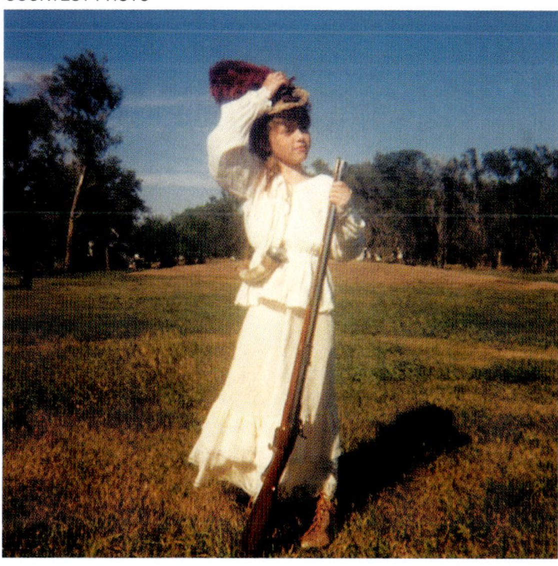

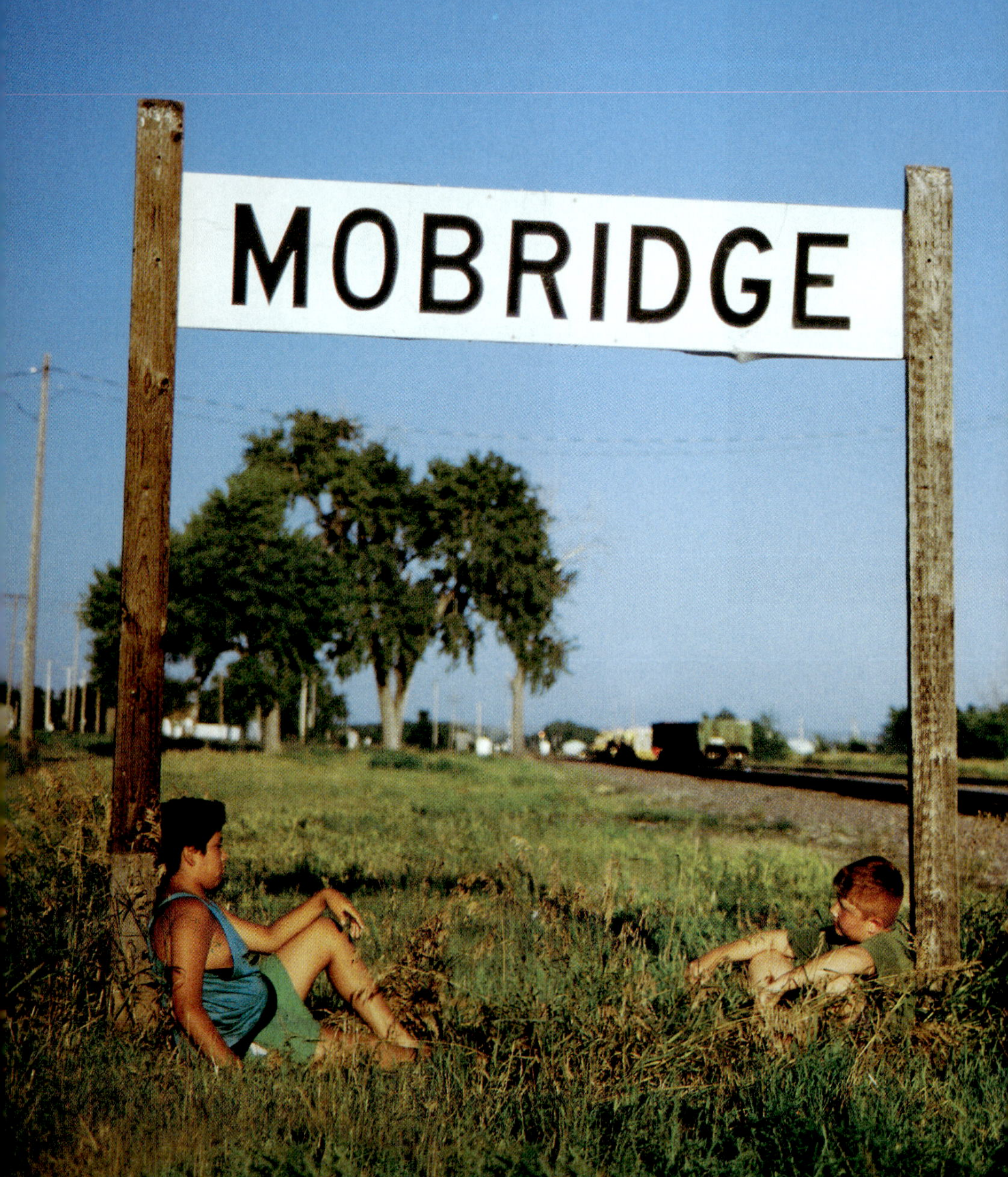
MOBRIDGE

BEN HANTEN

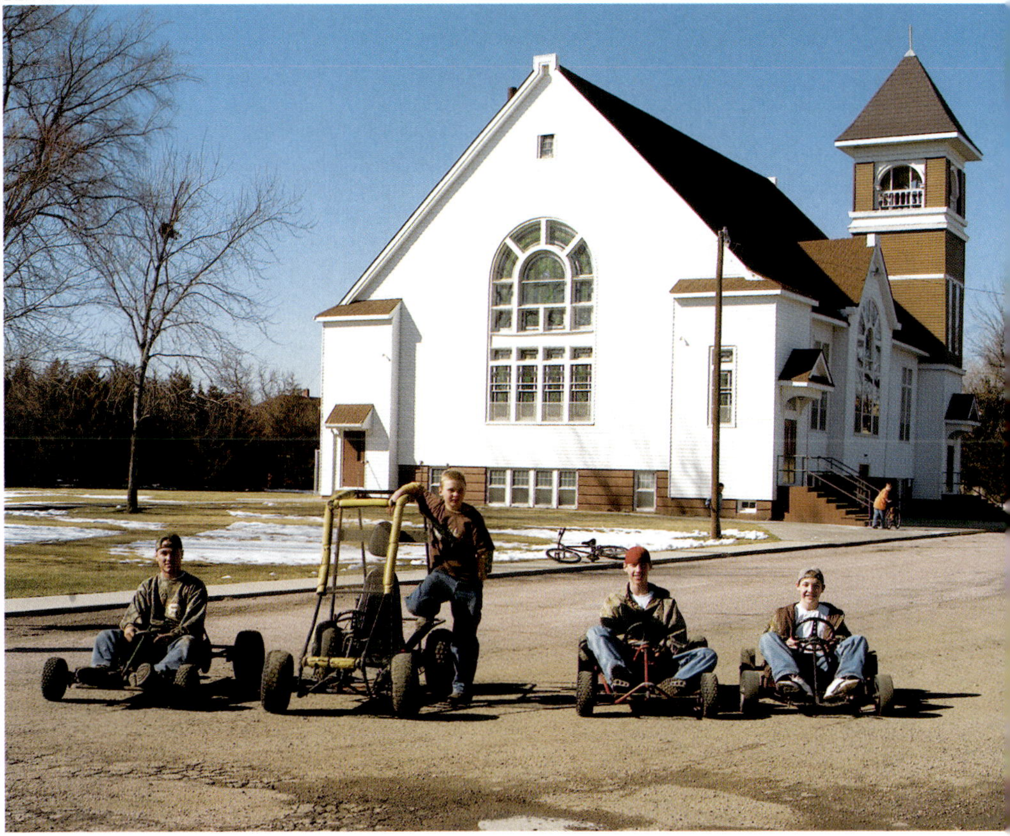

Modern life is more structured than ever for youngsters, but there's still time to hang out around the railroad tracks at Mobridge, or go-cart in the small town of New Holland, or just fiddle on a Pearl Street porch in Yankton.

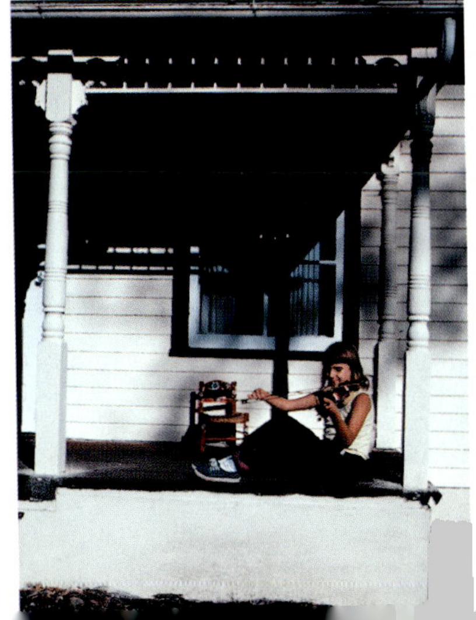

BERNIE HUNHOFF

SD TOURISM

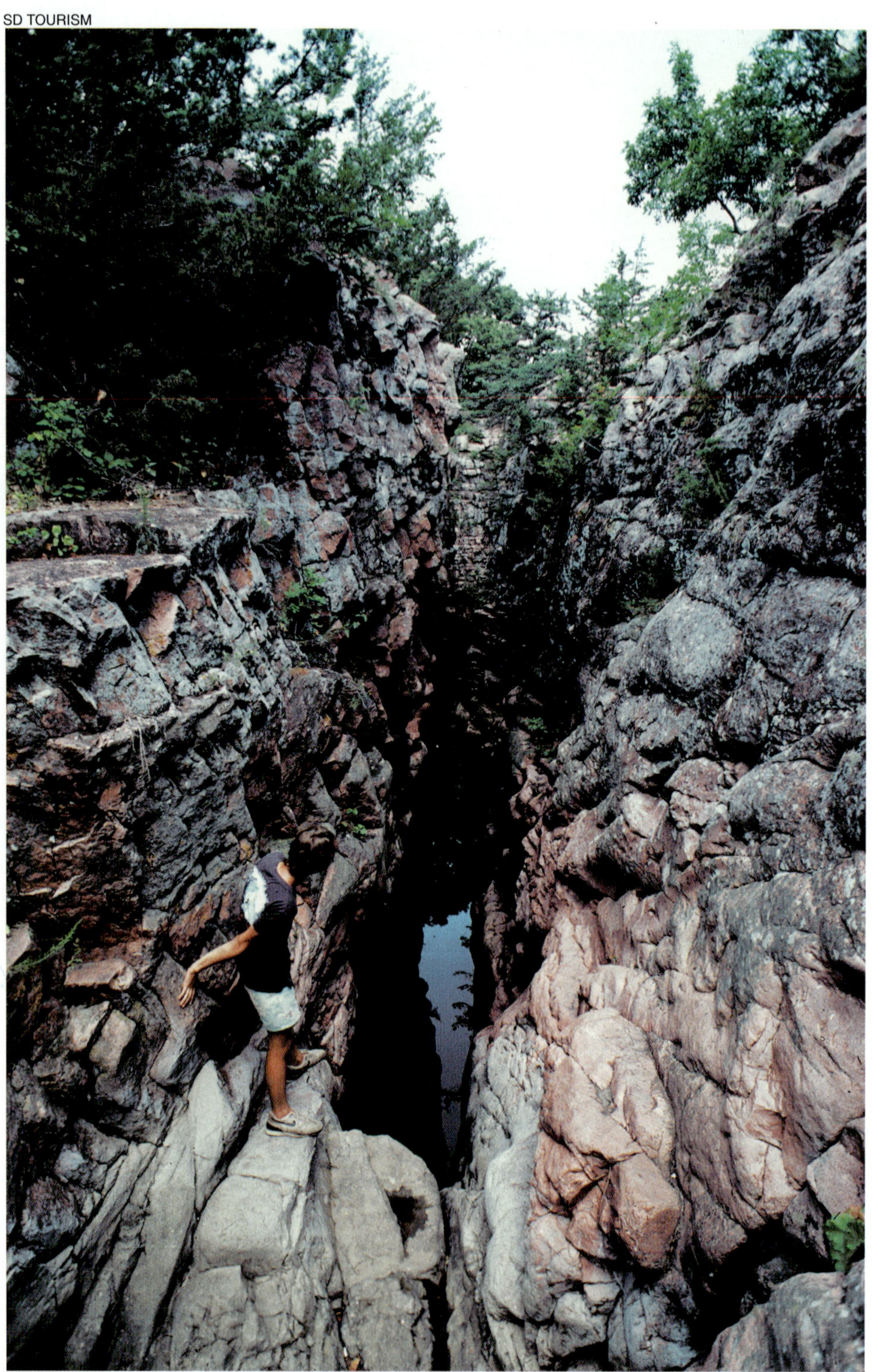

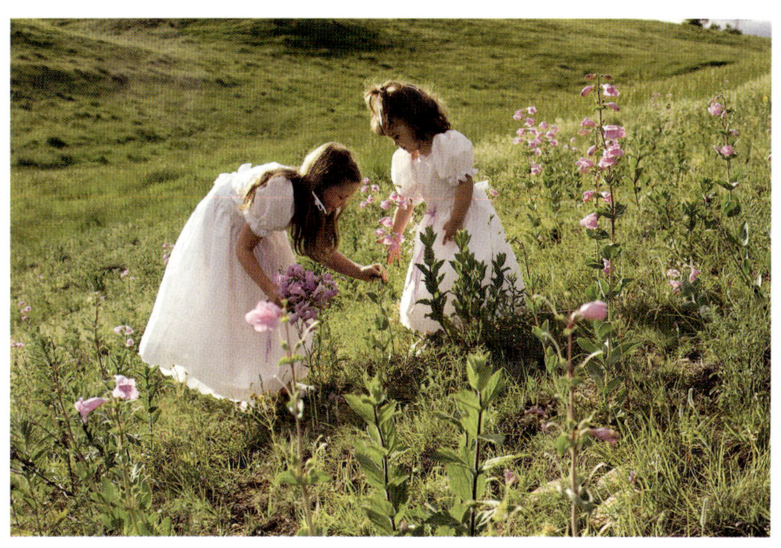

Adventure comes in many ways — like rock climbing (opposite page) in the quartzite of northern Minnehaha County; or searching for wildflowers on a Yankton County hillside; or even burrowing into a pile of "reject" potato chips at the Dakota-style Chips factory near Clark.

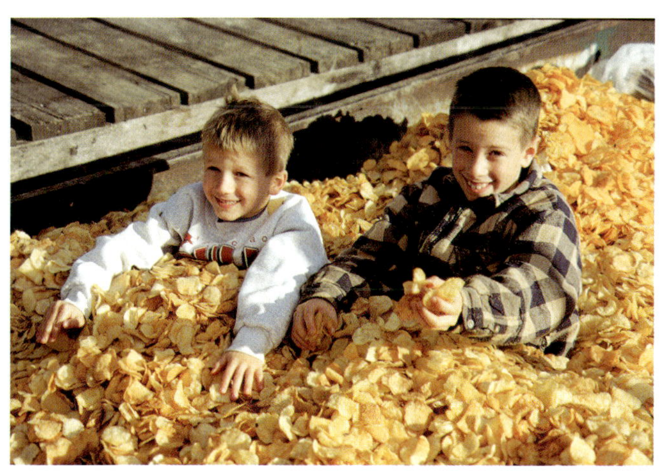

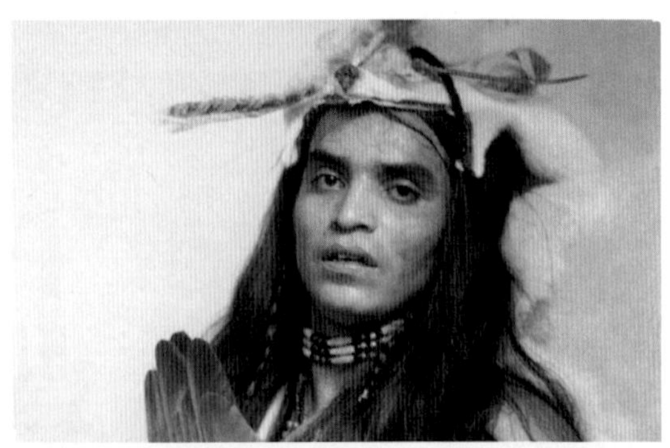

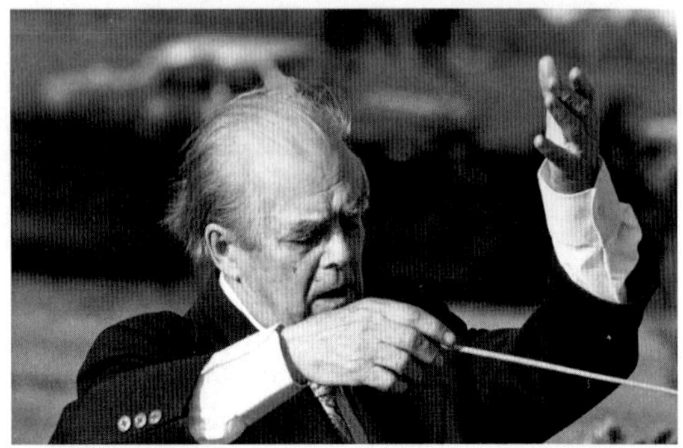

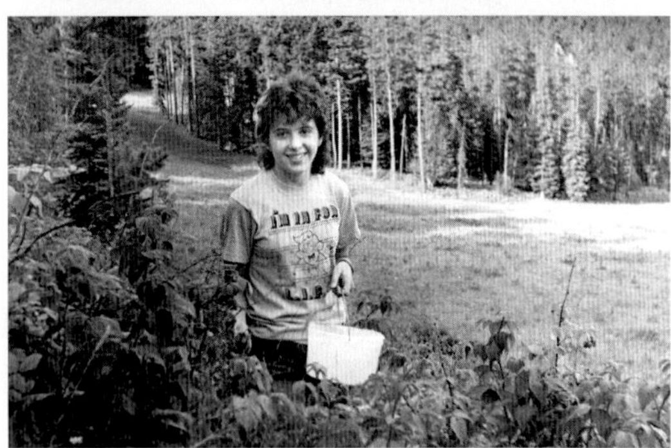

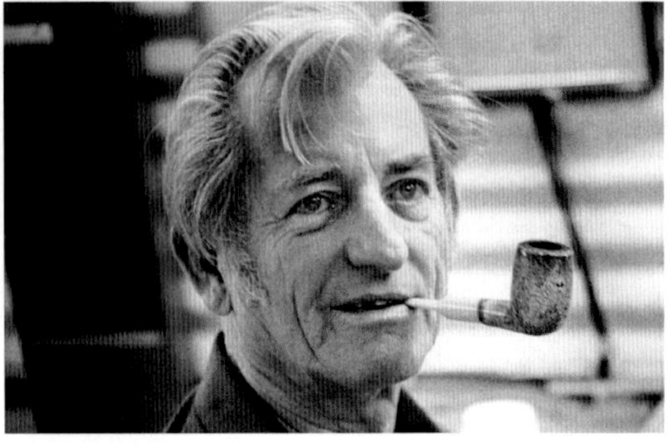

Photos from top: Lower Brule Native Michael Ziegler learned traditional Lakota dancing. Arne Larson founded the National Music Museum in Vermillion. A young lady picks buffaloberries on Terry Peak. Ed Yost set records in ballooning. Opposite page: Avon farmer George Voigt.

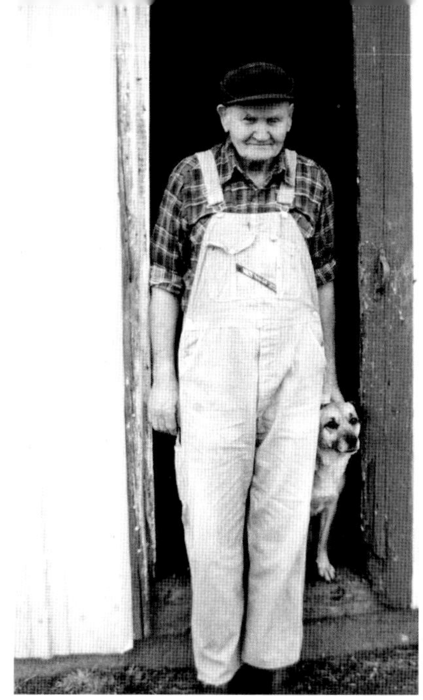

The Early Years

IN BLACK AND WHITE

By Bernie Hunhoff

We had a 35 millimeter Olympus camera with a 50 millimeter lens when we started to plan *South Dakota Magazine's* first issue in the winter of 1984. In exchange for a full page advertisement, Harold's Photography of Sioux Falls traded us a darkroom enlarger, and we used a bank vault in downtown Yankton for a darkroom. I should clarify that last sentence. It was a vault in a defunct bank. We were not tempted by stacks of greenbacks.

Most of the photographs in this chapter were shot by me with that camera and enlarged in that empty vault or, later, in the refurbished bathroom of the 130-year-old Pennington House in Yankton, which we bought and moved to in 1987. We built a counter top over a claw-foot tub and taped black paper over the window glass to trap the darkness. The vault was blacker, but its thick, steel door always worried me, because no one knew the combination.

Digital photography was merely a twinkle in someone's eye then. Printing color pictures in magazines was very expensive. We used color on the covers, but nearly all the inside pages were black and white. In the 1990s, as our readership grew, we could afford more color pages. But we continued to use some black and whites, and even do so on occasion today. A black and white photograph leaves something for the imagination — like a pretty woman in a fine dress. The mood inspires the mind to fill the details. Furthermore, in today's cluttered colored world, black and white seems refreshingly simple.

In those early years, we knew we didn't have the equipment or the expertise to copy Ansel Adams-style landscapes, so we didn't try. We focused mostly on people in our black and white days. Our modest Olympus worked fine at catching them in their city and rural environments. We photographed famous people and hermits and everyone in between. Eventually we bought a pair of used Nikons and a few more lenses, a tripod and some special lights (that mysteriously exploded in the living room of Redfield mystery writer Kathleen Taylor when we were taking her picture for a story).

Today, black and white photography is a nearly-lost art, thanks to the convenience of the computer digit. A darkroom is now the equivalent of the weaver's loom or the potter's wheel; all were necessities at one time and today they are primarily used by fine artists.

We didn't consider it to be art when we shot these pictures. It was just an affordable way for us to show off South Dakota. Here she is in black and white.

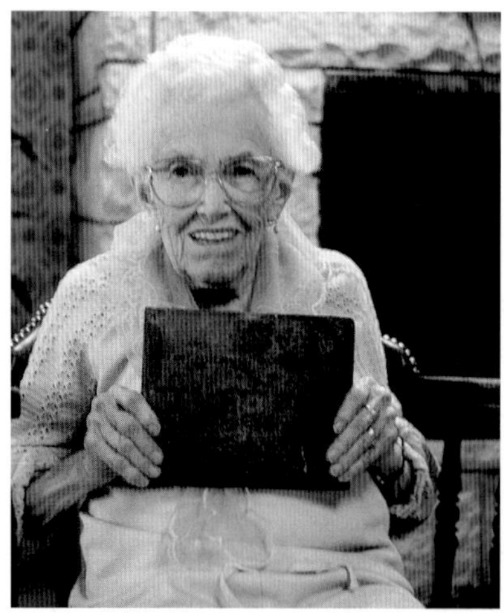

Ethel Roberts, pictured in 1989 at Howard, was one of three youngsters to discover the historic Verendrye Plate near Fort Pierre. The lead plate is one of three left behind by French explorers in 1743.

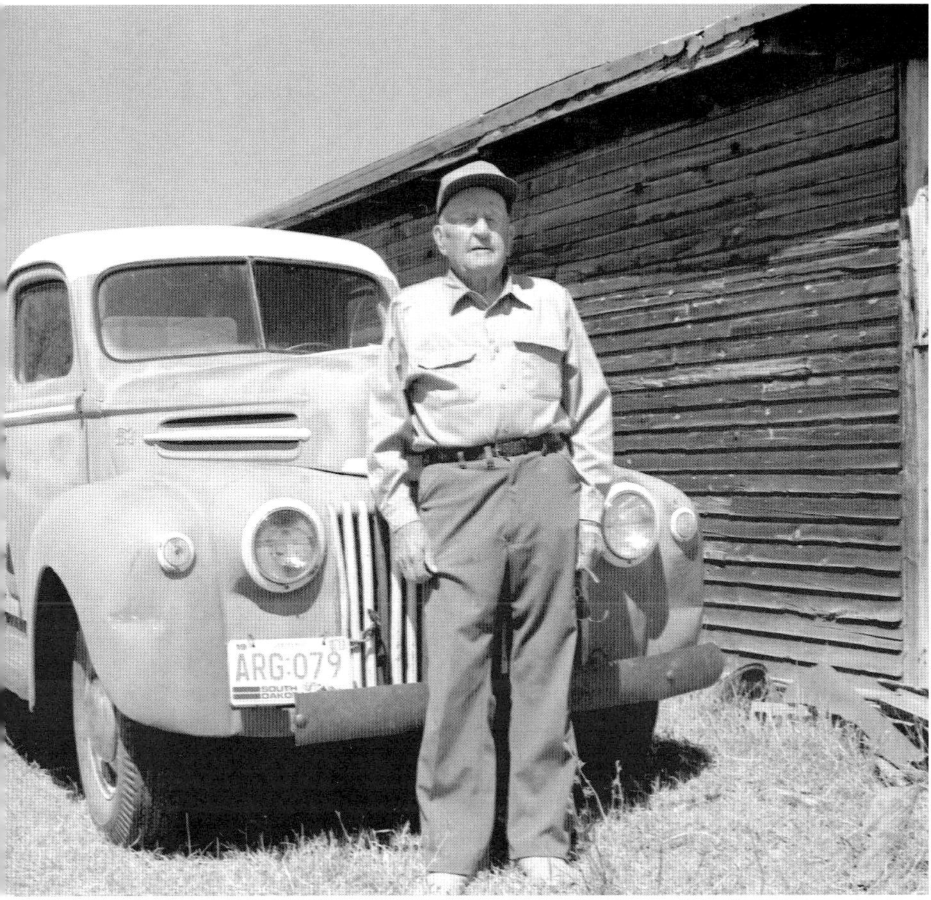

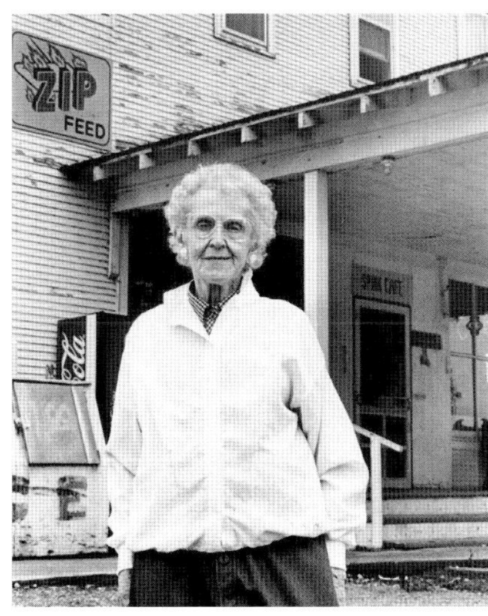

Pioneer aviator Clyde Ice (above), interviewed in 1986, was a well-known barnstormer who gave many South Dakotans their first plane ride. He also flew countless mercy missions, bringing doctors to patients or vice versa. At right, Myrtle Twedt was more stationary. She painted pictures of Spink, a tiny place in Union County.

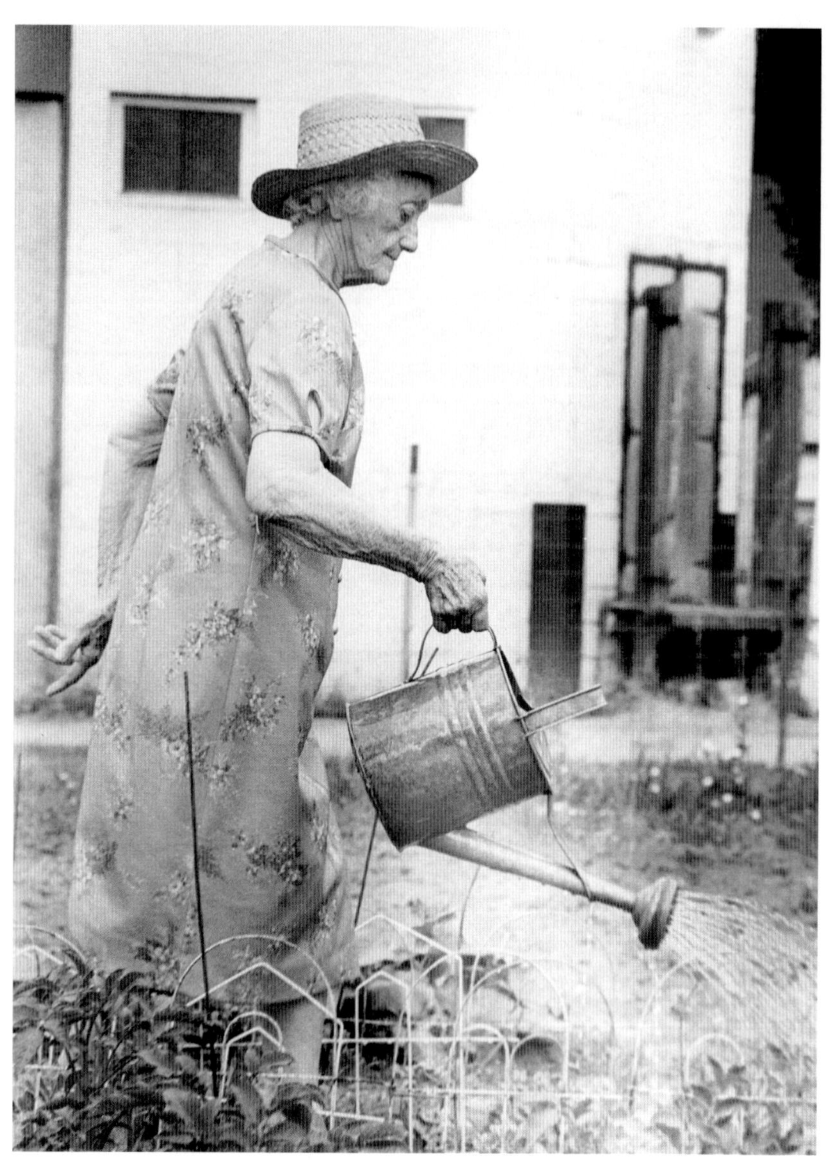

Mary Kaiser lived next door to South Dakota Magazine's office in Yankton. She was an avid flower gardener who prayed rosaries for those who did her favors.

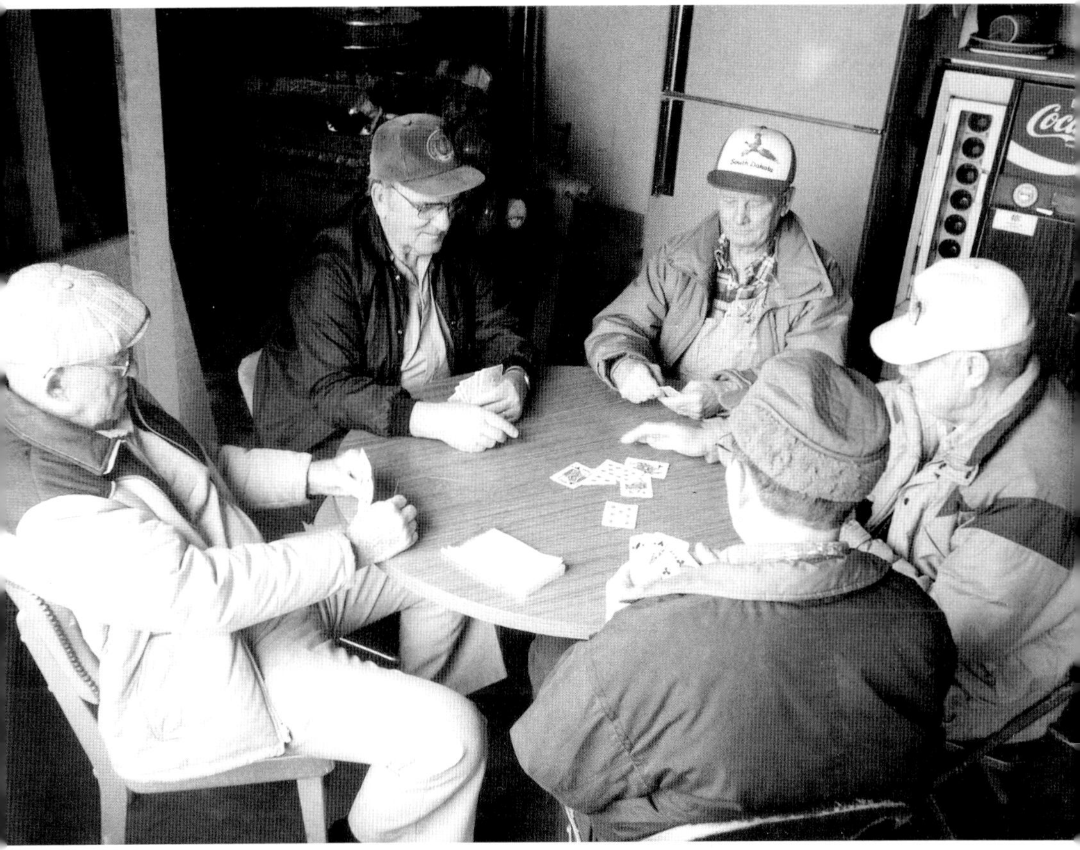

The largest Danish colony in the United States in the late 19th century was in Turner County, so it's no surprise that men still play Sevensil, a card game from the Old Country, on main street in Viborg. At right: St. Francis Mission on the Rosebud Reservation.

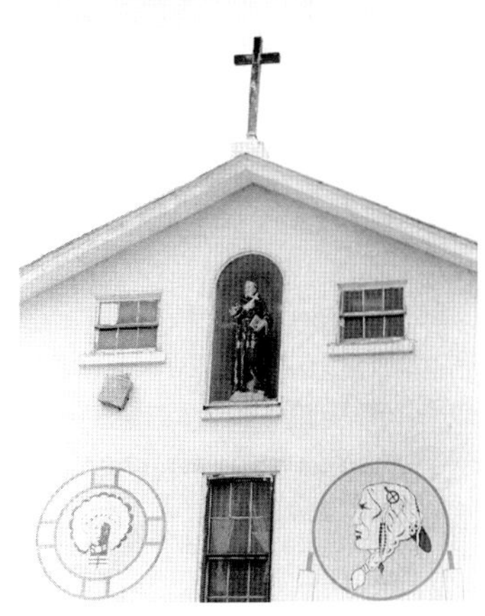

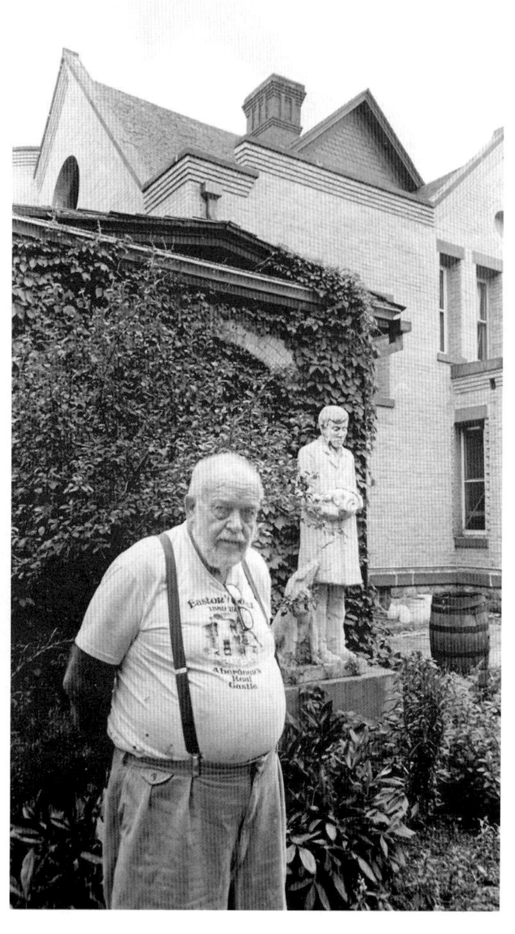

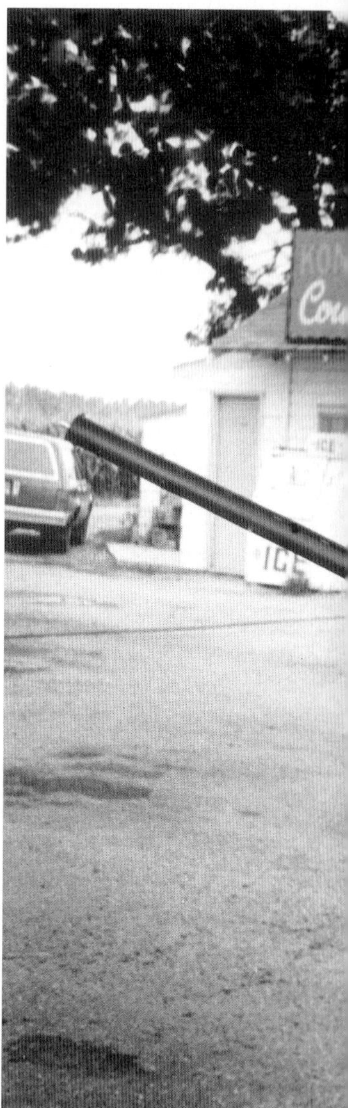

Easton's Castle was built on the outskirts of Aberdeen in 1889. The big Victorian house with gingerbread trim later fell into disrepair, but veterinarian Sam Holman and his family bought it in the 1960s and lovingly restored the yellow brick landmark, inside and out.

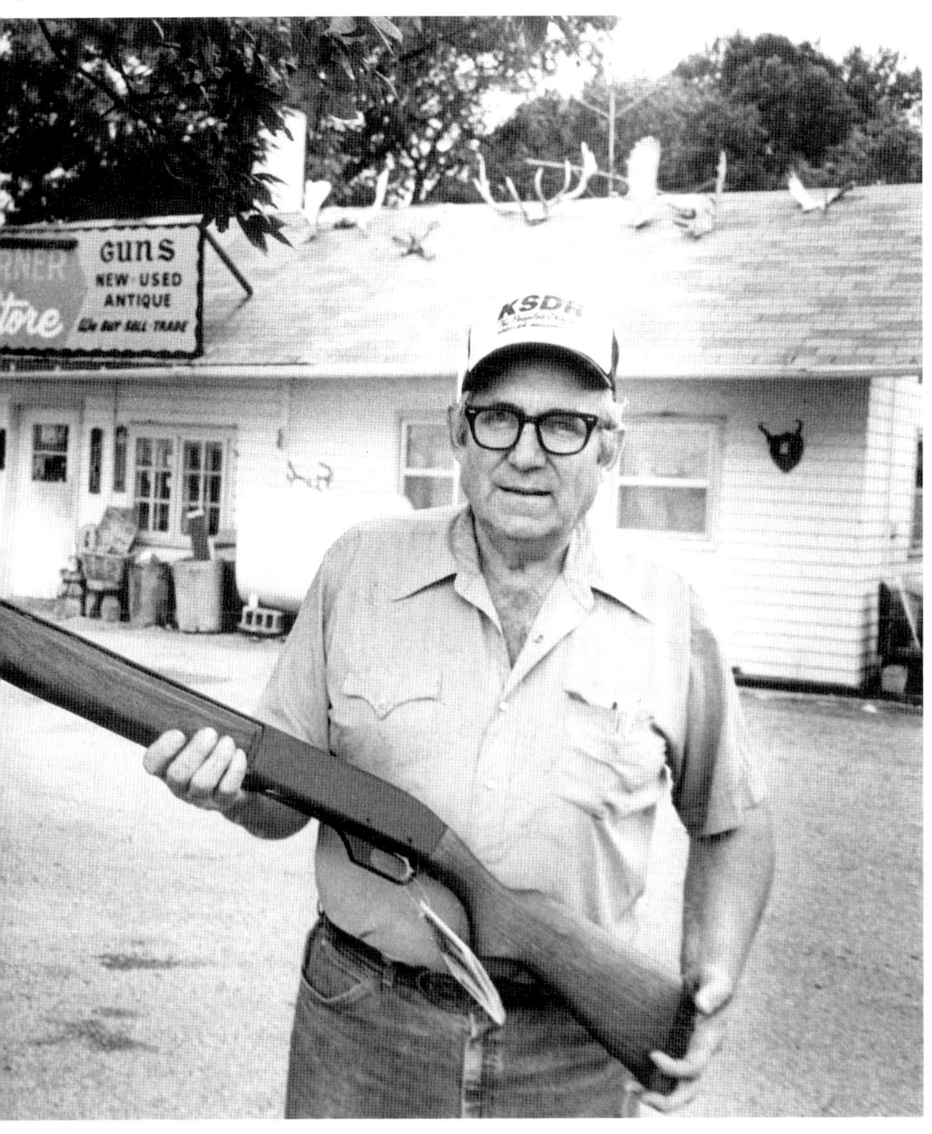

In 1964, Curt Carter bought his uncle's gas station, south of Watertown on U.S. Highway 81, and hung a few guns on the wall to sell. They sold, so he hung a few more. The business boomed into one of the Midwest's biggest gun shops.

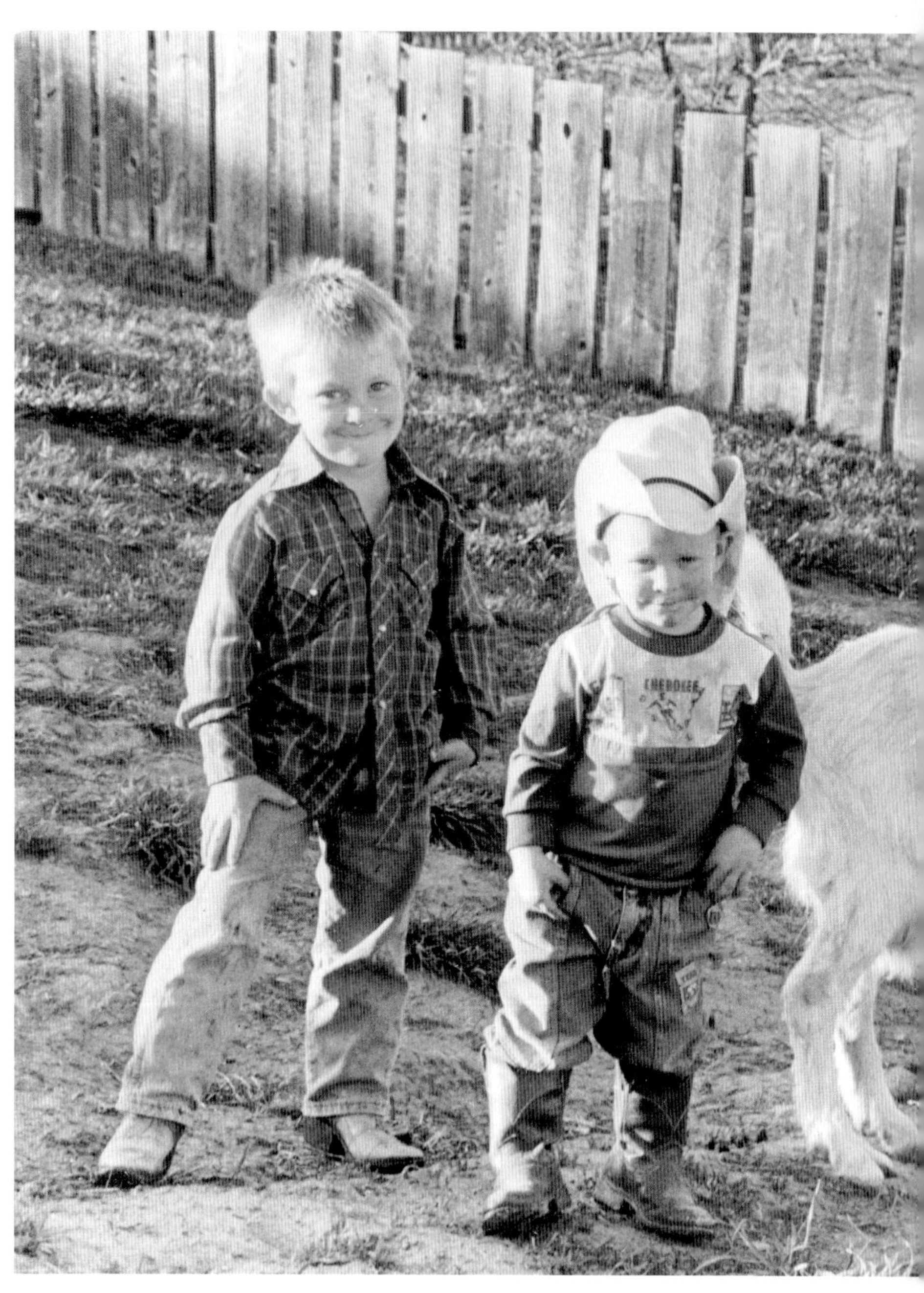

Just as our writer-photographer arrived at the Lawrence Brown ranch near Buffalo on a summer's evening in 1993, Lawrence's three grandchildren stepped out of the barn to milk their goat, Eugenia Blue Flower. The boys are (from left) Nathan, Joseph and Justin.

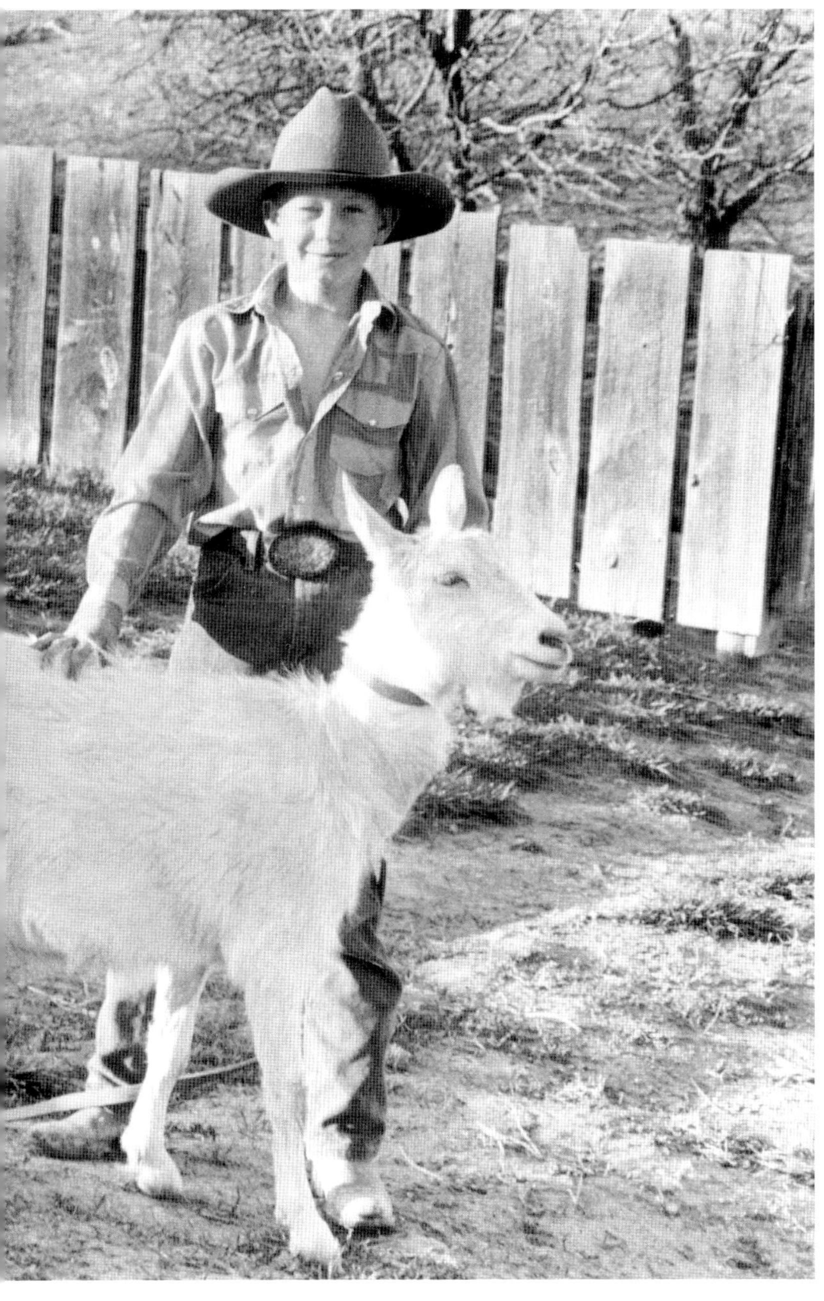

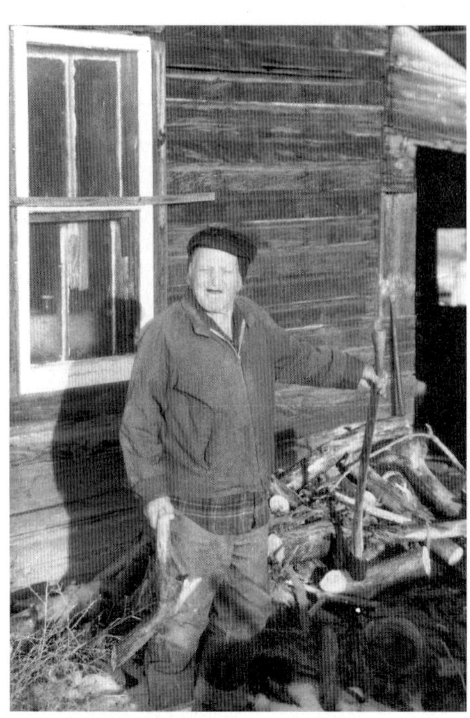

We visited Beryle Seaman in his small house along the Bad River, southwest of Fort Pierre, in 1997. He had survived a long and terrible winter and, anxious for company, told us about his life. Readers loved his simple and unusual aphorisms.

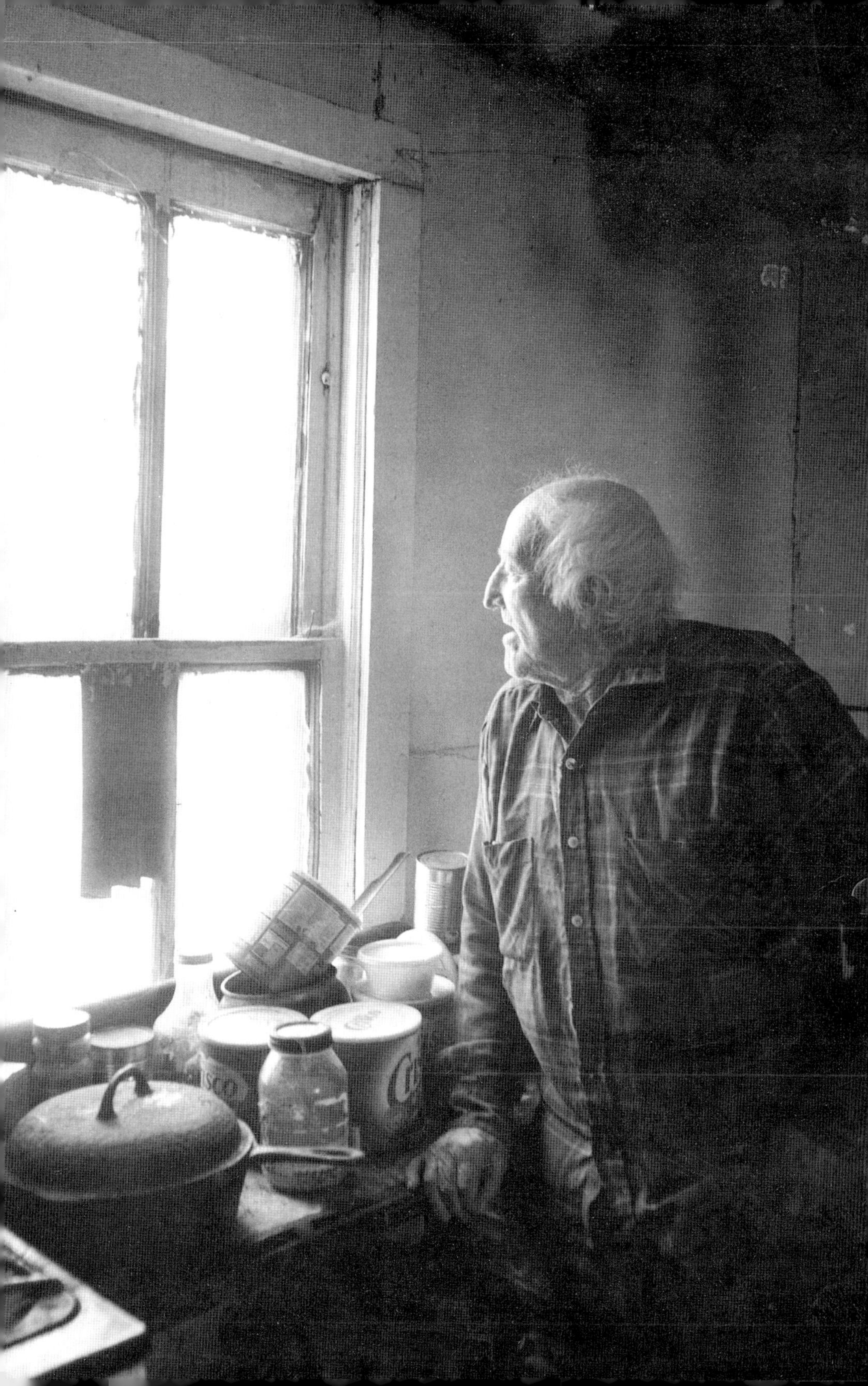

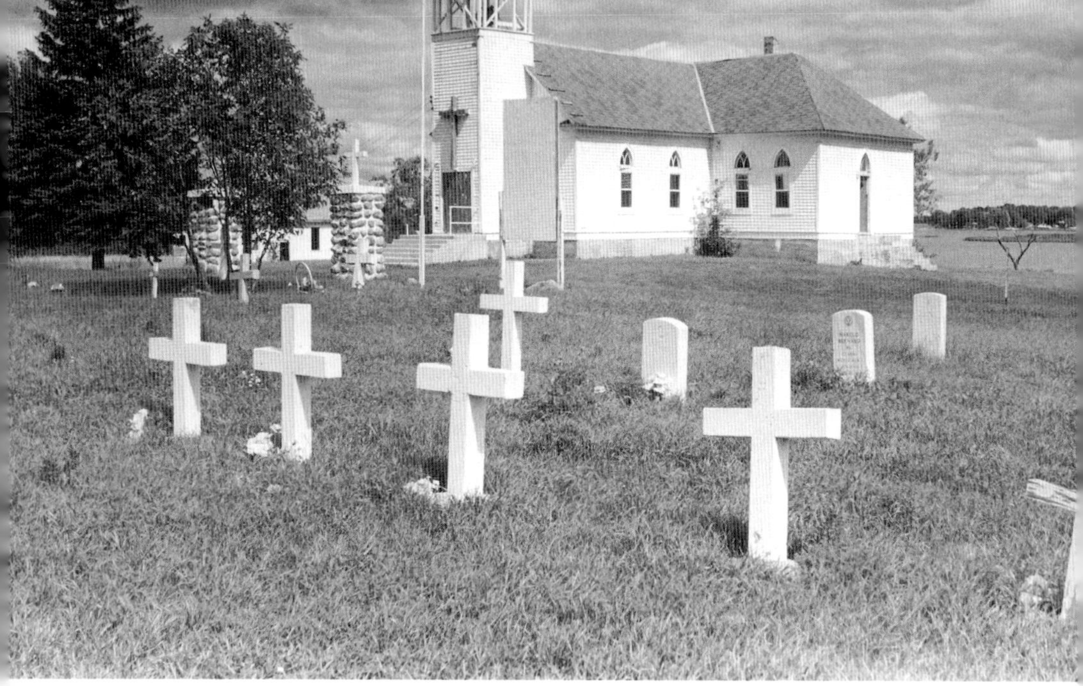

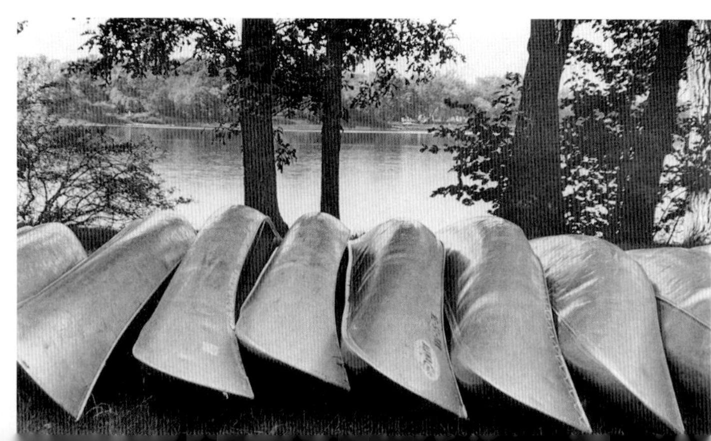

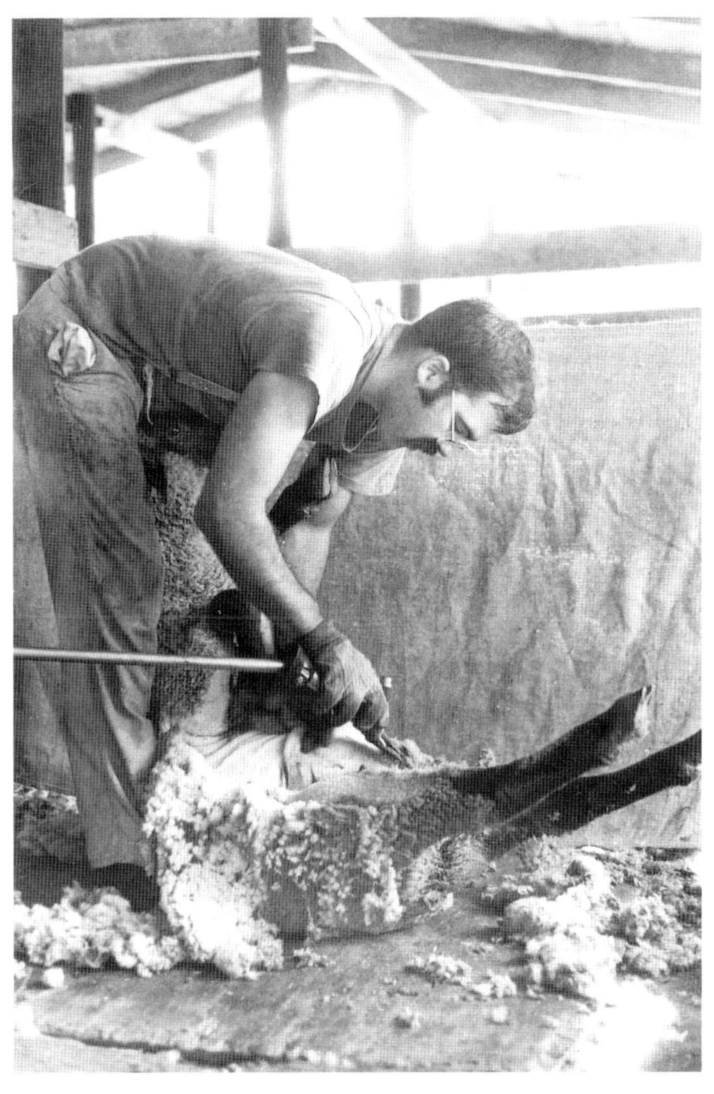

More than two million pounds of wool are sheared and sold in South Dakota every summer. The total sheep herd numbers about 375,000.

St. James Episcopal Church attracts worshipers to the west shore of Enemy Swim Lake in South Dakota's glacial lakes region. Below, canoes from the Ne-So-Dak Bible Camp lay waiting.

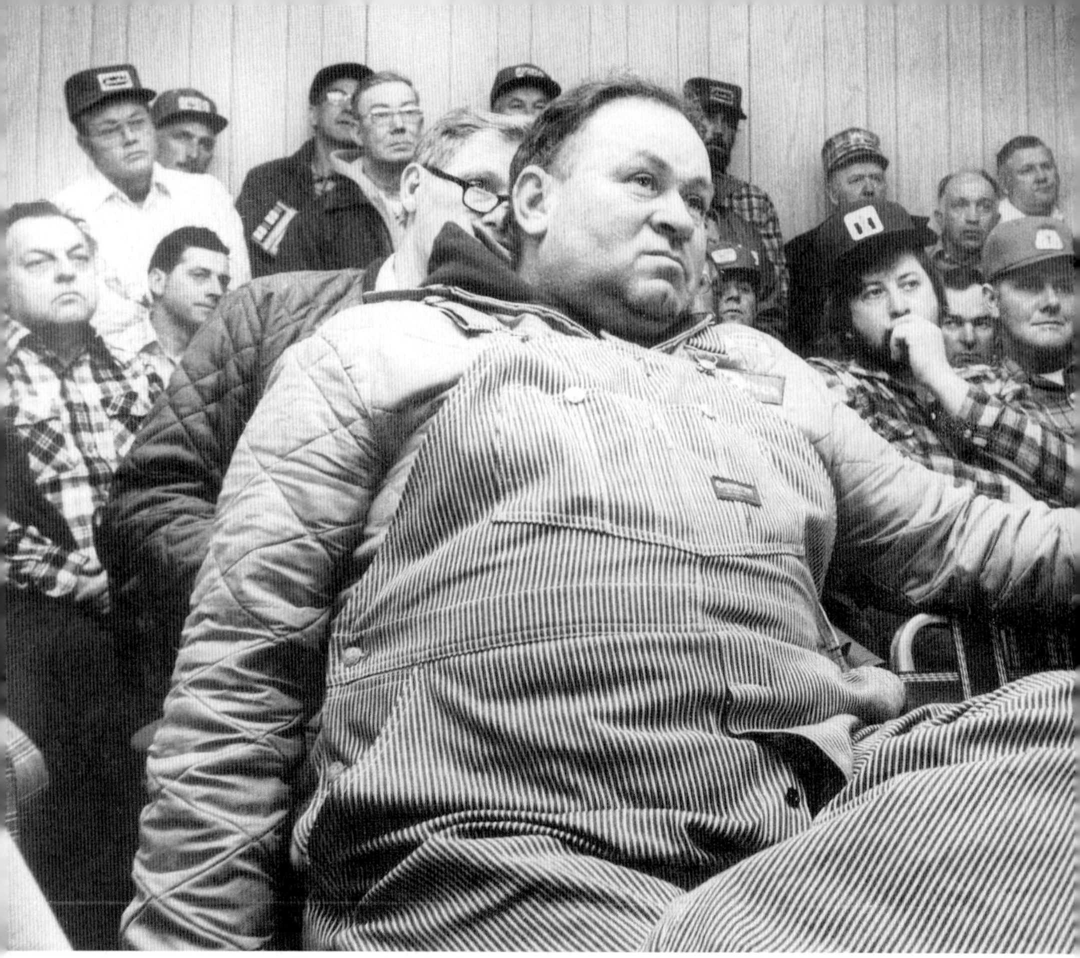

When word that a big mining company was secretly exploring for uranium in Yankton County, a roomful of irate landowners met in Irene and demanded information.

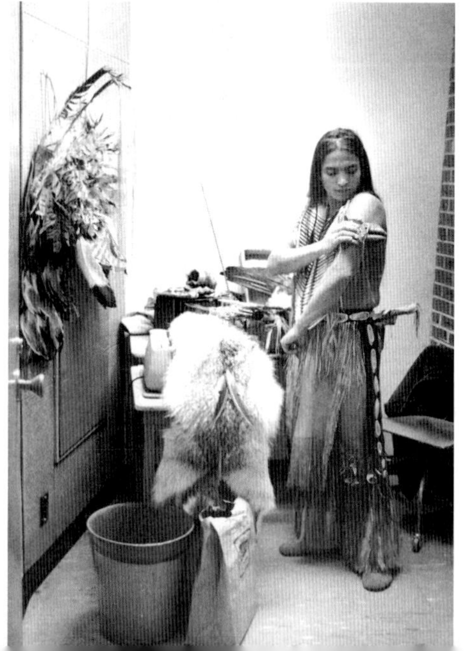

Michael Ziegler faced drug and alcohol troubles as a young man on the Lower Brule reservation. But he found himself when he donned the outfit of traditional Lakota dance and performed for audiences far and wide.

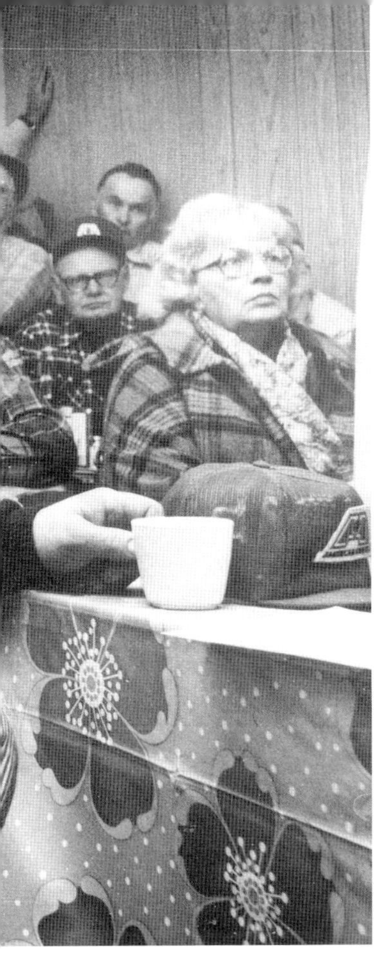

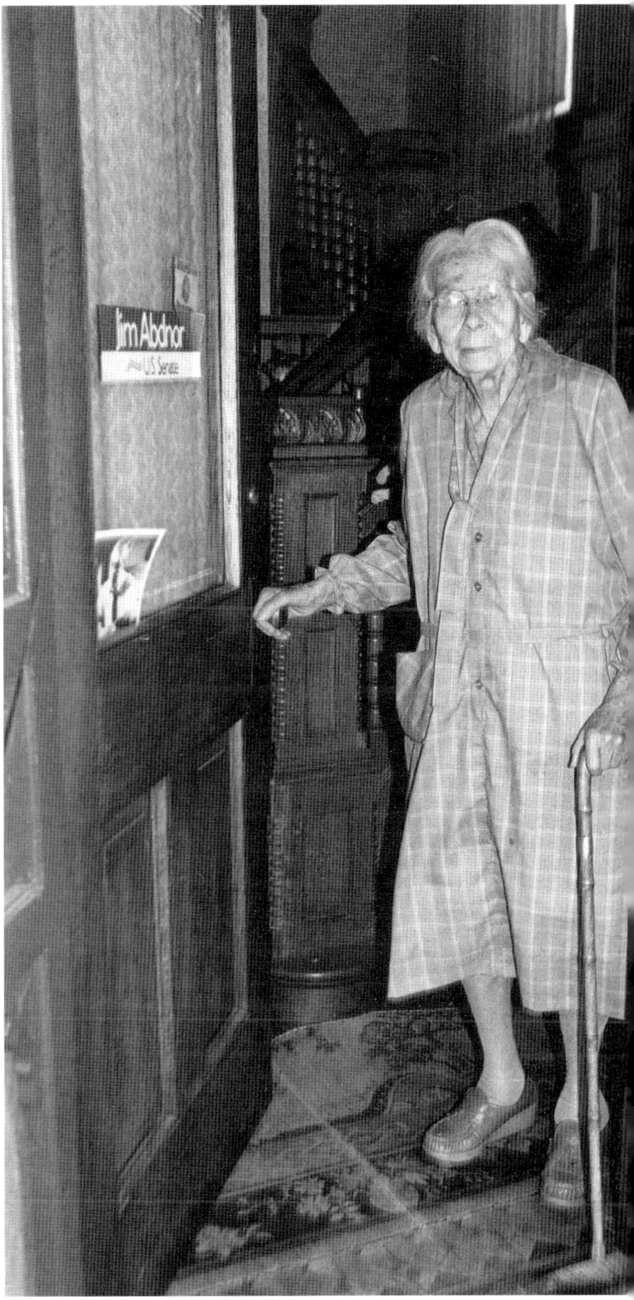

Gladys Pyle of Huron fought for women's right to vote, served in the state legislature, nearly became governor, and in 1938 became the first South Dakota woman elected to the U.S. Senate.

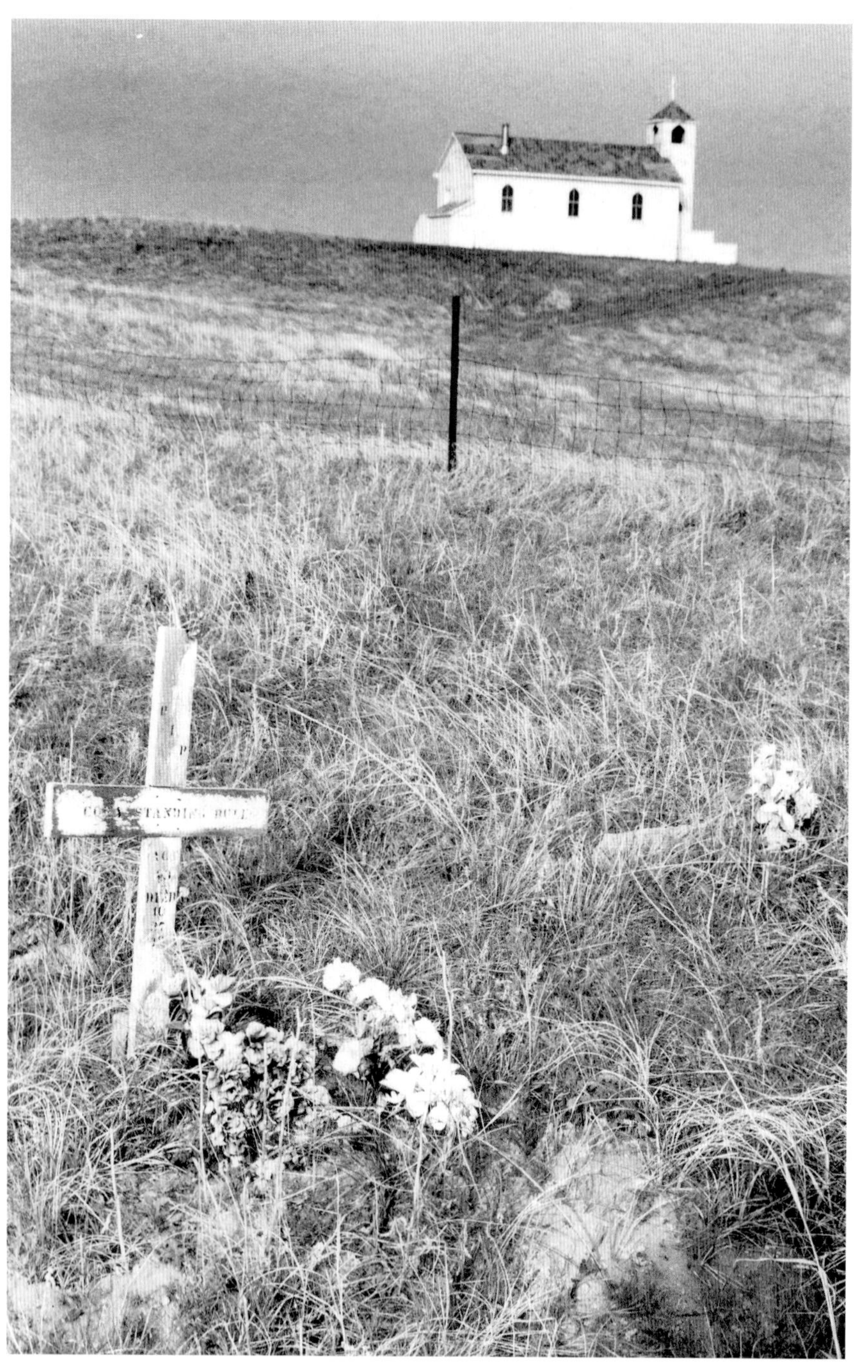

Highway 18, South Dakota's southern route to the Black Hills, is also called The Oyate Trail. Motorists pass through three Sioux reservations — the Yankton, Rosebud and Pine Ridge. Rural churches, small towns, ranch land and wildlife mark the landscape.

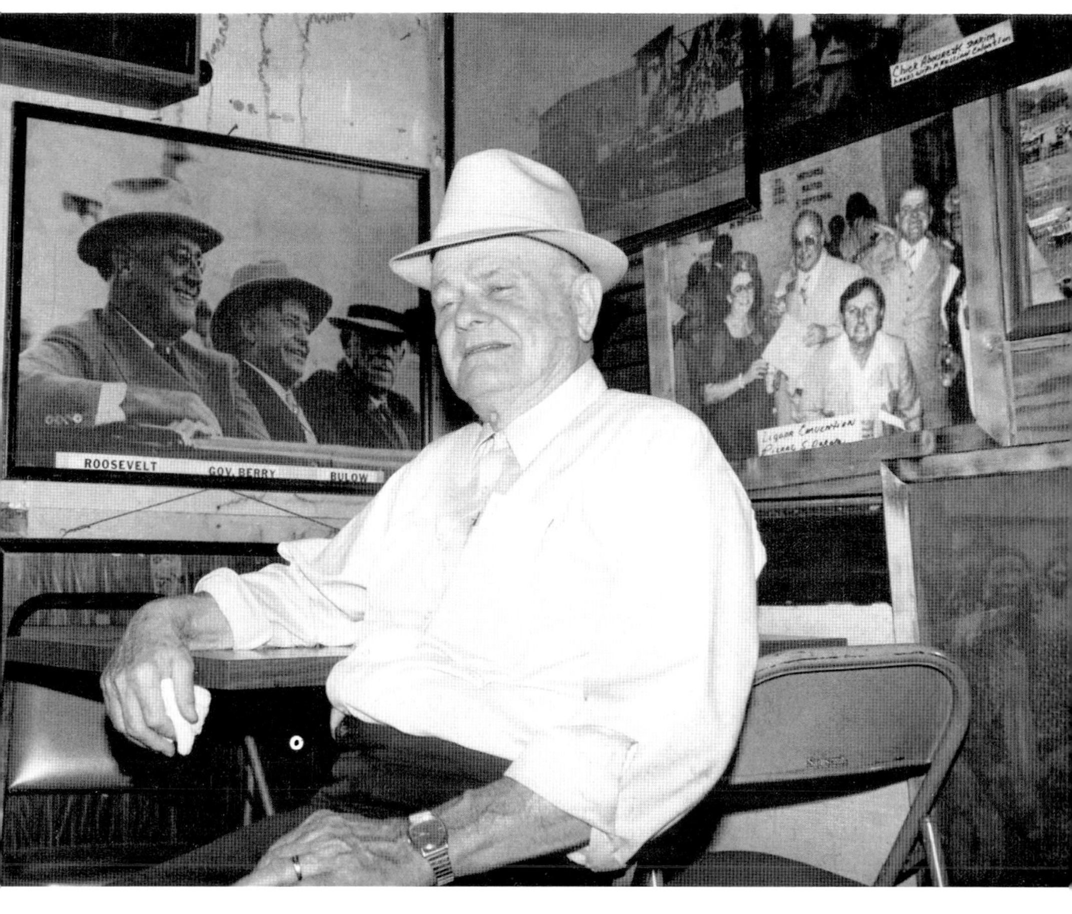

Frank Day came to Dallas, on Highway 18, in 1946 and started a bar that eventually grew to include historical photos and cowboy collectibles — like big belt buckles, boots, hats and fire arms.

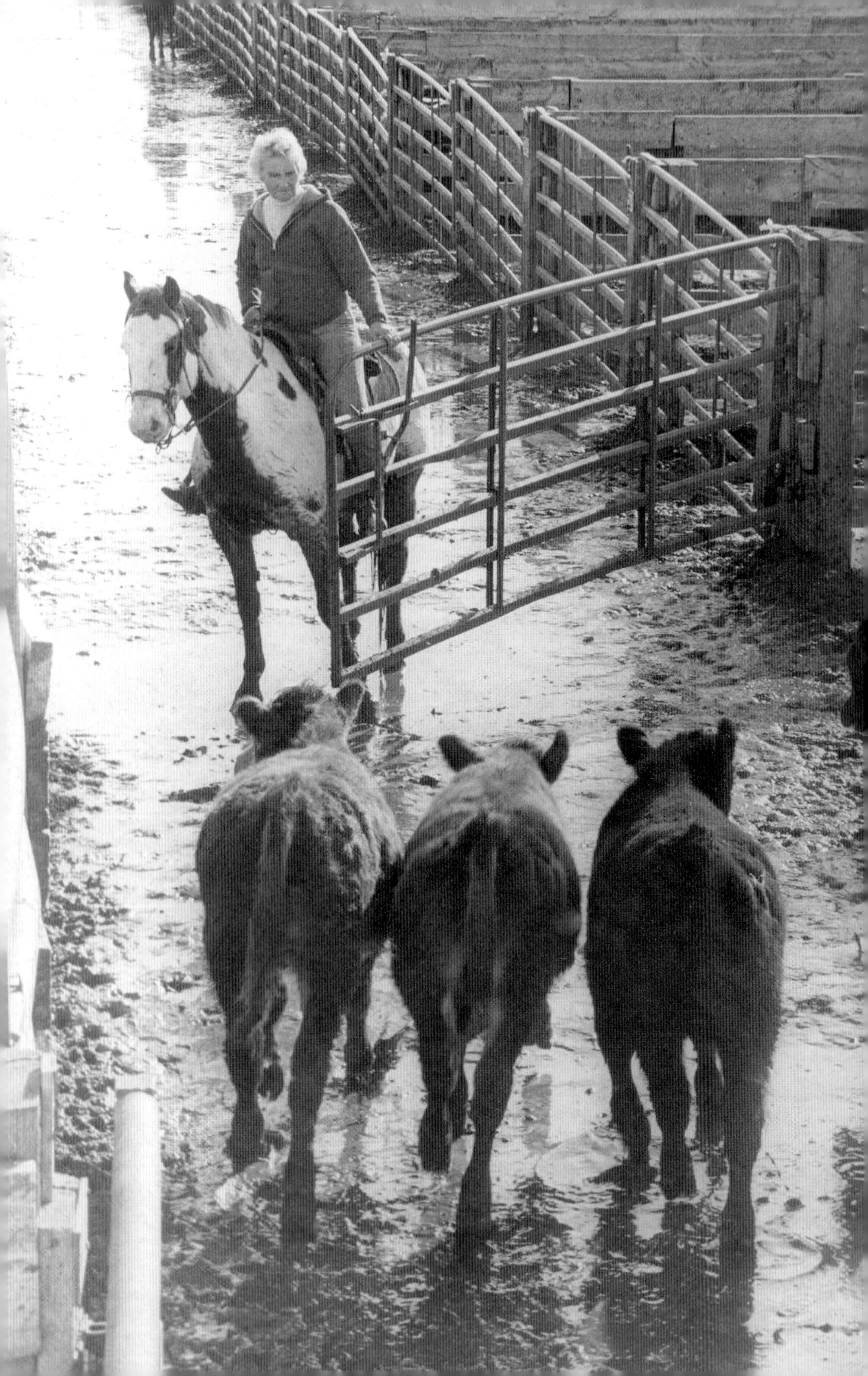

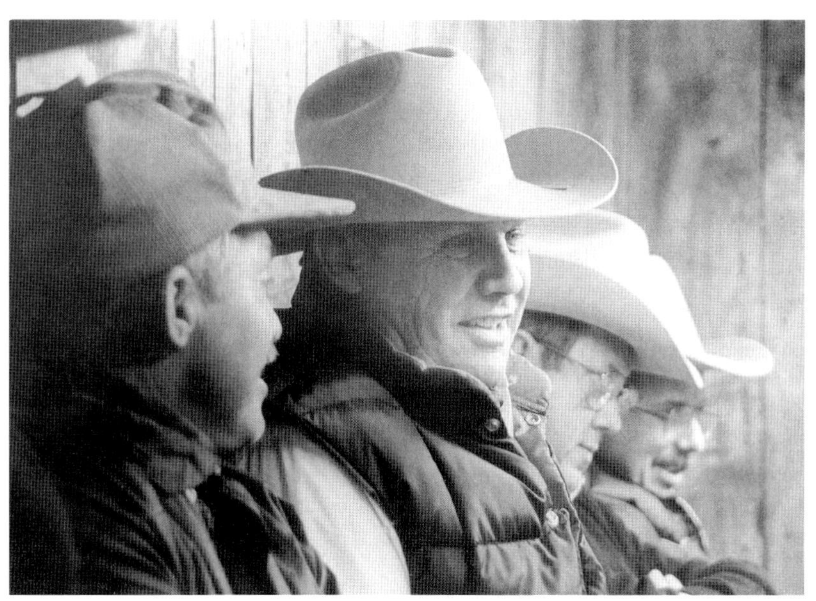

Sale day at a livestock auction is like lunch at Rotary, the bank board meeting, golf in the afternoon and Thanksgiving Day — all rolled into one. St. Onge Livestock Auction in the northern Black Hills is among the busiest. Cattle are escorted to pens (left) while buyers josh in the seats. Ranchers get one big paycheck a year, and its size is determined in a minute or two. Winning the lottery would be fine for a cattleman, but getting $1.10 a pound at St. Onge — now that's real excitement.

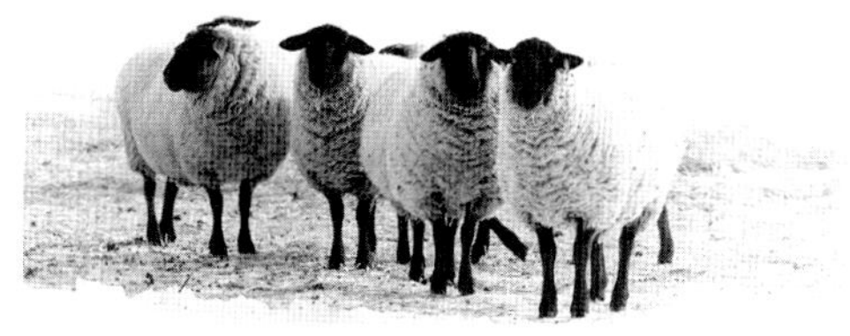

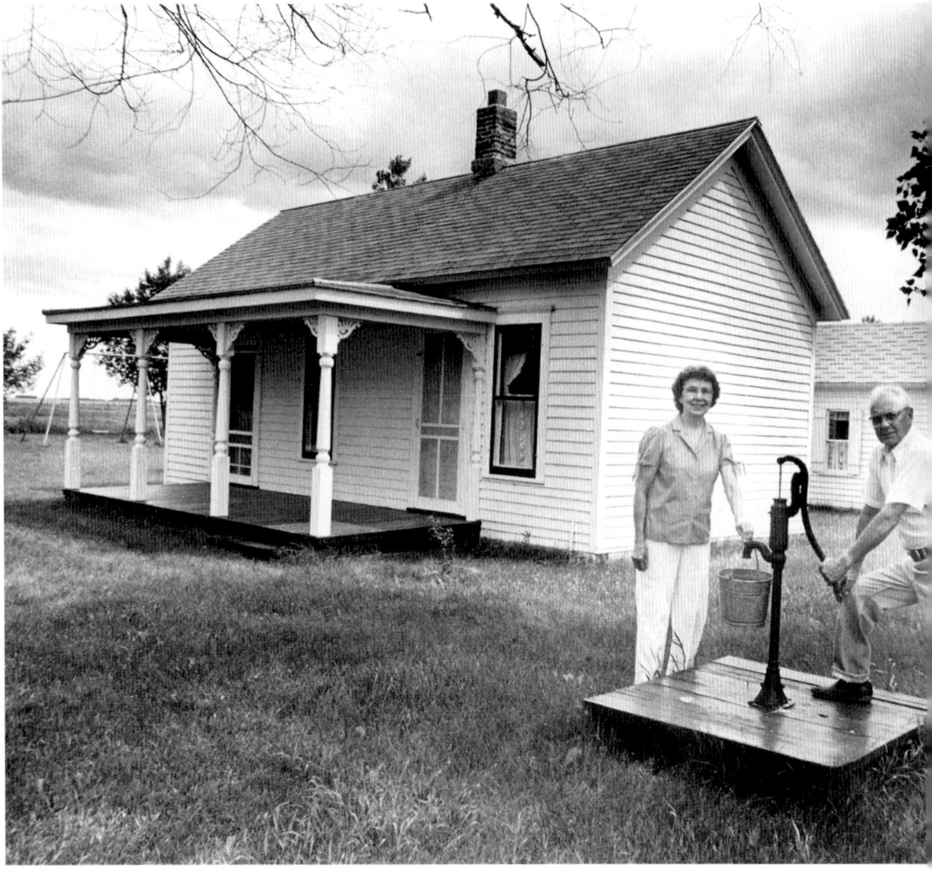

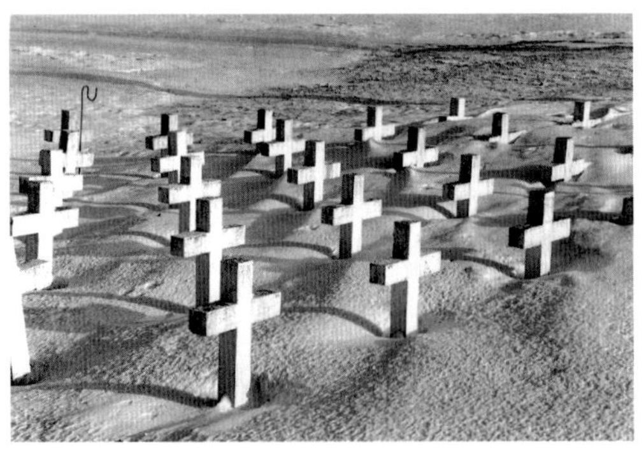

Bob and Bonnie Palmer created Mansfield's own pioneer village (above) when they moved old structures to their property and restored them. Snow blankets a cemetery near Big Stone City (left).

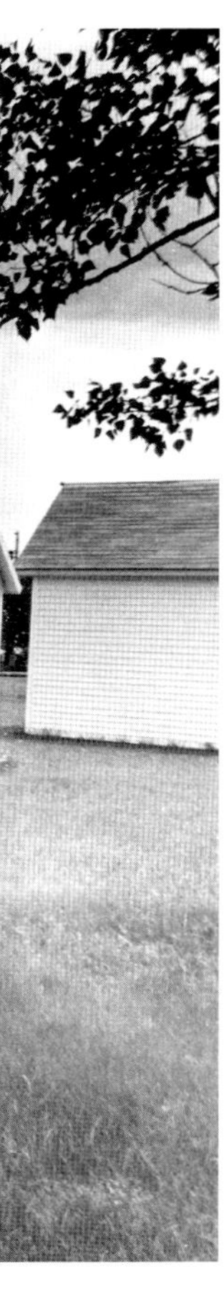

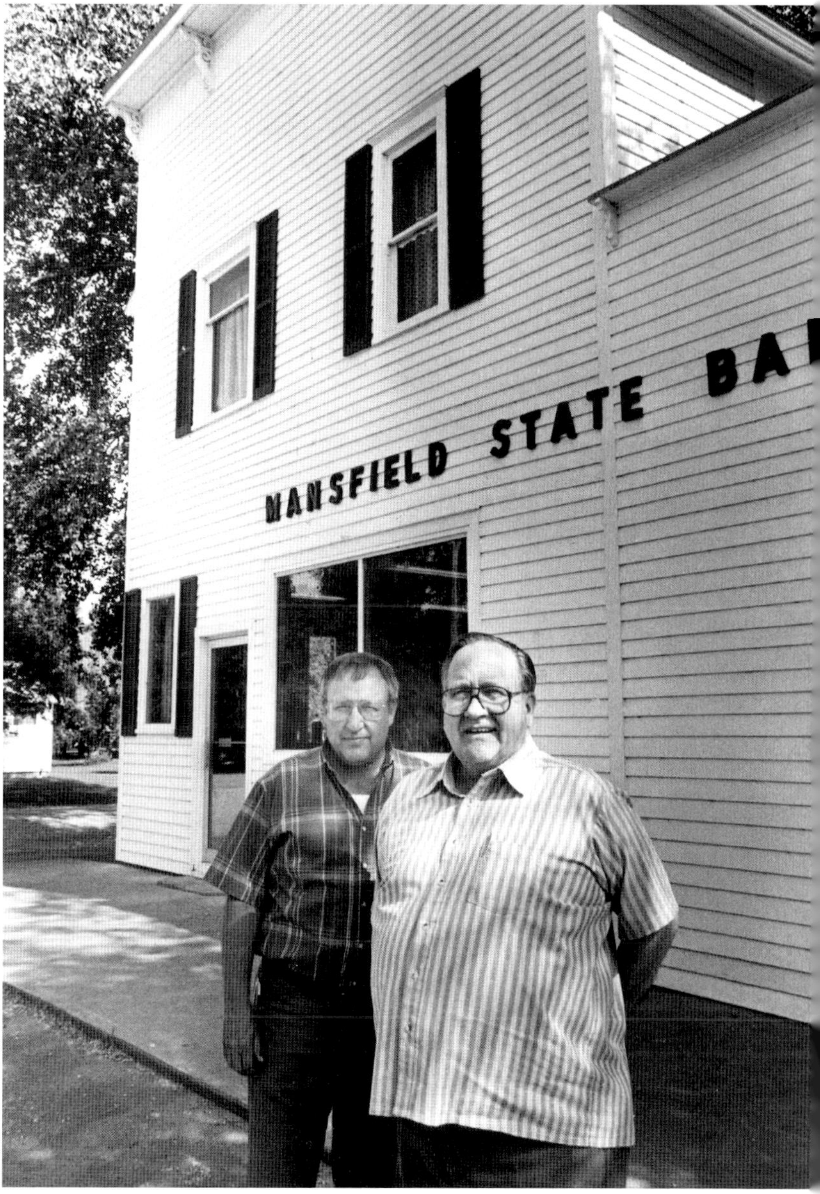

John Forsyth and his father, Bob, ran the Mansfield State Bank decades after their predecessor kept the bank open on a bluff. An alarmist gossiped that the bank was broke in the 1930s, so the bank president showed the townspeople bags of money to calm their fears. Months later, the town learned the banker had bought bags full of washers in Aberdeen.

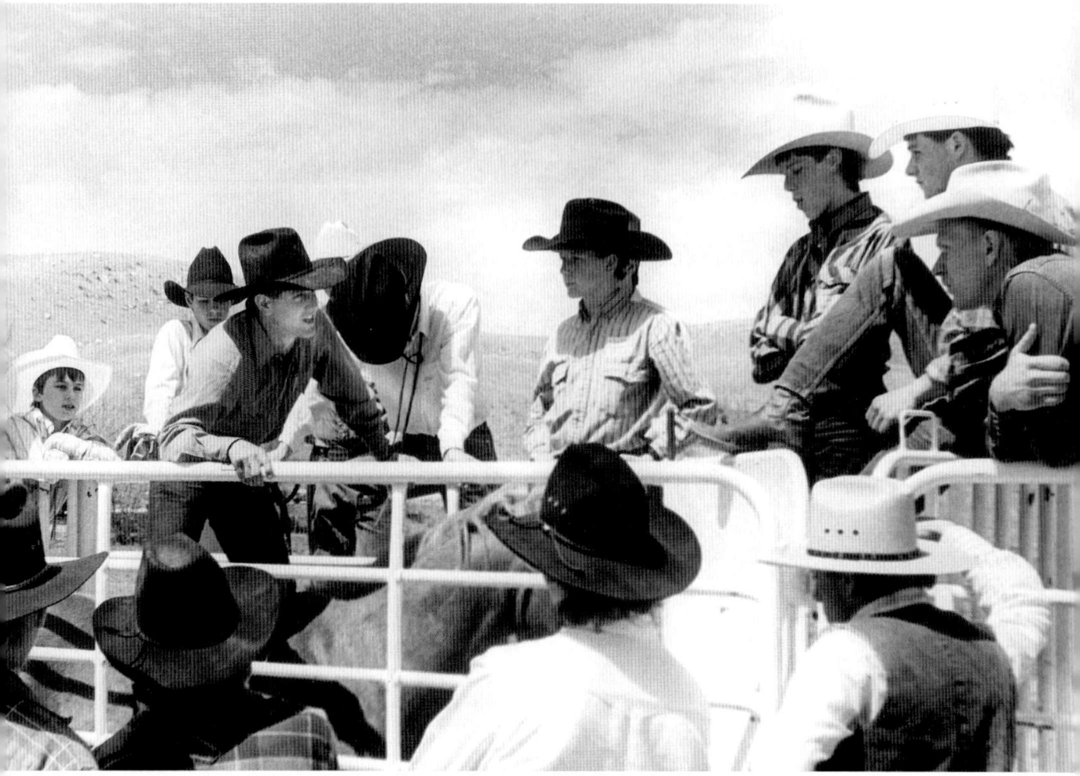

The Korkows of Blunt raise bucking broncs and bulls for rodeos. They also host a rodeo school at the ranch to teach youngsters how to stay on the critters, or how to fall off properly. The school seems to encourage some of the youth, and it discourages others. Either way, the tuition is money well spent.

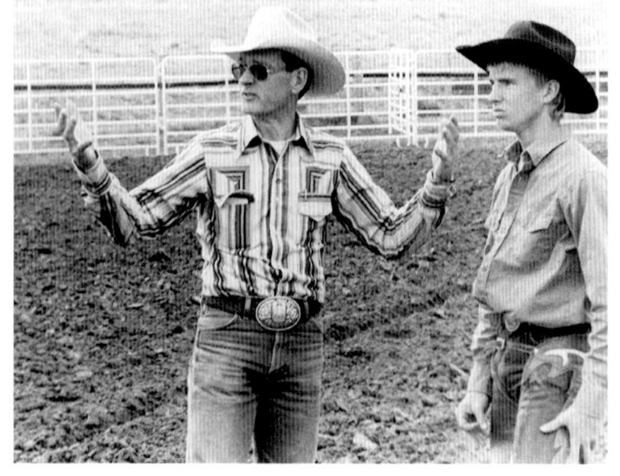

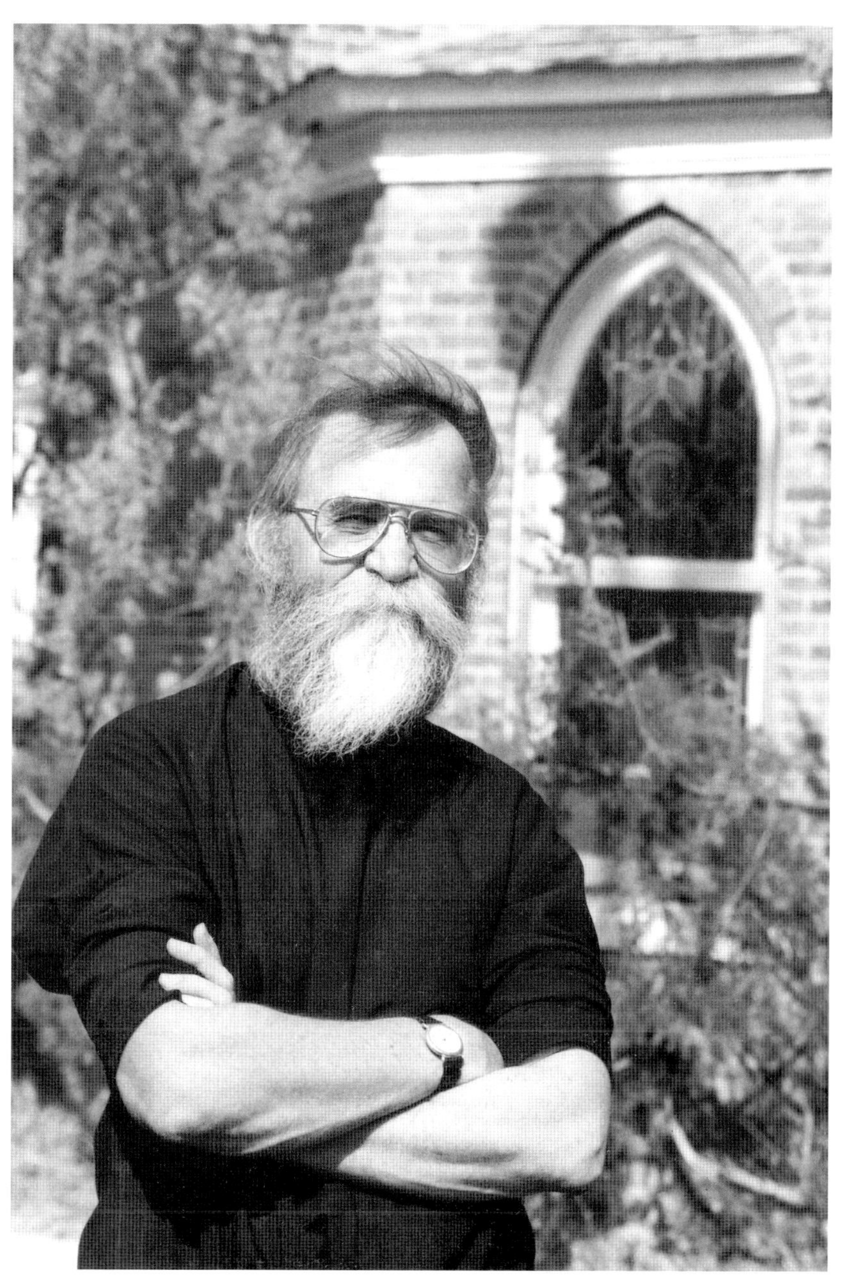

Brother Simon's Heritage Center at Red Cloud Mission, near Pine Ridge, encourages Lakota artists and helps them to market their work. The big, brick mission buildings date to the 1880s.

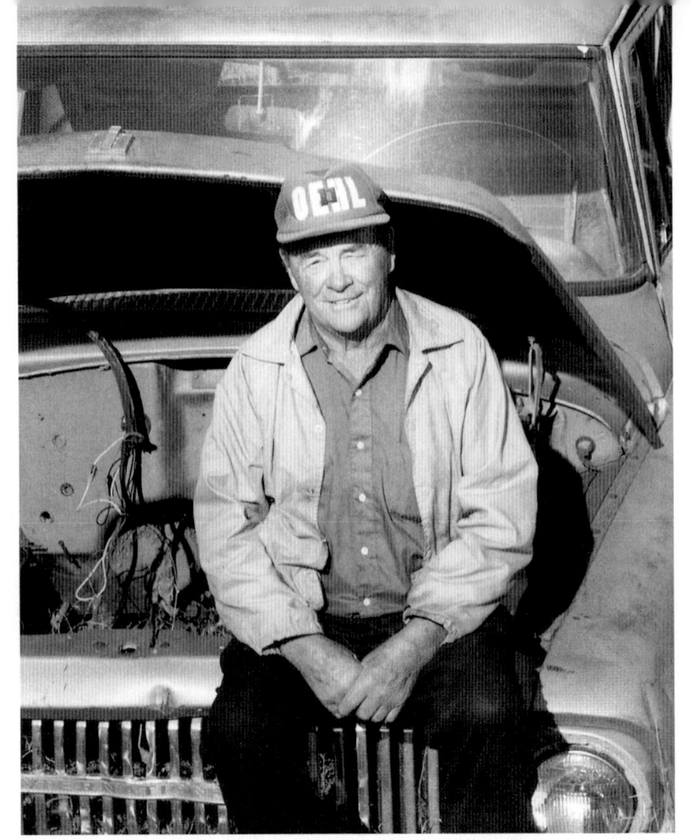

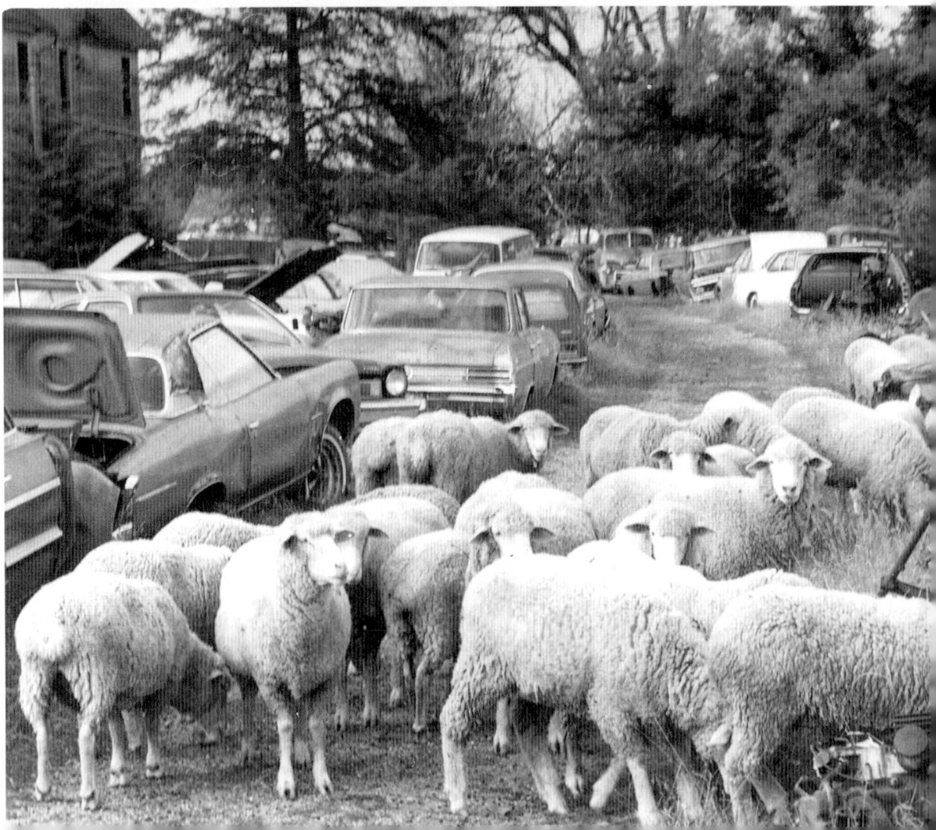

King Ziegler liked old cars. He collected them before they became collectibles. Eventually he started a unique salvage yard near Scotland. Sheep kept the grass short. "If I'd known I was going to get so many cars I'd have put them in better rows," he said.

Grass Mountain School on the Rosebud Reservation was built, partly of straw bales, by the youngsters who studied there.

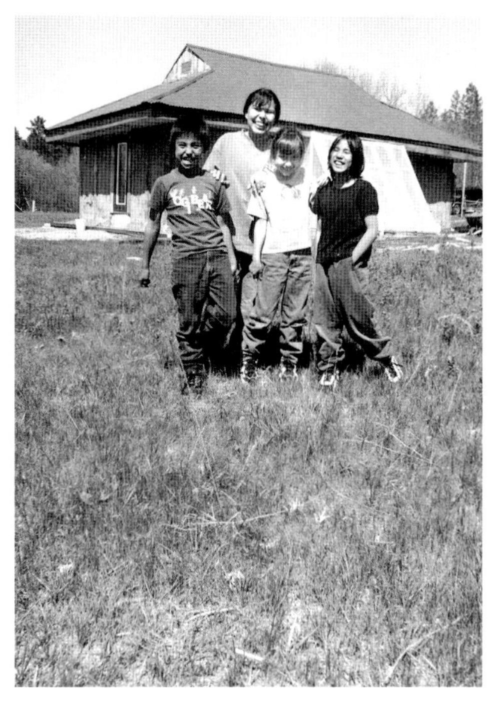

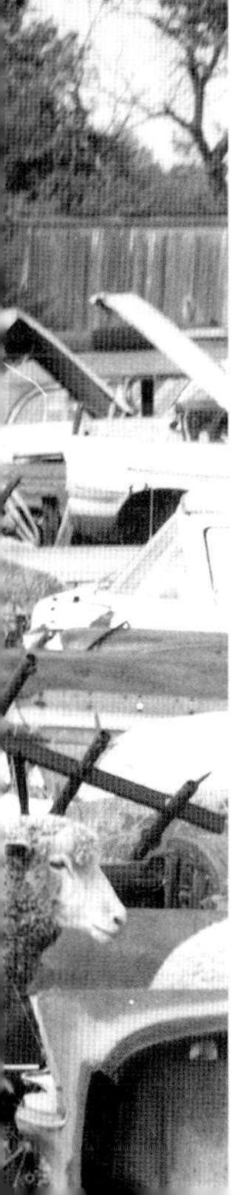

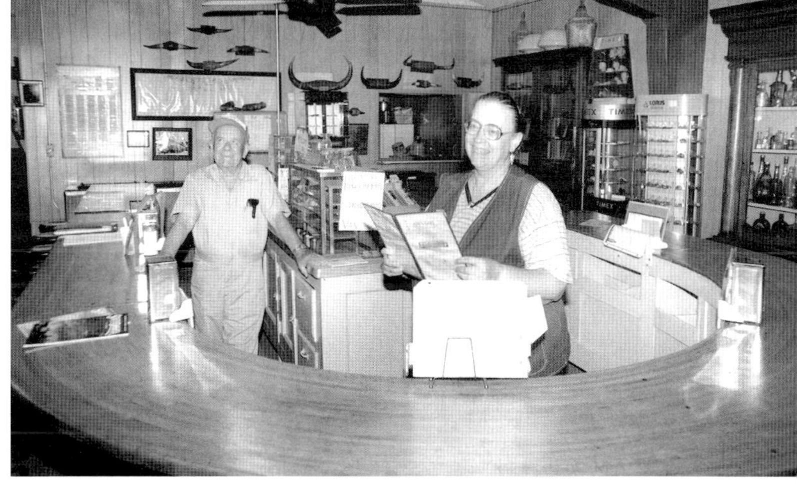

Visitors to Winner's museum are welcomed around a wood horseshoe-shaped bar that came from Joe's Cafe. The museum also has a two-headed, six-legged calf.

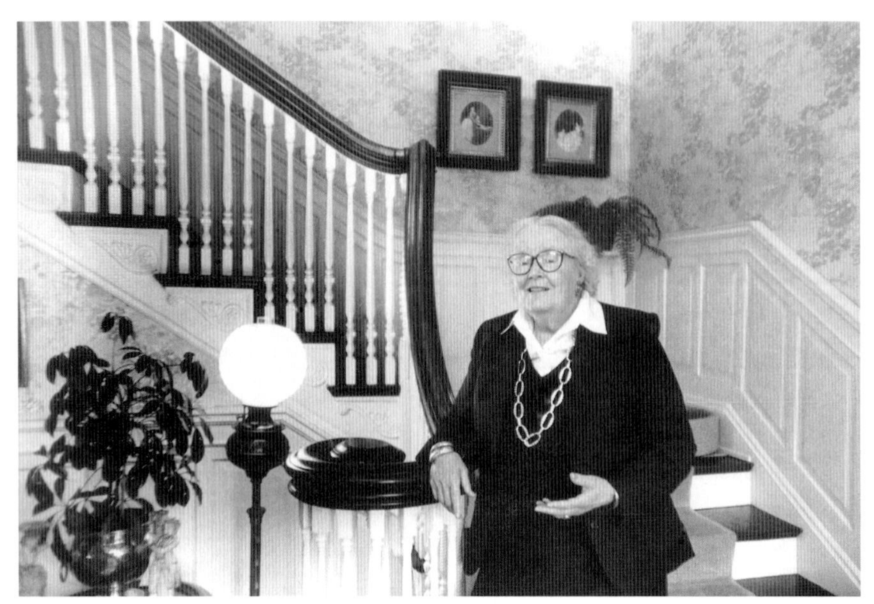

Dona Brown restored Huron's 28-room Campbell mansion, built by attorney J.W. Campbell. He was an Illinois native who was a neighbor of Abraham Lincoln's family. Miss Brown featured Lincoln memorabilia and the works of South Dakota's top artists — such as Oscar Howe, Harvey Dunn and Charles Greener — in the house, which regained its status as a social center for Huron.

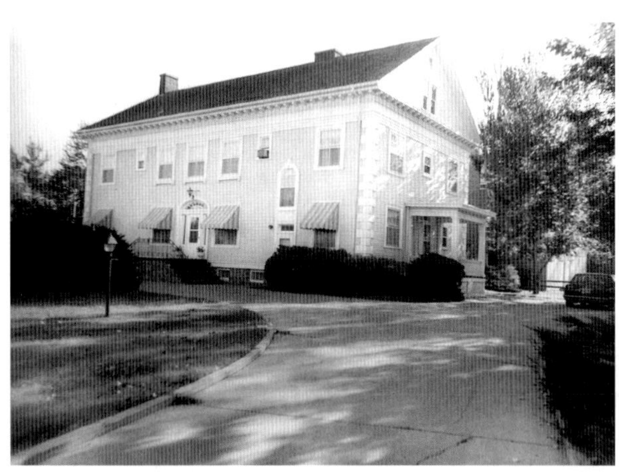

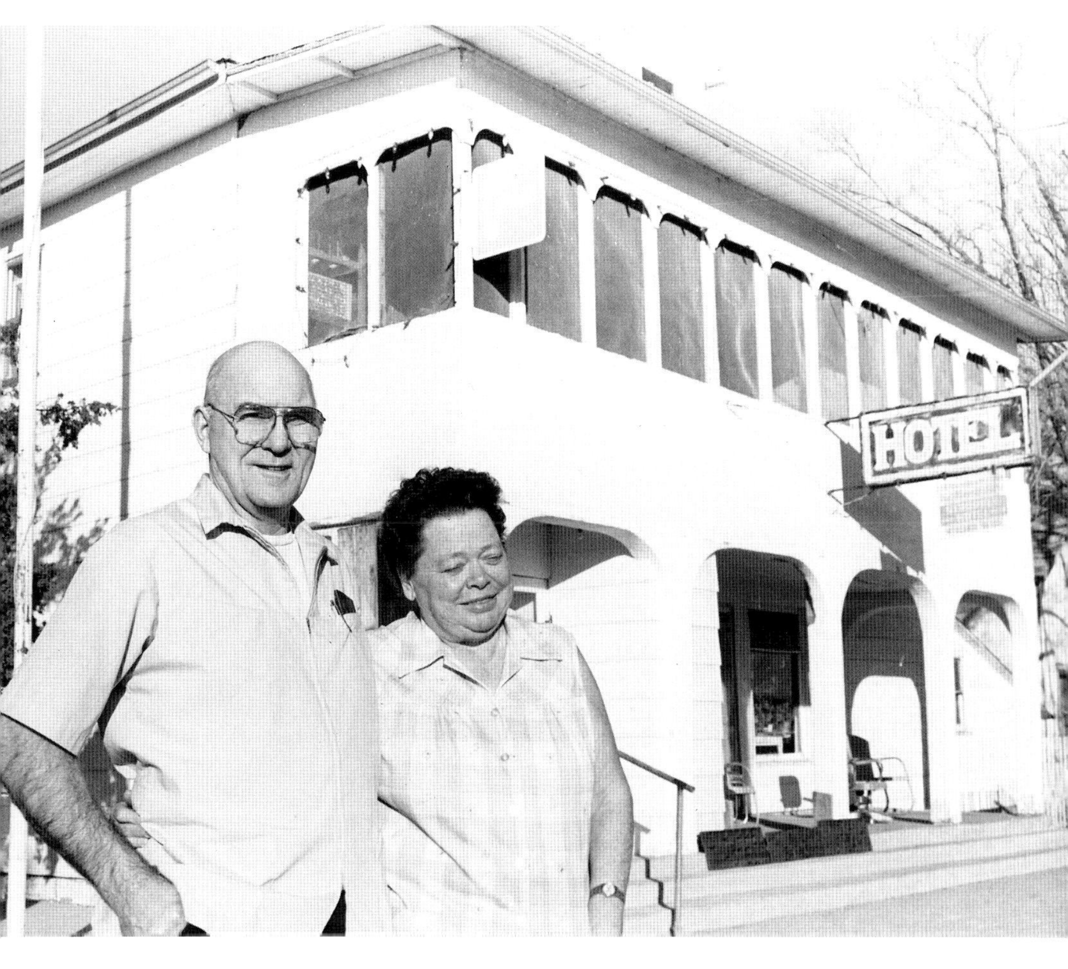

Hot mineral baths attracted thousands of people to George and Alice Stroppel's historic hotel in Midland. The geothermal water is 119 degrees before it comes out of the ground. Some people believe the water's large amounts of sodium chloride and sodium bicarbonate give it a medicinal quality, especially for sufferers of arthritis, rheumatism, back aches and kidney troubles.

Mark Kayser / SD Tc

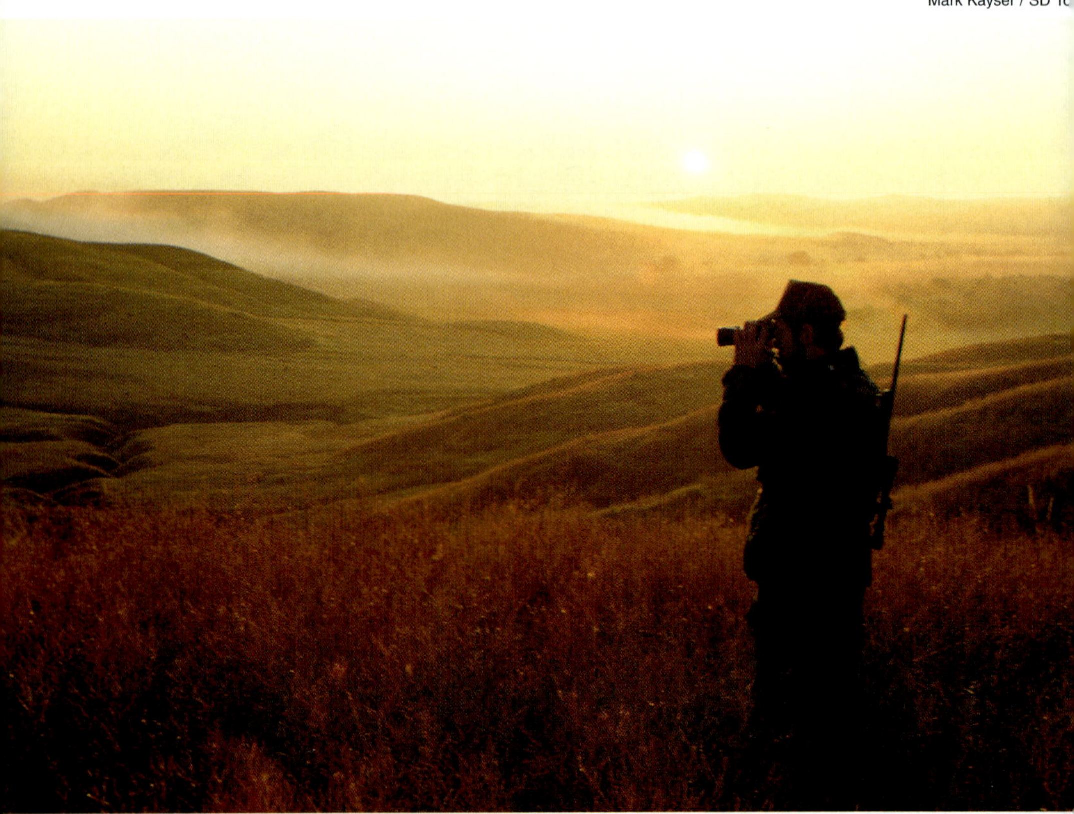

A hunter surveys the Bad River Valley in Stanley County.

Postscript

By Roger Holtzmann

WE LIVE IN the age of video. We can choose between scores of entertainment channels on our televisions. News footage comes to us by satellite, 24 hours a day, from every spot on the globe. Music is no longer merely tone and instrumentation and harmony; to young people especially, a song hasn't really been experienced until it's seen in its video version.

Yet photographs retain their impact. There's something about lifting a moment from the stream of life that focuses our attention on what's essential and freezes it forever. When we return to the pictures pasted in our family albums, children are always two years old and staring with wide-eyed wonder at the candles on a birthday cake, or smiling self-consciously, trying to look grown up while standing next to their date for the senior prom. Photographs, in a very real sense, become our memories.

When we set out to collect the photos for this book, we were hoping to accomplish that for the state we call home. Through the magic of photography, Arne Larson will forever be directing the Dalesburg Community Band. King Ziegler will never have to climb down off the hood of that pickup and rummage through the rusty relics of his Scotland junkyard for the rear door hinge of a '59 Buick Roadmaster. Nathan, Joseph and Justin Brown will always be happy to grin and pose for a stranger while Eugenia Blue Flower waits patiently to be milked.

Though we can hardly claim to have captured all of South Dakota in one slim volume — the state is too big and too diverse for that — we hope we've captured something of our essence. And become part of your memories.

Index

Contributors

Peter Carrels
Chad Coppess
Jay Davis
Tom Dempster
Dave Dringman
Roy David Farris
John Front
Stephen Gassman
Pat Hansen
Ben Hanten
Phillip Henry
Paul Higbee
Bill Honerkamp
Paul Horsted
C.A. Hosmer
Bernie Hunhoff
Chris Hunhoff
Katie Hunhoff
Mark Kayser
Marianne Larsen
Greg Latza
Troy McQuillen
Jim Peterson
Chuck Post
Rob Powell
Robin Reinhold
Simon Spicer
Joel Strasser
Johnny Sundby
Paul Wasserman
Juli Wilcox
Jerry Wilson
Ruby R. Wilson
Arnold Wold
Robert Wong